t

PATHS TO GLORY

W9-BYH-604

PATHS TO GLORY

HOW GREAT BASEBALL TEAMS GOT THAT WAY

MARK L. ARMOUR AND DANIEL R. LEVITT

Brassey's, Inc.
Washington, D.C.

Library of Congress Cataloging-in-Publication Data

Armour, Mark L.
  Paths to glory : how great baseball teams got that way / Mark L. Armour and Daniel R. Levitt.— 1st ed.
    p. cm.
Includes index.
  ISBN 1-57488-560-X (cloth : alk. paper)
  1. Baseball teams—United States—History—20th century. 2. Baseball—United States—Management. I. Levitt, Daniel R. II. Title.

GV875.A1A76 2003
796.357'06—dc21
ISBN 1-57488-805-6 (paper)   2003000062

Printed in the United States of America on acid-free paper that meets the American National Standards Institute Z39-48 Standard.

Brassey's, Inc.
22841 Quicksilver Drive
Dulles, Virginia 20166

First edition.

10 9 8 7 6 5 4 3 2 1

To Jane, who has tolerated my passion with humor and grace.—M.A.

To Suzanne, my best friend and wife.—D.L.

CONTENTS

Foreword *by Rob Neyer*   ix

Preface   xi

Acknowledgments   xiii

Introduction   1

1   Ned Hanlon, Opportunist: The 1899 Brooklyn Superbas   5

2   A Great Off-Season: The 1915 Philadelphia Phillies   21

3   Turmoil and Determination: The 1917 Chicago White Sox   39

4   Clark Griffith—Patience: The 1924 Washington Senators   75

5   Rags to Riches: A History of the Relief Pitcher   91

6   The Height of Folly: The 1930s Boston Red Sox   112

7   Following the Recipe: The 1948 Boston Braves   128

8   What Happened? The Vagaries of History:
The Postwar Boston Red Sox   148

9   An Unexpected Drop-off: The 1960s Minnesota Twins   176

10   Player Growth and Decline: Patterns in Aging   204

11   Plans Gone Awry: The 1971 California Angels   217

12   Brilliance and Bombast: The 1970s Oakland Athletics   233

13   The New Specialist: The Fireman vs. the Closer   260

14   Unfulfilled Promise: The Early 1980s Montreal Expos   276

15   A Change of Plans: The 1997 Florida Marlins   295

16   Translating Minor League Ability: An Outside View   311

17   Unheralded Dynasty: The 1990s Atlanta Braves   321

Conclusion   341

Appendix 1   Player Valuation Methodology   347

Appendix 2   Measuring Park Effects   357

Appendix 3   Defensive Efficiency Record   364

Appendix 4   S-Curve Methodology   365

Appendix 5   Win Probability Added   371

Appendix 6   Offensive Winning Percentage   374

Appendix 7   Minor League Translation Methodology   377

Bibliography   381

Index   391

About the Authors   407

FOREWORD

I've read a lot of books about baseball teams. Not as many as some, but more than most. Comes with the job, I guess.

But I've read all sorts of other books, too. (I'd rather read a book than write one, but I haven't been able to figure out a way to make reading pay more than writing can.) I've read books about great men, I've read books about great bridges, I've read books about great documents, I've read books about . . . well, you get the idea. And if there's one question that all of these books strive to answer, it's how was this man—or this bridge or this document—*built*. That's what we really want to know, right? After all, most of us know the big stuff, the famous stuff. What we really want to know is how this thing went from *nothing* to *something*.

Yet for some reason, when we read a book about a baseball team, we rarely learn much about what happened before the team became famous. It's almost as if the '27 Yankees and the '29 Athletics and the '75 Reds just . . . appeared on the scene fully formed from nothing, just as Athena leapt from the brow of Zeus. There are even books about what happened to the team years later.

As you know, I'm nearly as guilty as anybody. A few years ago, I wrote a book called *Baseball Dynasties* with Eddie Epstein, with a chapter on each of the fifteen teams we considered the greatest of the twentieth century. And though we didn't completely ignore what came before—each chapter contained a small section on how the team was built—it now occurs to me that we probably should have written twice as much as we did, and it also occurs to me that we rarely even mentioned the names of the men who put those teams together.

Which reminds me, there's another reason that I'm excited about this book, which is that it should get people thinking about a group of men who are sadly neglected when people talk about the game.

No, not scouts. You may think that they belong in the Hall of Fame, and I won't bother arguing with you. But the fact that there is a debate about scouts means they're not really that underappreciated. On the other hand, when was the last time somebody got a plaque in Cooperstown because he built a great baseball team? I don't know either, so let me consult *Total Baseball*. . . . Well, it looks to me like it's been about twenty-five years, as Larry McPhail was elected to the Hall of Fame in 1978. (McPhail, as you probably know, put together the early-'40s Dodgers and the late '40s Yankees, though he may have been enshrined for introducing night ball to the majors as much as for anything else.)

That's not to say this book is about who belongs in the Hall of Fame and who doesn't. We've got plenty of those books already. No, this book is about something far more interesting, far more fundamental. This book is about how the teams that still live in our memories reached the point at which they could do enough to live in our memories. Some of them were great and some of them weren't so great, but all of them were *built*, and it's the building that can tell us some fundamental things about the sport.

I've already read this book, which makes me a lucky guy. And you know what? I can't wait for the sequel. Because I've already come up with thirteen more teams whose stories should be told.

Rob Neyer
Senior writer and
baseball columnist, ESPN.com

PREFACE

We began corresponding a number of years ago about baseball questions that we found interesting and mostly unaddressed. After some time we recognized a pattern to our correspondence in that it often related to why some teams became winners while others could never seem to get over the hump. As we began to expand and research some of the points we were debating, we realized that our discussion might have some interest to a wider audience than just the two of us. After all, many of the concepts inherent in building a winning team—evaluating, acquiring, using, and developing ballplayers—are at the very heart of what many baseball fans care about.

Both of us have been baseball fans and avid readers of baseball books since we were old enough to know which way to run to get to first base. We further gained an appreciation for applying an analytical approach to baseball questions from Bill James's revolutionary *Baseball Abstracts* of the early 1980s.

In our analysis of how teams are built and why some had more success than others, we use a variety of techniques. In most instances, we present the story in conjunction with some statistical analysis; in other cases we use more of a comparative method. By looking at these teams' stories from different angles, we hope to provide interesting insights into the process of creating a team.

One finds no shortage of baseball books in libraries or bookstores, and we hope that ours will add something to an already crowded shelf. We have enjoyed the process of delving into the history of a number of great and a few not-so-great teams. We hope that the reader will find value in our synthesis of team construction and maintenance along with our historical and numerical diversions.

ACKNOWLEDGMENTS

A number of people have provided assistance in the production of this book. Tom Ruane, Pete Palmer, Sean Forman, Evelyn Begley, and David Smith all provided significant help with the necessary research. Lyle Spatz, Bill Deane, Jeff Bower, Lou Scialpi, Paul Andresen, and Stew Thornley each read one or more chapters or otherwise helped them along.

Much of the analysis in this book relied on information from Retrosheet (www.retrosheet.org), a wonderfully selfless organization whose goal is no less than the computerization of the play-by-play for every major league baseball game ever played. Most of the statistical work in these pages used data from Sean Lahman's database, downloadable from www.baseball1.com.

This book would not have been possible without the existence of the Society for American Baseball Research, whose individual members have engaged us in countless conversations and e-mail exchanges. While always enriching us, these relationships have often provided ideas that have left no discernible footprints from whence they came.

We need to thank our patient and supportive editor, Chris Kahrl, who believed in our concept for a book and helped make it a reality. He provided a lot of needed guidance to a couple of novice authors. Along with the usual editing functions, he also gave a number of insightful and valuable baseball-related suggestions.

Finally, neither of us could have undertaken this project without the support of our families. Each of us has two young children (Maya and Drew, and Charlie and Joey) who probably wondered why their dads were spending so much time on the computer. And, of course, our wives took on an additional share of the household burden while we buried ourselves in the book.

INTRODUCTION

*W*e *have read many books, some of them outstanding, devoted to telling the* stories of great baseball teams. Most of these works have dealt primarily with what the teams accomplished: thrilling victories, hard-fought pennant races, and postseason heroics. In 1948 Tom Meany wrote a wonderful book, *Baseball's Greatest Teams*, which explored the histories of many of baseball's famous clubs. Meany generally began his discussions with the team already in place and then presented the highlights of the season and the World Series. The story of the 1927 Yankees began in April and ended in October.

As recently as 2000, Rob Neyer and Eddie Epstein wrote *Baseball Dynasties*, in which they select the fifteen greatest teams in baseball history and present their stories. The backbone of the book was an interesting statistical justification of their selections, and it included a discussion of some of the noteworthy players on those clubs. Most books on great teams address largely the same things: What did they do? How good were they?

What has gone largely untold, it seems to us, is the stories of how teams have been constructed. If you begin the story of the 1927 Yankees in April, a reader is likely to think, "Well, of course they are going to win, they have Babe Ruth and Lou Gehrig and Tony Lazzeri and Bob Meusel and Herb Pennock and Waite Hoyt. It hardly seems fair." If one wants to understand why the Yankees became so dominant, the discussion should begin in January 1920 when owner Jake Ruppert bought Babe Ruth from the Boston Red Sox.

Many baseball fans have imagined themselves running a baseball team and formed opinions about how they would proceed: sign a bunch

1

of free agents, trade for more pitching, build a great farm system, acquire veteran leadership, or some combination of these and many other alternatives. We hope to provide insights into some of these strategies by presenting the stories of the building of several successful teams—and a few that fell short.

Fortunately, baseball history has produced more than two hundred league champions, each with a story of how its management built the team. By studying the decisions of these past champions and isolating those responsible for their success, some of the most worthwhile strategies become apparent. Conversely, by examining the formation of teams that disappointed, we can focus on common mistakes and decisions that did not work as intended.

Our book is not a comprehensive study but a presentation of the stories of several interesting ball clubs. We make no attempt to choose the best teams or the even the best-built teams. The clubs were selected largely because we found their stories compelling, facets of their stories have not been well told, and lessons can be learned from them. We also chose teams that represent many different baseball eras and therefore a wide variety of contexts in which teams have competed. Along the way, we also meander off to discuss other topics we believe are instructive in understanding the stories of these and other teams.

◇   ◇   ◇

In the broadest sense, creating and maintaining a successful baseball team depends on several factors, but especially the following: (1) sound baseball judgment; (2) an understanding of the existing and potential future economic structure of the game; (3) the willingness and the wherewithal to work within that structure; and (4) luck. We make no claim that any of these requirements are particularly profound, but they offer a good general framework to examine specific issues surrounding the assembly and decline of baseball teams.

Saying that a team has sound judgment implies an understanding of a whole gamut of assessments that a baseball team's management might be called upon to make. Where is the franchise in the development cycle: does it need to start rebuilding or can it fine tune its existing personnel? Is it trying to remain on top for a couple of more years? How much are the players on the current team contributing right now to the winning of games? Can a particular player handle the role assigned him? Which of a team's veteran players are likely to decline in the next year or two? (In this book, when we refer to a player's age, we mean his age as of July 1 unless noted otherwise.) Will a team's young players develop in the way the team expected? Does the organization have a plan? In today's game, these assessments often need to be made throughout the entire organization, from the owners down to the field manager and his coaches.

Economics has always played a significant role in the rise and fall of baseball clubs. In the nineteenth century, franchises banded together to form "syndicates": teams that combined players and management to better insure financial success. Many times in baseball history, most recently during the reign of the Federal League in the 1910s, owners have had to deal with an unfriendly competitive league. The Great Depression saw many major league teams willing to sell nearly anyone on their roster in order to keep afloat, creating opportunities for clubs that still had capital. The 1960s brought the first wave of expansion, allowing a group to create a team from scratch for the first time since early in the century. In the past twenty-five years, teams have had to understand a new reality: the end of the reserve clause that tied a player to a club for life. In each of these eras some teams have operated more successfully than others.

Luck, unfortunately, might be just as critical as anything else. In a world with thirty major league teams, or even sixteen, there can be only one champion and the difference between that champion and the next several teams might be razor thin.

The Minnesota Twins in the 1960s saw a rapid decline of many regulars after their 1965 pennant. By the time the team had been successfully rebuilt in 1969, the Baltimore Orioles had assembled a juggernaut, effectively squashing any realistic pennant hopes for the rest of the league. The 1971 California Angels suffered through one stroke of bad luck after another.

Baseball history is replete with teams that missed out on the Holy Grail because they picked the wrong year to become competitive. The 1993 San Francisco Giants won 102 games, the most in their history, only to lose the division race to the Atlanta Braves. On the other hand, the 2000 Yankees won 87 games in a weak division, played well in October, and enjoyed another parade. Building a solid baseball team requires smarts, money, and determination, but sometimes the time and place can make a critical difference.

Every baseball team is assembled by making numerous decisions, both large and small, conscious and unconscious, regarding many potential options. Sometimes these decisions occur within the framework of a larger plan; oftentimes they are simply made on an ad hoc basis. With a number of interesting teams as the backdrop, the following chapters delve into the choices, logic, and results of various team building strategies and decisions.

1

NED HANLON, OPPORTUNIST:
THE 1899 BROOKLYN SUPERBAS

The 1898 Brooklyn Dodgers finished tenth in the twelve-team National League, forty-six games behind the league champion Boston Beaneaters. This result was no doubt a disappointment to the fans in Flatbush, but it could not have been much of a surprise—the club had finished more than thirty games out of first place in each of the prior two years.

On the eve of the 1899 baseball season, the *Brooklyn Daily Eagle* nonetheless suggested, without a trace of irony, that the latest Brooklyn entry, led by new manager Ned Hanlon, might just be the greatest National League team ever—better even than the champion Chicago clubs of the 1880s and the famous recent contingents from Baltimore and Boston. It had obviously been an interesting off-season for the Dodgers. Therein lies a tale.

In 1892, for the first time in ten years, the National League found itself as baseball's only major league. Only two years earlier three major leagues vied for fans, but the stronger ownership of the National League prevailed over the Players League, which survived only the single season of 1890, and the American Association, which had hung around for ten years. Technically the association, after dropping its four weakest members, "merged" with the established league, forming "The National League and American Association of Professional Baseball Clubs." But no one called it that; it was the "Big League" or simply "the League."

In keeping with the times (this was, after all, the age of Rockefeller, Carnegie, Frick, and Morgan), team owners were never more on center stage than they were in the 1890s. Arthur Soden in Boston, John T. Brush in Cincinnati, Charles Byrne in Brooklyn, Andrew Freedman in New York, Harry Von der Horst in Baltimore—these were all competent and successful men. All that these men needed was a strong and capable leader, but no such person emerged. The league president, Nick Young, a figurehead who operated more as a secretary and treasurer, had little authority or inclination to lead. The league was composed of a group of strong-willed men looking out for themselves. The results were predictable.

Several difficult issues divided the league into factions. With the entrance of the four association clubs, the small-market teams formed a majority bloc. They won an even split of gate receipts between the home and visiting teams, an uneven split of the war debt—the league had bought out the four dissolved association teams—and the option to play ball on Sunday.

One thing that all owners could agree on was that the players needed to be paid less money. After a decade of competition for their services, players were faced with an ugly reality during the National League monopoly. Roster sizes were reduced, long-term contracts were abolished, and in 1894 the league instituted a maximum annual salary of $2,400. The reserve clause, which essentially bound a player to his team as long as it wanted to have him, was in effect again after the demise of the rival leagues.

In order to create more excitement in the game, owners made a few changes to introduce more offense. Most important, in 1893 the pitcher's rubber was placed 60 feet 6 inches away from home plate, replacing a pitcher's box whose front edge was 50 feet away—effectively moving the pitcher about 5 feet further from the batter. Runs per game leapt from 5.1 in 1892 to 6.6 in 1893 and then 7.4 in 1894. The Boston Beaneaters and the Baltimore Orioles, who between them won all of the pennants between 1891 and 1898, each averaged more than 9 runs per game in 1894. Within a few years, pitchers had adjusted to the new distance and the offenses returned to their previous levels.

The biggest problem facing the Big League was that is was so big. Numerous poor teams have existed throughout baseball history, but only in the 1890s could those teams finish twelfth. Louisville, for example, never rose above ninth or climbed within twenty-eight games of first. Washington never finished closer than thirty-two games. With the country in an economic depression, baseball fans increasingly showed little appetite for paying to watch so many uncompetitive baseball teams. Attendance was stagnant for most of the mid-1890s but dropped dramatically in 1898, averaging only 2,576 fans per game, compared with 3,568 just the previous year.

John T. Brush, the owner of the Cincinnati Reds, blamed the poor attendance on the conduct and language of the players. The Baltimore Orioles of the 1890s have long been romanticized for their skill, scientific play, and "inside baseball," but they were also, in the main, a bunch of vulgar and violent hoodlums. Several other clubs were not much better. In an attempt to combat the growing unruliness of the hired hands, Brush drew up a set of puritanical rules—a code of conduct—for all players to abide by. An obscene word uttered within earshot of a spectator, for example, would result in a hearing and possible punishment. The league adopted the rules but never enforced or honored them.

New York's Andrew Freedman favored a different solution to the sagging interest and attendance. In 1899, he suggested the league owners form a trust. Each team would hold a percentage, depending on its market size, of the single company. The teams in the biggest cities, like Freedman's Giants, would have larger stakes and would get most of the best players. The league would discard the teams in the smallest cities. The teams in the middle would survive, but only to give the large markets someone to play. Freedman was suggesting, in effect, that the owners drop the silly pretense of competition and instead run baseball strictly as a business enterprise. According to his plan, the league would hold an annual redistribution of talent to ensure that a small-market team did not suddenly become too good.

The plan was not absurd—most industries did or tried to do similar things in the 1890s—and the league might even have considered it if it had been someone else's idea. But Freedman had spent the previous five years insulting and belittling the other owners (along with his players and managers and the press), so most of his fellow magnates did not take his plan seriously.

Instead, a few of the league owners created "syndicates," essentially smaller versions of Freedman's proposal. One man who grasped how such a combination could work was Frank Robison, owner of the Cleveland Spiders. Upset at the attendance for his generally competitive team, he bought the St. Louis Browns at auction after the 1898 season. A great club in the American Association in the 1880s, the Browns had been awful in their seven years in the league—the 1898 team had finished 63 1/2 games out of first place. The fortunes of the team had paralleled those of their owner, Chris Von der Ahe, for whom life was one long party in the 1880s and whose senseless spending and living had led to debt and personal disgrace in the 1890s.

Robison now controlled two teams and thought more profits could be made if his new club in St. Louis had all the good players. He promptly transferred several Cleveland contracts to the Browns, including those of Cy Young, the best pitcher in the league and not yet half way to his record 511 pitching victories; Jesse Burkett, one of baseball's best hitters who had hit .400 in both 1895 and 1896; and Patsy Tebeau, the first baseman and manager. The press appropriately dubbed the resulting Cleveland team "the Leftovers." St. Louis rose to fifth in 1899, but the Leftovers finished 20–134, the worst record in major league history.

In the meantime, another combination was played out in Brooklyn and Baltimore, with much more interesting results.

◇   ◇   ◇

Ned Hanlon had a fine twelve-year major league career as a center fielder, mainly with the Detroit Wolverines in the 1880s. He was not a star but earned a reputation as a clever player and leader at a young age and became team captain at only twenty-four. After moving to Pittsburgh in 1889, he was soon named the team's player-manager. He jumped to manage the Pittsburgh team in the Players League in 1890, regained his old job with the Pirates when that league folded, and was fired in mid-1891. Just before the start of the 1892 season, he snapped a tendon in his leg, effectively ending his playing career. While recovering, the lowly Baltimore Orioles offered him their manager's job.

The Orioles' principal owner, Harry Von der Horst, made a fortune brewing and selling beer but had yet to find success with his baseball team. Von der Horst soon had enough faith in his new manager that he let Hanlon acquire a 25 percent share in the Orioles and become their president. Hanlon signed the players, made all transactions, and decided who played. Von der Horst took to wearing a button that read "Ask Hanlon." When asked about his team, he pointed to his lapel.

Before the introduction of farm systems in the 1920s, many of the better baseball players were playing in the minor leagues. A team with money to spend and astute baseball judgment could often find good players with a little effort. Additionally, since so many major league owners were having trouble making money, good players were often available because an owner did not feel like paying them anymore.

The team that Hanlon inherited in 1892 finished 46–101, but he soon proceeded to turn over the personnel. John McGraw was a scrawny, intense nineteen-year-old kid sitting on the bench when Hanlon arrived. Hanlon put him into the lineup immediately. Wilbert Robinson was a

Willie Keeler

journeyman catcher who became the team captain and leader. Hanlon soon discarded or dealt away most of the rest of team, bringing in players with little on their resumes.

Near the end of his first season Hanlon traded George Van Haltren, a .300-hitting center fielder who had started the year as the team's manager, to the Pirates for Joe Kelley, a twenty-year-old rookie who was hitting .239. While with the Pirates in the spring, Hanlon had trained with Kelley and must have liked what he saw.

In June 1893, Hanlon traded outfielder Tim O'Rourke, who was hitting .363, to Louisville for twenty-three-year-old shortstop Hughie Jennings, who was hitting just .136. Late in the year Hanlon bought Steve Brodie, a fine offensive and defensive center fielder, from St. Louis, where he was having salary problems. None of these moves caused much of a stir.

Hanlon wasn't finished. The next winter he dealt his third baseman, Billy Shindle, and center fielder, George Treadway, to Brooklyn for two players the Dodgers did not really want. One, Dan Brouthers, had been a star hitter for many years but seemed about finished at age thirty-five. The other, Willie Keeler, a tiny twenty-one-year-old left-handed third baseman, was still recovering from a broken ankle that earned his release from the Giants in early 1893.

The 1894 Orioles rose from eighth to first and repeated as champions the next two years as well. Ned Hanlon's assembling of this team was astonishing. Most of the players he acquired were not even starting for their old teams, none of them was in demand, some of them were playing positions that they could not play, and all of them came cheap. If one or two of these men had turned out to be useful players, it could be chalked up to good fortune. The fact that Hanlon continuously turned players with no reputation into stars must be attributed to his baseball genius. Virtually unknown when Hanlon got hold of them, Kelley, Keeler, McGraw, and Jennings within a very short time developed into four of the greatest players in the game. All of them, along with Brouthers and Robinson and Hanlon himself, are now in the Hall of Fame.

More than for its extraordinary collection of players, the Orioles became legendary as early proponents of "inside baseball." Ned Hanlon and his team have been variously credited with either inventing or popularizing the hit-and-run, the pickoff, cutoff plays, the pitcher covering first base on a ground ball to the right side, the pitcher cutting off the catcher's throw to prevent a double steal, the Baltimore chop, the bunt, and the suicide squeeze. Several historians have suggested that some of this credit is misplaced and owes much of its currency to the recollections of its famous players. Either way, the team clearly executed all of these plays and was very successful doing so.

Some of the players' behavior was less respectable: hiding balls in the outfield grass that could be put in play on a moment's notice, skipping bases on the way around the diamond, and tripping opposition base runners. They used their spikes on opponents and umpires alike, screamed vile language, and started full-scale brawls. Outside of Baltimore, everyone hated the Orioles.

After three straight championships, the team slipped to second place in 1897 and 1898, much to the delight of almost everyone. This was no disgrace—the first-place Boston Beaneaters were a marvelous team—but the fans of Baltimore had apparently become spoiled. Attendance had dropped dramatically once the Orioles were no longer winning pennants. In 1898 only 123,000 fans showed up at Union Park, less than half the number of the previous year. Since the team had several star players to pay, Von der Horst was losing a lot of money.

◇   ◇   ◇

By the late 1890s, the Brooklyn Dodgers had fallen on even harder times. After two straight seasons finishing more than thirty games out of first place, Charles Ebbets established control of the team upon the death of Charles Byrne in January 1898, although Ferdinand Abell still held the majority stake. Ebbets had started out selling tickets for the Dodgers and slowly moved his way up in the organization over fifteen years. In the few months prior to the start of the new season, he built his team a new ballpark, Washington Park, located in the heart of Brooklyn. He expected the faithful to flock there to see his Dodgers.

The faithful did no such thing. Attendance was down 40 percent from 1897 and Ebbets lost more than $20,000 in his first year at the helm. He employed a succession of managers, including Ebbets himself, but could not prevent the team from falling to tenth place. In a league that averaged .271, the Dodgers had only three regulars hit over .250—outfielders Fielder Jones, Mike Griffin, and Jimmy Sheckard. They had three league average pitchers—Brickyard Kennedy, Jack Dunn, and Joe Yeager—and a few lousy ones.

Sources differ as to who first hatched the idea, but in early 1899 the Brooklyn and Baltimore franchises effectively merged into a single entity. Rumors had been rampant for a year that Baltimore would combine with New York or Philadelphia, and Von der Horst apparently turned down multiple advances before finally being convinced of the profits he was missing out on. Per the agreement, Von der Horst and Abell each owned 40 percent of the stock in each team, and Hanlon and Ebbets each owned 10 percent. Hanlon, president of the Orioles, essentially performed the functions of a modern general manager for that club, and also became the manager of the Dodgers.

The former city of Brooklyn had recently become a borough of New York, a "merger" orchestrated by the merchants in Manhattan, and would soon connect to the mass transit system. The money men of the two teams essentially decided that there were more fans, and more profits, available in Brooklyn. Hanlon planned to transfer all the Oriole stars to the Dodgers and send some of Brooklyn's lesser players to Baltimore in exchange. From a business perspective this lopsided deal made sense. The value of the Brooklyn team and ballpark was much higher, and the imbalance of the players exchanged was intended, in part, to compensate for this.

Not surprisingly, Baltimore's star players had mixed feelings about moving to Brooklyn. The deal thrilled the great Wee Willie Keeler—he had grown up and still lived in Brooklyn and had long been a hero to the fans there. Just twenty-seven years old, Keeler was already the most famous player in baseball. Standing only 5 feet, 4 inches and weighing but 140 pounds, he used a 30-inch, 29-ounce bat and choked up so much that Sam

Crawford later observed: "He only used half his bat." Nonetheless, the speedy right fielder with a strong throwing arm had yet to hit below .371 or garner fewer than 210 hits in his first 5 full seasons. On a team of rascals, Keeler was quiet and reserved on the field, beloved and respected off of it.

Joe Kelley and Hughie Jennings both expressed reservations, but were persuaded to go along with the transfers. Kelley played left field, and if he did not quite achieve the batting averages of Keeler, hitting .360 every year instead of .380, he could provide good power for the time. In keeping with the reputation of his team, Kelley was a fine fielder, aggressive base runner, and first-class umpire baiter.

Jennings was a great defensive player who made more plays per nine innings (6.16) than any shortstop in history. He had hit .401 in 1896 (the only shortstop to ever top .400) and averaged about .350 in the surrounding seasons. He was a master at getting hit by the pitch—three times he was hit more than forty-five times in a season. The formulas used by *Total Baseball* rank Jennings as the best player in the National League in 1895, 1896, and 1897. Jennings was loud and hyperactive on the field and his nickname, "Ee-yah," came from the trademark blood-curdling yell that he used to enliven his team. He was a bright man, a practicing attorney in the off-season, but he annoyed the opposition as much as any other Oriole.

The player most responsible for giving the Orioles their reputation for cunning and ruthlessness was third baseman John McGraw, who was an excellent ballplayer as well. Sporting a gaudy .334 lifetime batting average, he walked so much and was hit by so many pitches that he was able to record a .466 career on-base percentage. McGraw owned a pool hall with Wilbert Robinson, the Orioles' popular catcher, and their ties to Baltimore made McGraw and Robinson reluctant to leave the Orioles. After several attempts to persuade the two stars to move, Hanlon reluctantly named McGraw manager of the Baltimore club and Robinson as his captain. Hanlon, as Orioles president, was McGraw's boss. Before the Baltimore-Brooklyn deal was finalized, Hanlon, as manager of the Orioles, traded infielder Gene DeMontreville for Bill Dahlen, the star shortstop of the Chicago White Stockings. Once everything was settled with the stock transfers, Hanlon moved Dahlen to Brooklyn to play third base (since McGraw was not coming) and began to organize his team.

Outfielder Mike Griffin had hit .300 for the Dodgers in 1898 and signed a contract to be captain in 1899. When he expressed his ire to Ebbets about the new situation, Hanlon sold Griffin to St. Louis. Rather than report, Griffin sued Ebbets for breach of contract and later settled for $2,250. Griffin never again played in the major leagues. Hanlon had planned to play

Kelley at first base with Griffin, Fielder Jones, and Keeler in the outfield. Instead, he moved Kelley back to left field and grabbed first baseman Dan McGann from the Orioles roster. Hanlon elected to keep the Dodgers' incumbent second baseman, Tom Daly.

When the smoke cleared, Hanlon had transferred seven Baltimore players of note to Brooklyn: Keeler, Kelley, Jennings, McGann—who had hit .301 for the Orioles in 1898—and three pitchers who each won twenty games the previous season—Doc McJames, Jim Hughes, and Al Maul. In exchange, Hanlon sent several Dodger players to the Orioles, the only ones of note being center fielder Jimmy Sheckard, first baseman Candy LaChance, and shortstop George Magoon.

No matter how one analyzes it, this trade has to be considered one of the most one-sided ever. On offense, Brooklyn upgraded substantially at five positions. On the mound, they received three pitchers who had won seventy games in 1898 for three others who had won four.

Theoretically, these moves were only the beginning. Because Hanlon controlled the rosters of both clubs, he could decide to exchange players throughout the year. In fact, just before the teams came north to start the season Hanlon realized that he needed another pitcher and took Dan McFarlan off the Oriole roster, passing over the untried Joe McGinnity. This would prove one of Hanlon's few mistakes; McGinnity won twenty-eight games for McGraw. After this trade, Hanlon assured the Orioles and their fans he would leave the team alone during the season.

In the spring Hanlon had to adjust to some unexpected misfortune. Hugh Jennings showed up with a sore arm and was unavailable until July. To replace his great shortstop, Hanlon used Bill Dahlen, originally acquired to play third. Dahlen, a star player then in the prime of his career, remains one of the better players from this era excluded from the Hall of Fame. He made more errors than any player in major league history, principally because in this age shortstops made a lot of errors and Dahlen played over two thousand games. He had very good fielding statistics (putouts and assists), and was a solid .290 hitter.

A popular vaudeville troupe by the name of Hanlon's Superbas happened to be playing in Brooklyn at the time. The imaginative press corps applied the name to Brooklyn's ball club, and the name stuck for as long as Hanlon managed the team. The 1899 Superbas were justifiably favored to win Brooklyn's first pennant since 1890, and a Brooklyn record twenty thousand fans came out to see the home opener.

The Superbas started slowly and just days into the season Hanlon reacted by acquiring third baseman Doc Casey and catcher Duke Farrell

Table 1.1 1898–1899 Brooklyn Personnel

	1898	1899
C	John Ryan	Duke Farrell
1B	Candy LaChance	Dan McGann
2B	Bill Hallman	Tom Daly
3B	Billy Shindle	Doc Casey
SS	George Magoon	Bill Dahlen
LF	Jimmy Sheckard	Joe Kelley
CF	Mike Griffin	Fielder Jones
RF	Fielder Jones	Willie Keeler
P	Brickyard Kennedy	Brickyard Kennedy
P	Jack Dunn	Jack Dunn
P	Joe Yeager	Jim Hughes
P	Ralph Miller	Doc McJames

from the Washington Senators for two unneeded players. Casey had only thirty-seven major league games behind him and did not turn out to be much of a player. Farrell, a ten-year veteran who caught over a thousand games in the major leagues, was still a fine player. Both immediately assumed full-time duties for Hanlon.

In the 1890s, many teams did not really consider themselves contenders and were merely trying to make a little money. This environment made it easier for an astute manager like Hanlon to find available talent on other teams. It would be highly unusual for a contending team today to acquire regular players for virtually nothing during the season. Hanlon was able to do this repeatedly with the Superbas, as he had done with the Orioles several years earlier.

Table 1.1 shows the change in Brooklyn's regular lineup and frontline pitchers from 1898 to early 1899. Only Fielder Jones, who moved from right field to center field, remained from the previous year's offense. Jones was Hanlon's kind of player—an intense .300 hitter who played fine defense. He later gained fame for managing the 1906 Chicago White Sox to an upset victory over the crosstown Cubs in the World Series.

The Brooklyn fans, enthusiastic early in the season, soon became jaded. When the Superbas hit another rough patch in June, a few supporters wrote to the *Brooklyn Daily Eagle* wondering if they were throwing games.

Hugh Jennings was not able to take the field until July, and when he did he still could not throw or, for that matter, hit. Hanlon attempted to trade Jennings to Louisville for young third baseman Hans Wagner and might have done so if not for the interference of his player. Jennings wrote a letter to Louisville Colonels owner Barney Dreyfus saying, "Don't consent to deal. Am in no condition. Will play no more this season. Bad arm." Jennings was being coy; he told a newspaperman that he was concerned that Louisville might be dropped from the league at season's end, which in fact it was. Hanlon was so upset he wanted to release Jennings.

John McGraw considered Jennings his greatest friend in baseball and made it known that he wanted him back in Baltimore. Hanlon wired his price: George Magoon, who had played shortstop for Brooklyn the previous year. McGraw considered this a great deal, but unfortunately he had just traded Magoon to Chicago for Gene DeMontreville and had neglected to mention this trade to Hanlon, his boss. A furious Hanlon reacted by transferring both DeMontreville and pitcher Jerry Nops to Brooklyn in exchange for Jennings.

McGraw, now livid, claimed that Hanlon had promised him he would not interfere with the Orioles during the season. Promise or no, McGraw had no recourse. Practically speaking, he managed a farm team, with the added detail that he had to compete with his major league affiliate. Jennings was hitting just .171 in forty-one at-bats at the time of the trade, but McGraw installed him as the team's second baseman.

Several interesting events soon followed. First, the Oriole fans and media were understandably angered. The *Baltimore Sun* reported a "torrent of indignant protest from Baltimore lovers of baseball, as well as enthusiasts all over the country, who want to see the national game on a higher level than that of mere dollars and cents." Second, the trade angered the Brooklyn fans as well—they liked the famous Hugh Jennings and did not see how their team benefited by acquiring two obscure players for him. They also may have grown embarrassed of the whole syndicate arrangement. And third, Jennings played two games for McGraw, fielded a flawless second base, and managed three hits, including two triples.

Hanlon decided to reverse the trade. His stated reason was that the criticism from all quarters, including his own fans, so overwhelmed him that he had to back down. He blamed Von der Horst for not letting him release Jennings in the first place. Hanlon almost certainly recognized, however, as did McGraw, that a healthy Jennings changed the one-sided nature of the trade. In fact, a healthy Jennings would have been the best player on the Orioles.

With the recuperated Jennings back in the fold, the Superbas made one last change to their lineup. They moved Jennings to first, since he still could not throw, and traded Dan McGann to Washington for catcher Deacon McGuire. Jennings played first base for the remainder of the season and rebounded to hit .326 in fifty-one games.

From May 23 until the end of the year the Superbas held first place but did not shake the Beaneaters until very late in the season. When the lead had shrunk to one game in August, New York Giants owner Andrew Freedman, who did not hide his distaste for the success of the team in Brooklyn, sold pitcher Jouette Meekin to Boston for $5,000, far below his market value. Meekin won seven games for the Beaneaters down the stretch. In retaliation, Hanlon was urged to get McGinnity from Baltimore, but he still felt a little gun-shy after the Jennings fiasco.

Brooklyn's attendance more than doubled from the previous season, but the team never achieved the financial success that Hanlon and Ebbets anticipated. According to Burt Solomon in his wonderful book *Where They Ain't*, the hometown crowd derided the team any time it struggled and often cheered on the opposition. A local writer claimed, "Without any question the merging of the Baltimore club with the Brooklyn club was never a satisfactory move to the patrons of the sport in this city. They looked upon it as a hold-up game to get their quarters and half-dollars."

According to historian David Q. Voight, the club drew poorly on the road as people grew tired of watching such a good team. Writer Henry Chadwick declared that the team had bored its own fans. When Brooklyn finally clinched the pennant on October 7, Admiral George Dewey's flagship had come into New York Harbor and the locals considered the new hero more deserving of their attention and affection.

The 1899 Superbas won 111 games and lost 47, finishing 8 games ahead of the second-place team from Boston. The team was very balanced, scoring the most runs per game in the league and allowing the second fewest. Keeler, who hit .379, and Kelley were the two offensive stars. Jim Hughes, another transfer from the Orioles, won 28 games and led a strong four-man rotation.

Obviously, much of the improvement of the team had little to do with the baseball acumen of Ned Hanlon. Most managers would do well with a club created by combining the best players from two teams. A lot of the turnaround, however, was unrelated to the former Orioles. Among the regular players from the Orioles, only Keeler and Kelley made a large impact. Hugh Jennings, on the other hand, played less than half the season and contributed nothing before August. Dan McGann hit only .243 over sixty games before Hanlon traded him for McGuire. Hanlon's non-Oriole additions, especially Farrell, Dahlen, and Casey, once again demonstrated Hanlon's excellent judgment and improved the offense significantly. Hanlon was given free reign to spend money to acquire players, and he did not stop after transferring his players from Baltimore.

Among the three pitchers taken from the Orioles, Jim Hughes had an excellent season, but Doc McJames proved less effective than in Baltimore and Al Maul won only two games. Much of the pitching improvement can be attributed to the holdover pitchers, especially Brickyard Kennedy.

As an interesting side note, the performance of the Baltimore Orioles in 1899 became the biggest story of the baseball season. Stripped bare of most of his best players, McGraw nonetheless cajoled his team into the first division—not quite in contention, but not quite out of it either. Incidents like the Jennings trade only added to the national attention, particularly for first-year manager McGraw, already labeled a genius.

In late August, tragedy intervened. McGraw's twenty-two-year-old wife died suddenly of complications from a burst appendix, and McGraw left the team for two weeks. When he returned, he did not play for almost two more weeks. Baltimore finished a surprising fourth, fifteen games behind the Superbas, but many observers suggested that the Orioles would have been much closer had this painful event not befallen McGraw.

◇   ◇   ◇

The 1899 season was a disaster for the National League as a whole. The Cleveland Spiders, winners of only twenty games, were an embarrassment, but the team was only the worst example of what had become a grossly uncompetitive league. At the league meetings in March 1900, the magnates made official what had been rumored for some time: they cast off four teams—Washington, Baltimore, Cleveland, and Louisville—and became an eight-team league for 1900. After twenty-four years of constant change, the makeup of the National League would remain constant for the next fifty-three years.

The biggest beneficiary of the contraction was the Pittsburgh Pirates. Concerned about rumors that he was going to lose his team, Louisville owner Barney Dreyfus bought control of the Pirates and transferred the contracts of several Louisville players, including Hans Wagner, Fred Clarke, Tommy Leach, Claude Ritchey, Deacon Phillippe, and Rube Waddell, to Pittsburgh.

Brooklyn, of course, acquired the best of the rest of the Baltimore team. The newest Superbas included Joe McGinnity, Jimmy Sheckard, and Gene DeMontreville, but John McGraw and Wilbert Robinson received their release and moved to St. Louis. In 1899, McGinnity had rewarded

Table 1.2 1899–1900 Records

	W	L	Pct
1899	101	47	.682
vs. dissolvers	44	12	.786
vs. rest	57	35	.619
1900	82	54	.603

John McGraw with a league-leading twenty-eight victories and somehow managed to avoid the clutches of Ned Hanlon all year. Jimmy Sheckard, a fine outfielder, had been transferred from Brooklyn to Baltimore in 1899 to make room for Keeler and Kelley. Now back in Brooklyn, he and De-Montreville provided depth for the Superbas.

Hanlon kept working. He considered third baseman Doc Casey the weakest link on his team, so, just days into the 1900 season, Hanlon acquired Lave Cross from the St. Louis Cardinals. A good hitter and an excellent defender, Cross was in the middle of a career that spanned twenty-one years.

The 1900 Superbas waltzed to a record of 82–54 and finished four and a half games ahead of the Pirates. Although the team's winning percentage dropped from .682 to .603, it was playing in a much more competitive league.

In the previous season Brooklyn had played fourteen games against the hapless Cleveland Spiders and won them all. Table 1.2 separates from the record of the 1899 Superbas the games played against the teams dissolved after the season. Without these fifty-six games, the team still had an impressive record, but not to the same degree.

Additionally, the transfer of the best players from the dissolved teams made the remaining seven opponents that much stronger. The Pittsburgh Pirates, to name one, had been strengthened by the addition of three future Hall of Famers and several other star players.

In 1900, for the first time since 1881, major league baseball consisted of only eight teams, and it seems likely that the National League was one of the strongest collections of teams ever put together. The last-place team, the New York Giants, finished only twenty-three games behind Brooklyn, and its .435 winning percentage is one of the best ever for a cellar dweller.

The newly added Joe McGinnity supplied a 28–8 record as the best pitcher in the National League. The team would likely have been even better had it not lost the services of Jim Hughes, its 1899 ace pitcher. Hughes tried to get a big raise from Hanlon after his twenty-eight-win season but received only a token increase. Rather than reporting in 1900, Hughes pitched for his hometown team in Sacramento and led it to the California League title. He would return to Brooklyn the next year.

The 1900 Superbas, unlike the previous club that Hanlon had continually improved throughout the season, remained stable. Only eleven non-pitchers played more than ten games. Farrell and McGuire shared the catching duties. Jennings, Daly, Dahlen, and Cross played the infield. Keeler, Kelley, Jones, and Sheckard shared the three outfield positions, with Kelley occasionally filling in at first base as well. Gene DeMontreville, the eleventh man, backed up the infielders.

The 1899–1900 Superbas are clearly among the more neglected of baseball's great teams. Many baseball histories ignore the nineteenth century completely, but even those that reference the era rarely devote much space to the Superbas. Brooklyn dominated the last twelve-team league and repeated when the league consolidated to eight teams. Its Hall of Fame manager, Ned Hanlon, remains much more famous for the three pennants he won in Baltimore than for the two he won in Brooklyn. The team included several Hall of Fame players (Keeler, Kelley, Jennings, and McGinnity) and many other stars (Dahlen, Jones, Hughes, Cross, Daly, and McGuire).

Writing in 1946, longtime sportswriter and historian Fred Lieb called the 1900 Superbas the greatest Brooklyn outfit ever. The Dodgers were about to enter their most successful period as Lieb wrote this, but that should not detract from the high regard in which he held this team. The notorious story of its creation, while interesting, has overshadowed the quality of the team.

In 1901 the American League, after several years as a strong minor league, declared itself "major" and began to compete with the National League for players. As it had done successfully with the rival leagues of the 1880s and 1890s, the senior circuit once again went through the motions of a war. Fortunately for the future of baseball, the American League not only had much better leadership than the previous challengers, it also had better leadership than the National League itself. Within three years, the old league gave up the fight and joined together with the Americans to form the strongest major league organization yet devised.

This great Brooklyn team was like a supernova. If its creation can be largely attributed to conditions unique to its time and place, so, too, can its dissolution. In 1901 the American League signed several players from the Superbas, including McGinnity, Jones, and Cross, and Brooklyn fell to third place. Within two more years Brooklyn lost several more players, including stars such as Keeler, Daly, McGuire, and Kelley. The team held on in the

first division for a few years—everyone other than the Pirates suffered losses as well—but failed to contend for the pennant again until it won in 1916.

Along the way Ned Hanlon and Charlie Ebbets became embroiled in a
power struggle for control of the team. Hanlon stayed on out of loyalty to
Von der Horst, who continued to keep away from operations despite
holding 40 percent of the stock. Ebbets was the team president and Hanlon's boss, but while Ebbets's salary was $4,000, Hanlon made three times
as much and was probably the highest paid person in baseball. Ebbets believed that he knew as much about baseball as Hanlon (he had even managed the team for a while in 1898), and the two were destined to clash, especially as the manager received all the credit for the success of the team.
Ebbets controlled the purse, and he denied his rival the means to compete
in a highly competitive environment.

For a while Hanlon wanted to move the team to Baltimore, which had
been granted an American League franchise in 1901 but lost it by the middle of 1902. Within a few years Ebbets came up with the money to buy out
Abell and Von der Horst. Hanlon became merely a field manager, and the
Brooklyn ball club stopped competing for pennants.

It is interesting to contemplate what might have happened had the
Brooklyn-Baltimore merger never occurred. Looking closer at the construction of the 1899 Superbas, Hanlon would have likely accomplished
similar results in Baltimore with his Oriole players. In 1899, he used only
three men from the 1898 Dodgers, Fielder Jones and pitchers Jack Dunn
and Brickyard Kennedy. The rest of team came from either Baltimore or
Hanlon's shrewd dealing.

If he had stayed in Baltimore, Hanlon might have had McGraw, Robinson, and McGinnity instead of Jones, Dunn, and Kennedy. Assuming
some of the moves he made in Brooklyn—picking up the likes of Deacon
McGuire—could have been made in Baltimore, Hanlon might have had
another Orioles pennant winner and saved the franchise. Whether Hanlon
would have been given the financial resources to keep his Orioles stocked
is doubtful; whether he had the baseball knowledge to do so is not.

The men who created the great Brooklyn teams of 1899 and 1900, especially Ned Hanlon, creatively and successfully took advantage of the pre-
vailing rules. The rules have been changed—no person today can have an
interest in more than one team—and Ned Hanlon, more than anyone else,
showed why the system needed to be changed. He did not need help finding baseball players, but if help came his way, he knew how to use it.

2

A GREAT OFF-SEASON:
THE 1915 PHILADELPHIA PHILLIES

Baseball in the early twentieth century held a prominent place in American life. The other professional team sports that are so popular today did not have more than a small, regionally concentrated following in that era. Only college football and boxing enjoyed widespread national appeal, but both fell far short of major league baseball. After the introduction of the American League in 1901, the structure of the major leagues stayed remarkably consistent. The sixteen franchises remained in the same cities from 1903 until 1952. Most baseball fans would have viewed a game in 1940 as remarkably similar to one in 1905.

The decade beginning with the 1903 peace agreement between the American and National Leagues was baseball's most prosperous and tranquil era since the sport first organized in the 1870s. Many historians define the beginning of the twentieth century as the start of "modern" baseball, as it saw the introduction of the current two-league system and an associated explosion of attendance. As an illustration, attendance per team increased by more than 50 percent between 1895 (an average of 241,000 per team) and 1905 (368,000 per team).

Another key change over the first decade of the twentieth century was the drop in hooliganism and abusive behavior by both players and fans. AL president Ban Johnson, the most powerful man in baseball over this period, championed the reduction in the thuglike conduct that the Baltimore Orioles and others made commonplace in the previous decade. Largely successful in this crusade, Johnson benefited the game immensely through his efforts.

A new generation of stars debuted and matured at this time. Four of the original five Hall of Fame inductees, Hans Wagner, Ty Cobb, Christy Mathewson, and Walter Johnson, experienced some of their very best seasons during this period. Attendance reflected the fans' excitement with the game; it reached its pre-1920 peak in 1909 (7,236,000 total or 452,000 per team) and remained strong for several more years.

The minor league system, as we know it today, did not exist. Teams basically acquired players from three sources: other teams, via trades or outright purchases; the minor leagues, in the form of purchases, the minor league draft, or even a trade of players under the major league team's control; and the signing of amateur players. Major league teams acquired most of the top minor league players by buying them directly, although a minor league draft did exist in various forms.

Roster and player control limits varied throughout the period. Prior to the 1920s, in-season major league rosters typically numbered in the low twenties. Additionally, teams could control other players, usually ranging from eight to twenty.

Teams of this era typically did not employ anyone who performed the functions of a modern general manager. The principal owner and the manager made most of the player personnel decisions. The allocation of authority depended upon the balance of power between the two men. In Chicago, White Sox owner Charles Comiskey, with a long history in the game and a domineering personality, was clearly in charge. In Philadelphia, Phillies manager Pat Moran was allowed quite a bit of leeway in making personnel moves.

This period of relative peace and tranquility ended abruptly in 1914. Competition from a third major league, the disruption caused by World War I, and the Black Sox scandal combined to make the next several years one of the most tumultuous periods in baseball history.

The first disturbance of baseball's serenity was the emergence of the Federal League as a third major league during the middle of the decade. A regional minor league in 1913, the league expanded geographically and announced it would challenge the existing baseball structure as a major league for the 1914 season. The league lasted two seasons; a peace settlement after the 1915 season effectively closed it down.

The birth of the Federal League had three significant consequences for the established major leagues. First and most obviously, it led to a drain on talent from the existing major leagues to the new league. The talent level in the Federal League never reached the level of the American and National Leagues, but several major league teams lost key players to the

Pat Moran

new circuit. Second, the competition for players led to an increase in salaries and multiyear contracts. Not surprisingly, this run-up in player compensation led to much consternation among the owners, to the point where several of them decided not to pay. Finally, the new major league put attendance pressure on existing major league franchises, especially in cities such as Chicago where the new league went head-to-head with existing teams. Attendance in the two established major leagues plummeted from 6.36 million in 1913 to 4.45 million in 1914.

◇   ◇   ◇

Over the first dozen years of the twentieth century, three teams dominated the National League. The Pittsburgh Pirates, the New York Giants, and the Chicago Cubs each won four pennants during these twelve years; no other team won any. Furthermore, over the last five of these years, from 1908 through 1912, these three teams finished first, second, and third every year.

While never a threat to win the pennant during these years, the Philadelphia Phillies usually fielded a competitive team. From 1908 to 1912, the Phillies consistently played right around .500 baseball and typically finished either fourth or fifth, right behind the big three.

Prior to the start of the 1913 season a syndicate headed by Pittsburgh Pirates secretary William Locke purchased the Philadelphia Phillies. In

1913 the Phillies broke through with an 88–63 record and finished second. Unfortunately for the long-term success of the team, Locke died during the season and was replaced as club president by another syndicate member, former New York City police commissioner William Baker.

In late June 1913, with the Phillies in first place, New York Giants manager John McGraw disparaged the Phillies by noting: "If a team like the Phillies can win a pennant in the National League, then the League is a joke." Shortly thereafter the Giants came to Philadelphia for a series and beat the Phillies to take over first place for good. During the game McGraw viciously heckled the Phillies' bench and particularly pitcher Ad Brennan, who was scheduled to pitch the next day. After the game Brennan caught up to McGraw as he was leaving the field and hit him twice in the head, knocking McGraw unconscious. McGraw turned out not to be seriously hurt, and both he and Brennan were fined and given five-day suspensions.

By the end of the 1913 season the Phillies had assembled a strong club. The offense was led by three sluggers: first baseman Fred Luderus, left fielder Sherry Magee, and right fielder Gavvy Cravath, almost surely the best non-pitcher in the National League in the mid-teens. Cravath led the league in home runs six times, and in runs batted in (RBI) and slugging percentage twice each. His 119 career home runs constituted the twentieth-century record prior to the emergence of Babe Ruth. His chances for Hall of Fame recognition, however, are remote, since he did not play regularly until he was thirty years old in 1912. Catcher Bill Killefer would soon be recognized as one of the National League's better backstops.

The pitching staff included several exceptional hurlers. Eppa Rixey finished 9–5 in his second year in the majors, although it would be several years until he rounded into his Hall of Fame form. Pitcher Tom Seaton completed one of his two excellent major league seasons with a 27–12 record and a 2.60 earned-run average (ERA). Journeyman pitcher Brennan had his best year in the majors despite his altercation with McGraw and finished 14–12 with a 2.39 ERA. Erskine Mayer delivered a 9–9 record in his rookie year; he would go on to have several very good seasons in the 1910s.

Finally, the staff was anchored by one of the top half-dozen pitchers of all time, Grover Cleveland "Pete" Alexander. Alexander broke into the majors in 1911 with one of the greatest rookie seasons ever: twenty-eight wins, 367 innings pitched, seven shutouts (all league highs), and an ERA of 2.57. That season set the tone for the remainder of his career; he went on to compile a number of tremendous seasons during the teens.

In the meantime, the Federal League began raiding the established major leagues for players. Baker's syndicate was not particularly well capitalized, and whether because of financial constraints or simply an un-willingness to compete, the Phillies suffered losses to the new league as large as any other team. Defections included the starting keystone combination of Otto Knabe and Mickey Doolan and two of the key rotation starters (Seaton and Brennan).

In 1914 the team fell all the way to sixth (74–80) as manager and reserve catcher Red Dooin proved unable to make up for the lost talent. Rixey turned in his worst year at 2–11; Magee and Cravath, however, produced excellent years, finishing first and second in the league in both slugging percentage and RBI. Overall the offense remained strong, but the defense collapsed and the Phillies led the league in runs allowed by a large margin.

Much of the defensive decline was due to terrible fielding (as opposed to pitching). Career third baseman Bobby Byrne played second base in 1914, his only year at the position during his eleven years in the majors. The team's shortstop play was so inadequate that outfielder Magee played thirty-nine games there. Hans Lobert, a mediocre fielder, started at third.

Fielding is an often-overlooked facet of a team's ability to prevent runs. While no straightforward, well-established measure exists to assess a team's fielding, two statistics permit us a good conjecture as to the tightness of a team's defense. The first is fielding percentage, which measures the percentage of chances the team fields cleanly. The higher a team's fielding percentage, the less likely the team was to make an error.

The second measure of team fielding is defensive efficiency record (DER), introduced over twenty years ago by Bill James. DER measures the percentage of balls in play that the defense turns into outs. A good defense will field a greater percentage of the balls in play and thus register a higher DER. (Details on the calculation of DER can be found in appendix 3.)

Table 2.1 indicates both the Phillies' fielding percentage and DER and their rank within the league for 1913 and 1914.

In 1913 the Phillies fielded 96.8 percent of their chances cleanly or, in other words, made errors on 3.2 percent of their chances. The decline to 95 percent in 1914 indicates considerable defensive backsliding. In absolute terms, the Phillies error total jumped from 214 in 1913 to 324 the next year. Similarly, the 1913 team converted 68.5 percent of all balls put in play against them into outs. Because balls in play not fielded result in a hit, the decline of 2.9 percentage points from 1913 and 1914 represents a significant falloff.

Although no simple method exists for separating defense into pitching and fielding, it seems clear that fielding played a greater role in the dead-

Table 2.1 Phillies' Defense

Year	Pct	Rank	DER	Rank
1913	.968	1	.685	3T
1914	.950	8	.656	8

ball era than it does today. In *The Hidden Game of Baseball* John Thorn and Pete Palmer quantify the split by looking at the percentage of runs that are unearned. At the time they wrote the book in the early 1980s, unearned runs accounted for about 12 percent of the total runs scored (today it has fallen to just below 10 percent). Thus, they estimated the fielding component of defense to be 12 percent. Many believe that this estimate of the importance of fielding is too low and that fielders are responsible for many plays that do not show up as unearned runs. For example, in calculating win shares, Bill James estimates fielding to be 32.5 percent of defense for the typical team.

In the mid-1910s unearned runs accounted for around 25 percent of the total runs, more than twice as many as today. Regardless of its precision as a measure of fielding, this dramatic change in the percentage of unearned runs provides strong evidence that fielding was a much more important component of defense at that time. Furthermore, and perhaps more important, a plate appearance was much more likely to result in a ball in play in the deadball era. Home runs, strikeouts, and bases on balls—three events that require no defensive participation—have risen dramatically throughout the past several decades.

◇   ◇   ◇

During the 1914–15 off-season, the Philadelphia Phillies made five moves that ultimately turned them into a pennant winner. In mid-October Baker fired Dooin as manager and promoted Pat Moran to run the club. Moran, ostensibly a reserve catcher for the past several years, in reality served as the pitching coach. A tough but fair thirty-nine-year-old, Moran became a great manager.

There was a lot of doubt as to how well Moran, who was given only a one-year contract for $4,500, would perform with a mostly veteran team with many long-term contracts. The Philadelphia correspondent of *The Sporting News*, William Weart, noted that the Phillies were "not keen for keeping the rules of training and . . . they were mighty hard to handle." Weart expressed less-than-unconditional approval of the new manager, writing that Moran was "doubtless the best selection that could have been made from the men who wore the Quaker garb last season." The players, however, recognized their teammate's capabilities and expressed strong support for Moran's elevation to manager.

Moran proved up to the task of instilling discipline into the club. He ran a strict spring training and oversaw the players' diet and exercise. Moran also showed himself an excellent judge of baseball talent, as evidenced by the rest of the off-season moves. Although not particularly celebrated at the time, one year later *The Sporting News* deemed his series of transactions "so successful they could be counted as 'once in a lifetime' affairs." The trades resulted in three new position players and one new rotation starter by the end of 1915. Moran was actually handicapped by the fact that two of the trades were more or less forced on the club.

A couple of weeks after Moran's hiring, the Phillies purchased the contract of shortstop Dave Bancroft from Portland in the Pacific Coast League. The twenty-four-year-old Bancroft had been named to that league's year-end all-star team in 1914 after hitting .277; he was viewed as an excellent fielder, particularly on bad hops. Moran installed the rookie Bancroft at shortstop from the start, and he proved more than up to the task. He followed up a strong rookie year with a Hall of Fame career.

In December, Moran and Brooklyn Dodgers manager Wilbert Robinson agreed to a trade of Dooin, recently deposed as manager but still regarded as a decent reserve catcher, for second baseman George Cutshaw. This trade had to be called off, however, when Dooin claimed he would jump to the Federal League rather than go to Brooklyn. The Phillies later traded him to the Cincinnati Reds for third baseman Bert Niehoff, whom Moran smartly shifted to plug the second base hole.

Another forced trade was the shipping of star outfielder Sherry Magee to the Boston Braves. Magee, who had some hope of being named manager himself, wanted out of Philadelphia. In order to forestall any action by the Federal League, the Phillies sent Magee to Boston several weeks before the two teams could agree on whom the Braves would remit to the Phillies. After some negotiation, the Phillies and Braves settled on Oscar Dugey, a reserve infielder, and twenty-five-year-old outfielder George "Possum" Whitted. Although not a slugger of Magee's caliber, Whitted had more speed and turned in several fairly good years for the Phillies.

The final major off-season move was the most successful. The Phillies traded a fair thirty-three-year-old third baseman, Hans Lobert, to the New York Giants for Al Demaree, a solid middle-of-the-rotation starting pitcher; Milt Stock, a twenty-two-year-old third baseman who would be a

THE TALENT LEVEL OF THE FEDERAL LEAGUE

Nearly all sources except *The Sporting News* credit the Federal League with major league status and include Federal League statistics in player career totals. While certainly willing to spend money for major league stars, the Federal League remained materially inferior to the established major leagues— enough so that we have significant skepticism regarding its claim to major league status. We offer three arguments for the league's inferiority.

1. The Federal League's recognizable players mostly consisted of veterans near the end of their careers. Of the top ten finishers in the 1913 MVP voting in both major leagues, none of the twenty ever played in the Federal League.

2. A disproportionate share of the Federal League's players did not remain in the established major leagues after 1915. Table 1 summarizes the status of all players who appeared in the three leagues in 1914 or 1915. Nearly two-thirds of the players who appeared in the Federal League never again appeared in the major leagues after 1915. For the two established leagues, the percentage was less than 40 percent.

In order to verify that the Federal League did not land excellent front-line talent and then fill in with whoever might be available, we also checked the fate of regulars only (defined as at least 400 AB or 150 IP). Here (see table 2) the picture is even starker. Of the regulars in the Federal League, fully 45 percent never even appeared in the established major leagues after 1915, much less as starters. For the established major leagues this number ran below 15 percent.

Charlie Carr is a good example. A thirty-seven-year-old in 1914, Carr won the regular first-base job for Indianapolis after a number of years with the minor league Indianapolis Indians despite the fact that he had not appeared in the major leagues since 1906, when he was a reserve for the Cincinnati Reds. Nevertheless, Carr hit .293 with twenty-four extra-base hits in 441 at-bats.

3. The peace settlement that ended the Federal League after the 1915

Table 1 1914–1915 Major Leaguers

	FL	AL	NL
Only appeared 1914–15	32%	23%	17%
Last played 1914–15; played before 1914	34%	16%	20%
First played 1914–15; played beyond 1915	11%	22%	19%
Played before and after 1914–15	24%	39%	44%
All	100%	100%	100%

Table 2 1914–1915 Regulars

	FL	AL	NL
Only appeared 1914–15	10%	1%	1%
Last played 1914–15; played before 1914	35%	10%	13%
First played 1914–15; played beyond 1915	10%	19%	14%
Played before and after 1914–15	44%	71%	72%
All	100%	100%	100%

season allowed the league to maintain the rights to its players. As a further part of the agreement, the owners of the Federal League's Chicago and St. Louis franchises, Charles Weeghman and Phil Ball, were allowed to buy the National League's Chicago Cubs and American League's St. Louis Browns, respectively. Because the new owners controlled their Federal League players, the 1916 Cubs and Browns each effectively represented the merging of two teams.

In 1915 the Chicago and St. Louis clubs were the best two teams in the Federal League and finished in a virtual tie for first place. The Chicago club, managed by Hall of Fame shortstop Joe Tinker, won the league with a record of 86–66 (.566), just barely ahead of St. Louis, managed by 1906 World Series champion manager Fielder Jones, at 87–67 (.565).

In 1915 the Chicago Cubs finished fourth with a record of 73–80. In 1916 the Cubs, now managed by Joe Tinker and including the players from both the 1915 Cubs and the 1915 Chicago Federal League pennant winner, actually regressed to a 67–86 record and a fifth-place finish. In other words, the 1916 Cubs, composed of the 1915 squad bolstered by the 1915 Federal League champions, actually won fewer games than the year before.

The 1915 Browns finished sixth with a record of 63–91. The 1916 team under Fielder Jones, augmented by the influx of the second-place team from the FL, advanced no further than fifth place and a record of 79–75. It is unlikely that this improvement owed much to the new Federal Leaguers. First, 1916 was star first baseman George Sisler's first year as a regular (he had not been a Federal Leaguer). Second, in 1916 the Philadelphia Athletics set a twentieth-century record for futility with a record of 36–117 (.235). The Athletics were so inept that no other team in the American League finished with a winning percentage below .497.

In the middle of the decade, the emergence of the Federal League and associated consequences shook up all of organized baseball, both the major and minor leagues. But the record provides no evidence that the caliber of play was close to that in the established major leagues.

valuable starter by the end of the year; backup catcher Jack Adams; and cash. Demaree later became a widely syndicated sports cartoonist. The partially deaf Stock went on to a long and successful career lasting over sixteen hundred games. At the time of the trade it was noted, "He handled more chances per game than the man the Phillies let go." (This turned out to be an accurate assessment.) Stock took over as the regular third baseman late in the 1915 season when an injury sidelined now-journeyman regular Bobby Byrne. Stock held onto the job as the regular third baseman until traded several years later.

After all the off-season moves, Moran had assembled an excellent outfit for the 1915 season: Bill Killefer at catcher; the hard-hitting Luderus at first base; Niehoff, the newcomer, at second base; Bobby Byrne, who eventually gave way to Stock, at third base; rookie Bancroft at shortstop; slugger Cravath in right; and the solid Whitted joining Dode Paskert and Beals Becker in center and left fields. Pete Alexander and Erskine Mayer returned as the top two starting pitchers. Eppa Rixey developed into a first-rate pitcher, and the newly acquired Al Demaree completed the rotation.

◇　◇　◇

Though almost forgotten today, Clifford "Gavvy" Cravath was the first real slugger of modern baseball. He led the National League in home runs six times in the seven years between 1913 and 1919 and missed by only one in 1916. Cravath was no one-dimensional hitter; he could draw a walk and hit for average as well. In 1913 he nearly won the triple crown; he led the league in home runs and RBI and finished second in batting average at .341, nine points behind Jake Daubert.

Cravath was probably the best position player in the National League during the teens. Table 2.2 lists the top National League hitters by wins above replacement (WAR) per 150 games for the seasons 1911 through 1919 (minimum 30 WAR).

In 1902, at age twenty, Cravath joined his hometown San Diego club of the independent California League, the top league then active in the Golden State. When the league reorganized the next year into the Pacific Coast League (PCL), Cravath moved to the Los Angeles Angels. Over the next several years Cravath developed into a very good minor-league player. By 1907 the PCL was recognized at the highest minor league classification, and Cravath led the Angels to the PCL title with ten home runs, a .303 batting average and fifty stolen bases. For comparison, fourteen home runs topped the league that year, and Cravath's batting average was fourth best.

Table 2.2 Best NL Hitters, 1911–1919 (minimum 1,000 games)

	G	AVG	OBP	SLG	R	HR	RBI	SB	RC	WAAv	WAR	War/ 150
Gavvy Cravath	1057	.291	.381	.490	523	116	665	80	694	31	42	5.9
George Burns	1059	.289	.366	.388	651	24	351	293	652	26	38	5.4
Larry Doyle	1158	.290	.358	.419	648	56	576	197	706	24	37	4.8
Heinie Groh	1000	.294	.377	.391	531	17	314	126	560	21	32	4.7
Sherry Magee	1103	.287	.360	.423	560	55	623	154	628	20	32	4.3
Zack Wheat	1192	.301	.352	.421	542	49	581	145	672	20	34	4.2
Heinie Zimmerman	1241	.297	.334	.426	620	55	727	159	703	20	34	4.1
Jake Daubert	1209	.306	.364	.390	660	27	409	175	680	18	32	4.0

Note: Throughout this book, along with several traditional measurements, we use newer or "sabermetric" statistics. These stats represent the translation of the player's traditional statistics (hits, home runs, stolen bases, etc.) first into a run value (runs created, or RC) and second into a win value (wins above replacement, or WAR; in many tables we also include WAAv, or wins above average). RC estimates how many runs a player's offense was worth to his team and WAR estimates how many wins those runs were worth. WAR/150 puts the statistic into a seasonal context of 150 games played. Please see appendix 2 for a more detailed description of our valuation methodology.

The Boston Red Sox purchased Cravath in the fall of 1907 and he had a fair year in 277 at-bats in 1908. The Red Sox, however, let him go for a nominal fee to the Chicago White Sox. After he started slowly in 1909, the White Sox included Cravath in a three-for-one trade with the Washington Senators. He lasted only three games with the Senators before they farmed him out to the Minneapolis Millers of the American Association (AA), with whom they had a working relationship.

At the start of the 1910 season Cravath was twenty-eight years old and still one step away from the major leagues. Over the next two seasons, Cravath led the Millers to pennants and registered a couple of the greatest hitting seasons seen in the minor leagues up to that time. In 1910, Cravath led the AA in hits, doubles, triples, home runs, and batting average. The next year he again led the league in home runs with 29 and batting average at .363. Only two other players in the league had as many as 10 home runs, and each had only 14. His 221 hits, league-leading 53 doubles, and 13 triples gave Cravath an almost unheard-of deadball era total of 387 total bases.

After his great 1911 season, the Phillies paid $9,000 to acquire Cravath. Although the top going rate for minor leaguers could approach and even exceed $20,000, Cravath's cost represented a significant outlay for a minor leaguer, particularly one who would be thirty years old by the start of the 1912 season. For the next eight years, Cravath dominated the major leagues in home run hitting. The 1916 *Reach Guide* noted that Cravath "is now looked upon as the greatest slugger in the game."

Many years later, near the end of Cravath's playing career, Baker named him manager of the Phillies, but he lasted only one and a half seasons at the helm of a much-reduced team. Nicknamed "Cactus" because of his bristly personality, he is also often remembered as an enjoyable clubhouse presence. Cravath actually had a reputation for being too lenient as a manager. After his major league playing days, Cravath played two more years in the high minors before returning to his native California, where he sold real estate and became a judge. According to one story, Cravath once fined a man just two cents for illegally catching a fish because the judge did not like the approach of the fish and game wardens.

The Phillies' home ballpark in the 1910s, Baker Bowl, was regarded as a hitters' haven due its short right field fence—a 40-foot-high tin wall only 272 feet from home plate. Cravath has little chance at Hall of Fame induction because of his late start and resulting career totals that fall short of those of many Hall of Famers. Cravath's reputation is also dimmed by Baker Bowl's reputation as an extreme offensive ballpark, and his numerous home run titles are often discounted.

In fact, in the mid-1910s Baker Bowl was not the hitters' paradise it would later become. Table 2.3 summarizes the park factor for Baker Bowl from 1912 through 1917, Cravath's top years. In 1914, for example, the Phillies and their opponents combined to score 6 percent more runs in Phillies home games than in road games. A park factor of 1.04 over the six-year period means that 4 percent more runs were scored at Baker Bowl than in Phillies road-game stadiums. Because teams play half their games on the road, Cravath's statistics benefited by only one-half the Baker Bowl effect, or 2 percent.

Although run scoring was only a little higher in Baker Bowl, the park did allow many more home runs. Upon a closer look, however, Cravath's accomplishments still stand up to scrutiny. In the Phillies' pennant-winning year of 1915, Cravath hit twenty-four home runs, the highest twentieth-century season total prior to Babe Ruth. And while nineteen of them were hit at home, visiting teams in Baker Bowl hit a total of eighteen home runs that year, one fewer than Cravath hit all by himself.

It is rather surprising that Cravath, a right-handed hitter, could take such advantage of the short right field in his home park. In the 1999 edition of *Baseball Research Journal*, published by the Society for American Baseball Research, Bill Swank argues that Cravath tailored his swing while playing minor league baseball in Minneapolis's Nicollet Park, which also had a short right field. Cravath's unique ability to take advantage of Baker Bowl should not be disregarded simply because he landed in the perfect park for his skills.

The Sporting News reported the location of home runs in Philadelphia for the 1915 season. The results are summarized in table 2.4. (As a technical note, the current encyclopedias credit the Phillies with forty-six home runs at home.)

Cravath hit nearly twice as many home runs to right and center fields as all the visiting players combined, and this ability won a lot of games for his team. He was considered a star, and deservedly so.

Table 2.3 Baker Bowl Park Factors

Year	GH	GA	RH	RA	PF
1912	75	77	670	718	0.96
1913	76	75	727	602	1.19
1914	78	76	698	640	1.06
1915	76	76	548	504	1.09
1916	79	74	514	556	0.87
1917	77	77	567	511	1.11
Total	461	465	3724	3531	1.04

GH = number of home games   GA = number of road games

RH = runs scored by both teams in Phillies home games

RA = runs scored by both teams in Phillies road games

PF = park factor (runs per game in Phillies home games divided by

runs per game in Phillies road games).

◇ ◇ ◇

The 1915 Phillies gained the league lead on July 14 and never looked back. They finished 90–62 and won the pennant by seven games over the defending champion Boston Braves. Beyond Moran's successful blending of talent, the team owed its success to the National League's two best players, Alexander and Cravath. Alexander had a tremendous season, finishing 31–10 and leading the league in wins, ERA (1.22), winning percentage, innings pitched, strikeouts, and shutouts. Cravath led the league in RBI, runs, slugging percentage, on-base percentage, walks, and home runs. His 115 RBI were 28 more than the second-best total, and his 25 home runs nearly doubled the 13 recorded by the runner-up. Slugging first baseman Luderus further propelled the offense. In his best season he hit .315 and missed the batting title by .005. Additionally he finished second in the league behind Cravath in both slugging percentage and on-base percentage.

While the offense improved slightly from third in the league to second, the team posted one of the most dramatic defensive turnarounds ever. The Phillies leapt from last in the league in runs allowed in 1914 with 687 to a league-low 463. Much of this improvement should be attributed to Alexander's monster season, an improved Rixey, and the addition of Demaree. A large share of the credit, however, must be assigned to a remarkable improvement in fielding.

Table 2.5 indicates the Phillies' DER and fielding percentage and their

Table 2.4 1915 Baker Bowl Home Runs

	RF	CF	LF	Total
G. Cravath	10	5	4	19
B. Becker	7	0	1	8
F. Luderus	1	0	4	5
D. Bancroft	2	0	2	4
D. Paskert	0	0	2	2
B. Niehoff	0	0	2	2
G. Alexander	0	1	0	1
P. Whitted	0	0	1	1
E. Mayer	0	0	1	1
Phillies Total	20	6	17	43
Visitor Total	6	2	10	18

Table 2.5 Phillies Defense, 1914–1915

Year	Pct	Rank	DER	Rank
1914	.950	8	.656	8
1915	.966	T1	.709	1

rank within the league for 1914 and 1915.

In 1915 Moran brilliantly turned the Phillies from the worst-fielding team in the league into the best. He rectified his weak infield defense by importing Niehoff to play second, shifting Byrne back to third (later replaced by the excellent fielding Stock), and bringing in Bancroft at shortstop. The Phillies' fielding upgrade should not be overlooked when evaluating the outstanding defensive improvement. At a time when fielding was critical to a strong defense, Moran understood its importance and reconstructed his fielders into the league's top unit.

For the World Series, the Phillies faced the American League champion Boston Red Sox. The Phillies won the first game 3–1 behind the excellent pitching of Alexander. The Phillies then lost the second, third, and fourth games, each by the score of 2–1. In both the second and third games, Boston scored in the ninth inning to win the game.

With the Red Sox up three games to one, the series returned to Philadelphia for game five. Moran called on Alexander, who had lost the closely contested game three only two days earlier, to start for the third time. When Alexander felt pain in his shoulder while warming up, Moran scratched him and brought back game two starter Erskine Mayer. The Phillies jumped out to the lead, but once again the Red Sox came back, scoring two in the eighth and one in the ninth, to win 5–4. Alexander later revealed that he had wrenched his shoulder during a Labor Day series against the Brooklyn Dodgers and had been hurting ever since.

Attendance in Baker Bowl for games one, two, and five averaged about 20,000 per game, similar to the year before, when the American League's Philadelphia Athletics, playing in Shibe Park, were in the World Series. In Boston, however, the series drew exceptionally well. The Red Sox had elected to play their games in the newly opened Braves Field, which held more people than their own Fenway Park. Games three and four each attracted over 40,000 spectators, and game three set a World Series record with 42,300.

Despite the series loss, the Phillies' prospects for the future looked bright: they had a great manager, the league's two best players, and a good supporting cast. As a harbinger of things to come, however, Baker took his time about re-signing Moran to a new contract. After some fairly arduous negotiations, Moran signed a three-year deal for $25,000.

Unfortunately for Phillies fans, the club essentially stood pat over the next couple of years and made few moves to improve the team. In 1916 the Phillies actually upped their record to 91–62 but finished second, two and a half games behind the Brooklyn Dodgers. An injury to Bancroft late in the year helped to derail the Phillies' pennant drive. The club finished second again in 1917 at 87–65, ten games behind the New York Giants.

Financial pressures and other economic disruptions from the Federal League war led to an unprecedented sale of players between major league teams. Philadelphia Athletics owner Connie Mack started the trend when he dismantled his 1914 American League pennant winner. Mack sold most of his best players, including Hall of Fame second baseman Eddie Collins to the White Sox for $50,000, Hall of Fame third baseman Frank "Home Run" Baker to the Yankees for $37,500, pitcher Bob Shawkey to the Yankees for $18,000, and shortstop Jack Barry to the Red Sox for $8,000.

After the demise of the Federal League, the New York Giants purchased outfielder Benny Kauff from the Brooklyn Federal League club for $35,000. The Yankees acquired Lee Magee from the same club for around $25,000. In April 1916 Cleveland obtained Hall of Fame center fielder Tris Speaker for $55,000 plus players. There were other deals. The sale of players, including a number of all-time greats, from one major league club to another became quite common at this time.

After the 1917 season Baker entered this market as a seller and never weaned himself from the profits. His first sale signaled a trend that would plague the Phillies franchise for the next thirty years. He sold the National League's best player, Alexander, and one of its better catchers, Killefer, to the Chicago Cubs for $55,000 and two marginal players. Other players soon followed, and the Phillies fell to sixth in the war-muddled 1918 season.

With his three-year contract now expired and Baker selling players to make money, Moran was probably not too disappointed when Baker released him after the season. Moran would go to Cincinnati for the 1919 season, where he would once again perform his off-season magic and lead the newly rebuilt Reds to ninety-six wins (their highest win total prior to 1939) and their first World Series title.

By 1919 the Phillies had descended into last place, a position the club would find familiar over the next several decades. Baker would run the Phillies until 1933, and under his parsimonious oversight the club plunged to the bottom of the National League for the next thirty years. He paid his players as little as any other major league owner and continued to sell off his player talent as fast it could be developed.

Baker was not financially forced to dismantle the Phillies. After the 1915 season, *The Sporting News* reviewed the National League ownership as follows:

> Boston—Owned by James Gaffney, wealthy New York contractor and builder, who still runs his contracting business as a side line and is engaged in construction work that will net him when completed, it is said, several million dollars.
>
> Chicago—Owned principally by Charles P. Taft, who, counting his own fortune and that of his wife, is rated as the richest man in Cincinnati and probably could cash in if pressed hard for 50 millions.
>
> Cincinnati—Backed by Fleischmanns, wealthy manufacturers of Cincinnati, who are perfectly satisfied to continue backing the club, provided certain changes are made in its business management; otherwise, prefer to retire from baseball.
>
> Pittsburg—Owned principally by Barney Dreyfus, wealthy in his own right and connected by family ties with rich distilling interests.
>
> New York—Considered the best paying investment in baseball, owned by Brush heirs and others, the former having besides their baseball interests a chain of stores that pay large profits.
>
> Philadelphia—Owned by a stock company, with president of club reported to be wealthy and with connections that represent much money in both Philadelphia and New York.
>
> St. Louis—Owned by the heirs of the Robisons, former street railway magnates. Owners recently disposed of certain outside interests for $200,000. Club has made money in nearly every year of its operation. Owns its park property, valued at nearly a quarter of a million. May have been embarrassed financially at times, but only because of estate being tied up in court.

Brooklyn was left off this list, but principal owner Charles Ebbets had finally acquired full ownership in 1912. At that same time, however, he built his team a new stadium that became Ebbets Field. He ultimately had to sell half of the club to meet some of his financial obligations.

The Phillies ownership group was not materially inferior to several other teams in the league. Boston, St. Louis, and Brooklyn were also owned by entities of limited capital, and Cincinnati's wealthy Fleischmanns were looking to sell. In addition, after the demise of the Federal

League prior to the 1916 season, the financial pressure on many of the organized baseball owners was much reduced. Thus, there is little reason to believe that Baker could not have continued to compete, had he wished to do so.

◇   ◇   ◇

By 1913 the Phillies had assembled a pretty good ball club. Over the previous couple of years they had added Alexander and Cravath, who became two of the National League's best players. The 1914 team, after having suffered heavy defections to the Federal League, dropped from second place to sixth. Before the 1915 season, new manager Pat Moran made four key personnel moves that rearranged the talent enough to dramatically improve the club. Offensive stars Cravath and Luderus responded in 1915 with excellent seasons. Their strong performance helped overcome the forced trade of Sherry Magee during the off-season. The remarkable turnaround of the defense, however, best exemplifies Moran's genius. Combined with the improved seasons from the holdover pitchers and the addition of Demaree, the team jumped from last to first in runs allowed.

Moran's accomplishment with the 1915 Phillies was impressive. In an era when competition from a third league put pressure on some of the less-capitalized teams, he successfully built a pennant winner. Moran is often overlooked as a great manager because of his short career; he died at age forty-eight in 1924 while managing at spring training for the Cincinnati Reds. In his nine-year career, however, Moran turned two also-ran franchises into pennant winners.

Numerous times in baseball history teams have found themselves with a couple of great players but proved incapable of converting that head start into a winner. The Phillies showed the value of intelligent management as they took advantage of the presence of Alexander and Cravath to construct a champion.

3

TURMOIL AND DETERMINATION: THE 1917 CHICAGO WHITE SOX

*E*ven after more than eighty years, the notoriety of the "Black Sox" in Ameri-can consciousness can hardly be overestimated. The agreement of a number of the 1919 American League pennant–winning Chicago White Sox players to throw the World Series to the Cincinnati Reds remains one of baseball's most notorious and debated events. The amount of money involved, reported at the time to be $100,000, and the idea that the premier event in American sports, the World Series, could be fixed stunned the baseball world and the American public.

Several years ago, at a breakfast function, keynote speaker Bud Selig, baseball's commissioner, spoke on the key issues facing the game, including the revenue disparity between teams in large and small markets, work stoppages, interleague play, and spiraling player salaries. After about an hour, he asked for questions from the audience. One of the first people to be called on, a young woman, wanted to know when "Shoeless" Joe Jackson would be admitted to the Baseball Hall of Fame.

In the words of baseball historians Alison Danzig and Joe Reichler, the scandal "broke up one of the best teams ever fielded. It threw club owners, fearful that the disgrace would wreck baseball and ruin them, into hysteria bordering on panic. . . . They put themselves and organized baseball into the keeping of Judge Kenesaw Mountain Landis and invested him with the dictatorial powers of an autocrat."

For their role in the fix, eight White Sox players were banned from organized baseball for life: ringleader Chick Gandil, Joe Jackson, Buck Weaver, Eddie Cicotte, Swede Risberg, Happy Felsch, Lefty Williams, and

Fred McMullin; none would play after the 1920 season. The relative guilt of each is debated to this day.

The Black Sox team that lost the 1919 World Series was fundamentally the same group that won in 1917. The two teams played the same eight regular position players and top two reserves. Three of the top four starting pitchers were common between the two years.

Many books and articles have been written on the story of the fix and its aftermath, although quite a bit still remains unknown. Naturally, much effort has gone into analyzing the team's undoing, but relatively less into how owner Charles Comiskey assembled this great team.

◇ ◇ ◇

One of the central figures of the first half-century of organized baseball, Chicago White Sox owner Charles A. Comiskey by the 1910s had become an extremely powerful man and a complex personality. Comiskey was born August 15, 1859, at Union and Maxwell Streets on the old West Side of Chicago. He had six brothers and one sister. His father, nicknamed "Honest John," was described in *The Sporting News* as one of the "interesting characters" of Chicago's early days. An alderman for twelve years, he also held the office of county clerk and assistant county treasurer. Comiskey's father disliked baseball, and his mother, whom Comiskey often called his best friend, died when he was still a youngster.

Honest John sent Comiskey to St. Mary's College in Kansas at age fifteen to give him a thorough schooling and (hopefully) to get him away from baseball. Like many parental plans, this one went awry. At St. Mary's, Comiskey joined the baseball club and, along with his brother Jim, played baseball often.

After the close of the 1876 college year, Comiskey's father apprenticed him to a plumber. This plan fared little better than the first in keeping Comiskey away from baseball. When Ted Sullivan, a St. Mary's teammate and mentor, organized a team in Dubuque, Iowa, Comiskey gave up plumbing and followed him.

In 1882 a new major league, the American Association, was formed to challenge the National League. Chris Von der Ahe, the owner of a local beer hall and one of the most colorful characters of the era, owned the St. Louis club. A German immigrant, Von der Ahe spoke with what has been described as a "comic strip" accent.

Sullivan met with Von der Ahe and Alfred H. Spink, a St. Louis sports personage who four years later established *The Sporting News*. Sullivan convinced them to sign his friend, and Spink then sent a letter asking Comiskey to join the Browns for $75 per month. Disappointed in the proposed salary and reluctant to leave his future bride, Comiskey initially hesitated but eventually accepted the offer with the encouragement of Sullivan. Comiskey remembered, "After working for Von der Ahe for awhile, I was surprised to receive a pay envelope containing $125, a raise of $50, without a word from Chris. Von der Ahe was one of the most liberal men ever associated with baseball. Nothing was too good for his players."

Comiskey played first base for the Browns for several years and advanced the techniques used to play the position. He was one of the first to play off the bag at first base and helped originate the strategy of having the pitcher cover first on ground balls to the right side of the infield. In mid-1884 Von der Ahe gave Comiskey, still only twenty-four, the manager's job. Not a great player himself, Comiskey managed his Browns to four straight American Association pennants. Not surprisingly, Comiskey remembered those Browns as one of the best teams of all time.

In 1890, frustrated by low salaries and their lack of basic rights, a number of players found financial backers and formed a third major league, the Players League. Although not an organizer of the new league, Comiskey signed on as manager of his hometown Chicago club for an $8,000 salary. Comiskey later claimed that he had a great team that was "just getting on our feet," but that the Players League was destined to fail because it "wasn't constructed along the right lines."

The league folded after one year and Comiskey went back to Van der Ahe, who, not surprisingly, still harbored resentment over Comiskey's jumping to the fledgling league. After one year back with the Browns, Comiskey negotiated a three-year contract at $7,500 per year as manager of the National League's Cincinnati Reds. Working for John T. Brush, Comiskey managed in Cincinnati from 1892 through 1894.

While in Cincinnati, Comiskey met Ban Johnson, sporting editor and baseball writer for the *Commercial Gazette,* and the two became friends. Despite numerous quarrels and rocky periods, this friendship survived nearly twenty-five years. A strong, complex, and driven man in his own right, Johnson harbored larger designs for the future.

In 1894, Johnson reorganized the Western League and became its president. A year later, his Cincinnati contract having expired, Comiskey acquired the Sioux City franchise in Johnson's league and transferred it to St. Paul, Minnesota. In 1900 Comiskey transferred his club again, this time to his hometown of Chicago. He brought most of his players from St. Paul

Comiskey and the White Sox Salaries

Nearly all accounts that attempt to establish the causes of the Black Sox scandal vilify Comiskey for the low salaries he paid his players. After the collapse of the Federal League and the consequent rollback of salaries, players generally earned less than their true economic value. In evaluating Comiskey's miserliness as an owner, the proper comparison is between the White Sox salaries and those of the other major league teams. When one examines it in this way, one finds that Comiskey rewarded his players no less generously than his fellow owners.

Fortuitously, quite a bit of salary information on the White Sox became available forty years later when, Bill Veeck, who then owned the team, found a hardcover ledger book that included White Sox player salaries. In *The Hustler's Handbook*, Veeck published a number of the figures from the salary list for 1918:

- Second baseman Eddie Collins: a five-year contract at $15,000/year
- Catcher Ray Schalk: a three-year contract at $7,083/year
- Left fielder Joe Jackson: $6,000
- Third baseman Buck Weaver: $6,000
- Pitcher Eddie Cicotte: $5,000, plus a $2,000 signing bonus.
- First baseman Chick Gandil: $4,000
- Outfielder Happy Felsch: a two-year contract at $3,750/year
- Pitcher Lefty Williams: $3,000
- Reserve third baseman Fred McMullin: $2,750
- Shortstop Swede Risberg: $2,500
- Manager Pants Rowland: $7,500

Much of the salary information available in the contemporary press was for the 1917 season. This should not unfairly skew any comparison with 1918 because of the strong downward pressure on salaries at this time. The uncertainty from American involvement in World War I and the end of the competition from the Federal League both militated strongly against any salary increases.

The average salary for 1917 was estimated in *The Sporting News* at $3,000. Not surprisingly, Ty Cobb was the highest-paid player at around $17,500. Tris Speaker was second at $16,000 and Eddie Collins of the White Sox third highest at $15,000. Walter Johnson was probably the game's highest-paid pitcher at $12,000. Veteran outfielder Sam Crawford, now in the Hall of Fame, was making $7,500.

In the National League, the highest-paid player was probably Pete Alexander at about $12,000. He needed to engage in a nasty holdout to receive even this salary after being offered $8,000 for the season. His 1915 and 1916 salaries had been only $6,000 per year, although he had received a $1,000 bonus each year for winning at least twenty-five games. His new contract had a unique clause that his salary could be cut to $10,000 should the Phillies have a "bad season financially, owing to international complications." Boston Braves' veteran second baseman Johnny Evers, described as one of the National League's "very best assets" and "a big drawing card the circuit over," was one of the highest-paid National League players at $10,000. While Evers was clearly not the National League's best player, his Braves were referred to as "one of the highest priced teams in captivity in 1916." Even Hans Wagner, the greatest shortstop of all time, saw his salary plateau at $10,000; he was nearing the end of his career and the Pirates wanted to cut his salary further.

Buck Weaver, at $6,000, was probably the game's highest-paid third baseman in 1918. Heinie Groh made only $4,000 in 1916, and the Reds offered him $4,600 for 1917. Groh wanted a three-year contract for $5,500 per year; it is unlikely that he received it. Rogers Hornsby broke in at third base for the St. Louis Cardinals in 1916 and had a great rookie season; he settled for around $5,000 for 1917.

At over $7,000, Ray Schalk, was almost certainly baseball's most highly paid catcher. One of the National League's top catchers, Phillie Bill Killefer, made $6,500 in 1916. In tandem with Alexander, he held out in 1917 after being offered only $4,500. Chicago Cub catcher Jimmy Archer saw his pay reduced from $7,500 to $4,000 for 1917. Brooklyn Dodger owner Charles Ebbets showed his pettiness by cutting Chief Meyers's $6,000 contract by the amount of his World Series share.

Joe Jackson was underpaid in comparison with other outfielders, but it is hard to lay all the blame on Comiskey. Jackson, described by Veeck as "the world's worst negotiator," signed a three-year contract with the Cleveland Indians for 1914 through 1916 at $6,500 per year. At that point, Jackson was coming off his great first three seasons and had the added negotiating leverage of the Federal League. Before being traded in 1915 in the midst of the Federal League war, he apparently signed another contract for 1917 though 1919 at $7,500 per year. This contradicts Veeck's information but does offer some insight into how Jackson felt about his salary level. Second baseman/outfielder Lee Magee, while not in Jackson's class as a hitter, had been a highly sought-after player in 1916 when the Yankees paid $25,000 for him. Now making $8,000, he was traded in 1917 in what was likely a salary dump.

Journeyman first baseman Chick Gandil, with a $4,000 salary, compares well with his contemporaries. First baseman and cleanup hitter Dick Hoblitzel of the 1916 pennant-winning Boston Red Sox made $5,000 in 1917. Jake Daubert won the MVP award in 1913 and finished second in the league in batting for the pennant-winning 1916 Brooklyn Dodgers. The press held up his contract at $9,000 per year as an example of Federal League–inspired excess. Only the select few earned salaries above the $7,000–$8,000 range.

Swede Risberg, coming off of a feeble rookie year, made $2,500 in 1918. This figure fits into the league's structure. While acknowledging shortstop as the most difficult position to rank, Irving Sanborn selected Everett Scott as the major league's best shortstop following the 1916 season. He received $5,000 for 1917.

Eddie Cicotte was underpaid in 1918, but his $7,000 was $1,000 above the three-year contract he signed at the end of 1914 in the midst of the Federal League war. In those negotiations, Cicotte had asked for $7,000 per year for the three years but settled for $5,000 per year. After reaching the agreement, Comiskey surprised Cicotte with a $3,000 bonus for his loyalty.

Salary information on managers suggests that Rowland, too, was fairly paid. Pat Moran, after leading the Phillies to the 1915 National League flag, signed a three-year contract at $8,333 per year after some heated negotiations. While this was slightly more than Rowland received, until nearly the start of the 1916 season uncertainty still surrounded the demise of the Federal League, and the magnates' reaction against the wartime salaries did not really begin until well into that season.

Summing up, of the White Sox players, three were probably the highest-paid players in baseball at their positions. Three other infielders, Risberg, Gandil, and McMullin, had salaries that fit right into baseball's salary scale. Jackson made nearly as much as he had in Cleveland, when he held additional negotiating power. Cicotte was underpaid but still made a comparable salary to all but the most elite players. Comiskey had his faults, but in comparing the salaries of his White Sox to the rest of baseball, the evidence suggests that he paid no less than his peers.

Transcendental Graphics

Charles Comiskey

with him and won the 1900 pennant in the now-renamed, but still minor, American League.

Shortly after Comiskey's return to Chicago, he purchased a large hunting lodge in Wisconsin called the Woodland Bards where he entertained many of his friends and Chicago celebrities. Prior to the Black Sox scandal, Comiskey could claim to be one of the most popular men in Chicago, and his sympathetic press treatment owed much to including sportswriters among his lodge guests.

Prior to the 1901 season, Johnson declared his American League a major league and announced that it would compete with the established National League for players. With better organization and leadership, the American League thrived and soon overtook the Nationals in attendance. A peace settlement in 1903 resulted in a two-league, sixteen-team structure that would last over fifty years.

There can be little doubt that Comiskey was important to the success of the new league. Witt K. Cochrane, secretary to Comiskey's club in St. Paul, observed in *The Sporting News:*

> Comiskey is the greatest mind in baseball. I was with him day after day and knew his thoughts. Comiskey planned the American League many years before it came into existence. . . . Comiskey saw in Ban Johnson, the Cincinnati baseball writer, the making of a league leader, and he coached his man for the Western League presidency and leadership. It was Comiskey who brought Johnson into the American League and pushed him into the leadership.

Cochrane, no doubt, exaggerates somewhat the relative importance of

Comiskey and Johnson in the formation of the AL, but the strength, vision, and manipulative nature of Comiskey's character comes through in these comments.

In the American League's first season as a major league, Comiskey's White Sox, now managed by pitcher Clark Griffith, won the pennant again. In 1906, Fielder Jones managed the White Sox, then known as the "Hitless Wonders," to a pennant and World Series victory. Comiskey commented on the reasons for that team's success: "Great pitching, wonderful fielding and clever managing won the world's flag for us that year. It was a great tribute to brains and fielding ability for the White Sox to win. It was also an achievement for the Sox pitchers." Comiskey was an extremely competitive, driven man who planned his future and did not like losing.

Over the next several years, as the team remained competitive, Comiskey embarked on two pet projects. In 1909 he purchased a site in Chicago's Bridgeport neighborhood and began construction of Comiskey Park, one of America's first concrete and steel ballparks. Now affectionately known as the "Old Roman," Comiskey on July 1, 1910, opened what the *Reach Guide* called the "Finest Ball Park in the United States" to a laudatory reception. Built at a cost of $750,000, the park stood until the 1990s. Comiskey would let Chicago groups use his new facility free of charge—like many men of self-made wealth, he could be generous, but only on his own terms.

Comiskey achieved another dream after the 1913 season when he took the White Sox on a world tour with John McGraw's New York Giants. Comiskey organized the 38,000-mile tour, a tremendous undertaking for the time. The voyage included stops in Japan, the Philippines, Australia, Ceylon, Egypt, Italy, France, and England and lasted more than four months.

After recovering from his remarkable trip, Comiskey rededicated himself to building a winner for one of the league's flagship franchises. At this point, the White Sox were a mediocre team with an excellent pitching staff. They consistently drew some of the league's highest turnouts: the team led the league in attendance by a wide margin in 1913 and in 1914 finished second in attendance despite direct competition from the new Federal League.

The arrival of the Federal League and the resulting economic dislocation resulted in many of baseball's top stars being available for purchase. Comiskey, a sharp baseball talent evaluator, took advantage of these circumstances to acquire two of the American League's biggest stars, Eddie Collins and Joe Jackson. In addition, he recognized which of his existing players he could win with and successfully filled in the rest of the spots with valuable players and a skilled manager.

The story of how Comiskey put together the 1917 world championship club breaks down into four episodes. First, at the time of his around-the-world tour, Comiskey had already landed two crucial position players. Second, prior to the trip he had assembled most of the key components of his championship pitching staff. Third, Comiskey spent about a year after the 1914 season ended aggressively acquiring several players, including two of baseball's greatest players and a new manager. Finally, he spent 1916 and 1917 attempting to fill the remaining holes.

◇ ◇ ◇

Although several scouts thought Ray Schalk too small (five feet, seven inches and around 150 pounds), Comiskey purchased the catcher from Milwaukee of the American Association in the middle of the 1912 season. Comiskey paid approximately $15,000 in cash and players for the twenty-year-old, the highest price ever paid for a catcher up to that time. *The Sporting News* described Schalk as "quick in mind and body, has a great throwing arm and is full of ginger." He was quickly put to the test in Chicago. Staff veteran Ed Walsh looked at the undersized Schalk and made several disparaging remarks regarding Schalk's ability to handle Walsh's spitball. According to Chicago sportswriter Warren Brown, Schalk responded, "Warm up, you big fathead, and I'll show you." He won Walsh over, and from then on Walsh wanted no one else to catch him.

One of the top backstops of the time, Schalk is one of only two dead-ball-era catchers in the Hall of Fame. In an age when catching over 120 games was a rarity—it was done only forty-one times through the 1920 season—Schalk accomplished the feat six times. He caught over 120 games every year from 1914 through 1923 except for the war-shortened 1918 season. In the deadball era, even more so than today, teams viewed the catcher as the key defensive player and an important partner of the pitcher. While his batting statistics may appear less than impressive to a modern reader, in his day Schalk was viewed as one of baseball's most valuable commodities. Schalk is also generally credited with being the first catcher to back up infield throws to first base.

After Schalk's second full season in 1914, he finished sixth in the most valuable player (MVP) voting—the highest finish for any catcher that year. The MVP vote was then discontinued until 1922, when the thirty-two-year-old Schalk came in third, again the highest finish of any catcher. These particular seasons were in no way exceptional for Schalk. Irving Sanborn, called the "baseball sage of the *Chicago Tribune*" by *The Sporting News*, named Schalk his clear-cut choice as the major league's best catcher on his year-end all-star team in 1916.

The White Sox signed Buck Weaver as a teenager after a couple of minor league seasons and sent him to San Francisco of the Pacific Coast League for the 1911 season. A shortstop with a wild arm, he made fifty-seven errors in ninety-four games that first year. He hit well and the White Sox must have been satisfied with his defense because the team installed him as the starting shortstop in 1912. Over the next several years, Weaver was regarded as one of baseball's better shortstops, but his fielding was often described as erratic. There was enough concern about his defense that by the middle of the decade the team moved him to third base, where he was soon regarded among the league's best.

Among baseball analysts, debate still surrounds how valuable fielding statistics are for evaluating a ballplayer's defensive ability. As the interpretation of baseball statistics has become more sophisticated over the past thirty years, the calculation of successful chances per game, also called range factor, has gained some acceptance as a measure, albeit an imperfect one, of the ability to make plays in the field.

Using chances per game as a measure of fielding, however, is not new. During Weaver's time, when objective attempts were made to assess fielding ability, chances per game (total chances divided by games) was often used along with the well-established fielding percentage. For example, a comparison of Hans and Heinie Wagner in *The Sporting News* used both measures in its discussion of their relative abilities. At the end of the 1916 season the same magazine evaluated second basemen by chances per game.

In a 1914 article *The Sporting News* again evaluated American League infielders using chances per game. The headline read "Donie Bush Still Covers the Ground in Short Field," with a subheading "Percentage of Fielding Chances to Game Prove Tigers' Little Star More Active Than Any Other Man in Position in American League."

And in discussing shortstops in that article, *The Sporting News* wrote: "Though Bush doesn't top the list of American League shortstops in fielding perfection [fielding percent], he is the real master of them all in covering ground, . . . Which means that Bush cut off a great many more hits

Table 3.1 Buck Weaver's Fielding

Year	Fld Pct	Rank	Ch/G	Rank
1912	.915	6 of 6	5.70	3 of 6
1913	.929	7 of 7	6.50	1 of 7
1914	.928	6 of 6	6.08	2 of 6
1915	.939	5 of 7	5.41	5 of 7

per game than any rival shortstop, consequently stopped many more runs, and consequently helped to win a few more games by his brilliant defensive work."

While chances per game offers insights into a player's range, it should be regarded with some skepticism as a precise measurement. Chances per game measures exactly that: how many plays a player made or should have made (i.e., errors); it does not reflect a player's opportunities. Opportunities depend on many variables, including the makeup of the pitching staff and how often the player appears in less than a full game. The more opportunities vary between players, the less useful chances per game is as a gauge of fielding range.

Table 3.1 reviews Buck Weaver's fielding and ranks him against his American League peers who appeared in at least eighty games at shortstop. The statistics seem to bear out the general perception that Weaver was error prone but could get to balls, at least until he appeared to slow down in 1915. As will be discussed, the Sox first attempted to move him to third base in 1916. As a third baseman, Weaver was generally regarded as the best in the American League, although the National League's Heinie Zimmerman and Heinie Groh were usually considered the major league's top two at the hot corner.

◇ ◇ ◇

Over the first twenty years of the twentieth century, the White Sox consistently had strong pitching. The team proved highly adept at replacing the nucleus of the 1906 championship staff as it aged and lost effectiveness. From 1906 through 1917, the club never finished lower than third in ERA.

Over a period of less than two years, from mid-1912 through the start of the 1914 season, the White Sox added three pitchers who would form the core of the 1917 rotation. In July 1912, the White Sox purchased Eddie

Cicotte on waivers from the Boston Red Sox. Cicotte had been an average rotation starter for several years but started the season only 1–3, with an ERA of 5.67, and Boston was looking to move him. According to White Sox historian Richard Lindberg, Cicotte had "earned the reputation of a troublemaker, having been suspended several times by Boston management." Comiskey would later acquire a few other players fitting this description.With the White Sox, Cicotte would develop into one of the league's best starters.

Cicotte threw a variety of curves and a knuckleball but was most famous for his "shine" ball. At that time the spitball was permissible, but the rules prohibited intentionally discoloring the ball. Connie Mack, longtime owner and manager of the Philadelphia Athletics, described the shine ball and spitball pitching in general in *The Sporting News* after the 1917 season.

> No matter what the shine ball is, how it is delivered by a pitcher or when it is used, it is illegal. They should rule it out of the game. There is only one way this can be done. First, eliminate the spitball which should never have been allowed in baseball, and then it will be easy to put the skids on the freak delivery. Chicago pitchers are not the only ones using this "shine" ball. Lots of pitchers have been experimenting with it. To try to get something new is only natural, and since they have been talking so much about this particular delivery I have seen pitchers all over the circuit trying to master it.
>
> I don't know why they pick on the White Sox and accuse them of its promiscuous use. This is probably because Eddie Cicotte is credited with having introduced it.
>
> To my way of thinking, the "shine" ball is nothing more than a particular discoloration of the ball. To discolor the ball is legal as long as the spitball is sanctioned. You can't rule against the one and not the other. From my personal observations, pitchers using the "shine" ball, shine one side of it along the seam, making it dark and heavy by soaking it. The other side, or half of the ball is light, in its natural state. They then grasp the dry or lighter side and with the heavier side as a sort of propeller, deliver the ball to the batsman.

Mack's comments help illustrate the confusion over the legality of the shine ball. Opposing managers often sent balls they believed to be illegal to AL president Ban Johnson for adjudication. Usually no action would be taken, although occasionally a small fine might be imposed. Any confusion was ended in 1920, when all foreign substances were explicitly made illegal.

• • •

In 1913 Reb Russell joined the team as a twenty-four-year-old rookie after one year of organized ball in Texas. He had one of the great rookie pitching seasons of the era: a record of 22–16, an ERA of 1.90, and a league-leading fifty-two appearances. He finished in the top four in wins, innings pitched, ERA, complete games, and shutouts. This workload might have been too much for Russell; he could pitch only 167 innings the following year.

Recovered by 1915, in 1916 he had another stellar year and finished 18–11 while splitting time between starting and relieving. For his 1916 all-star team Sanborn named Babe Ruth his left-handed pitcher, although he observed that Ruth was not a great deal better than Russell. Like Ruth, but obviously not to the same degree, Russell was also an excellent hitter.

In the fall of 1913, Comiskey signed another spitballer, Urban "Red" Faber, after his second season pitching for Des Moines in the Western League. For the world baseball tour the Giants were short of pitchers, so Comiskey lent McGraw the newly acquired Faber for the trip. According to Warren Brown, Faber so impressed McGraw on the voyage that he offered $50,000 for the pitcher.

In his first years on the White Sox, Faber was in danger of being overworked like several Sox pitchers before him. Ed Walsh was the top White Sox pitcher for several years after the 1906 championship season. He had averaged an incredible 375 innings pitched per year over the six seasons of 1907 through 1912. The two top pitchers of the era, Walter Johnson and Christy Mathewson, had only one single season between them in which they exceeded 375 innings. Not surprisingly, after the 1912 season Walsh never again surpassed 100 innings in a season, even though he was only thirty-three years old. To some extent, Walsh became the model for the type of pitcher the White Sox looked for: a workhorse spitball pitcher who would also relieve.

In 1914 *The Sporting News* summarized the history of this pitcher usage problem on the White Sox after Faber pitched a full game Friday and finished games on Saturday, Sunday, and Monday:

> Once upon a time the White Sox had an iron man. His name was Walsh. His fate is a familiar and pathetic story. Then the White Sox got another iron man. His name was Russell. The box scores tell the story of his undoing. Now the Sox have another iron man. His name is Urban Faber. White Sox followers "hail with glee" the amount of work he is now doing . . . forgetting the history of iron men who did similar stunts and broke under the strain.

In 1915 it looked like Faber was next in line, as he had pitched 180 innings through about half the season. *The Sporting News* commented, "hopefully he will last," and once again observed that Ed Walsh first broke under the strain, followed by Reb Russell, and next Joe Benz, "though last year [Jim] Scott and Cicotte did somewhat share the burden with Butcher Joe [Benz]." Faber finished the year with 300 innings, but the White Sox appeared to take note of his workload, and he would not reach that level again until 1920, as a thirty-one-year-old. Faber pitched well in 1916, finishing fifth in the league with his 2.02 ERA.

◇ ◇ ◇

The White Sox had assembled a pennant-quality pitching staff and a couple of very good position players by 1914, but they still lacked enough offensive talent to win. The team had finished last in the league in runs scored in both 1913 and 1914. Between the end of the 1914 season and the end of the 1915 season, Comiskey made four vital moves that helped round his team into one of the greatest of the era.

In his first major transaction, Comiskey purchased second baseman Eddie Collins from the Philadelphia Athletics for $50,000. After being swept in the 1914 World Series, and fearing the defection of his players to the Federal League, Philadelphia team owner and manager Connie Mack decided to break up his great team by selling off his stars. The Athletics, who would descend over the next couple of years into the worst team of the twentieth century, may not have had the financial resources to compete with the Federal League. A fairly wide disparity in financial wherewithal existed among the league's franchises. The competition from the Federal League exacerbated this gap. Comiskey had both the financial resources and baseball acumen to take advantage of this state of affairs. At the end of the 1915 season, *The Sporting News* evaluated the ownership of the American League:

> Boston—Owned by Joseph Lannin, one of the wealthiest men in all New England.
> Chicago—Charles Comiskey, still able to write a check for $50,000 that any bank will cash without taking the trouble to make inquiries as to how his account stands.
> Cleveland—Owned by Charles Somers, wealth in coal and manufacturing investments that temporarily have been embarrassed, but are being rapidly put on their feet by a committee of bankers, who state that his properties are going to be worth a hundred cents on the dollar and that their total

value is upwards of three millions.

Detroit—Owned chiefly by Yawkey and Navin, former being rated as worth $20,000,000. Club made a pile of money last year.

New York—Owned by Messrs. Ruppert and Huston. Former recently became principal heir to estate of $50,000,000 left by his father, to say nothing of wealth in his own right. Huston is a millionaire.

Philadelphia—Owned by Shibes and Connie Mack, former wealthy men and Mack himself listed as worth a quarter of a million, made out of profits of the club.

St. Louis—Owned principally by R. L. Hedges, recently elected president of one of the largest manufacturing concerns in his home city through holdings of a large part of its stock, to say nothing of other investments.

Washington—Owned by a considerable body of stockholders, none of them of great individual wealth, but taken together representing a credit of several millions.

Half of the teams—Cleveland, Philadelphia, St. Louis, Washington—were significantly less well capitalized than the other four. This discrepancy in the financial strength of the teams, along with the added financial pressures of the Federal League, created the unique environment in which several star players became available for purchase.

Not only did Comiskey pay $50,000 for Eddie Collins, but with the lingering threat of player defections to the Federal League, he also signed Collins to a five-year, $75,000 contract and a $15,000 signing bonus.

Many thought the college-educated Collins, nicknamed "Cocky," would be named manager for 1915 after Comiskey jettisoned Jimmy Callahan. In fact, Comiskey surprised everybody by hiring Clarence "Pants" Rowland, one of the few managers at that time with no major league experience. Comiskey had known Rowland for several years and was impressed by his ability to judge talent. Additionally, a strong personality like Comiskey may have wanted a manager who might be more pliant in implementing his wishes than some of the more established men who had managed for him over the previous decade. In the event, Comiskey got the perfect man for what was to become an extremely fractious group of players.

Rowland had spent a number of years managing in the minors around the Midwest. His teams reportedly always had speed, an ability to score runs on few hits, and good ballplayers. George Robbins, Chicago correspondent for *The Sporting News*, wrote that Rowland "seems to have the exceptional talent of knowing a ballplayer when he sees one." Rowland also practiced what was described as "'harmony theory': a pat on the back is worth ten times more than profane attacks and verbal abuse."

Rowland understood other important elements in managing as well. He recognized the value of getting on base, especially for leadoff hitters. Nemo Leibold, the right fielder against right-handed pitching, was a career .266 hitter, but Rowland appreciated the value of his .357 career on-base percentage. In his four seasons as a White Sox regular, he averaged sixty-six walks per season. Rowland also understood the value of platooning and alternated the left-handed Leibold with the right-handed John "Shano" Collins in right field. Collins, a mediocre starter since 1910, was less taxed in a platoon role.

When Rowland took over the team, one of its weaknesses was fielding. With Jack Fournier at first and Weaver at shortstop, many questioned the tightness of the White Sox infield. As discussed in the previous chapter, we evaluate team fielding by looking at both the defensive efficiency record and fielding percentage. Table 3.2 lists both statistics for the White Sox and their rank within the league for 1914 through 1917.

The White Sox appear to have improved their defense over Rowland's first two years. The Boston Red Sox, who won four World Series in the decade, led the league in DER in all four of the years in question.

With the dismantling of the Athletics, there was no clear-cut favorite to win the 1915 American League pennant. With the addition of Eddie Collins to go along with the strong pitching and catching, Rowland came under some pressure to win. Rowland proved up to the challenge and dramatically turned the team around. The White Sox finished third, improving their record by 23 games from 70–84 to 93–61. Most of the improvement derived from the rejuvenated offense, which improved from 487 runs to 717.

Despite the turnaround, Rowland received some flack. *The Sporting News* reported that he had been criticized for possible overwork of the pitching staff, such as Faber's high workload early in the season. His

Table 3.2 White Sox Fielding, 1914–1917

Year	Pct	Rank	DER	Rank
1914	.955	6	.692	4
1915	.965	2	.692	5
1916	.968	2	.708	2
1917	.967	2	.701	2

pitchers supported him, however. Faber claimed his arm was in "perfect condition to pitch." Cicotte noted that the fact that "every pitcher on the club, except Walsh and Wolfgang, have been ready for service all season ought to be conclusive. The Big Moose [Walsh] has been in better condition than for two years. [Spot starter Red] Wolfgang has been bothered by boils all season, which has kept him from being used to finish games."

Eddie Collins, again rumored to be in line for the manager's job, gave his support, although somewhat less than unconditionally: "Rowland did the best he could with the team in a constant state of change and, considering everything, we did well to finish third."

Rowland supposedly had difficulty selecting coaches and often had inexperienced men, or players with poor judgment, as his base coaches. Near the end of the 1916 season Comiskey brought back Kid Gleason, a coach prior to the hiring of Rowland, to lend a hand. Gleason had spent over twenty years as a player in the majors, first as a pitcher and later as a second baseman, and had last played regularly in 1907. A fighter and a disciplinarian, Gleason reportedly worked well with pitchers.

The White Sox made one other major player acquisition prior to the 1915 season when they purchased Oscar "Happy" Felsch from Milwaukee of the American Association for $12,000. A Milwaukee native, Felsch earned his nickname as a youth due to his habitual smile. He liked his whiskey, had a wild streak, and destroyed at least one hotel room.

The twenty-three-year-old Felsch became a very good player and one of the best defensive center fielders of the time. Most observers rated Tris Speaker as the greatest defensive center fielder of the era. Eventually, however, many witnesses viewed Felsch in Speaker's class. Warren Brown wrote in 1952, "He [Felsch] lasted to take his place with Bill Lange [a noted nineteenth-century center fielder], Tris Speaker, and in baseball's later stages, Joe DiMaggio, as the greatest of centerfielders." The 1920 *Reach Guide* added: "[Felsch is] a rival of Tris Speaker as the leading outfielder of the American League, and who by some is said to be greater than the Cleveland star." Finally, even Babe Ruth pointed out, "He was far superior to Cobb on defense and a greater ball hawk than Speaker, and what an arm he had!" As to Felsch's arm, he still holds the major league record for most double plays in a season by an outfielder, with fifteen in the shortened 1919 season.

As with Buck Weaver, Felsch's statistics agree with the perceptions. Although this is getting ahead of the story, table 3.3 lists the ten players who spent considerable time patrolling center field in the American League

Table 3.3 AL Center Fielders, 1915–1920

	Games	PO	A	E	DP	FldPct	Ch/G
Happy Felsch	741	1921	116	53	41	.975	2.75
Tris Speaker	852	2192	133	54	43	.977	2.73
Baby Doll Jacobson	398	964	46	32	13	.969	2.54
Clyde Milan	786	1848	99	79	20	.961	2.48
Tilly Walker	736	1661	122	97	29	.948	2.42
Ty Cobb	781	1769	106	69	31	.965	2.40
Armando Marsans	253	570	30	19	8	.969	2.37
Amos Strunk	615	1307	76	25	18	.982	2.25
Ping Bodie	498	996	74	39	18	.965	2.15
Tim Hendryx	297	577	30	22	4	.965	2.04

from 1915 through 1920 during Felsch's six years in the majors.

Chances per game can be misleading because opportunities vary among players. Time spent in either right or left field, where chances are fewer, can further skew an outfielder's data. Hendryx and Bodie both spent considerable time in right and left fields, respectively; Jacobson, Milan, Walker, and Strunk also played a little in the corner outfield spots. Nevertheless, all the evidence suggests that Felsch was an exceptional fielder.

Felsch could hit some, too. A career .293 hitter, Felsch actually led the 1917 White Sox in batting average despite the presence of more famous teammates like Eddie Collins and Joe Jackson. Although not a home run threat, he consistently rapped out doubles and triples. Table 3.4 ranks the twenty-four major league hitters from 1915 through 1920 who contributed at least 4.0 WAR per 150 games (minimum 1,500 at-bats). Felsch joins Jackson and Collins as one of the top twenty hitters of the time.

Felsch was one of the best center fielders, offensively and defensively, in baseball.

After the off-season acquisitions of Collins, Rowland, and Felsch, Comiskey landed outfielder Joe Jackson during the 1915 season as the final crucial addition to the team. One of the greatest hitters of the dead-ball era, Jackson was one of the very few at the time to challenge Ty Cobb's hitting dominance. He hit .408, .395, and .373 in his first three full seasons, 1911 to 1913, without ever taking the batting crown from Cobb.

Table 3.4 Top Hitters 1915–1920 by Wins above Replacement (minimum 1,500 AB)

	G	AB	AVG	OBP	SLG	R	HR	RBI	SB	WAR/150
Babe Ruth	528	1558	.329	.451	.652	359	103	365	27	9.5
Ty Cobb	800	3039	.372	.447	.507	625	20	466	296	9.3
Tris Speaker	854	3133	.345	.435	.473	593	14	439	146	7.5
Joe Jackson	731	2742	.338	.405	.495	438	33	471	74	7.3
Ross Youngs	411	1570	.324	.395	.430	240	9	147	53	6.9
Rogers Hornsby	704	2592	.323	.384	.467	369	36	360	71	6.4
George Sisler	767	2987	.347	.390	.484	473	40	403	196	6.2
Eddie Collins	856	3080	.319	.418	.410	551	13	382	214	6.1
Benny Kauff	700	2512	.297	.375	.431	397	41	357	158	6.0
Gavvy Cravath	677	2158	.279	.375	.472	308	68	378	41	5.7
George Burns	874	3472	.288	.362	.391	572	25	280	206	5.7
Bobby Veach	876	3355	.313	.373	.452	490	31	598	112	5.5
Edd Roush	784	2932	.319	.366	.429	408	20	370	148	5.4
Heinie Groh	858	3230	.298	.378	.398	499	12	280	88	5.2
Zack Wheat	794	2986	.306	.358	.419	376	29	366	77	4.8
Larry Doyle	732	2655	.284	.343	.395	342	27	323	79	4.5
Harry Hooper	844	3201	.271	.371	.376	502	17	279	133	4.3
Happy Felsch	749	2812	.293	.347	.427	385	38	446	88	4.2
Joe Judge	608	2286	.283	.372	.391	353	10	195	92	4.1
Sam Rice	518	1995	.319	.371	.401	269	7	240	129	4.1
Fred Luderus	720	2538	.286	.355	.390	279	27	307	32	4.1
Hal Chase	623	2378	.299	.325	.430	310	32	340	87	4.1
Frank Baker	513	1984	.289	.348	.394	238	32	268	54	4.0
Harry Heilmann	650	2373	.296	.353	.424	288	29	380	43	4.0

WAR/150 = wins above replacement per 150 games

After acquiring outfielder Harry "Nemo" Leibold on waivers from the Cleveland Indians in July, Comiskey returned to the cash-strapped Charles Somers to try to pry Jackson loose. The trade was consummated on August 21, when Comiskey sent Braggo Roth, Larry Chappell, and Ed Klepfer plus $31,500 to the Indians for Jackson. Roth was a pretty good ballplayer; only twenty-two years old at the time, he ended up leading the league with seven home runs in 1915. Cleveland had the choice between Roth and rookie center fielder Felsch, and selected Roth. One can speculate on how the future of the Indians might have differed had they selected Happy Felsch instead; the Indians would have been unlikely to send $55,000 plus two players to the Red Sox for center fielder Tris Speaker in the following off-season.

Comiskey had completed an extraordinary series of expenditures. From the end of the 1914 season through 1915, he had spent upwards of $110,000, plus several players, to upgrade his club. Collins had cost $50,000 and Jackson $31,500 plus players. Leibold came from Cleveland for $8,000, outfielder Eddie Murphy from Philadelphia cost $10,000, and Felsch required an outlay of $12,000. In normal economic times teams rarely make the truly elite players available. Comiskey took advantage of the disruption caused by the Federal League to acquire two of the league's best players while scouting around to pick valuable additions like Felsch and Leibold.

◇   ◇   ◇

By the end of the 1915 season, Comiskey and Rowland had put in place the nucleus of a championship team. The squad had an excellent pitching staff to which they would add in 1916. In addition, the club had assembled stars at five of the eight defensive positions: catcher Ray Schalk, second baseman Eddie Collins, shortstop Buck Weaver, left fielder Joe Jackson, and center fielder Happy Felsch.

Many felt the team still needed to fill a few holes, particularly at first and third base, and probably in right field as well. The team's solutions for these positions in 1916 produced little improvement, and the solutions tried the following year were only marginally more successful. Nevertheless, the team's acquisition strategy showed an intelligent approach, and the rest of the team was so strong that weakness at these positions turned out to be inconsequential.

Prior to the 1916 season, the White Sox added two significant left-handed pitchers to their staff. The first, Claude "Lefty" Williams, would

Happy Felsch

develop into a big winner for the White Sox before baseball banned him for his role in the series fix. A pretty good pitcher with high win totals, he has been overrated historically. In his four seasons as an ERA qualifier, he only once produced an ERA below the league average.

The White Sox acquired Williams from Salt Lake City after the 1915 season. He recorded statistics only seen in the long season of the old Pacific Coast League: 33–12 with 419 innings pitched, 294 strikeouts, and an ERA of 2.84. Despite his small stature (five feet, nine inches), he became a regular starter for the Sox as a twenty-three-year-old in 1916 and won 13 games.

The team also brought in spitballer Dave Danforth, who had appeared briefly in the majors in 1911 and 1912 before returning to the minors. The White Sox acquired the strikeout pitcher after his 1915 season at Louisville, where he finished 12–8 in 189 innings, with 172 strikeouts and an ERA of 3.00. Rowland used Danforth mostly in relief, and he excelled in that role.

Comiskey had long been trying to improve his team's first-base play. In 1915 slugger Jack Fournier started at first for the White Sox. He hit well but had a reputation as an incompetent fielder. In 1916 the White Sox acquired Jack Ness, a thirty-year-old right-handed-hitting minor league veteran coming off a record forty-nine-game hitting streak in 1915, to platoon with the left-handed-hitting Fournier. Neither hit much in 1916, and

Fournier again fielded atrociously. When Ness refused a $500 pay cut, he lost his spot on the club.

Desiring a more stable solution, Comiskey acquired veteran Chick Gandil from Cleveland for $3,500. Gandil swung the heaviest bat in the majors at fifty-six ounces and had turned in a couple of .300 seasons earlier in the decade. Comiskey had considered purchasing or trading for Gandil the year before from Washington, but the Indians had jumped in and bought him for $7,500. The reduction in Gandil's purchase price clearly signified some dissatisfaction with the player. Gandil was a self-described "wild rough kid" and "roughhouse character."

The Sporting News noted that Gandil would be a good addition for the Sox if they could "secure the best efforts of Gandil all season and if that player works with his head up and his heart in his work." When Clark Griffith sold Gandil to the Indians prior to the 1916 season, he claimed that it was to make room for young first baseman Joe Judge. It appears more than coincidental, however, that approximately three weeks before the sale Griffith was quoted saying that he wanted some "young, hustling, honest players." Until he decided to throw the 1919 World Series, Gandil offered a slightly above-average answer at first base, but he also added another divisive influence to the team.

Table 3.5 examines the hitting by the team's first basemen from 1915 to 1917. Fournier was easily the best hitter of the lot, but Rowland believed his horrific fielding more than offset any batting advantage. So the team made a change, and for the next few years the White Sox received league-average hitting along with respectable defense.

• • •

Table 3.5 Chicago White Sox First Baseman Hitting, 1915–1917

	AB	AVG	OBP	SLG	R	HR	RBI	SB	RC	WAAv	WAR
1915											
Jack Fournier	422	.322	.429	.491	86	5	77	21	100	5.5	6.8
1916											
Jack Fournier	313	.240	.328	.367	36	3	44	19	41	0.7	1.7
Jack Ness	258	.267	.310	.345	32	1	34	4	29	0.1	0.9
Total	571	.252	.320	.357	68	4	78	23	70	0.8	2.6
1917											
Chick Gandil	553	.273	.316	.315	53	0	57	16	64	0.4	2.1

RC = runs created   WAAv = runs above average   WAR = wins above replacement

Table 3.6 Chicago White Sox Hitting by Right Fielders, 1915–1917

	AB	AVG	OBP	SLG	R	HR	RBI	SB	RC	WAAv	WAR
1915											
Shano Collins	576	.257	.298	.368	73	2	85	38	72	-0.3	1.8
1916											
Shano Collins	527	.243	.323	.342	74	0	42	16	64	0.5	2.2
Nemo Leibold	82	.244	.303	.305	5	0	13	7	8	-0.1	0.1
Total	609	.243	.320	.337	79	0	55	23	72	0.4	2.3
1917											
Nemo Leibold	428	.236	.350	.292	59	0	29	27	57	1.0	2.4
Shano Collins	252	.234	.269	.321	38	1	14	14	24	-0.5	0.3
Total	680	.235	.322	.303	97	1	43	41	81	0.5	2.7

RC = runs created   WAAv = runs above average   WAR = wins above replacement

Veteran Shano Collins had manned right field since 1911. An average player both in the field and at the plate, Collins turned in a lengthy career of nearly seventeen hundred games and sixty-four hundred at-bats. For 1916 the team stuck with Collins in right field, but he did not have one of his better years, hitting only .243 with no home runs (although he did have fifty-nine walks, his career high—in no other season did he have more than thirty-two).

For the 1917 season, Rowland hit on the happy solution of platooning the left-handed-hitting Leibold and the right-handed-hitting Collins. The team was looking for a leadoff hitter, and the diminutive Leibold fit the role perfectly. As one of the shorter players in major league baseball at five feet, six and a half inches, Leibold used his size to draw walks. A good fielder as well, Leibold had started in center field for Cleveland. He hit just .236 in 1917, but his .350 OBA that year was higher than for any season of Collins's career.

Table 3.6 examines the hitting by the team's right fielders over the years 1915 to 1917.

The improvement at the position was marginal, but the platoon was at least an intelligent approach to the problem. Leibold, who finished his career with a .357 on-base percentage, gave Rowland the leadoff hitter he wanted. In 1917 the average on-base percentage in the AL was only .318. Nevertheless, every team except the Senators began the season with a leadoff hitter who would finish his career with an on-base percentage between .350 and .370.

Rowland's platoon also kept the veteran Shano Collins involved by getting him 250 at-bats. Although only average as a starter, Collins offered a strong reserve option—a player who can hit and field residing on the bench is a valuable commodity. The right field platoon ended up providing offense that was better than the major league average. Given the strength of the remainder of the club, this was more than satisfactory.

In 1915 the black hole of the White Sox had been third base. The nominal regular was Lena Blackburn, who batted .214 with six extra-base hits (no home runs) in 283 at-bats. The situation became so bad that Rowland played outfielder Braggo Roth at third for thirty-five games. Roth's fielding percentage of .837 is the lowest since 1910 for anyone who played in at least thirty games. Roth made an error on nearly one of every six chances.

For 1916 the White Sox needed to land a quality third baseman. The three best third basemen in the league were Boston's Larry Gardner, Washington's Eddie Foster, and New York's Fritz Maisel. None was available at a reasonable price.

The club worked hardest to acquire the twenty-six-year-old Maisel, who hit .281 in 1915 and stole fifty-one bases; he led the league with seventy-four steals in 1914. The Yankees held out for Joe Jackson; as an indication of how far Jackson's stock had fallen after hitting just .308 in 1915, quite a few observers believed the White Sox should make the trade. Chicago's *Sporting News* correspondent, George Robbins, believed Rowland was actually in favor of the trade. The most frequent opinion heard around the winter meetings was that the deal would "make both clubs." The White Sox, of course, were extremely fortunate that Comiskey vetoed this trade; Maisel never again hit above .232 and was out of the majors by 1919. One can only speculate on the future of the Yankees had they acquired Jackson at this time. Would they have purchased Babe Ruth several years later?

Without another third-base option, the team elected to move Weaver to third and bring in Zeb Terry, a slick-fielding shortstop from the Pacific Coast League, for 1916. The success of the Phillies in importing shortstop Dave Bancroft from the West Coast for 1915 almost surely influenced the White Sox to try a similar strategy. Unfortunately, Terry hit only .190 with few extra base hits the next year. The White Sox acquired twenty-two-year-old Charles "Swede" Risberg from Vernon in the Pacific Coast League to play shortstop. The results differed little from the year before: Risberg hit an anemic .203 and fielded only .913.

Table 3.7 examines the changes in the offensive contributions over the

Table 3.7 Hitting By Weaver's Infield Partners, 1915–1917

	AB	AVG	OBP	SLG	R	HR	RBI	SB	RC	WAAv	WAR
1915											
Lena											
Blackburne	283	.216	.304	.240	33	0	25	13	26	-1.4	-0.3
1916											
Zeb Terry	269	.190	.292	.249	20	0	17	4	22	-1.2	-0.2
Fred											
McMullin	187	.257	.332	.273	8	0	10	9	19	-0.2	0.4
Total	456	.217	.308	.259	28	0	27	13	42	-1.4	0.1
1917											
Swede											
Risberg	474	.203	.297	.285	59	1	45	16	49	-1.0	0.7

RC = runs created   WAAv = runs above average   WAR = wins above replacement

three years 1915 to 1917 by Weaver's partners on the left side of the infield.

Risberg's performance in 1917 was barely adequate, but the best the Sox received in the three years. For the World Series, in fact, Rowland benched Risberg, moved Weaver back to shortstop, and played utility infielder McMullin at third base. It is a cliché that great teams are strong up the middle. With catcher Schalk, second baseman Collins, and center fielder Felsch, the White Sox had three of the best, but Risberg was still a year or two away from becoming a quality regular.

The team that Comiskey had assembled by 1917 included four players recognized as the best in the league at their positions: Ray Schalk at catcher, Collins at second, Weaver at third, and Jackson in left. Center fielder Happy Felsch was a great player but was overshadowed by Ty Cobb and Tris Speaker, two of the best of all time. First baseman Chick Gandil and the right field platoon of Nemo Leibold and Shano Collins were both solid. Of the starting eight, only rookie shortstop Swede Risberg was below average at his position.

Two of the league's best pitchers, Eddie Cicotte and Red Faber, anchored the 1917 pitching staff. Two other excellent pitchers, Lefty Williams and Reb Russell, rounded out the rotation. The staff was also deep. The White Sox boasted two veteran pitchers with career ERAs below 2.50 now limited to spot duty, Joe Benz and Jim Scott, as well as Dave Danforth, an outstanding reliever.

In the spring of 1917, Russell, only twenty-eight years old, showed up with a crooked left arm and a growth on his elbow. The team sent him to an x-ray specialist who proclaimed the arm trouble not serious and prescribed heavy lifting as a remedy. One has to wonder whether the diagnosis and cure might not have been worse than the affliction. Despite his arm troubles, he tossed 189 innings and led the league in winning percentage.

The 1917 pennant race was basically a two-team battle between the White Sox and the Boston Red Sox, the 1916 champions. The Red Sox jumped out to an early lead and held it until early June. From June to mid-August, Boston and Chicago struggled back and forth for the lead, with the White Sox regaining first place for good on August 18. They did so without much help from Weaver, who missed time with a broken finger. A strong run down the stretch gave Chicago a nine-game margin over Boston at season's end.

The team finished 1917 with a record of 100–54, the highest winning percentage of any White Sox team ever. Chicago's excellent season was a product of both strong hitting and pitching, as the team led the league in runs scored and ERA.

It is a tribute to the quality of this ball club that it led the league in offense despite less-than-exceptional years from their two offensive stars, Jackson and Collins. Jackson hit only .301, the lowest of his career. Collins hit .289, the only season of his long career in which he hit less than .300 in over 350 at-bats. Felsch was the offensive spark plug; he led the team in batting at .308, home runs with six (league leader Wally Pipp had only nine), and RBI with 102 (only one behind league leader Bobby Veach).

Cicotte anchored the pitching staff and led the league in ERA, wins, and innings pitched. Faber and Russell also finished in the top five in ERA. Lefty Williams finished 17–8. Danforth went 11–6 in 173 innings pitched with only nine starts but a record forty-one relief appearances.

In the World Series, the White Sox defeated John McGraw's New York Giants four games to two. The White Sox took the first two games in Chicago behind complete games from Cicotte and Faber, but lost the next two in New York. The Sox won game five in Chicago, forcing a sixth game in New York. Red Faber became the World Series hero by pitching a complete game and winning his third game of the series.

In that final game, the White Sox jumped out to a lead by scoring three runs in the fourth inning. One of those runs came on one of the most famous "bonehead" plays in World Series history. With no one out, Eddie

Collins on third and Joe Jackson on first, Felsch bounced to the pitcher Rube Benton. Benton threw to third baseman Heinie Zimmerman, catching Collins off the bag. Felsch and Jackson kept running, and rather than concentrating on putting Collins out, the entire Giant infield seemed to converge between second and third bases. Collins broke for home and ran past catcher Bill Rariden. The Giants had no one behind Rariden, and Collins crossed the plate with the game's first run, Zimmerman in hot pursuit.

The 1917 World Series victory would be the high–water mark for this great team; no White Sox team has won it since.

◇　◇　◇

In addition to the fledgling Federal League, baseball was also disrupted by the First World War during the teens. In April 1917, the United States officially entered the the Great War as a cobelligerent with the Allies. Baseball seemed to escape much of the discomfort of the war until May 23, 1918, when provost marshal Enoch Crowder issued a "work-or-fight" order requiring all draft age men either to find essential war work by July 1 or risk induction into the armed services. Baseball appealed the application of the work-or-fight order to the national game. Near the end of July, Secretary of War Newton Baker ruled against baseball but extended the deadline until September 1. At this point the migration of players out of baseball and into defense work accelerated dramatically.

The 1918 White Sox fell back to sixth, and the *Spalding Guide* reported they "suffered more through loss to the essential industries than any other team in the league." Lefty Williams started only fifteen games and Joe Jackson played in only seventeen before taking wartime production jobs. Additionally, several stars went into the military: Eddie Collins enlisted in the Marines and played in only ninety-seven games, and Red Faber, who joined the Navy, started only eleven.

The dichotomy between the players who chose to work and the players who chose to fight led to further divisions on the club. The press was particularly unsympathetic to Joe Jackson's decision to opt for war work over the armed forces. As a further setback, Reb Russell's arm gave out completely in 1918. Despite the player losses to war work and the military, Comiskey was unhappy with the sixth-place finish in 1918 and released manager Rowland after the season.

Comiskey named coach Kid Gleason to replace Rowland as manager for 1919. Dickie Kerr was the other major addition for the season. Kerr took over the rotation slot vacated by the injured Russell and pitched well.

By the time the season began, the club was virtually divided into armed camps between what would become the Clean Sox and the Black Sox. The Clean Sox group was led by Eddie Collins, whom Gleason named team captain. The team finished the 1919 season three and a half games ahead of Cleveland, with a record of 88–52. The White Sox took over first place for good in July and were never seriously threatened thereafter.

The White Sox led the league in runs scored and finished third in ERA. Cicotte almost repeated his 1917 feat by leading the league in wins and innings pitched and finishing second in ERA. Faber battled arm problems much of the year and was unavailable for the World Series.

The mystery of the 1919 World Series fix still fascinates baseball fans and the public alike. The White Sox lost the World Series that year to the Cincinnati Reds, who cruised through the National League season with a record of 96–44. After acknowledging that anything can happen in a short series and that the Reds had an exceptional record that year, the evidence strongly suggests that Chicago was a better club than Cincinnati.

In the first place, the Reds appear to have been a decent team that broke through for one year based on exceptional performances from some pretty good players. As table 3.8 indicates, in the four years surrounding 1919, the Reds played just above .500 ball.

The Reds had only two outstanding position players, Edd Roush and Heinie Groh, and each had one of his best seasons in 1919. The club had a fairly deep array of pretty good pitchers, but none of them was of Hall of Fame caliber. Several of these hurlers had their best or nearly best season in 1919. Cincinnati did have one of the era's best managers, Pat Moran, who was in his first year with the Reds.

Second, the American League was significantly better than the Nation-

Table 3.8 Cincinnati Reds Record, 1917–1921

Year	Wins	Losses	Pct
1917	78	76	.506
1918	68	60	.531
1919	96	44	.686
1920	82	71	.536
1921	70	83	.458

al. Excepting 1919, of the ten World Series between 1910 and 1920, the American League won nine. The American League won nearly two-thirds of the games, with an overall record of 37–19–1.

This sentiment was strongly felt at the time by most observers. In naming his 1916 all-star team, Irving Sanborn wrote: "Picking an All-American baseball team this year means merely selecting the best team in the American League and looking over that National League field to see if it can be strengthened anywhere. The Ban Johnson circuit has demonstrated its superiority in playing strength for so many seasons that there is no way to controvert the results of the inter-league contests."

Finally, knowledgeable contemporary observers believed the White Sox were a truly great team. Ed Barrow, one of the most successful baseball executives of the first half of the twentieth century, claimed, "The greatest team of all time was the Chicago White Sox of 1919." And he went on to add, "Those 1917–1919 White Sox were without equal. They had pitching, power, defense, and perfect balance. They didn't have a weakness. I would put the 1927 Yankees right behind them." Manager of the world champion 1918 Boston Red Sox, Barrow later served as the top Yankee executive for twenty-two years and assembled many of the Yankee juggernauts of the 1920s and 1930s. Nevertheless, he ranked these White Sox over any of his own squads.

A top baseball writer of the time, Fred Lieb, wrote of these White Sox, "The White Sox club was one of the most compact ever put together. It is said of some players: 'He can be as good as he wants to be.' Well, one could almost say that about this club. Whenever it felt inclined to extend itself, it could turn on the heat." In 1944, when *The Sporting News* polled 140 sportswriters as to the greatest team of all time, the 1927 Yankees finished first with seventy-one votes, and the White Sox of 1919 finished second with fifteen.

This highly regarded team did not post great winning percentages mainly because the club was in constant turmoil. The White Sox divided into factions, and the factions then divided into cliques. Many of the players were tough, strong-willed men, and when they did not get along, the situation could become very chaotic. Warren Brown later wrote of Rowland's departure after the 1918 season to buy into the minor league Milwaukee franchise: "Manager Rowland, for all of the fact that he had led the team to a world's championship, was not too happy with his lot. He felt that he was getting room and board in a den of jaguars, with a hyena or two and a few wolves tossed in for good measure."

Star second baseman Eddie Collins told Ed Barrow, "Gandil and I didn't speak to each other for two years while playing side by side. Some of the pitchers didn't like Schalk. Many a time bad throws or wrong throws were written into the records because the thrower didn't care for the guy he was throwing to and wouldn't give him a chance to make the catch." He added. "Can you imagine that? We played like a lot of school kids. Yet, we won going away."

The White Sox were the best team in the best league. Including Hall of Famer Schalk, the team had five of the top twenty players in baseball. Comparing teams over many years is fraught with difficulty; nevertheless, these White Sox are correctly recognized as one of the best of their generation.

◇ ◇ ◇

In the aftermath of the 1919 World Series, the relationship between the White Sox factions degenerated even further. The Clean Sox clique obviously suspected some of their teammates of the World Series shenanigans, especially when the 1920 season itself appeared suspect. Historian Lindberg suggested that the Sox "would have probably won the [1920] pennant if Rothstein [New York gambler Arnold Rothstein, who had been involved in the 1919 series fix] and his friends hadn't decided on Cleveland as their choice." After taking over the lead briefly near the end of August, the Sox lost several games. Eddie Collins reflected on the season many years later:

> It was in Boston the incident happened that cost us the 1920 pennant. Some gamblers got panicky that we'd win again and they must have gone to the players they had under the thumb and ordered the rest of the games thrown. We were leading by three games with seven to go [Collins's memory of the timing of these games may be faulty here—the Sox lost the three straight to Boston at the end of August, and Cleveland never lost the lead after mid-September]. We knew something was wrong but couldn't put our finger on it. The feeling between the players was very bad. Dickie Kerr was pitching for us and doing well. A Boston player hit a ball that fell between Jackson and Felsch. We thought it should have been caught. The next batter bunted and Kerr made a perfect throw to Weaver for a force out. The ball pops out of Weaver's glove. When the inning was over Kerr scaled his glove across the diamond.
>
> He looks at Weaver and Risberg who are standing together and says, "If you'd told me you wanted to lose this game, I could have done it a lot easier." There is almost a riot on the bench. Kid Gleason breaks up two fights. That was the end. We lose four more games the same way.

While Collins's memory may be a bit hazy on some of the specifics, it does illustrate the extreme turmoil on the White Sox. Note that despite being banned with the rest of the Black Sox and despite Collins's recollection, Weaver has never been implicated as a participant in the World Series fix. He was exiled from baseball for knowledge of the plan, not involvement.

Upon his return to Chicago, Collins confronted Comiskey with his suspicion that the Boston series had been fixed. Comiskey failed to start any sort of investigation, but events now overtook him. On September 7, 1920, a grand jury in Cook County, Illinois, was called to investigate allegations of a fix in the Cubs-Phillies game of August 31, 1920. The grand jury testimony soon expanded to include the 1919 World Series, and a newspaper scoop on September 27 implicated the Sox players even further. Several of the conspirators were then paraded before the grand jury to give their now-famous testimony on the fix. The eight conspirators appeared in their last game on September 27. At the end of that day the White Sox trailed the Cleveland Indians by only half a game. Comiskey suspended the Black Sox the next day. None would ever return to organized baseball.

The 1920 season ended approximately one week later, with the White Sox finishing second, two games back. The team would not again contend for a pennant for many years.

The banning of Jackson, Weaver, Felsch, Cicotte, and Williams represented an especially severe loss to the White Sox. Had Jackson, one of the great offensive ballplayers prior to the live-ball era, been able to play in the major leagues past 1920, he would almost surely have finished with a hit total among the highest of all-time (see sidebar) and landed in the Hall of Fame before World War II. Table 3.9 ranks the top ten hitters by wins above replacement per 150 games for all seasons through 1920 (minimum 30 WAR).

It should be pointed out, however, that his first three seasons were Jackson's greatest. As table 3.10 indicates, he never again posted a WAR as high as he recorded in 1913.

In the late 1910s Jackson was still a great player. While unlikely to ever recreate the monster totals of his early days, he would probably have remained a dominant player for several years.

Weaver's hitting dramatically increased in 1917 and he sustained this new level through the 1920 season. Had he been able to maintain the hitting increase—a strong possibility with the overall increase in batting averages in the 1920s—his career statistics would have improved consider-

Table 3.9 Top Ten Hitters by WAR through 1920

	G	AVG	OBP	SLG	R	HR	RBI	SB	RC	WAAv	WAR	War/ 150
Ty Cobb	2041	.370	.433	.512	1502	69	1274	780	1783	107	128	9.4
Babe Ruth	533	.328	.450	.650	360	103	367	27	449	29	33	9.4
Dan Brouthers	1673	.342	.439	.519	1523	106	1296	256	1806	73	95	8.5
Billy Hamilton	1591	.344	.455	.432	1690	40	736	912	1727	66	87	8.2
Joe Jackson	1332	.356	.423	.517	873	54	785	202	1094	57	72	8.1
Tris Speaker	1769	.342	.424	.484	1189	53	912	384	1385	70	89	7.6
Pete Browning	1183	.341	.403	.467	954	46	659	258	1154	42	58	7.3
Ed Delahanty	1835	.346	.411	.505	1599	101	1464	455	1792	64	89	7.3
Hans Wagner	2792	.327	.391	.466	1736	101	1732	722	2161	100	132	7.1
Eddie Collins	1869	.329	.419	.426	1253	28	1856	584	1379	67	88	7.1

ably. When banned after 1920, Weaver was twenty-nine years old and had a career batting average of .272 (although after 1916 he never hit below .284) and 1,308 hits. In the new live-ball environment of the 1920s, he could easily have put together a run of five or six years of .300 batting averages.

Felsch, like his teammates Weaver and Jackson, would have dramatically enhanced his career statistics in the live-ball era had baseball not barred him for being in on the fix of the 1919 World Series. Only twenty-nine years old heading into the 1921 season, he would have likely ended up with a career batting average above .300, high doubles and triples totals, and a deserved reputation as one of the best center fielders of the era.

Although Cicotte was thirty-six when banned, he had shown no signs of slowing down; he won 50 games over the 1919 and 1920 seasons. A couple of more winning seasons on top of his 208–149 lifetime record and 2.38 ERA would have built a compelling case for the Hall of Fame.

Lefty Williams won forty-five games between the 1919 and 1920 seasons and would also likely have put together a number of fine seasons in the 1920s. As table 3.11 indicates, the 1920 White Sox pitching staff finished with four pitchers winning at least twenty games.

Table 3.10 Joe Jackson, 1911–1920

	Team	AB	G	AVG	OBP	SLG	R	HR	RBI	SB	RC	WAAv	WAR
1911	CLE	571	147	.408	.468	.590	126	7	83	41	147	8.3	9.9
1912	CLE	572	154	.395	.458	.579	121	3	90	35	149	8.3	10.0
1913	CLE	528	148	.373	.460	.551	109	7	71	26	133	8.2	9.7
1914	CLE	453	122	.338	.399	.464	61	3	53	22	85	4.1	5.4
1915	CLE & CHI	461	128	.308	.385	.445	63	5	81	16	84	3.2	4.7
1916	CHI	592	155	.341	.393	.495	91	3	78	24	115	6.1	7.8
1917	CHI	538	146	.301	.375	.429	91	5	75	13	100	4.7	6.3
1918	CHI	65	17	.354	.425	.492	9	1	20	3	14	0.8	1.0
1919	CHI	516	139	.351	.422	.506	79	7	96	9	110	5.7	7.2
1920	CHI	570	146	.382	.444	.589	105	12	121	9	138	6.8	8.5

For a team with so much history, the 1920 White Sox were surprisingly young. Of the key regulars, only Eddie Collins, Red Faber, and Eddie Cicotte were over thirty years old, and the first two proved to have quite a bit of baseball left. Collins stayed a star for another five years, even finishing second in the 1924 MVP balloting.

Faber would go on to pitch well for the hapless White Sox of the 1920s and early 1930s. He was one of several spitball pitchers grandfathered after his specialty pitch was banned in 1920. Faber retired in 1933 as the last legal American League spitballer.

After winning the 1917 championship, Comiskey had remained active in obtaining new talent despite having a young, established team. In 1919 he brought in Kerr, a World Series bright spot and twenty-one-game winner in 1920. Johnny Mostil, who became a mainstay of Chicago's outfield throughout the 1920s, first appeared in ten games during 1918.

After losing the eight banned players, it is not surprising that the White Sox collapsed into mediocrity during the 1920s—the team did not finish higher than fifth until 1936. The scandal would cost Comiskey his health, some of his fortune, and, after his indecisive response to the scandal, his reputation.

Prior to the scandal Comiskey was one of the most intelligent, wealthy, competitive, and powerful of baseball's magnates. Although feuding with

Table 3.11 Starting Pitchers in 1920

Pitcher	Win-Loss	Win Pct	ERA
Faber	23-13	.639	2.99
Cicotte	21-10	.677	3.27
Kerr	21-9	.700	3.37
Williams	22-14	.611	3.91

his old friend Ban Johnson, Comiskey was also a force in the league's boardrooms. If there had been no Black Sox scandal, there is little reason to believe the White Sox would not have challenged the Yankees as one of the league's dominant clubs throughout the 1920s.

WHAT WOULD JOE JACKSON'S FINAL HIT TOTAL AND BATTING AVERAGE HAVE LOOKED LIKE IF HE HADN'T BEEN BANNED?

Joe Jackson, banned after the 1920 season for his part in the World Series fix, currently holds the third highest career batting average at .356. Only Ty Cobb at .366 and Rogers Hornsby at .358 are higher. With the caveat that alternative history is by its very nature completely speculative, we hypothesize here on Jackson's lifetime hit total and batting average had his career been allowed to run its natural course.

Most baseball analysts who have studied aging patterns recognize that hitters typically peak between the ages of twenty-six and twenty-nine, and Jackson was already thirty-one by 1920. On the other hand, a historic transformation in the batter/pitcher matchup occurred around 1920, and run scoring increased dramatically.

According to *Total Baseball*, Joe Jackson was born in 1889. We found eight other players born between 1888 and 1890 who had at least twelve hundred at-bats and a .300 average through 1920. Benny Kauff, who himself was banned, and Vin Campbell, a Federal Leaguer who was unable to get back into the majors after the Federal League folded, never played after 1920. The batting averages of the remaining six through 1920 are listed in table 1. Table 2 shows how each of the six performed after 1920.

The average of at-bats after 1920 was 3,805 and the average (unweighted) increase in batting average for the six players was .014. Assuming that post-1920 Jackson hit .014 better than his average through 1920, table 3 shows his hypothetical career:

Table 1 Batting Averages through 1920

	Birth Year	AB	H	AVG
Baby Doll Jacobson	1890	1773	532	.300
Stuffy McInnis	1890	5231	1607	.307
Sam Rice	1890	1995	637	.319
Tris Speaker	1888	6521	2232	.342
Bobby Veach	1888	4456	1356	.304
Zack Wheat	1888	5749	1738	.302
Weighted Average		4288	1350	.315
Arithmetic Average				.313

Table 2 Batting Averages after 1920

	Birth Year	AB	H	AVG	dAVG
Baby Doll Jacobson	1890	3734	1182	.317	0.016
Stuffy McInnis	1890	2591	798	.308	0.001
Sam Rice	1890	7274	2350	.323	0.004
Tris Speaker	1888	3674	1282	.349	0.007
Bobby Veach	1888	2200	707	.321	0.017
Zack Wheat	1888	3357	1146	.341	0.039
Weighted Average		3805	1244	.327	0.012
Arithmetic Average				.327	0.014

dAVG = increase in batting average after 1920

Thus, our methodology suggests Jackson may have finished with nearly 3,200 hits and a career batting average of around .362. For Jackson to have hit .367 over the course of his career and recorded the highest all-time average would have required him to hit .382 (1,453 for 3,805) after 1920. An increase of .026 would have been unlikely, but not outside the realm of possibility. After all, one of the six, Wheat, improved by much more than this.

Table 3 Hypothetical Joe Jackson Career Batting Average

	AB	H	AVG
Actual career	4981	1772	.356
Plus post-1920 estimate	3805	1406	.369
Hypothetical career	8786	3178	.362

4

CLARK GRIFFITH—PATIENCE: THE 1924 WASHINGTON SENATORS

*A*s *the 1924 season approached, the New York Yankees were a prohibitive* favorite to win the American League pennant. Rarely remembered after subsequent decades of Yankee success, the early-1920s clubs won three straight pennants and the 1923 World Series. There was every reason to expect that they would keep right on winning.

The 1923 powerhouse won by sixteen games, the largest margin of victory in a major league since the 1907 Chicago Cubs, and the Yankees were not particularly old. Among the regular players and pitchers, only catcher Wally Schang and pitcher Bob Shawkey were older than thirty. Babe Ruth had one of his greatest years (forty-one home runs, 131 RBI, .393), playing in the brand-new Yankee Stadium, dubbed "The House That Ruth Built" by Fred Lieb. A strong and deep pitching staff included five hurlers who won at least sixteen games: Sam Jones, Herb Pennock, Joe Bush, Waite Hoyt, and Shawkey.

The Yankees built this team largely through the generosity and largesse of the Boston Red Sox. Over a period of three years, New York acquired Ruth, Jones, Pennock, Bush, Hoyt, Schang, third baseman Joe Dugan, and shortstop Everett Scott from the Red Sox for a combination of lesser players and money. These trades unquestionably destroyed the Red Sox, winners of four World Series in the 1910s, and provided the foundation for the Yankee dynasty.

Meanwhile, the 1923 Washington Senators had finished in fourth place, 23 1/2 games behind New York. Unlike the Yankees, the Senators were an aging team, both on the mound and in their lineup. Walter Johnson and

George Mogridge, the team's two best starting pitchers, were thirty-five and thirty-four, respectively. Washington also started three players who were in their thirties: shortstop Roger Peckinpaugh and outfielders Sam Rice and Nemo Leibold.

For the third straight season Washington owner Clark Griffith fired his manager, this time Donie Bush. He then hired Bucky Harris, his scrappy twenty-six-year-old second baseman and one of the younger players on the team. Other than a new manager, the team Washington would field in 1924 was essentially the same outfit as the one that had fallen well short in 1923. Even if they had predicted that a team would challenge the Yankees in 1924, few would have chosen the Senators as the challenger.

◇ ◇ ◇

By 1924 Washington's reputation as a baseball wasteland was firmly in place. Not only had the Senators never won an American League pennant, but the city had also failed with several other major league clubs. In the first year of the National Association (sometimes considered a major league), the 1871 Washington Olympics ended the season 16–15, the last Washington team to finish above .500 for more than forty years. In the remaining four seasons of the National Association, Washington fielded four different clubs that combined for a record of 15–72.

With the demise of the National Association, Washington was without major league baseball until 1884, when the city fielded *two* teams. The Nationals of the American Association ended up 12–51 and failed to finish the season. The Nationals of the Union Association fared little better, finishing 47–65 in a dreadfully unsuccessful league. When the UA folded, the Nationals moved to the minor Eastern League for one season before resurfacing in 1886 in the National League. This franchise, the first Senators, finished (successively) last, next-to-last, last, and last in its four years. After the 1889 campaign, the NL mercifully dropped Washington from the league.

When the American Association gave Washington another try in 1891, the city's entry finished solidly in last place. For the 1892 season this team joined the National League as part of the AA merger. This second NL Washington club, also called the Senators, competed for eight years and never ended a season closer to first than thirty-two games. When the National League contracted from twelve teams to eight before the 1900 season, Washington once again lost its league franchise.

• • •

As a charter member of the American League in 1901, Washington picked up right where all of its predecessors had left off. In the first eleven years of the league, the Senators finished eighth (last) four times, seventh five times, and sixth twice. At this point (after the 1911 season), the nation's capital had been represented in all but twelve of the forty-one years of major league baseball (thirty-one different seasons), and had an aggregate won-loss record of 1,317–2,335. In those years in which the Washington team completed the season, it finished last ten times. The city boasted a winning record only once.

A legendary scouting trip by backup catcher Cliff Blankenship in 1907 was the highlight of the first decade of the American League's Washington Senators. Blankenship had broken his finger, and in those days teams did not like to pay players to sit around and heal. Manager Joe Cantillon sent the catcher to Wichita, Kansas, and Weiser, Idaho, to take a look at a couple of prospects he had glowing reports on. Blankenship liked what he saw of the youngsters, outfielder Clyde Milan and pitcher Walter Johnson, and signed them both to Senators contracts.

An excellent outfielder, Milan spent his entire sixteen-year career with the Senators. With no power but good plate discipline, Milan twice led the league in stolen bases, hit .285 lifetime, and played a great center field. For the acquisition of Milan alone Blankenship's trip justified the trouble and expense. Until Milan became player-manager in 1922, he would room with his fellow Blankenship signee, Walter Johnson, for fifteen years. Their sixteen years as teammates set a major league record.

The story of Walter Johnson has been told and retold. Johnson played twenty-one years in the major leagues, all of them with the Senators. Toiling for teams that were generally mediocre, he won 417 games. Understanding that he often needed to take matters into his own hands, Johnson tossed 110 shutouts, 20 more than his closest challenger, Pete Alexander. Johnson could also help his own cause at the plate, rarely hitting below .200, and once finishing as high as .433 in 97 at-bats.

Johnson and Milan each joined the Senators in 1907, but Washington remained lousy for a few more years. About this time vaudevillians popularized the joke that Washington was "first in war, first in peace, and last in the American League." This quip is often used to represent the entire sixty-year history of the first American League Senators franchise, but the truth is much more interesting.

In 1912, Clark Griffith became the Senators' manager and a leading stockholder. First as manager and later as owner, Griffith essentially ran the team until his death in October 1955. The Senators did not finish in last place in his first thirty-two years in charge, and the team was often quite competitive. For Griffith, it became a matter of pride and principle that the team would *never* finish last. He succeeded in this goal until 1944, when World War II scrambled major league rosters.

Griffith started his major league pitching career as a twenty-year-old in 1891, when he won fourteen games for St. Louis and Boston in the American Association. Despite this fine start, he was a victim of the elimination of four teams (and 25 percent of major league jobs) in the 1892 merger of the American Association and National League. Resurfacing at the end of the 1893 season with Cap Anson's Chicago Cubs, Griffith ran off six consecutive seasons of twenty or more victories and had ERAs about a run less than the league average.

Griffith soon earned the nickname "The Old Fox" because of, in the words of sportswriter Shirley Povich, "his canny pitching, his awareness of the batters' weaknesses, his sly tampering with the ball, and all the other tricks which in those days were permissible." He used a vast repertoire of pitches, delivery points, and windups, giving him a reputation much like that of Luis Tiant eight decades later. Griffith claimed to have invented the screwball. He compiled an impressive won-loss record of 237–146 over a pitching career that did not completely end until 1914.

In the winter of 1900–1901, Griffith played a critical role in the formation of the American League. An outspoken critic of the established National League's treatment of players and its maximum $2,400 salary, Griffith reportedly traveled all over the country to talk fellow National Leaguers into joining the new league. After convincing more than thirty players to switch leagues, he became the player-manager for Charles Comiskey's Chicago club. In 1901, Griffith led the White Sox to the pennant in the AL's first year as a major league, while also winning twenty-four games as a pitcher.

After the 1902 season, Ban Johnson, who ran the new league like a czar, played another card in the league's war with the National League. Johnson dissolved the Baltimore team, created a new club in New York, and installed Griffith as the New York manager. Griffith led the newly christened Highlanders for six years, then spent three years as manager of the NL Cincinnati Reds. After the 1911 season, Griffith wanted to return to the American League, and he leapt at the chance to buy into the struggling Senators.

Under the guidance of the Old Fox, the Senators placed in the first division for the next four years, topped by second-place finishes in both

1912 and 1913. Griffith deserves a lot of the credit; other than Johnson and Milan, the team had no star players. Chick Gandil, who later achieved infamy with the Black Sox, was probably the Senators' next best player. The 1911 team, which finished 64–90, might have been a good minor league outfit without Johnson's 25–13 record and 1.90 ERA.

Almost alone, Walter Johnson lifted the team out of mediocrity. The 1912 and 1913 Senators finished with successive records of 91–61 and 90–64, the best two records the team posted prior to 1924. At a glance, one could conclude that Walter Johnson finally had a good team behind him and that he responded with two of his biggest years. In reality, the team had good records *because* Johnson pitched so well.

In the two seasons, the team had an essentially league-average offense. The team was successful largely because it led the league in ERA in 1912 (2.69 against an average of 3.34) and finished third in 1913 (2.73 against an average of 2.93). The Senators won because of their pitching and their defense. Table 4.1 illustrates Johnson's effect on the statistics of these two pitching staffs.

Over the two seasons, the Senators were fifty-six games above .500; Johnson was fifty games above average, and the rest of the pitchers six. Playing in what was essentially a neutral park (favoring neither the hitter nor the pitcher), the ERA of "Everyone Else" was .17 lower than the league in 1912, and .32 higher in 1913. The Senators were a mediocre team that Walter Johnson pushed to thirty games over .500.

Griffith continued to make progress improving his club. His initial contribution after taking over the club was to provide Walter Johnson with an average supporting cast. In order to compete for championships, Griffith needed to find a few more stars.

Griffith found two in 1915. He first acquired pitcher Sam Rice from Pe-

Table 4.1 Walter Johnson in 1912 and 1913

	Wins	Losses	Pct.	IP	ERA	LgERA
1912 Senators	91	61	.599	1376.2	2.69	3.34
Walter Johnson	33	12	.733	369.0	1.39	
Everyone else	58	49	.542	1007.2	3.17	
1913 Senators	90	64	.584	1396.1	2.73	2.93
Walter Johnson	36	7	.837	346.0	1.14	
Everyone else	54	57	.486	1050.1	3.25	

tersburg of the Virginia League. After thirty-nine innings on the mound, the Old Fox slyly moved Rice to left field, a position he patrolled until 1933. Griffith also purchased first sacker Joe Judge from Buffalo of the International League. Judge claimed the first-base job through 1932. He and Rice played as teammates for eighteen years to break the record set by Johnson and Milan. Their record would last until Lou Whitaker and Alan Trammell broke it in 1995 with the Detroit Tigers.

Rice would end up in the Hall of Fame and Judge would not, but they were very similar offensive players. Rice had a higher batting average (.322 vs. .298) but Judge had more power and walked more, so their slugging percentages (.427 vs. .420) and on-base percentages (.374 vs. .378) were nearly identical. Judge would suffer a few nagging injuries, so Rice ended up with a thousand more plate appearances and more impressive career statistics.

In 1919 the team bought Bucky Harris from Buffalo, and he held the second-base job for nine years. Though not a great player, Harris was a defensive star (Walter Johnson thought he was without peer at second) who played with the aggressive, cocky attitude that Griffith loved. Years later, Griffith called Harris "the gamest ballplayer I ever saw in fifty years of baseball. He was the smartest player I ever had."

Griffith had not signed any superstars, but he had found good players who could contribute to a good team for a decade or more. It stands to reason that if a team secures players who can play a major role for ten or fifteen years, it does not need to find as many players. When Griffith plugged a hole, it stayed plugged. By staffing the team with long-term solutions, when a season arose with no dominant club, the Senators could be assured of a competitive team with a minimum of flaws to address. To Griffith's credit, he also found a couple of Hall of Fame–caliber players.

The team staggered a bit in the late teens and fell to seventh place in 1919, but Griffith was assembling the pieces of a championship team one at a time.

◇ ◇ ◇

After the 1920 season, Griffith bought enough additional stock to assume complete control of the team and resigned his post as manager. After twenty years as a big league manager and thirty years in baseball, Griffith had earned a reputation as a firebrand and a man who rivaled John McGraw as a pest to umpires. After leaving the dugout for the front office, he seemed to transform overnight into a quiet, gray-haired gentleman in a

Table 4.2 Increase in Run Scoring, 1917–1921

Year	Runs/G	AVG	HR/G
1917	3.59	.249	.13
1918	3.63	.254	.12
1919	3.87	.263	.20
1920	4.36	.277	.25
1921	4.76	.291	.39

three-piece suit. Nonetheless, the fire still burned. Griffith hired four managers in his first four years as owner as he sought someone who could stir up the team as he had ten years before.

The game of baseball changed substantially after the Great War, when the dramatic emergence of Babe Ruth in New York ushered in the "Big Bang" era. Table 4.2 shows the increase in run scoring from 1917 to 1921.

Ruth was a trailblazer who showed that holding your hands at the end of the bat while taking a good healthy cut, contrary to how players had been taught for generations, was an effective way of generating some offense.

Equally significant factors in the increased run scoring were the decisions to outlaw the spitball and other trick pitches, as well as a new policy requiring fresh baseballs to be in play at all times. Fresh baseballs, especially those not defaced with mud, traveled more predictably and could be hit more solidly.

The new era required a different breed of player. Accordingly, in late 1921 Griffith bought outfielder Leon "Goose" Goslin from Columbia (South Carolina) of the Sally League. In one version of the signing, Griffith had never heard of Goslin, but a golfing partner alerted him that Jack Dunn of the International League's Baltimore Orioles was about to buy Goslin. Showing due respect for the acumen of Dunn, Griffith called Columbia himself and made a higher offer. Goslin hit .300 his first year and became the best hitter the Senators ever had.

That same summer, longtime Senator scout Joe Engel discovered twenty-three-year-old third baseman Ossie Bluege playing for Peoria in the Three-I League. Bluege failed to hit much in his first few years but he was considered one of the best defensive players of his time. Clark Griffith later called him the best defensive player ever, at any position. Following a general pattern, Bluege played for the Senators for the next eighteen years.

Griffith also made gradual progress building his pitching staff. He signed Tom Zachary, with two games of experience behind him and eighteen years ahead, in 1919. On the other hand, thirty-two-year-old George Mogridge was apparently washed up when acquired from the Yankees for outfielder Braggo Roth. Zachary and Mogridge won twelve to eighteen games each year for the next several years and, along with Walter Johnson, formed the core of the rotation through 1924.

Prior to the 1922 season Griffith engineered a three-team trade with Philadelphia and Boston that brought in Roger Peckinpaugh, arguably past his prime at thirty-one but one of the most respected and accomplished shortstops in the game. Along with Judge, Harris, and Bluege, this gave the Senators an infield of which Griffith later said, "When the ball is hit in their direction, everyone is out."

Before the 1923 season, Griffith filled another big hole by trading three players to the Red Sox for twenty-seven-year-old catcher Muddy Ruel. His pitchers loved him, and Ruel also turned into one of the better hitting backstops of the time. Ruel was a bright man, a practicing attorney in the off-season, and is credited for coining the term "the tools of ignorance" to refer to a catcher's equipment. He lasted as the regular catcher through 1928.

One of the most interesting players on the 1923 Senators was Allan Russell, who had previously pitched for several years with the Red Sox and Yankees and who was one of the few pitchers still allowed to throw a spitball. Manager Donie Bush (likely with the urging of Griffith) turned Russell into one of the first full-time relief specialists. He started five games, relieved in forty-seven (a new record), finished 10–7 and "saved" nine games. (Saves were not recorded in 1923, but were retroactively figured in the 1960s.) Of his 181 innings pitched, 144 came in relief (also a new record), meaning he pitched an average of 3 innings every time he came in as a reliever. His record indicates he was used with the game in doubt, as a critical member of the Senators pitching staff.

In 1923 scout Joe Engel found Fred Marberry pitching for Little Rock in the Southern Association. Nicknamed Firpo for his resemblance to Argentine boxer Luis Firpo, Marberry joined the Senators at the end of 1923 and finished 4–0 in eleven games with a 2.80 ERA. Then twenty-four, he had only been pitching for a few years.

A big man for his time at six feet, one inch, and 210 pounds, Marberry stomped around the mound, threw dirt around, and glared angrily at the batter. He relied on no fancy stuff—he basically just reared back with a high leg kick and fired the ball to the catcher. His style and reputation was

Firpo Marberry

like that of Rich Gossage in the 1970s. When Marberry warmed up between innings, Ruel caught every pitch in the center of his glove to maximize the noise of his fastball. Along with the sound that could be heard in the opposing dugout, Ruel allowed his body to stagger as each pitch hit his glove. On an otherwise aging pitching staff, young Marberry began the 1924 season as a spot starter and backup reliever for Russell.

Heading into the 1924 season, Washington had a core of excellent regulars (Judge, Goslin, Rice, Peckinpaugh) and a group of young players with promise (Harris, Bluege, Ruel). The one hole was in center field. Clyde Milan finally retired in 1922 and the team had not yet found an adequate replacement. The core of the pitching staff was good, but beginning to age. The Senators also had the makings of a strong bullpen. On the other hand, in the previous three years Washington had finished fourth, sixth, and fourth in the American League. A team of some talent, the Senators fell short of the Yankees, who looked much better and were largely in their prime. *Baseball* magazine picked Washington to finish seventh in the eight-team American League.

Clark Griffith also needed to find a new manager, having just fired Donie Bush. He first offered the position to Eddie Collins, whose acceptance at least would have helped the offense. The thirty-seven-year-old Collins was still a great player; he hit .360 in 1923 and would top .340 the next three years. Had Collins accepted the job, the Senators planned to move Harris to third base or trade him. Griffith also reportedly offered the job to Jack Barry, manager of the 1917 Red Sox.

When Griffith finally named Harris his manager, it surprised everyone, including the nominee. Griffith wanted a fiery, aggressive manager in his own image. When he let manager Clyde Milan go after one year in 1922, Griffith suggested that Milan had let the players walk all over him. Harris certainly had the personality for the position, but he was younger than virtually everyone else on the team. He supposedly approached Johnson and Rice for their support, received it, and got the rest of the team behind him.

◇ ◇ ◇

The Senators started slowly in 1924, and the local press was soon referring to Harris as "Griffith's Folly." The team languished below .500 until late June before catching fire and moving into first place. They spent the next couple of months jockeying with New York and Detroit for the league lead.

Griffith made two in-season acquisitions that helped immensely. On June 19, he claimed sore-armed twenty-three-year-old pitcher Curly Ogden from the Philadelphia Athletics on waivers. Ogden's career record at the time stood at 2–9, and he had lost his three 1924 decisions. Nonetheless, he started sixteen games in the second half of the season, winning eight in a row at one point, and finished 9–5 with a 2.58 ERA.

The second pickup came about as Griffith searched for a better solution in center field. Scout Joe Engel was ordered to scour the minor leagues. He and Griffith finally settled on Earl McNeely, who was hitting .333 for Sacramento in the Pacific Coast League. Griffith paid $35,000 for the outfielder in August and also sent three players to Sacramento in exchange. Although neither Griffith nor Harris had ever seen him play, McNeely was installed as the center fielder and leadoff hitter. He responded by hitting .330 over forty-three games.

The pickup of McNeely further illustrates the additional options a team had in the days of strong independent minor leagues. There were numerous good players in the minors, many of whom could have been regulars, or even stars, in the majors. Clark Griffith generally did not have a lot of money to spend, but he sensed the Senators had an opportunity to win and he opened his purse.

The Senators took over first place for good in late August when they beat the Yankees three out of four in New York and hung on to the end.

The Senators ultimately won the pennant over the Yankees by two games. They finished 92–62, an improvement of seventeen wins over 1923.

The Senators went on to beat the New York Giants in one of the best and most dramatic World Series ever played. Washington scored the deciding run in the bottom of the twelfth inning in the seventh game after Earl McNeely's hard ground ball hit a pebble and bounced over the head of Giant third baseman Fred Lindstrom, scoring Muddy Ruel from second base. Washington and Walter Johnson, the winning pitcher in the final game, had finally won a world championship.

◇　◇　◇

One of the principal reasons for the Senators' improvement in 1924 was the resurgence of Walter Johnson. Johnson finished 23–7 and led the league in both strikeouts and ERA (2.72). Johnson had pitched many years like this in the 1910s, but most felt his best seasons were behind him. His record in the previous four years had been 57–52. His ERAs in these years were still better than the league average but no longer the celebrated numbers of his prime. His won-lost record, of course, was partially a reflection of his supporting cast, but he had once been good enough to overcome the mediocrity of his teammates.

In 1924, he returned to being the best pitcher in the league, especially down the stretch when he won thirteen consecutive decisions. For his efforts he was recognized as the league's Most Valuable Player.

The baseball world was caught up in the story of the Senators, principally because everyone wanted to see old Walter Johnson finally reach the World Series. In September, Will Rogers wrote in his syndicated column that after 150 years, Washington had finally found an honest man: "So good luck, Walter; win or lose, you will have the satisfaction of knowing that you carry more good wishes that any man that ever entered any event in the history of our country, and we will love you just the same if you never see a World Series, because you are an example to the American boy, the same as Abraham Lincoln *should be* to the politicians."

Overall, strong pitching keyed the team's success. In addition to Johnson, both Mogridge (16–11) and Zachary (15–9) had good seasons, and the team allowed a full run per game fewer than the average American League team. Ogden was a great fourth starter down the stretch.

Meanwhile, the offense improved at several positions and included excellent years from Judge (.324) and Rice (.334, with a league-leading 216 hits). Nemo Leibold, one of the honest members of the Black Sox, played center field most of the year. Young McNeely hit .330 after his acquisition to play the position.

The biggest offensive improvement came from left fielder Goose Goslin. Goslin hit .344, with twelve home runs and a league-leading 129 RBI. Twelve home runs may not seem that impressive, but he hit only one at home—the only home run a Senator hit at home all season. Large home-road home run splits were not unusual for Goslin in cavernous Griffith Stadium; in 1926 he hit seventeen home runs, all on the road. Goslin was a power hitter whose statistics suffered from his home ball-park more than almost any other player in baseball history.

Griffith Stadium was one of the worst parks for home runs in the twentieth century. Although ballpark dimensions often vary from source to source, they were listed in the 1920s at about 407 feet down the left field line, increasing to 421 feet in dead center field, and cutting back to just 320 feet, with a 30-foot-high concrete wall, at the right field line. Although it was theoretically easier for a left-handed hitter like Goslin to hit one right down the line, he seldom did so. The park factor for home runs was often .50 or lower (meaning that more than twice as many home runs were hit in Senator road games than at home).

There were a lot of doubles and triples hit into the alleys at Griffith Stadium, enough to make up for many of the lost home runs. Still, about 3 percent to 5 percent fewer runs were scored there than in an average park.

With the offensive explosion of the early 1920s, many teams began to place an increased emphasis on sluggers. Clark Griffith, on the other hand—perhaps with his stadium in mind—continued to place a premium on defensive ability. Most of his long-service players, like Judge, Ruel, Bluege, and Harris, had very good defensive reputations. When Griffith spoke, later in life, about his favorite players, he always mentioned their defensive talents first.

An exception to this philosophy was Goslin, a fair defensive player who hit a ton. Many players had eye-popping offensive statistics in the 1920s, but Goslin was a truly great hitter. Table 4.3 summarizes Goslin's statistics for his seven full seasons with the Senators. In these seasons, Goslin hit twenty home runs at home and sixty-nine on the road. Goslin finished in the top five in triples each of his first five full seasons, leading twice. In a different home ballpark, many of these would likely have been home runs.

Goslin consistently provided enough offense to bring an average team (one that would finish 77–77) to five games above average (to a record of 82–72).

Table 4.3 Goose Goslin, 1922–1928

	Age	AB	AVG	OBP	SLG	R	HR	RBI	SB	RC	WAAv	WAR
1922	21	358	.324	.373	.441	44	3	53	4	57	1.3	2.4
1923	22	600	.330	.347	.452	86	9	99	7	97	2.2	4.1
1924	23	579	.344	.421	.516	100	12	129	15	118	4.0	5.9
1925	24	601	.334	.394	.547	116	18	113	27	127	4.3	6.2
1926	25	568	.354	.425	.542	105	17	108	8	128	5.7	7.5
1927	26	581	.334	.392	.516	96	13	120	21	119	3.9	5.9
1928	27	456	.379	.442	.614	80	17	102	16	111	5.4	6.8

RC = runs created   WAAv = wins above average   WAR = wins above replacement

◇ ◇ ◇

The 1923 Senators had led the American League with sixteen saves. In this era teams that needed a pitcher to enter a game with the lead typically turned to another starting pitcher; it was very unusual prior to the 1930s for a team to employ a quality relief pitcher. The league leader in saves in 1922 was the Yankees' Sam Jones, who saved eight but also had twenty complete games. Allan Russell, who led the league for the Senators in 1923, was a true relief pitcher who set records for relief games and innings. (There is much more on the history of relief pitching in the next chapter.)

Harris used his bullpen as aggressively as Bush had. As the season wore on, he shortened the pitching rotation so that Johnson could pitch more often, but Harris did not expect him to finish every game. When Allan Russell struggled in the role of primary relief ace, Harris turned the job over to Firpo Marberry, and Marberry responded sensationally. He pitched in fifty games, thirty-five in relief, won eleven, saved (as retroactively calculated) fifteen, and pitched 195 innings, fourth most on the team. Harris used Marberry like Bush had used Russell the previous year: an average of three innings per appearance and as early as the second inning if needed. Russell finished second in the league with eight saves, and the Senators set an all-time team record with twenty-five.

The success of Marberry had a significant effect on the way Harris used Walter Johnson. Over the course of his career, Johnson usually relieved six to ten times a year on top of his thirty to forty starts. In 1924, for the first time in his career, the thirty-five-year-old star was strictly a starting pitcher, and he responded with his best season in years. When Harris needed a star pitcher to secure a victory, he turned to Russell early in the year, and eventually to Marberry.

In *The Bill James Guide to Baseball Managers,* James discusses the evolution of bullpen strategy. James wonders why the success of Marberry failed to immediately revolutionize the way managers used their relief pitchers. He was the first excellent pitcher to be used primarily in a relief role, and it worked. He was the only player of consequence added to the 1924 Senators, and the team improved by seventeen games and won the World Series. When the team repeated in 1925, Marberry excelled again; this time exclusively in relief. He received very little credit for the team's success and no other great relief pitchers emerged for many years.

The 1925 *Reach Guide* makes little mention of Marberry's work: "In that respect [relieving] Marberry was the greatest in the American League, as he appeared in about 50 games, the great majority of which he either saved or won." Note that the word "save" was already part of the baseball lexicon by 1925. The *Spalding Guide* did not mention Marberry at all in its recap of the Senators' season.

In Shirley Povich's definitive 1954 team history, *The Washington Senators,* the author (who had witnessed most of the events) presents Marberry as little more than a figure coming in and out of games, not as a key member of two pennant winners. In 1994, *seventy years* after the event, he wrote a column for the *Washington Post* about the 1924 season, claiming, "That was the year too when the relief pitcher was invented by Harris. For that job he selected the big Texan, right-handed Firpo Marberry, whose delivery included sticking a huge (size 13) shoe into the batter's face, and then letting loose his steaming fastball. Marberry set an AL record by appearing in 50 games." Between 1954 and 1994 Povich elevated Marberry to one of the team's stars. Of course in the years after Povich wrote his book the importance of relief pitching had become universally accepted.

◇   ◇   ◇

Flush with success, in the off-season Griffith purchased two more aging pitchers, thirty-six-year-old Stan Coveleski from the Indians and thirty-one-year-old Dutch Ruether from the Dodgers. Since the pitching staff was somewhat old already and had been the strength of the team the previous season, these moves may at first appear a bit illogical. In the event, they proved invaluable: Ruether finished 18–7 and Coveleski chalked up a 20–5 record and a league-leading 2.84 ERA. Along with Walter Johnson, who won twenty games again despite missing a month with tonsillitis, the two newcomers once again gave the Senators the best pitching in the league. Marberry pitched fifty-five games in relief, a new record, and was credited (retroactively) with fifteen saves.

The lineup remained essentially unchanged from 1924 to 1925, but the acquisition of Joe Harris from the Red Sox further fortified the team. An excellent right-handed hitter, Harris spelled Judge or McNeely in the lineup and hit .323 with twelve home runs in only three hundred at-bats. Most of the regulars played as well, or better, than they had in 1924 and the team scored 829 runs, an increase of 74 from the previous year. Shortstop Roger Peckinpaugh hit .294 and was named the league's MVP.

In 1925 the Senators won a less-competitive pennant race. Waging a battle for much of the season with the resurgent Philadelphia Athletics, the Senators pulled ahead in late August and finished eight and a half games in front. Babe Ruth (.290, twenty-five home runs, multiple disciplinary problems) and the Yankees (seventh place) collapsed, leading baseball fans to consider their short reign over. (In fact, no Yankee team would finish below .500 for another forty years.)

The 1925 World Series was another thrilling fall classic. The NL champion Pittsburgh Pirates bounced back from a three-games-to-one deficit to win the championship. Walter Johnson won the first and fourth games easily, allowing only one run and eleven hits in the two games. In the seventh game Johnson and the Senators jumped out in front 4–0, but Johnson failed to hold the lead and the team lost, 9–7. Inexplicably, Harris had failed to use Marberry even as Johnson was increasingly ineffective as the game progressed. A furious Ban Johnson, the American League president, accused Harris of relying on sentimentality at the expense of his team and league.

The 1925 World Series was the last hurrah for Walter Johnson and this Senators team. Johnson fell to 15–16 the next year and 5–6 in 1927, before finally retiring. The offensive stars, particularly Goslin and Rice, continued to hit, but the aging pitching rotation petered out fairly quickly, and the team fell out of contention.

One could overlook these Senators as a team that slipped in while the Yankee dynasty sputtered. As it turned out, the fall of the Yankees was short-lived, and the team just ahead (1926 through 1928) would be one of the best teams ever assembled. Once the Yankees rebounded, nothing short of a truly great team could harbor realistic pennant hopes, but for two years a strong, well-constructed ball club had an opening. Clark Griffith, slowly, patiently, and piece by piece, built an outstanding team that stood ready when the two-year window opened.

The 1924 and 1925 Senators were excellent teams. They had future Hall of Fame players enjoying outstanding seasons (Johnson, Goslin, Rice, and Coveleski), other star players at their peaks (Judge, Marberry, and Peckinpaugh), and several other good players who enjoyed long careers (Ruel, Bluege, Harris, Mogridge, and Zachary). They had a good bench in both seasons. Furthermore, the team captured the pennants without any player having a season that was out of the ordinary for him.

The drop-off of the New York Yankees created a window, but the Washington Senators were ready to step through it. The Senators earned their perch atop the baseball world, a place to which they never returned.

5

RAGS TO RICHES:
A HISTORY OF THE RELIEF PITCHER

In his classic 1967 book The Thinking Man's Guide to Baseball, *Leonard* Koppett allotted one page to relief pitching and described the reliever's job as "to get one or two outs in the middle of an inning with men on base, and to pitch a scoreless inning or two." In 1999 Johnny Bench authored a book (apparently for a different audience) entitled *The Complete Idiot's Guide to Baseball,* which included subsections on "Long and Middle Relievers," "Setup Men," and "Closers." The closer was to be used "when they're ahead in the ninth inning." Things had obviously changed in thirty-two years.

In the history of baseball, no facet of strategy has evolved as continually as has the use of the bullpen. Fifty years ago a manager made an average of one pitching change per game; today he makes two and a half. Fifty years ago, even twenty-five years ago, a team generally filled its bullpen with failed starters. Today a manager constructs a highly organized bullpen with several pitchers in well-defined roles. One of these pitchers is a "closer," who might be paid as much as a top starter and with a great seventy innings might win the Cy Young or MVP award.

While building his great teams, Ned Hanlon could ignore relief pitchers, since the role did not yet exist. When the Florida Marlins participated in the 1992 expansion draft to stock their team, the most famous player they drafted was a relief ace, Bryan Harvey. In the intervening hundred years, the importance of relievers had gradually increased. As relievers took on a larger role in the game on the field, general managers began to consider the bullpen when constructing a ball club.

◇ ◇ ◇

Two key statistics useful for understanding the changing role of the bullpen are relief appearances (appearances by pitchers other than starters) and saves. Since the definition and importance of a "save" has evolved over time, the following digression into its history is needed to illuminate how the statistic has been used in each era. The evolution of the save rule influences the evaluation of pitchers historically and also directly affects how teams use and value relievers today.

At the instigation of Jerome Holtzman of the *Chicago Sun-Times*, *The Sporting News* began keeping and publicizing saves in 1960. According to the 1961 *Official Baseball Guide*, "pitching saves had been compiled by some club statisticians for several years on a helter-skelter basis." The first *Sporting News* save rule required that a pitcher enter the game with the lead and face a batter who was the potential tying or lead run, but did not require that he finish the game. According to *The Sporting News* records, the 1960 league leaders in saves were the Cardinals' Lindy McDaniel with twenty-two and the Red Sox's Mike Fornieles with twelve.

The rule was soon liberalized to allow for a save if the reliever entered the game with a two-run lead and pitched at least one inning. By 1964 a reliever could also earn a save by entering with a three-run lead and pitching at least two innings. *The Sporting News* 1965 league leaders were Eddie Fisher of the White Sox with twenty-two and Ted Abernathy of the Cubs with twenty-four.

In 1969 major league baseball officially recognized and codified the "save" statistic. Ignoring the nine-year history of *The Sporting News* rule, scorers awarded a save to a pitcher who entered the game with the lead and held it. He also had either to finish the game or be removed for a pinch hitter or pinch runner. If more than one pitcher qualified for a save, the official scorer awarded it to the pitcher deemed most deserving.

That same year, Macmillan published the first addition of the classic *Baseball Encyclopedia*. The researchers who created it, Information Concepts Inc., retroactively applied the new save rule to every game in major league history. As historically figured, a pitcher was required to have finished the game. The researchers did not feel it was appropriate to make a judgment of effectiveness by looking at game logs. A save was automatic if a reliever finished a victory for another pitcher.

The unofficial save totals calculated by *The Sporting News* for 1960 through 1968 were all modified. Eddie Fisher's AL-leading twenty-two saves in 1965 were adjusted upwards to twenty-four, but Ron Kline of the

Senators was awarded twenty-nine, and all modern sources consider Kline to have been the league leader.

In the five years (1969–1973) that this rule was in effect, on at least five occasions a save was awarded to a pitcher who did not finish the game. (We know this because Retrosheet has score sheets for 98 percent of the games for those seasons.) For example, on April 29, 1970, at Yankee Stadium, Angel pitcher Paul Doyle was awarded the save for pitching a scoreless seventh and eighth inning, as opposed to teammate Ken Tatum, who allowed a run in the ninth. The other four cases are similar.

The official rule was first changed in 1974, though previously published totals were not refigured. The new rule was quite strict: the reliever now had either to face the potential tying or lead run or pitch at least three effective innings. He still did not have to finish the game. Predictably, save totals plummeted back to the level that *The Sporting News* recorded in the 1960s. Only three pitchers posted twenty saves in 1974. Had this rule applied to Dennis Eckersley's 1992 season, in which he saved fifty-one games, Eckersley would instead have been credited with only twelve saves.

In 1975 the rule was liberalized to the one in use today. A relief pitcher must enter with a lead, hold it, and finish the game. He also must also either (a) face the potential tying or lead run, (b) protect a three-run lead for at least one inning, or (c) pitch three or more effective innings.

It is important to understand that all the save totals listed in the modern record books for seasons before 1960 had no meaning at the time they occurred. Although the official records indicate that Joe Page recorded twenty-seven saves in 1949, no one was keeping track of such things at the time. The same could be said for runs batted in or ERA for the first forty years of professional baseball. The statistics are nonetheless likely to be bandied about.

◇   ◇   ◇

The most obvious reason for the increased importance of the bullpen has been the declining frequency of the complete game. As figure 5.1 shows, the decrease has been steady, and not simply a recent phenomenon. A pitcher from the 1960s might lament the drop in complete games ("back in my day, we were expected to finish what we started"), but his predecessors likely said the same things about their era. (The tables in this chapter were developed and derived from Sean Lahman's baseball database. A few are similar to ones compiled independently by David W. Smith in his research presentation, "From Exile to Specialist: The Evolution of the

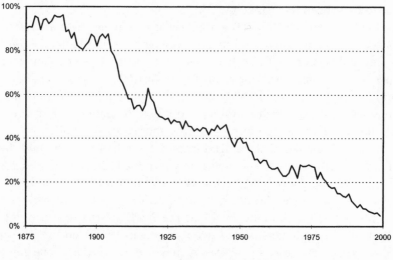

Figure 5.1

Relief Pitcher," given at the 2000 convention of the Society for American Baseball Research.)

One hundred years ago the use of the bullpen was an afterthought, something to worry about if the starter was hit hard or hurt. Today, constructing a solid collection of relievers is an important task for a front office, and many consider its supervision one of the manager's more important jobs. A modern manager knows that he will likely have to use his bullpen in nearly every game and may need some of the same pitchers in the next game as well.

In the nineteenth century, the bullpen did not yet exist, nor did the concept of a relief pitcher. As a matter of fact, until 1889 the rules did not allow for substitutions except in cases of illness or injury. Jack Manning is credited with being baseball's first outstanding relief pitcher, based solely on his performance for the 1876 Boston Red Stockings. That season Manning relieved fourteen times, pitched forty innings, and was later credited with five saves. Five saves might not seem like a lot, but the entire league had only thirteen, and no one broke this record until 1905, when Claude Elliot of the New York Giants posted six. It is not really accurate to call Manning a relief pitcher, since he was the starting pitcher twenty times, and in his "spare" time he was the starting right fielder. When Jack Manning the reliever entered the game to pitch, he did so by jogging in from the outfield.

Obviously, if the starting pitcher is completing more than 90 percent of his games, not much work remains for a full-time reliever. If the starter got hurt or pounded, a team had only two options: bring in someone from another position or call in the pitcher scheduled to start the next day. Kid Nichols of the Boston Beaneaters, perhaps the greatest of all nineteenth-century pitchers, started forty to fifty games a year, completed almost all of them, and relieved a handful of games a year; he led the National League in saves four times.

In 1908 the National League waged one of the most famous pennant races in its long history, which culminated in a winner-take-all game between the Cubs and the Giants. The leaders in saves for the NL that season were Christy Mathewson and Joe McGinnity of the Giants and Mordecai Brown of the Cubs, three great starting pitchers. Brown held both the single season (thirteen) and lifetime (forty-nine) records for saves until the first real relief star, Fred Marberry, surpassed both in the 1920s. Ed Walsh, another top starting pitcher from the deadball era, became the first to pitch one hundred games in relief .

Table 5.1 summarizes the frequency of the use of a good starter as an occasional relief ace—a "starter/closer" if you will. For this analysis a starter/closer is defined as a pitcher who started at least thirty games and recorded at least four saves. As the table indicates, this profile was common in the 1910s and did not die out until the 1960s. Phil Niekro finished 13–10 with four saves for the 1973 Braves. Before him it had been eight years since Sam McDowell won seventeen and saved four for the 1965 Cleveland Indians.

The first man to gain a measure of fame based solely on his performance as a reliever may have been Otis "Doc" Crandall. He pitched 20 to 30 games a year in relief for the Giants from 1909 to 1912 and then established a record with 33 relief appearances in 1913. Damon Runyan championed Crandall in the pages of the New York American as "the greatest relief pitcher in baseball." Though certainly a quality pitcher, Crandall ex-

Table 5.1 Starter/Closers

Years	No.	Years	No.
pre–1900	2	1940–1949	12
1900–1909	10	1950–1959	16
1910–1919	38	1960–1969	4
1920–1929	24	1970–present	1
1930–1939	31		

celled for only five years. Crandall pitched in relief 168 times in his career, a record at the time.

Ernie Shore turned in one of the worst performances ever by a relief pitcher in his major league debut in late 1912 for the Giants. He entered in the ninth inning with a big lead but allowed eight hits and ten runs (three earned) in his one inning. Since he protected the lead, he was duly rewarded in 1969 with a save.

While pitching for the Boston Red Sox on June 23, 1917, Shore made up for his 1912 performance with the greatest effort ever by a relief pitcher. After starter Babe Ruth walked the first batter of the game, he was ejected for slugging home plate umpire Brick Owens. Shore relieved Ruth. The base runner was immediately caught stealing, and Ernie retired the remaining twenty-six men in order. For many years the record books quixotically considered this a "perfect game."

Fred Marberry of the Washington Senators deserves recognition as the first great long-term relief pitcher. In *The Bill James Historical Baseball Abstract*, James suggests that Marberry was second only to Lefty Grove as the most valuable pitcher in baseball during his career. Marberry set the all-time record for saves with fifteen in his first full season, 1924, and followed that up with fifteen more in 1925 and twenty-two in 1926. He held the single-season and career save records for more than twenty years.

When manager Bucky Harris made Marberry his primary relief pitcher in 1924, he was not trying to develop a new weapon. By this time most teams had a couple of pitchers available if the starter needed help. Marberry had been a starting pitcher in the minors, and Harris made him a relief pitcher because he could not win a job in the rotation. That Marberry turned out to be a great pitcher was likely as much of a surprise to Harris as to everyone else. Harris ignored tradition by leaving him in the relief role even after Marberry proved himself a quality pitcher. Had the Senators not possessed such an outstanding starting rotation, Harris most likely would have moved Marberry out of the reliever role.

As Bill James also noted, everyone received credit for the remarkable success of the Senators except Marberry. He was the first man regularly used to close out winning ball games, yet everyone forgot about it within a few years. Bucky Harris forgot about it within a few minutes. In the seventh game of the 1925 World Series, Harris let Walter Johnson finish a game in which he gave up fifteen hits and nine runs while a rested Marberry watched. The Senators led most of the game before the Pirates went ahead with their final three runs off Johnson in the eighth inning.

Throwing only fastballs in his early years, Marberry likely contributed to the notion that a reliever lacked a complete repertoire of pitches. Muddy Ruel, his longtime catcher, claimed that Marberry "was invincible for two or three innings, but he couldn't go the distance." His record as a starter, however, 94–52, suggests otherwise. He was not being spotted against weaker opponents. Of his 186 lifetime starts, 29 came against the New York Yankees, including a total of 7 (4 wins) against the world champions of 1927, 1928, and 1932.

By midcareer he started as often as not. In 1929 he started twenty-six times, finished 19–12 and still managed a league-leading eleven saves. Marberry excelled as both a starter and reliever for ten years. Had he been given one role or the other for his whole career, he would likely be in the Hall of Fame today.

The next pitcher to enjoy extended success in relief was Johnny Murphy, who starred for the New York Yankees in the 1930s and early 1940s. In Murphy's rookie season of 1934, he split his forty games between starting and relieving, finishing 14–10 and third in the league in ERA at 3.12. Despite this success, manager Joe McCarthy believed that a pitcher could not get by for long with only one out-pitch—in Murphy's case the curveball. McCarthy turned Murphy into a reliever, and he became the best in baseball for the next ten years. He usually pitched only thirty-five games per year but led the league in saves four times and broke Marberry's career save record. Additionally, pitching in the World Series every year made Murphy much more famous than Marberry had been.

At the time, neither Marberry nor Murphy was considered to be as important as the other players on the team. In Murphy's case, not until 1943, when most of his famous teammates were in the military, did he receive any mention in the MVP balloting, a single tenth-place vote. He was selected for the All-Star Game three times but never pitched, despite the fact that his manager ran the team every year.

By the 1930s, most teams had one or two pitchers used exclusively as relievers; nearly all were young players on the way up, old players on the way out, or pitchers with sore arms. Marberry and Murphy were exceptions—most teams changed relievers every year. The league-leading save totals, ten to fifteen in most years, indicates that teams brought in relief pitchers not to protect a lead but to rescue a faltering starter. Starters still completed over 40 percent of their starts, and this total includes both the winning and losing team. The winning team's starter obviously finished even more often.

By 1946 each manager used an average of one relief pitcher per game. As figure 5.2 indicates, the use of relief pitchers began to accelerate at this time.

Relief Pitchers Used Per Game Per Team

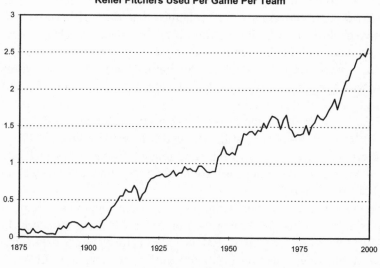

Figure 5.2

The dip in the 1970s is attributable entirely to the American League, almost certainly a result of the introduction of the designated hitter in 1973.

Joe Page, who starred for the New York Yankees in the late 1940s, represented another revolutionary figure in the history of relief pitching. Though he did not have the career that Marberry had, Page posted two outstanding seasons: 1947 (14–8, 17 saves) and 1949 (13–8, 27 saves). The first reliever to be considered an MVP candidate, Page finished fourth in 1947 and third in 1949. In 1947 he pitched in the All-Star Game and was later credited with the save by getting the last four outs in a 2–1 AL win.

The Yankees, as always, acted as a bellwether. After Murphy left, new Yankee manager Bucky Harris, Marberry's old boss, made Page his new relief ace, and he flourished. After Page's success, the notion that a team needed a relief ace to win finally began to take hold. Teams still did not develop relievers in the minors and generally used the best pitchers remaining after choosing the starting rotation. However, teams now recognized the relief ace as an important, even essential, part of a championship team.

In 1949 Page worked an average of 2.25 innings per outing. Casey Stengel did not bring in Page every time the Yankees had a lead to protect—his usage depended on the starting pitcher. If Vic Raschi (twenty-one complete games) was throwing well, Stengel let him finish the game. With Allie Reynolds (four complete games), he was more likely to bring in Page. (Of course, one did not ever want to bet on what Stengel would do—he let Reynolds go the route in the first game of the World Series, but relieved Raschi with Page in both of Raschi's wins.)

In 1949, the Phillies gave their relief job to a thirty-two-year-old career minor leaguer named Jim Konstanty and he responded with a fairly effective year (53 games, 9–5, 7 saves). The next year Konstanty had a great season (74 games, 152 innings, 16–7, 22 saves) and won the MVP award. After the Whiz Kids eked out the pennant on the last day of the season, manager Eddie Sawyer surprised almost everyone by starting Konstanty in the first game of the series. Sawyer's whole staff was pretty beat up at that point, but starting a man who had not made a start in four years was a rather bold decision. Konstanty pitched a great game, but lost 1–0 to Raschi, and the Yankees quickly swept the Phillies. Konstanty had a very ordinary career from that point forward.

In 1952, Joe Black, a twenty-eight-year-old rookie for Brooklyn, turned in a season comparable to Konstanty's; he relieved fifty-four times, won fourteen, and saved fifteen. Taking a page from Sawyer's book two years before, Dodger manager Charlie Dressen gave Black two late-season starts and then started him in games one, four, and seven of the World Series (with no off-days—he was pitching on two days rest). The Dodger staff was not having injury problems; Dressen believed the team had a better chance of winning with its best pitcher starting rather than relieving. Black pitched well all three times, but the Dodgers lost the series in seven games.

Ellis Kinder of the Red Sox represents a historically notable case as perhaps the first quality starter to be converted into a reliever. Kinder did not reach the majors until age thirty-one, but in 1949, at thirty-two, Kinder won twenty-three games pitching mostly as a starter (2–1 with four saves in thirteen relief appearances). The next year he split the two roles (twenty-three starts and twenty-five relief efforts) and again pitched effectively (14–12 with nine saves). For the next five years (1951–1955) he was Joe Page revisited, leading the league twice in saves, including a record-tying twenty-seven in 1953. Kinder's move to the bullpen signified a new belief in the importance of the relief pitcher. After the Red Sox finished second by one game to the Yankees in 1949, a perception emerged that Joe Page was a key difference in the two teams. As a result, the Red Sox moved their twenty-three-game winner to the bullpen.

Clem Labine's performance for the Dodgers in the 1955 World Series represented another important milestone in the story of relief pitching. That season Labine pitched mainly in relief and finished 13–5 with eleven saves in sixty games for the team that finally brought a championship home to Brooklyn. More importantly, in the World Series that year he had a win and a save in four appearances. In the Yankee clubhouse after the seventh game, Casey Stengel gave Duke Snider and Johnny Podres their due, but concluded, "that fella Labine . . . he was the difference."

Prior to the start of the series, rumors persisted that Brooklyn manager Walter Alston might start Labine in the first game, much like Dressen started Joe Black in 1952. After the series, Alston admitted, "I never did plan to use Clem in the opener, but for a time I thought I might have to start him in the fourth or fifth game. I didn't want to start him at all, because that would mean I wouldn't be able to use him for a couple of days. I wanted him ready in relief every day if he was needed . . . I think that's where we won it."

All of the top teams of the 1950s had strong bullpens, and baseball's front offices and managers began to notice. During the decade the percentage of starters completing their games dropped from above 40 percent to below 30 percent, one of the steeper drops in the century-long trend. As Frank Graham Jr. suggested in *Sport* magazine in 1956, "A manager with a Joe Page, a Joe Black, or a Clem Labine in his bullpen will not only pull a starter without a second thought—often he'd rather have his ace reliever in the game when trouble looms than any other pitcher on his staff."

◇   ◇   ◇

The best relief pitcher ever was Hoyt Wilhelm, and the competition is not particularly close. His ERA of 2.52 is the lowest (by far) of any pitcher who pitched most of his career after 1920. He pitched enough innings to qualify for the ERA title only twice and led the league each time. Mainly a relief pitcher, Wilhelm pitched 2,254 innings over the course of his career, only 70 fewer than Sandy Koufax.

One can hardly imagine two more dissimilar pitchers than Wilhelm, the dumpy right-handed knuckle-balling relief pitcher who pitched forever, and Koufax, the classic southpaw fireballer who retired at age thirty. When Wilhelm threw his first professional pitch, Koufax was in the first grade. When he threw his last, Koufax had already been elected to the Hall of Fame. Table 5.2 compares their basic raw statistics.

Although the style of these two pitchers could not have been more different, the results for the unfortunate hitters were similar. Koufax allowed slightly fewer hits but more home runs. Wilhelm actually allowed fewer walks. Although Wilhelm posted a better ERA, much of this difference evaporates when unearned runs are considered. More on this later.

Table 5.2 Koufax vs. Wilhelm

	IP	H/9	HR/9	BB/9	K/9	ERA	R/9
Koufax	2324.3	6.8	0.8	3.2	9.3	2.76	3.12
Wilhelm	2254.3	7.0	0.6	3.1	6.4	2.52	3.08

Sportswriter Jim Murray once pondered the difficulty in hitting Wilhelm: "Part of the trouble is, the ball comes to the plate like a kid on the way to a bath." Wilhelm had two deliveries: one sidearm and the other delivered about three-quarters. He claimed that the sidearm knuckleball sank and the other floated, but his catchers dispute this. Wilhelm also regularly admitted that he really had no idea where his pitch would end up, or when it would start to move. He generally tried to place the pitch in the upper half of the strike zone. Considering his uncertainty over the ball's flight, it is remarkable how often Wilhelm threw strikes.

Major league organizations have often had difficulty deciding how to use a knuckleball pitcher, so Wilhelm did not reach the majors until age twenty-eight. He pitched for several years in the minors as a starter and spent three years fighting in World War II. He was wounded at the Battle of the Bulge, received the Purple Heart, and went back to the front to finish up.

Wilhelm twice won twenty games in the low minors without impressing anyone in particular. While he was pitching for Mooresville of the Class D North Carolina State League, he was described by a Charlotte reporter this way: "Wilhelm is never going any place. He throws like a washer-woman." The New York Giants drafted him in 1947 and sent him to the minors for four more seasons before finally giving him a major league uniform in 1952.

The 1951 Giants won the National League pennant and featured a strong starting rotation, so manager Leo Durocher sent his new knuckleballer to the bullpen, reasoning, "The knuckler can fool 'em for four or five innings, even if Wilhelm doesn't have the hard stuff to go nine." After waiting ten years to get a shot, Wilhelm was in no position to complain.

In his first year, Wilhelm pitched seventy-one games (a rookie record since broken) and 159 innings, all in relief. He finished 15–3 with eleven saves and won the ERA title (2.43), the first and only time for either a full-time relief pitcher or a rookie. In Wilhelm's first major league at-bat, he homered—a feat he never repeated. He lost the Rookie of the Year award to Joe Black and finished fourth in the MVP voting, just behind Black.

After selecting Wilhelm to the 1953 All-Star team, National League

Hoyt Wilhelm

manager Charlie Dressen expressed concern that no one would be able to catch him, and he did not pitch. In 1954 Wilhelm had another great season (12–4, 2.10 ERA in 111 innings) and the Giants won the pennant and World Series. After two fair seasons, he was passed around for the next two years. He moved from the Giants to the Cardinals to the Indians and, finally, to the Orioles at the tail end of the 1958 season. Wilhelm was still pitching effectively, but now in his mid-thirties, he seemed to be nearing the end of his career. A thirty-five-year-old knuckleballer, even one with a 2.49 ERA, is not allowed many bad outings before being sent on his way.

Finding someone to catch him was a continual problem. In Wilhelm's first sixteen seasons (1952–1967), his team led its league in passed balls in every year but one (1953). The Giants' Ray Katt was charged with four passed balls in a single inning catching Wilhelm in 1954. The catchers of the 1958 Indians (mainly Russ Nixon and Dick Brown) allowed a league-leading thirty-five passed balls. The next year, without Wilhelm, the same catching corps permitted only six.

Orioles manager Paul Richards thought Wilhelm might make a good starter and acquired him in late 1958. Richards explained his reasoning: "I'd always wondered why he'd been used in relief, coming in with men on base where one passed ball could hurt him. I thought that perhaps, if Hoyt started, the runners wouldn't get on base to begin with."

According to Richards and his pitching coach, Harry Brecheen, Wilhelm had been tipping his pitches, allowing the batter to know when the occasional fastball was coming. He just needed a small mechanical adjustment to correct this problem. In September Wilhelm started four times and in his last game tossed a 1–0 no-hitter against the Yankees. The final batter, Hank Bauer, laid down two bunts that rolled foul before eventually popping to second base.

In 1959, as a full-time starter for the first time, Wilhelm finished 15–11 with a 2.19 ERA, earning his second ERA crown. He started the season 9–0 with an ERA under 1.00, prompting former manager Leo Durocher to express some regrets: "If I ever had any idea he could go the distance like that I'd have used him as a starter when I had him on the Giants. Maybe I made a big mistake."

After a slow start in 1960, Richards moved Wilhelm back to the bullpen, and he never again pitched in a major league rotation. The Orioles' reasoning appears sensible. A young team, the Orioles wanted to develop an impressive crop of young starters—Chuck Estrada, Steve Barber, Jack Fisher, Milt Pappas, and Jerry Walker. How could Richards have known that Wilhelm would outlast most of them? Had Wilhelm been a few years younger, or thrown a ninety-mile-per-hour fastball, Richards might have designed his rotation differently.

Wilhelm successfully returned to full-time relieving and was named to the All-Star team in each of the next two seasons. In 1961 he won nine, saved eighteen, and recorded a 2.30 ERA in 109 relief innings. The next year he pitched even better and finished with an ERA of 1.94 in 93 innings. *Total Baseball* ranks him the most valuable pitcher in the American League for that season.

During the off-season after 1962, the Orioles traded Wilhelm to the White Sox in a six-player swap in which the Orioles landed shortstop Luis Aparicio. Wilhelm was still one of the better relievers in the game but was now approaching forty; few could have imagined that he had more than a year or two left. In fact, he was just hitting his stride.

In 1963 major league baseball deployed a new strike zone that extended from the bottom of the knees to the top of the shoulders (formerly it reached from the top of the knees to the armpits). During the next six years, run scoring in both leagues dropped to levels not seen since 1919 (with the exception of the American League during World War II, when a different ball was used). A larger strike zone helps all pitchers, but especially those with no idea where the ball is going.

Over the next six years, while with the White Sox, Wilhelm put together one of the best sustained stretches of relief pitching ever. In 1963, his ERA "soared" to 2.64 in over 136 innings (he had three starts). Thereafter his ERA decreased for four consecutive years (1.99, 1.81, 1.66, and 1.33) before finally inching up to 1.73 in 1968—still not a bad year for a pitcher turning forty-five. More than a situational pitcher, Wilhelm averaged well over 100 innings a season, throwing 144 in 1965. Overall run production was historically low, but no one else consistently pitched as well. His ERA in the 1960s was 2.18.

Taking bunting practice during spring training in 1966, Wilhelm sustained the only significant injury of his career when a pitching machine broke the middle finger of his pitching hand. At the time, the White Sox had the best pitching staff in the league and an excellent bullpen. Accordingly, Wilhelm returned from his injury in mid-June to a reduced workload, having to share the late-inning situations that resulted in saves. The White Sox usually produced very high team save totals, but spread them around among an excellent relief corps that also included Jim Brosnan, Eddie Fisher, Bob Locker, and Wilbur Wood.

Using ERA as a measure for Wilhelm is slightly misleading, since many of the passed balls that occurred while he was on the mound led to unearned runs. Whether the scorer blamed Wilhelm or his catcher, the prevalence of passed balls led to more unearned runs with Wilhelm pitching. In the 1961 All-Star Game in San Francisco, Wilhelm entered a tie game in the eighth inning. After retiring the first two hitters in the ninth, he walked Ken Boyer. Paul Richards, managing the American League team, came to the mound and, in an unusual move, relieved catcher Yogi Berra. New catcher Elston Howard's passed ball in the tenth contributed to Wilhelm's loss.

When Wilhelm came to the American League in 1958, the league record for passed balls in a game was four, set by John Henry of the Washington Senators in 1911. Over the next five years, Wilhelm's team tied this record seven times while he was pitching. The 1959 Orioles were charged with forty-nine passed balls, thirty more than any other team. The forty-nine were split between Gus Triandos, with twenty-eight, and Joe Ginsberg, with twenty-one, the two highest totals for any catcher in the 1950s.

Catchers did not particularly enjoy being on the receiving end of Wilhelm's deliveries. Wes Westrum, his primary receiver with the Giants, later said that after catching Wilhelm he would wake up at night shaking. Catching him so baffled J. W. Porter that the catcher used a first baseman's mitt. In 1960, the Orioles began using a specially designed catcher's mitt for Wilhelm that measured forty-two inches in circumference. When the rules were changed to prohibit gloves larger than thirty-eight inches, the White Sox designed a new one with a hinged thumb, one of the first of its kind.

There were several other excellent knuckleball pitchers whose careers overlapped Wilhelm's, including Eddie Fisher, Phil Niekro, and Wilbur Wood. None of them had the consistent problems with catchers that Wilhelm had, an indication that Wilhelm's knuckleball moved much more than theirs did. Ted Williams, who knew a thing or two about pitchers, once stated categorically, "Don't let anybody tell you they saw a better knuckleball than Wilhelm's."

Over the course of Wilhelm's career, 18 percent of his runs allowed were unearned. His pitching teammates, on the other hand, were charged with unearned runs for only 12 percent of the runs they allowed. One can assume that Wilhelm's additional unearned runs are attributable to his knuckleball, mainly all of the passed balls charged to his catchers. If one arbitrarily recalculated 88 percent of Wilhelm's total runs as earned, his career ERA would move up to 2.71 rather than 2.52. One could argue that this revised figure better reflects his value.

Table 5.3 provides Wilhelm's basic statistics for his White Sox years and also compares his actual ERA with the theoretical ERA calculated by applying the above formula.

Because of the many passed balls Wilhelm induced, his ERA may slightly overstate his value. Nevertheless, even after attempting to adjust for this effect, during the mid-1960s he delivered one of the best-ever sustained stretches of excellence for a relief pitcher.

It is also interesting to examine more specifically how the White Sox

Table 5.3 Wilhelm with the White Sox

	G	W	L	SV	IP	ERA	ERA*
1963	55	5	8	21	136.3	2.64	2.78
1964	73	12	9	27	131.3	1.99	2.14
1965	66	7	7	20	144.0	1.81	1.89
1966	46	5	2	6	81.3	1.66	1.99
1967	49	8	3	12	89.0	1.31	1.78
1968	72	4	4	12	93.6	1.73	1.63

ERA* = ERA adjusted for additional unearned runs

Table 5.4 Inning When Wilhelm Entered

Inning	No.	Inning	No.
3–5	12	8	124
6	34	9	74
7	95	10–13	19

used Wilhelm. Thanks to Retrosheet (www.retrosheet.org) and Tom Ruane, we have play-by-play information for his White Sox years. Ruane provided the raw data for each of Wilhelm's 361 games pitched in this period (1963–1968). Table 5.4 shows the inning in which he entered the game in his 358 relief appearances.

Usually, though not always, the White Sox brought him in towards the end of the game, with the understanding that he was capable of pitching two or three innings if needed.

Setting aside his long appearances, table 5.5 indicates the Chicago lead (+) or deficit (-) when Wilhelm entered in the seventh inning or later (312 games).

Wilhelm entered tie games most frequently, and the White Sox brought him in to another eighty-seven games with the team trailing by three runs or fewer. He was brought in to win games, rather than to save them. Most teams used their relief ace this way—the save leader usually recorded a season total in the high teens or twenties. The whole notion of a save was new enough (still unofficially compiled by *The Sporting News*) that a manager did not feel obligated to let the "rule" dictate how he used his best relief pitcher.

Additionally, pitchers still threw a fair number of complete games. The White Sox won 526 games in these six years (about 87 per season) and pitched complete games in 34 percent of their victories. This was a low figure for the era that most likely can be attributed to Chicago's quality bullpen.

Examination of the Retrosheet data produces another interesting observation. In his first three years with the White Sox, catcher J. C. Martin often came in to the game with Wilhelm, even in the middle of an inning. From 1963–1965 on the ninety-one occasions Wilhelm entered a game and Martin was not already catching, Martin entered with Wilhelm fifty-nine times. Further subdividing the data, on the seventeen such occasions when Wilhelm came in with runners on base without Martin catching, Martin was brought in fourteen times.

Table 5.5 Situation When Wilhelm Entered

Lead/ Deficit	No. of Times	Lead/ Deficit	No. of Times
-4 or more	23	1	51
-3	16	2	38
-2	28	3	16
-1	43	4 or more	22
0	75		

Martin's adeptness at catching the knuckler cannot be determined at this date, but for his efforts he led the league in passed balls in 1964 and set the American League record in 1965. In the latter year, Eddie Fisher, another knuckleballer who threw 165 innings with a 2.40 ERA, joined Wilhelm in the bullpen. Fisher and Wilhelm threw 309 great innings of relief between them, an average of almost 2 innings per game.

The White Sox left Wilhelm unprotected in the 1968 expansion draft, most likely reasoning that no one would want a forty-five-year old knuckleballer. The Kansas City Royals drafted him and soon traded him to the Angels. Despite the newly reduced strike zone, he had another excellent season in Anaheim, throwing sixty-five innings with a 2.47 ERA.

In September 1969, Wilhelm was traded to the Atlanta Braves, who were trying to win the NL West and needed help in the bullpen. He provided it brilliantly, with two wins, four saves and a 0.73 ERA in eight games. When the Braves won the division by three games, Wilhelm received much of the credit. He arrived too late to be eligible for the NL playoffs, which the Braves lost in three straight to the Miracle Mets.

After three more seasons as a journeyman reliever (and a 1970 All-Star), Wilhelm finally retired after the Dodgers released him in 1972 just short of his forty-ninth birthday. A unique and wonderful twenty-one-year career had finally ended. In 1985, he was voted into the Hall of Fame, the first reliever so honored.

One can speculate on Wilhelm's career had he been a starter. He threw in a regular rotation only once in his career and led the league in ERA. Overall, he pitched 384 lifetime innings as a starter, with an ERA of 2.36. *Total Baseball*'s formulas suggest he was the fifteenth most valuable pitcher in history and sixty-first among all players.

Could he have had a Phil Niekro–type career? Might it have been better than Niekro's? Wilhelm was almost certainly a better pitcher than Niekro, but he pitched many fewer innings. It seems reasonable to conclude that had he stayed as healthy and effective as a starter for as long as he did as a reliever Wilhelm would have won well over three hundred games.

◇ ◇ ◇

By the 1960s, almost every team had a good pitcher or two in the bullpen who was considered an important part of the team. Figure 5.3 shows the rapid growth in the average number of relievers employed per team in a given season. For this analysis a reliever is defined as a pitcher who throws at least twenty games and starts fewer than five. (There is some double counting if a single player qualifies for more than one team in a given year.) This is a somewhat arbitrary definition, but a different one would not materially alter the trend.

Teams first employed a three-man bullpen in 1962 and had four relievers by 1984. By 1999 bullpens averaged six and a half pitchers and chairs were getting scarce out there.

More often than not, relief pitchers of the 1960s still had only one or two good years. Pitchers such as Stu Miller, Ted Abernathy, Phil Regan, and Ron Kline might have a spectacular season or two and then disappear for

Relief Pitchers Per Team

Figure 5.3

Table 5.6 Relief Workhorses

Years	No.	Years	No.
pre–1960	6	1980–1989	26
1960–1969	22	1990–1999	1
1970–1979	38		

a year or two or forever. All of these players, and several other similar pitchers, began as failed starters and joined the bullpen at an advanced age.

Next to Wilhelm, Roy Face and Lindy McDaniel were the best long-term relievers of this era; each led the National League in saves three times and retired ranked second and third to Wilhelm in saves and relief games. Face, of course, won eighteen games (against only one loss) in 1959, still a record for a reliever. In 1960 McDaniel became the first and only relief pitcher to be mentioned in the balloting for the Cy Young Award prior to 1970, when the process was expanded to include second- and third-place votes.

For a brief period in the 1960s, baseball's best relief pitcher was Boston's Dick Radatz. Over his first four years (1962–1965) Radatz won forty-nine games and saved one hundred for an otherwise awful team. His 1963 season reads like a great fluke year (15-6, 132 IP, 25 saves) until a glance at 1964 shows an even better season (16-9, 157 IP, 29 saves). When Radatz entered the game he threw smoke, averaging well over one strikeout per inning. After his last good season in 1965, he was basically washed up.

Radatz represented the best of a new style of relief ace. Table 5.6 shows the prevalence of this breed of workhorse (zero starts and at least 120 innings) beginning in the 1960s. Due to their workload, these pitchers were among the most valuable relievers ever.

The first qualifier was Joe Berry, who pitched 130 innings for the 1945 Philadelphia Athletics. Joe Page (1952), Jim Konstanty (1950), and Hoyt Wilhelm (1952 and 1953) each did it during the postwar era. It wasn't until the mid-1960s that it became fairly common, and there were generally two or three workhorses every year through the 1980s. The last person to fit this profile was Duane Ward in 1990, the setup man on the Blue Jays for Tom Henke. By this time, a team's star reliever (the "closer") was usually pitching fewer innings than one or more of his own reliever teammates.

The 1960s saw the creation of the workhorse fireman, but because teams typically assigned the role to an aging player, these pitchers often succeeded for only a year or two. In the 1970s teams began giving the relief ace position to young pitchers; the job was not merely a stepping-stone to a spot in the rotation or a haven for a failed starter. Prior to this time only a handful of pitchers maintained the role as a team's primary reliever for more than four or five years. The 1970s saw the emergence of the first group of career relief aces.

Rollie Fingers held down the primary relief position on his team for the final fourteen years of his career, which included seven All-Star selections and the MVP and Cy Young awards in 1981. A good reliever for the Red Sox, Sparky Lyle later starred with the Yankees for several years, including a thirty-five-save year in 1972 (and third place in the MVP balloting) and a Cy Young Award in 1977.

John Hiller was a serviceable reliever for several years for the Tigers but missed a year and a half after suffering a heart attack before the 1971 season. He came back with perhaps the best relief-pitching season ever in 1973—a record thirty-eight saves and a 1.44 ERA. In 1974, the one year that saves were calculated using the very strict rule, Hiller posted a record of 17–14 (both the second most wins and the second most losses ever by a relief pitcher) with only thirteen saves. The Tigers were using Hiller with the outcome of the game in doubt. Still only thirty-one years old, Hiller had several more quality seasons ahead.

Mike Marshall did not become a relief ace until age twenty-eight, but then delivered two wonderful seasons for the Montreal Expos. In 1972 he finished 14–8 with eighteen saves and a 1.78 ERA in 116 innings. The next year, he relieved in a record ninety-two games, pitched a record 179 innings, and finished 14–11 with thirty-one saves. In these two fine seasons, he came in fourth and second in the Cy Young award balloting.

During the following off-season, the Dodgers traded Willie Davis, a good outfielder coming off an all-star season, for Marshall, an indication of the importance the Dodgers placed on a quality relief ace. In 1974, Marshall pitched 106 games and 208 innings in relief (both still records), finished 15–12 with twenty-one saves (with the one-year strict save rule in place), and helped the Dodgers to the World Series. That year he became the first relief pitcher to win the Cy Young Award. Marshall had a few injury-plagued years in the mid-1970s but came back with two more strong seasons for the Twins in 1978 and 1979. He still holds the record for most games pitched in a season in both the National and American Leagues.

Rich "Goose" Gossage broke through with his first great season in 1975: twenty-six saves and a 1.84 ERA in 141 innings. In 1976, new manager Paul Richards decided to try him as a starter, as he had done with Wilhelm with success in 1959. It did not work—Gossage finished 9–17

Table 5.7 All-Time Relief Inning Leaders

Pitcher	IP	Pitcher	IP
Hoyt Wilhelm	1871.0	Kent Tekulve	1436.1
Lindy McDaniel	1694.0	Sparky Lyle	1390.1
Rich Gossage	1556.2	Tug McGraw	1301.1
Rollie Fingers	1500.1	Don McMahon	1297.0
Gene Garber	1452.2	Mike Marshall	1259.1

with a 3.94 ERA—and the White Sox traded him to the Pirates. Pittsburgh returned him to the bullpen, where he spent the next seventeen years. Gossage's next two seasons (1977 in Pittsburgh and 1978 for the Yankees) proved as successful as 1975. He remained a dominant pitcher through 1985, although his workload capped out at 100 innings rather than 140.

All of these pitchers deserve mention because of the high workloads they sustained for such a long time. Although many pitchers of the 1980s and 1990s generated high save totals with low ERAs, they typically pitched many fewer innings. Table 5.7 lists the ten pitchers who pitched the most innings in relief through 2001.

Of these ten pitchers, seven of them enjoyed their first success in the 1970s, the other three earlier. Able to withstand a much higher workload than present-day closers, their value was accordingly higher.

Two more great-quality firemen began their careers in the late 1970s. Bruce Sutter led the National League in saves five times for Chicago and St. Louis and won the Cy Young Award in 1979. Dan Quisenberry put together a string of six great seasons for the Royals (1980–1985), and was the last of the great one-hundred-plus-inning firemen. The voters regularly considered both of these men in Cy Young and MVP award balloting

By the mid-1980s the era of the one-hundred-plus-inning fireman was gone, and with it went some of the value of the star reliever. Baseball analysts today debate why this happened and whether or not it has been a productive change in strategy. We revisit the story of the modern relief ace and discuss the pros and cons of the strategy in chapter 13.

6

THE HEIGHT OF FOLLY: THE 1930s BOSTON RED SOX

*U*pon *his introduction to the local press corps in February 1933, Thomas A.*
Yawkey, the new owner of the downtrodden Boston Red Sox, cautioned that his new task would not be an easy one: "I don't believe the Red Sox . . . can be built up overnight," he said. "It would be the height of folly to dump a lot of money into the thing all at once."

Over the next few years, Yawkey dumped a great deal of money into his team. He bought every established player he could find in an ultimately futile attempt to turn a terrible team into a champion. Yawkey found a few great players, a few good players, and a whole lot of players of no good whatsoever.

Not only did the Red Sox fail to win, they never really contended until Yawkey changed course and the team established a farm system and began developing its own players. Other teams have purchased established players and subsequently won titles—the 1997 Florida Marlins are a recent example—but these Red Sox were the embodiment of the slogan, "You can't buy a championship." The mid-1930s Red Sox teams stand out both because of the depths to which they had fallen before they started ed spending and their single-mindedness in the pursuit of veteran players at the expense of finding and nurturing young talent.

By the end of the 1932 season, Boston's storied American League franchise had finished in last place for the ninth time in eleven seasons. The recent team was the worst yet—it won only forty-three games, its ballpark was falling apart, and its attendance was a franchise-low 182,000, an average of 2,800 per home date (including twelve doubleheaders).

Many major league teams were in financial trouble at this time, but as the 1933 *Reach Guide* pointed out, "those owners who sustained [losses] took them like men." Despite the losses, Tom Yawkey was willing and able to buy a team of his own.

Red Sox owner Bob Quinn had bought the team in 1923 at the behest of American League President Ban Johnson after Harry Frazee had traded or sold all his best players, including Babe Ruth. Previously an executive for the St. Louis Browns, Quinn put together a group of investors to rescue the dying club. Over the next decade, the team was spectacularly unsuccessful. By 1933, deeply in debt and in the middle of the Great Depression, Quinn had lost most of his life savings and needed to sell the team.

As luck would have it, Yawkey celebrated his thirtieth birthday on February 21, 1933, coming into an inheritance of several million dollars. In anticipation of this day, he had been looking around for a baseball team to purchase. His uncle and adopted father, William Yawkey, had owned the Tigers for a few years, and Tom had grown up loving baseball and idolizing baseball players. Now that he was one of the richest men in the country, it was only a matter of time before he satisfied his desire.

Bob Quinn had wanted to sell the Red Sox for a few years and recoup enough money to satisfy his debts and pay his taxes. He ultimately sold the team to Yawkey for $1.2 million. Quinn did not want to sell unless Yawkey's group included a baseball man, so Yawkey brought aboard the great Eddie Collins, his boyhood idol, to run the team. Collins would be the general manager of the Red Sox until 1947.

The 1932 Red Sox were not only a bad team (the 1933 *Spalding Guide* opined, "Boston had a team that did not rate with the others of the American League") but also a bad team without a future. With no farm system and no money to buy talent from independent teams, they were a collection of castoffs and other surplus players.

The major change in the structure of organized baseball between the wars was the introduction of the farm system. In response to Branch Rickey's initiative, the minor league system began to change by the late 1920s. In order to gain a wider, cheaper, and more secure source of young baseball talent, Rickey began acquiring both direct ownership and working relationships with minor league franchises. The model slowly took hold. Unfortunately, before Yawkey the Red Sox did not possess the capital required to construct a farm system.

From 1927 to 1933, only one player made his major league debut for the Red Sox and subsequently had a ten-year career: Rabbit Warstler, an excellent defensive shortstop who would hit only .229 for his eleven-year career. Over the same seven seasons, the Yankees introduced twelve ten-year players, including Bill Dickey, Lefty Gomez, Ben Chapman, Billy Werber, Red Rolfe, Johnny Allen, Johnny Murphy, and Frank Crosetti. Eddie Collins, with the aid of Tom Yawkey's wallet, was going to try to bridge this talent gap.

The 1932 Red Sox had two interesting players and, as was typical, other teams had discarded both early in the season. One was Smead Jolley, a six-time minor league batting champion who was such a terrible defensive player that he only played four major league seasons. Jolley spent much of 1932 driving in runs (ninety-nine RBI) and stumbling up and down the left field embankment in Fenway Park. The second, Dale Alexander, had just sixteen at-bats in mid-June when the Red Sox acquired him from the Tigers. Alexander wound up winning the batting title by hitting .367 for the year. Despite these two players, the Red Sox scored only 566 runs, 100 fewer than any other team in the league. They also led the league in runs allowed. Every player on the club was either in his prime, such as it was, or past it. There was no legitimate reason to expect the players on hand to get any better.

Despite his circumspection at the opening press conference, Yawkey soon settled on the quick fix. His purchase of the Red Sox did not become effective until after the 1933 season had started. At his first American League meeting in May, Yawkey stood up and announced, "I don't want to waste time quibbling here. I have $100,000 to spend and I intend to spend it." In retrospect, this may not have been the best negotiating stance.

Most of Yawkey's fellow owners were either broke or holding onto their money. When they of heard Yawkey's intentions, they practically tripped over themselves trying to get to him. St. Louis Browns owner Phil Ball got there first, and on May 9 sold catcher Rick Ferrell and pitcher Lloyd Brown for $25,000, an astronomical sum in 1933. The Red Sox badly needed a catcher, and Ferrell was one of the better catchers of the 1930s, but Brown was 1–6 with a 7.15 ERA at the time of the deal. This would become a trend in Yawkey deals—to acquire a useful player, the Red Sox would accept another player or two of dubious value.

In these years the rules allowed teams to keep a larger roster until May 15, when they were required to cut back to a twenty-three-man squad. The Yankees usually had tough decisions to make every year, but Yawkey helped them out in 1933. For $100,000, the Yankees sold to the Red Sox two players they might have had to release anyway, pitcher George Pipgras and third baseman Bill Werber. The impatient Yawkey neither looked for bargains nor waited to see who might get cut May 15. He had money to spend and, by God, he intended to spend it.

Red Sox fans were enthusiastic—it was not their money, after all. The Red Sox had spent many years selling players, and now they were buying them. Even better, they were getting them from the Yankees, the team that had built its dynasty largely by acquiring Red Sox players in the early 1920s. Better days were clearly ahead.

The 1933 Red Sox improved by twenty wins and advanced to seventh place. The additions of Werber and Ferrell enhanced the offense, and the team scored 700 runs, up from 566 in 1932. Led by five hurlers who were at least average—Pipgras, Brown, Gordon Rhodes, Bob Weiland, and Hank Johnson—the pitching also improved dramatically. At a rate of improvement of twenty wins a year, Yawkey probably figured the Red Sox could be the best team in the league in just two more seasons.

In 1933 the Red Sox second baseman, twenty-seven-year-old Johnny Hodapp, hit .312. Nevertheless, the team released him at the end of the season after trading Lloyd Brown to the Indians for an *older* second baseman, Bill Cissell. Two months later, the Red Sox acquired an even *older* one, Max Bishop. The Red Sox in this era made a habit of these fruitless transactions.

About the same time, Collins traded Jolley, pitcher Ivy Andrews, and cash to the Browns for thirty-year-old star outfielder Carl Reynolds. Yawkey also hired a new manager, Bucky Harris, without first checking with Collins. Had he inquired, he would have discovered that Collins and Harris hated each other.

Another high-impact change, the refurbishing of Fenway Park, took place in the off-season at a reported cost of $1.5 million. The largest building project in Boston during the 1930s other than the Mystic River Bridge in Charlestown, the effort transformed the park from a dilapidated old structure to one of baseball's most famous landmarks.

◇ ◇ ◇

Players like Rick Ferrell and Bill Werber were all well and good, but Yawkey really wanted a superstar. The place to get one turned out to be Philadelphia. Connie Mack, who had been hit harder than most other owners by the depression, decided to dismantle his great team, as he had done back in 1914. Mack informed Eddie Collins that Lefty Grove might be available for the right price. Grove was thirty-four but still the best pitcher in baseball; he had won twenty-four games for the Athletics in 1933.

On December 12, the Red Sox traded two players of little consequence (shortstop Rabbit Warstler and pitcher Bob Kline) and $125,000 for Grove, pitcher Rube Walberg, and second baseman Max Bishop. Once fine players, Walberg and Bishop were nearing the ends of their careers and not the type of players bad teams should acquire. Once they joined the club, they stood in the way of real solutions at their positions for a couple of years.

In the early days of his stewardship, Tom Yawkey was a hero worshipper. In particular he worshipped Lefty Grove, who was actually three years older than his new owner. Grove became Yawkey's closest friend in baseball. They drank together during the season and hunted and fished together afterwards. Grove could often be found before games in Yawkey's office with his feet up on the desk. Unfortunately, Grove gave his managers no respect at all, instead frequently treating them with contempt.

More important, Grove suddenly could not pitch, and at first both his teammates and the media questioned Grove's dedication. He reported to camp with a sore arm, the first of his long career, and the injury stayed with him all season. He had teeth pulled, tonsils removed, and teeth pulled again, but nothing worked. Grove finished the season with eight wins and a 6.52 ERA, and at thirty-four years old appeared washed up. The other two players Collins received from the Athletics were also disappointments—Walberg won six games and Bishop, despite an on-base percentage of .452, lost his job to Cissell in midseason. Connie Mack reportedly offered Yawkey a refund on his money for Grove.

In May, Collins acquired another tempestuous star pitcher by trading two players and $25,000 to the Indians for Wes Ferrell, Rick's brother. Ferrell had won twenty or more games his first four seasons, but had an off year in 1933 and was holding out rather than accepting the huge salary cut the Indians offered. In Boston, Ferrell found success immediately, pitching the way the Red Sox had expected Grove to pitch.

In 1934, many writers picked the Red Sox to finish third behind Washington and New York, largely because of the big trade with the Athletics. As the deal turned out to be a complete disaster that year, it is remarkable the team finished fourth at 76–76, 24 games behind the Tigers. In Yawkey's first two years, the Red Sox progressed from the worst team in the league to average. The Yawkey-Collins regime had clearly accomplished something. It is instructive to look at the team's improvement more closely.

The offense took another big step forward in 1934 and scored 820 runs, an increase of 254 runs over two years. The hitting star, Bill Werber, started the year at shortstop but moved back to third when Collins acquired Lyn Lary from the Yankees in May. Werber finished with 200 hits and 129 runs, hitting .320, and leading the league with forty steals.

Other than Werber and Rick and Wes Ferrell (the only regular pitcher with a winning record), the team was filled with mediocre players. The Red Sox improved a remarkable thirty-three games in two years, largely by replacing bad players with average players. The 1932 Red Sox had started a shortstop who hit .211 and an outfielder who hit .264 with no home runs. Two years later, the Red Sox had acceptable players across the entire roster. In order to contend, however, the Red Sox would need several *good* players. As they would soon discover, it is much easier to improve a team filled with bad players than it is one filled with average players.

When only nine games behind the Yankees in July 1934, manager Harris intimated that the team would have been in first with a healthy Grove: "We had every reason to expect Grove to win at least 20 games for us." This was nonsense. Even with Grove at his best, they were a long way from contending with teams like New York and Detroit, each of whom had several star players.

As the off-season approached, rumors were rampant that the Red Sox were going to buy Jimmie Foxx from the Athletics. Apparently Collins spoke to Mack about Foxx, but the great first baseman would remain in Philadelphia for one more year. Yawkey had his eye on another star player, a man who would help run the team for the next quarter century.

After the 1934 season, according to the oft-told story, Yawkey asked Collins to name the greatest player in the league, and Collins answered, "Joe Cronin." Yawkey then supposedly instructed Collins to acquire him. Cronin, manager and shortstop of the Washington Senators, was nowhere near the best player in the league, as Collins should have known. If Collins supported the acquisition of Cronin, it was more likely to get rid of Bucky Harris as the team's manager. Regardless of the reason, Collins approached Clark Griffith, the owner of the Senators and Cronin's father-in-law, and kept offering more and more money until Griffith finally said "yes" at $250,000.

It is impossible to overestimate the impact that this deal had on the baseball world. In inflation-adjusted dollars, it may be the most money paid for a player in baseball history. Cronin was still only twenty-seven years old, a star shortstop, and had won the pennant as the rookie manager of the 1933 Senators.

Transcendental Graphics

Joe Cronin

As it turned out, acquiring him was a mistake. Cronin remained an excellent hitter but was a terrible shortstop and the wrong manager for this team. The Red Sox were fast becoming a group of temperamental veterans, and the players gave Cronin, one of the club's younger players, even less respect than they had given Harris, which was very little. With a different team, Cronin might have been a good manager, but with the Red Sox he presided over a divided team for the next several years. The pitchers especially disliked Cronin for his poor defense and insistence on calling pitches from the shortstop position. Apart from the seemingly huge problems any shortstop would have calling pitches from the middle of the diamond, Grove and Ferrell didn't respect his baseball knowledge at all.

Other than the acquisition of Cronin, the off-season was fairly quiet. In 1935, for the first time in memory, the Red Sox actually had two young rookies in the starting lineup—twenty-three-year-old Babe Dahlgren at first base and twenty-two-year-old Mel Almada in center field. The team signed both players from the Pacific Coast League. The two were the first Red Sox regulars under twenty-five years old since Jack Rothrock in 1929. Collins seemed to be turning his attention to young players as well.

Once the season was under way, however, the Red Sox continued to acquire unneeded veterans. Cronin was unhappy with the play of Max Bishop and Bill Cissell at second base, so Collins bought Dib Williams and forty-year-old outfielder Bing Miller from the Athletics on May 1. Three weeks later, the Red Sox traded with the Browns for yet another second baseman, Oscar Melillo, who ended up getting most of the playing time.

Fresh off his disastrous 1934 season, Grove came into training camp healthy, determined, and confident. His left shoulder responded, and he won twenty games and the ERA title. Most accounts suggest that he was a different type of pitcher beginning in 1935; he now relied more on his curve ball, rather than his blazing fastball, to get batters out. As figure 6.1 clearly indicates, however, his strikeout rate actually dropped in 1933, the year before his injury. Once Grove recovered, his strikeout rate rose nearly to its old level before age finally began catching up with him about 1939.

Not to be outdone, Wes Ferrell finished 25–14. Likely the Red Sox's best hitter as well, he smacked seven home runs while hitting for a .347 average. Unfortunately, it was a two-man pitching staff, as table 6.1 shows. In 1935 the league ERA was 4.46, and the Red Sox played in a hitter's park, so a combined ERA of 3.14 for 45 percent of the team's innings was outstanding.

The Red Sox played atrociously in the field—the team led the league with 194 errors, and Cronin's shortstop play became a distraction. His pitchers, especially the veterans, grumbled that he was overpaid and should not be playing shortstop. Bill Cunningham, writing in the Boston

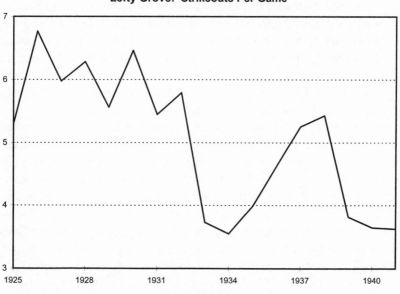

Figure 6.1

Table 6.1 1935 Red Sox Pitching

	IP	W	L	ERA
Grove + Ferrell	595.7	45	26	3.14
Rest of team	735.3	33	49	5.03

Post, suggested, "If first were guarded by a less agile and spectacular fielder than Babe Dahlgren, [Cronin] would stand charged with more errors than he has." The 1936 *Reach Guide*, not normally inclined to be critical of players, was forced to point out that Cronin's defense was not up to his usual standards, which is scary indeed.

In an interview with J. G. Taylor Spink for *The Sporting News* in October 1935, Yawkey indicated that Cronin's added weight and decreased speed meant that he was through as the team's shortstop—he would move to first base unless the Red Sox could get Foxx, in which case Cronin would play third base. Spink concluded, "Cronin will not play short and that is as definite as the fact that Joe will remain as manager of the Red Sox." Spink ought to have interviewed the manager himself—Joe Cronin had no intention of switching positions and would remain at shortstop for several more years.

Meanwhile, in Philadelphia, Connie Mack continued his fire sale. Although now depleted enough to have finished dead last in 1935, this once-great team still had several high-salaried veteran players. Accordingly, in two separate transactions, the Red Sox acquired Jimmie Foxx, shortstop Eric "Boob" McNair, outfielder Doc Cramer, and pitcher Johnny Marcum for a package of dubious replacements plus $225,000. Since Yawkey was the only one buying players in the 1930s, it is difficult to judge whether he was overpaying. Obviously, there were not many players the caliber of Jimmie Foxx and Lefty Grove in the league.

Second only to Lou Gehrig as the best hitter of the 1930s, Jimmie Foxx would turn in a number of excellent seasons for the Red Sox. He was a big, muscular twenty-eight-year-old slugger, but also a good defensive player and fast base runner. Capable of playing other positions, Foxx had actually started out the 1935 season as the catcher for the Athletics. Marcum, a twenty-seven-year-old starter, had won seventeen games for a bad team.

The other players were nothing special. Although a good center fielder (Fred Lieb called him "another Speaker"), Cramer was a weak offensive player. Players like Cramer who regularly hit .300 with no power were quite common in the 1930s. In fact, the 1935 Red Sox had three outfielders—Mel Almada, Dusty Cooke, and Roy Johnson—who all hit as well as

Cramer. McNair had a good defensive reputation but was a mediocre hitter. He had no power, and his lifetime on-base percentage of .318 offered little in an era when the league average was generally over .340.

At the time rumors persisted that Mack might be willing to sell everyone on his team. If true, the Red Sox missed a wonderful opportunity by not acquiring Bob Johnson. With the inflated run scoring, especially in the American League, the 1930s were replete with overrated offensive players, but Johnson was one of the rare *underrated* hitters. He regularly hit .300 with twenty-five or thirty home runs and ninety walks. Already thirty years old, he still had several All-Star seasons ahead and would have helped the Red Sox immensely over the next ten years. His availability, and the Red Sox's interest in him, is unknown.

Collins also traded outfielders Roy Johnson (Bob's brother) and Carl Reynolds to the Senators for Heinie Manush. Although destined for the Hall of Fame, Manush was thirty-four years old and coming off of a season in which he had hit just .274. In the 1930s, a left fielder with little power needed to hit .330 to be a star, and Clark Griffith correctly recognized that Manush was about finished.

After three years of steady improvement, the Red Sox heading into the 1936 season could boast of well-known players at nearly every position and on the mound. Foxx (who some predicted would surpass Ruth's record sixty home runs while in Boston), McNair, Cronin, and Werber would play the infield. Manush, Cramer, and Almada patrolled the outfield. Rick Ferrell was the catcher. The team had the two best pitchers in the league in Grove and Ferrell, and Marcum and Fritz Ostermueller gave them two decent young starters to fill out the rotation. The media began referring to the Red Sox as the "Millionaires" or the "Gold Sox." Boston fans dared dream of winning the American League pennant.

When the dust settled, the 1936 Red Sox finished 74–80 and in sixth place, twenty-eight and a half games behind the Yankees. As the 1937 *Reach Guide* proclaimed, "The most disappointing ball club and most dumbfounded fans can both be found in Boston." And what is more, "There probably never has been anything like it in baseball history. Mr. Yawkey, the liberal owner, paid a huge fortune in cash to get the best stars in sight, and his club is actually worse off in the percentage table than when he began his lavish spending." The last claim is patently untrue, but the sentiment is accurate: the 1936 Red Sox were expected to contend for the pennant, and they finished sixth.

The team may have been slightly unlucky. They outscored their opponents, 775–764, which would normally indicate a team that ought to win about half of its games. At this juncture, we can only speculate on whether this indicates simple bad luck. In any case, the shortfall was only a few wins, and the Red Sox needed another thirty to beat the Yankees.

The team suffered a few injuries. The Red Sox started the year by shifting Werber to right field and McNair to third base so that Cronin could remain at shortstop. Cronin broke his wrist early in the season and moved the fielders back to their preferred positions. Manush also got hurt and played only half the year. Late in the season the Red Sox recalled Babe Dahlgren from Syracuse to play first base and moved Foxx to left field.

The pitching was very good. Playing in a hitter's park, the Red Sox had an ERA of 4.19, second best in the league to the Yankees. Grove won his annual ERA title and seventeen games, and Ferrell won twenty. The young starters, Ostermueller and Marcum, had ERAs lower than the league average. The staff was not particularly deep, but the Red Sox may have had the best starting rotation in the league.

The offense was horrible. The Red Sox scored just 775 runs, 101 fewer than the average American League team. Considering that the team apparently had a star player at every position, most fans at the time and many historians today found this lack of offense inconceivable. In fact, this shortfall should not be viewed as surprising.

An average player, Bill Werber had had an excellent season in 1934 that was completely out of character; in 1936 he turned in his normal year. Heinie Manush's best days were obviously behind him. McNair had a decent year at shortstop as Cronin's replacement but was nothing special. Oscar Melillo finished the season as the regular second baseman despite hitting .226.

The lack of production from the outfielders was a huge problem. The Red Sox regulars—Almada, Cramer, and Cooke, plus Manush before he got hurt—hit .253, .292, .273, and .291, respectively, an aggregate .280, and combined for seven home runs. Each of the other seven American League teams had at least one outfielder who hit .320. Table 6.2 shows the cumulative statistics of each team's regular outfielders (in two cases four players are used) in 1936.

The next-to-last column, wins above average, compares each team's outfielders to the average American League hitter, a pool that includes all batters, even bench players and pitchers. Boston's outfielders provided offense six games below that supplied by average hitters. Compared to the Yankees, they were more than twelve games behind before considering the defense, pitching, and the hitters at other positions (Lou Gehrig, Bill Dickey, Tony Lazzeri, etc.).

A 1930s American League outfielder who hit .315 with ten home runs was nothing special—just an average hitter—and none of the Red Sox's options even approached this level of production. Had Cronin and Manush stayed healthy, conceivably the team could have won a few more games and finished third or fourth, but it's hard to see how it could have won ninety games.

The team also remained divided against the manager. After Cronin returned to the field, Wes Ferrell complained, "If we had a shortstop we'd win the pennant. Cronin has cost me four games already." Ferrell twice walked off the mound in the middle of innings because he was so frustrated with the defense. The second time, on August 21, he was fined and suspended by Cronin, although Yawkey reduced the penalty. At one point Ferrell threatened to "slug that damned Irishman [Cronin] right on his lantern jaw."

In Cronin's defense, Ferrell was not particularly easy to manage. He had problems in Cleveland with manager Roger Peckinpaugh and his conflicts with Cronin were persistent. All of Ferrell's teammates, on the other hand, spoke highly of him. He seemed to direct most of his tantrums at himself (Bill Werber claimed to have witnessed Ferrell knock himself out by punching himself in the jaw with both fists), and he was apparently quite reserved off the field. But he thought Cronin a terrible shortstop and manager, and it ate at him throughout his tenure in Boston.

Lefty Grove may have had an even worse relationship with Cronin. Grove's friend Tom Yawkey remained silent while Grove regularly blasted Cronin to the press and to Cronin's face. Doc Cramer overheard Grove tell Cronin he could not play shortstop for a high school team.

Ferrell and Grove may have had a point. In 1936, Cronin made twenty-three errors in only eighty-one games. He began getting down on one knee to field ground balls, causing Melillo to say, "For Christ's sakes, Joe, if you're going to miss 'em, you might as well stand up and miss 'em like a big leaguer." Grove had his whole team on edge most of the time. Oscar Melillo summed it up well:

> That Lefty was a terror. He was sore because we always seemed to be winning 10–8 for Wes Ferrell and losing the 1-0 games for Grove. So there we'd be in the ninth, and so scared of that wild man you could hear our knees knocking. I'd say to myself, 'I hope this guy hits it to Joe Cronin,' and I knew Cronin was hoping he'd hit it to Jimmie Foxx, and Foxx was hoping he'd hit it to Bill Werber.

In retrospect, the notion that the 1936 Red Sox had a chance to compete

Table 6.2 AL Outfielders, 1936

Team (Players)	AVG	OBP	SLG	HR	RBI	RC	WAAv	WAR
Detroit (Walker, Simmons, Goslin)	.331	.391	.515	49	330	336	7.4	13.2
Washington (Reynolds, Chapman, Stone, Hill)	.318	.399	.475	23	225	276	7.4	12.1
New York (DiMaggio, Selkirk, Powell)	.313	.380	.520	54	280	290	6.5	11.6
Cleveland (Weatherly, Averill, Vosmik)	.336	.402	.528	43	273	293	6.5	11.5
Philadelphia (Puccinelli, Moses, B Johnson)	.307	.391	.481	43	265	306	5.6	11.3
St. Louis (Bell, West, Solters)	.306	.375	.453	35	327	304	1.9	8.3
Chicago (Haas, Kreevich, Radcliff)	.312	.381	.419	13	197	278	1.8	7.6
Boston (Almada, Cramer, Cooke, Manush)	.280	.348	.367	7	154	213	-5.7	0.5
League Average Group	.313	.383	.470	33	256	287	3.9	9.5

RC = runs created   WAAAv = wins above average   WAR = wins above replacement with the Yankees is laughable. Although the brilliance of rookie Joe DiMaggio could not have been anticipated, the Yankees entered the season with excellent offensive players throughout the lineup, including Lou Gehrig, Tony Lazzeri, Bill Dickey, and George Selkirk. Realistically, the Red Sox had three players that could have been expected to be better than average offensively—Foxx at first, Cronin at shortstop, and Ferrell at catcher. Cronin got hurt, but Foxx and Ferrell had their typical seasons. It was not anywhere close to enough.

◇   ◇   ◇

As the team leveled off after its first burst of improvement under Yawkey, the owner shifted gears and decided that the team ought to develop some of its own players. Yawkey hired Billy Evans, former umpire and recently general manager of the Indians, as the team's first farm director. Early in 1936, the Red Sox took out an option on two players from the San Diego Padres of the Pacific Coast League—George Myatt and Bobby Doerr. When Eddie Collins went out west to scout the pair, he passed on Myatt, signed Doerr, and took an option on their teammate, Ted Williams.

During the winter of 1936–1937, Eddie Collins told *Baseball* magazine: "We have abandoned, definitely, the attempt to fight our way to the pennant by the purchase of ready-made stars." Although Yawkey's wealth would occasionally help the team out over the years, his general manager would now have other options available.

In preparing for the 1937 season, the team made only one immediately significant move, trading Bill Werber to the Athletics for Pinky Higgins. Bill James has called this type of transaction a "challenge" trade: the players traded played the same position, indicating not that the teams had different needs but that they evaluated the talents of the players differently. The Red Sox won the challenge: Werber was a year older than Higgins, not as good a player—he had never been able to duplicate 1934—and, by all accounts, a pain in the neck to manage.

The Red Sox made another big trade in June, dispensing of the Ferrell brothers and Mel Almada for Ben Chapman and Bobo Newsom. Although certainly happy to be rid of Wes Ferrell, Cronin received two players who managed to treat him even worse. Newsom disliked Cronin bothering him on the mound and reportedly would ask his manager, "Who's telling old Bobo how to pitch?" Chapman just ignored Cronin's instructions.

Doerr, a nineteen-year-old from Los Angeles, started the season as the second baseman, but he lost the job to McNair when he failed to hit. For most of the year the infield consisted of Foxx, McNair, Cronin, and Higgins. The outfield regulars were Chapman, Cramer, and Buster Mills, the last acquired from Rochester in the off-season. Gene DeSautels, a weak-hitting thirty-year-old rookie, replaced Rick Ferrell at catcher. The offense rebounded a bit and scored 821 runs despite an off year from Foxx (.285 and 35 HRs). Grove turned in another excellent year and won seventeen. The Red Sox also received good years out of a number of other pitchers, including rookie Jack Wilson (17 wins), Newsom (13), and Marcum (13). Again, the staff lacked depth, but few teams had strong bullpens in the 1930s. The team won eighty games—progress, but twenty-two games fewer than the Yankees.

Over the next few years, the Red Sox brought in a number of good young players. In 1938 rookie Jim Bagby Jr. was the team's best pitcher, and Bobby Doerr was a star by 1939. Ted Williams, destined to be the best player in team history, came up in 1939 and immediately hit like a Hall of Famer. Dom DiMaggio and Johnny Pesky arrived in 1940 and 1942, respectively. This was quite a group of players, and it came much cheaper than had the likes of George Pipgras and Bing Miller.

With the addition of this impressive young talent, the Red Sox began to win. They never caught the Yankees, but there is no shame in that—the Yankees of this era may have been the greatest team ever. Over the five years from 1938 to 1942, the Red Sox finished second four times and built the core of a team that would compete for several championships after the war. The Red Sox might have enjoyed great seasons from 1943 to 1945, but most of their players, like everyone else's, were in the military. In 1946, when the players returned, the Red Sox dominated the American League from start to finish.

Why did the Red Sox fail to win in Yawkey's early years? Essentially, the team needed better players. Yawkey and Collins acquired several good or excellent players—Grove, Foxx, the Ferrell brothers, and Cronin—who performed as well as one could reasonably have expected. The rest of the players acquired, however, were overrated or well past their primes, and the lofty expectations set for the Red Sox were unrealistic. Since they were not producing any talent of their own, they were left with several holes in their lineup and pitching staff. The Yankees, meanwhile, were at the very peak of their dynasty, with stars everywhere.

Yawkey's attempt to build a championship was doomed to fail for several reasons. First, before the advent of free agency, star players were rarely available for purchase. The 1917 White Sox took advantage of the availability of Eddie Collins and Joe Jackson but also acquired several other excellent players through more conventional means. Had Yawkey been able to purchase several other star players—say, Charlie Gehringer, Bob Johnson, and Earl Averill—his strategy might have worked. Players of this caliber are rarely on the market, and Yawkey was fortunate to find Foxx and Grove available.

Additionally, players purchased from other teams are normally on the downside of their careers. Veterans like Eric McNair and Doc Cramer, often of dubious value when acquired, usually require replacement themselves in a year or two. Even under the modern system of free agency, most players on the market are already in their thirties and likely to be dead weight by the end of their long-term contracts. Star free agents in their twenties, such as Greg Maddux and Barry Bonds, rarely disappoint but are a rare breed.

Tom Yawkey's wealth gave the Red Sox a big advantage over the rest of the American League, especially during the Great Depression. This advantage was not entirely squandered—the Red Sox were obviously a much strengthened organization with Yawkey aboard—but it has to be viewed as a missed opportunity nonetheless. While Yawkey was busy spending money on players who were declining in ability, owners with less money were scouting and signing players like Joe DiMaggio and Bob Feller. Once Yawkey changed course, the Red Sox system paid off quickly, but by that the time there were more owners willing to spend money again.

Tom Yawkey owned the Red Sox for forty-three years, until his death in 1976. He took over the worst team in the major leagues, a team on the verge of bankruptcy, and made it one of the most respected franchises in all of baseball. He completely rebuilt a dying ballpark into one of the best-loved sports facilities in the world. The Red Sox were a contender for most of the Yawkey years and did not finish in last place again until 1992. But the one overriding goal of Yawkey's life—to win a World Series—was never fulfilled, and that fact will always be part of his legacy.

7

FOLLOWING THE RECIPE:
THE 1948 BOSTON BRAVES

While the experience of Tom Yawkey in the 1930s showed that money alone would not create a champion, a large bankroll has always been helpful. The New York Yankees of the late 1970s and late 1990s won World Series titles due in part to a significantly larger operating budget than almost every other team. The Yankees enjoyed the same advantage in the late 1980s and were nevertheless one of the worst teams in baseball. Smart, capable management is as important as lots of money—and likely more so.

The Boston Braves of the early 1940s were a team nearly as unsuccessful as the Red Sox had been a decade earlier. Three wealthy men purchased the club in 1944 and then brought in capable decision makers to build the team. The Braves' transformation into a champion provides an instructive look at what can happen when a team is both willing to spend money and able to spend it wisely.

Charles Adams had assumed control of the Braves in 1935 from Judge Emil Fuchs, a man of modest means who was just about broke. Adams held large investments in horse tracks and therefore needed a front man to run the ball club. Adams turned to Bob Quinn, the man who had sold the Red Sox to Yawkey and who had spent the previous two years as the Brooklyn Dodgers' business manager.

The 1935 Braves team was the worst senior circuit team of the twentieth century, with a record of 38–115, a .248 winning percentage. Quinn's two most notable attempts to reverse this debacle were changing the team's name to the "Bees" and hiring Casey Stengel as manager. The team did show some improvement in the late 1930s, twice finishing above .500 and once even as high as fifth. But between 1939 and 1942, the team returned to its familiar seventh place—usually kept out of the cellar by the even more hapless Philadelphia Phillies.

Quinn—described by Boston sportswriter Harold Kaese as "one of the old school, kind and open, but aggressive and stubborn"—seemed to grow bitter with the Braves. He once said of himself, "Some men die in time to save their reputations. I lived too long. I've had a great reputation for developing teams and players, but 25 years ago I went to Boston, and since then . . ." Despite, or perhaps because of, this sentiment, in 1941 Quinn put together a syndicate to buy out Adams's interest. This new syndicate included three Boston area contractors who later became central to the Braves ownership: Louis Perini, Guido Rugo, and Joseph Maney.

The team's name reverted to "Braves" in 1941 with the buyout of Adams and for the next few years little real improvement seemed in the offing. Future Hall of Fame pitcher Warren Spahn appeared briefly for the team in 1942 before heading off to war. Many years later he played for Stengel with the expansion New York Mets. Spahn would later remark, "I played for Casey before and after he was a genius."

In January 1944, Perini, Rugo, and Maney purchased the team outright from Quinn's group for $750,000. Perini, who with his two brothers now owned 50 percent of the stock, headed the triumvirate and kept Quinn as president. Nicknamed the "Three Little Steam Shovels," the assertive trio had a business that had been strong during the war and the resources and desire to assemble a winning team.

Although Quinn remained with the team, Stengel was let go. Baseball historian Robert Creamer speculates that a conversation between Perini and Stengel at spring training in 1943 soured Perini when Stengel offered one of his notoriously convoluted explanations to a strategy question from the straightforward Perini.

With the war in full swing, the team made few other changes during 1944, although in May they moved the right field fence from 340 to 320 feet to increase run scoring. Near the end of the season, in a harbinger of the future the Braves paid $50,000 to acquire the keystone combination of Dick Culler and Tom Nelson from Milwaukee of the American Association. Culler started at shortstop for the next two years but fell far short of being a good major league regular. Nelson, too, disappointed; he hurt his arm and never played again after appearing briefly with the Braves in 1945.

After the 1944 season, Bob Quinn, then seventy-five, moved over to run the farm system so that his son John could become general manager. Upon his son's promotion, the elder Quinn remarked on the changes he had seen: "The world is upside down, with men wearing white shoes, white pants and silk shirts, and women wearing trousers. But the thing that surprised me most in my life was not the telephone, radio, or airplane. It was night baseball." Following the 1945 season, the elder Quinn finally left the employ of major league baseball in Boston, and the team hired William Sullivan Jr. (later to gain fame as the owner of football's New England Patriots) as public relations director. The Braves were not only gearing up to win but to entertain as well.

With the war still on, the Braves remained fairly quiet in 1945. They made only one major trade, but like the Culler-Nelson deal the year before, it signaled an ownership willing to spend. Near the end of May, the Braves traded starting pitcher Red Barrett, along with $60,000, to the St. Louis Cardinals for Mort Cooper, the best pitcher in the league at the time. Cooper's 1942–1944 record is summarized in table 7.1.

Unfortunately for the Braves, Barrett posted a record of 21–9 for the Cardinals over the rest of the season and led the league in wins in what would be the best season of his career. Even worse, in late August Cooper needed surgery to remove bone chips from his elbow, prematurely ending his season. This misfortune in the owners' initial foray into the trade market did not sour them on future deals.

The Braves ownership, it would turn out, had showed its hand and over the next few years would spend lots of money for players. Unlike several other attempts with this strategy, notably by Ray Kroc with the San Diego Padres and Gene Autry with the California Angels, Perini and general manager John Quinn exhibited enough baseball smarts to make it work.

Although the Braves made more trades and spent more money than

Table 7.1 Mort Cooper

	Won	Lost	IP	ERA	Lg ERA	MVP Rank
1942	22	7	278.2	1.78	3.31	1 (1)*
1943	21	8	274.0	2.30	3.38	5 (1)
1944	22	7	252.1	2.46	3.61	9 (3)

*MVP Rank is Cooper's ranking in the MVP vote, and the number in parentheses is his ranking among pitchers only.

most, the team was not alone in its activity. A syndicate that included Bing Crosby purchased the Pittsburgh Pirates in August 1946, and the Pirates also began spending money. In the first half of 1947, in two separate transactions, the Pirates spent $175,000 for six players, including aging slugger Hank Greenberg. Less than two years later, the Pirates spent another $125,000 on pitcher Murry Dickson and acquired numerous other players in this period. Yet the Pirates exhibited none of the Braves' aptitude in assembling a baseball team and never finished higher than fourth.

One intelligent decision by the Braves was hiring a first-class manager, both to advise on personnel moves and sort out the talent as it was acquired. Setting his sights high, Perini landed Billy Southworth, who had managed the St. Louis Cardinals to three pennants and two world championships from 1942 to 1944. Perini approached Southworth and Cardinals owner Sam Breadon at the 1945 World Series and managed to pry the manager away by offering a base salary of $35,000 plus a bonus based on the team's finish.

◇ ◇ ◇

Billy Southworth had played the game with a passionate, all-out style, but as a manager he showed a sensitivity to his players that was unusual for the era. Baseball historian Leonard Koppett described Southworth this way: "As a player, he had been known for fire and hustle and acquired the name 'Billy the Kid,' popularized by gunfighter legends. As a manager he was exactly the opposite: conciliation inside the clubhouse and careful handling of diverse personalities." Second baseman Connie Ryan would concur: "Southworth did a hell of job in those days. He was well ahead of his time. He had grievance committees for the players and those type of things off the field. He was a good man."

Although he played briefly for Cleveland in 1915, Southworth did not begin playing semi-regularly until 1918 with the Pittsburgh Pirates. In that war-shortened 1918 season, at a time when winning the batting title was regarded as the highest individual seasonal honor, some contemporary sources awarded the title to Southworth for hitting .341 in 62 games. NL President John Heydler said that owing to the shortened season (the Pirates played only 125 games because of World War I) he would not officially declare a winner among candidates Edd Roush, Zack Wheat, and Southworth. Modern sources award the batting title to Roush.

Traded to the New York Giants, Southworth got along well with John McGraw for a couple of years, but as an independent thinker, he eventu-

Transcendental Graphics

Billy Southworth

ally had a falling out with his dictatorial manager. The Giants traded Southworth to the Cardinals in the middle of 1926. Sportswriter and long-time friend Bob Hooey later wrote, "Billy found it impossible to subordinate his individuality to the rigorous system in vogue within the Giant clubhouse and dugout. To Southworth, the McGraw system was a continual pressure that never eased. It was lacking in sentiment and too coldly calculating for Southworth's best play."

After the June trade, Southworth had an excellent partial season for the Cardinals during their successful pennant drive and hit .345 in the World Series. In 1927 he injured his rib, and at thirty-four, his career appeared to be on the wane. General manager Branch Rickey and owner Sam Breadon recognized Southworth's leadership skills and offered him the manager's position at Rochester, the Cardinals' highest farm club, for 1928. Despite inheriting a mediocre team, Southworth won the International League pennant in his first season as a manager.

In 1929, Rickey and Breadon continued their long-running practice of not sticking with a field general. After winning the 1926 World Series, they had traded player-manager Rogers Hornsby to the Giants. After a second-place finish in 1927, they fired Bob O'Farrell. Finally, after winning the 1928 pennant but being swept in the World Series, they grew dissatisfied with skipper Bill McKechnie. For 1929, in an awkward move, Breadon and Rickey switched the managerial positions of McKechnie and Southworth. It's hardly surprising that the thirty-six-year-old Southworth, with no major league managerial experience, had difficulty taking over a pennant-winning team from the popular McKechnie. After a 43–45 start, the Cardinals sent Southworth back to Rochester and recalled McKechnie.

The Rochester team that McKechnie rejoined won another pennant in 1929 and then repeated in 1930 and 1931. In 1932, combative owner Larry McPhail hired Southworth to manage Columbus in the American Association, but the two did not get along. In 1933 Southworth joined the Giants as a coach under second-year manager Bill Terry, but he resigned at the end of spring training amid rumors of another fallout. Southworth remained out of baseball for a couple of years before Rickey offered him another position in the extremely deep Cardinal organization. Leo Durocher remembered that Southworth "had become an alcoholic and drifted down to the minors, but Rickey had stuck with him and Southworth had beaten it."

By 1939 Southworth had worked himself back up to Rochester, and in July 1940 Breadon again placed him in charge of the Cardinals. The team was languishing in seventh place when Southworth took over but ultimately climbed to third. In 1941 the Cardinals improved to 97 wins, finishing second to the Brooklyn Dodgers. From 1942 through 1944 the team won three straight pennants and two World Series, and never won fewer than 105 games. War or no war, it was an amazing run. In 1945 the team "slumped" to 95 wins and finished second behind the Chicago Cubs.

The 1942 Cardinals were one of the youngest pennant-winning teams ever. Of the ten position players with at least 250 at-bats, eight were younger than twenty-seven, and four were no older than twenty-four. Southworth seemed to prefer the young player to the veteran, thinking in 1940, "I'll get myself a club of kids—then watch us go to town."

In February 1945 Southworth suffered the death of his son, Billy Jr. A pilot and war hero, the younger Southworth crashed and died during a routine flight after having returned home from combat over Europe. Southworth apparently began drinking again after this tragedy and became more emotionally withdrawn. Braves pitcher Johnny Sain remembers Southworth going out to the airport and sitting for hours.

Southworth was a great builder of pitching staffs; under his leadership the Cardinals' pitching corps led the league in ERA every year from 1942 through 1944 and finished second in 1945. He would have similar success with the Braves as they paced the league in both 1947 and 1948. He ultimately played an integral part in the development of three pitchers who at various times could have been considered the best in the league: Mort Cooper, Warren Spahn, and Johnny Sain. Additionally, he managed great pitching seasons from an assortment of other Cardinals and Braves pitchers.

◇   ◇   ◇

Heading into the 1946 season, it was evident that the Braves ownership was committed to building a winner, but the team's talent made it difficult for a Braves fan to be optimistic. The 1945 team finished in sixth place with a record of 67–85, and its most experienced pitcher, Mort Cooper, was recovering from elbow surgery. Among the position players, only right fielder Tommy Holmes and catcher Phil Masi (who was selected to his first of four consecutive All-Star Games in 1945) appeared to have promising futures. Additionally, each major league team had twenty to thirty players returning from the military, and one would have been hard-pressed to get excited about the Braves contingent. Second baseman Connie Ryan, who had joined the Navy right after playing in the 1944 All-Star Game, was one of the few who offered hope.

Holmes was a left-handed line-drive hitter who had his career year in 1945, finishing second in the MVP balloting. Taking advantage of the shortened right field fence, Holmes hit a league-leading twenty-eight home runs (including nineteen at home), batted .352, and led the league in slugging percentage with a .577 mark. In 1944 with the fences shortened for only part of the season, Holmes hit thirteen home runs (ten at home). In no other year would he hit more than nine or have a slugging average over .450. In 1945 Holmes also set the post-1901 NL record (since broken by Pete Rose) by hitting safely in thirty-seven consecutive games.

The only other notable player on the 1945 Braves was third baseman Chuck Workman, who hit twenty-five home runs, second in the league to Holmes. Already twenty-eight when he first played regularly in 1943, Workman's major league career was essentially limited to the war years, although he did have some good minor league seasons before and after his years in the majors. Like Holmes, the left-handed-hitting Workman had taken advantage of the short right field fence, as nineteen of his home runs came at Braves Field.

Table 7.2 Johnny Sain

	W	L	IP	ERA	Lg ERA	MVP Rank
1946	20	14	265.0	2.21	3.41	5 (2)*
1947	21	12	266.0	3.52	4.06	17 (7)
1948	24	15	314.2	2.60	3.95	2 (1)

*MVP Rank is Sain's ranking in the MVP vote, and the number in parentheses is his ranking among pitchers only.

Boston had two excellent players in military service, pitchers Johnny Sain and Warren Spahn, but neither had particularly impressive resumes at the time. Manager Southworth deserves a lot of credit for recognizing their ability and for the hand he had in their development.

In his last two minor league seasons, 1940 and 1941, Sain was not especially impressive. In 236 innings over the two years, Sain had a record of 14–16, an ERA of four and a half, and a strikeout-to-walk ratio of just over one. Nevertheless, the pitching-poor Braves decided to give him a shot, and in 1942 Sain finished 4–7 with an ERA of 3.90 in ninety-seven innings for a seventh-place team. While this was not bad for a twenty-three-year-old rookie with no high minor league experience, it should be noted that the league ERA was 3.31 and Braves Field was still a pitcher's park.

Returning to the Braves after the war, from 1946 through 1948 Sain was probably the best pitcher in the National League. He won at least twenty games each year and was named in the MVP voting in each of the three years. Table 7.2 shows his record over this period.

Sain described his pitching style this way: "My speed was just above average. My hard curve was my best pitch, my out pitch. Then I threw a screwball and changed speeds and motion. I was an unorthodox, deceptive pitcher who kept batters off stride by throwing a variation of breaking balls, using different speeds, and using different deliveries and points of release."

Warren Spahn signed with the Braves (with no bonus) prior to the 1940 season. After a couple of great seasons in the low and middle minors, he made a brief appearance for the Braves in 1942. Spahn had a distinguished war record and did not receive his discharge until April 1946. He was the only major league ballplayer to be commissioned in the field, and as a combat engineer he fought in the Battle of the Bulge and at the Remagen Bridge over the Rhine. By the time he joined the team in 1946, the season was already well under way, but the twenty-five-year-old Spahn provided a glimpse of the future by finishing 8–5 with a 2.93 ERA in 126 innings. Despite Spahn's late start in the major leagues, he went on to become the winningest left-handed pitcher in major league history with 363 victories.

Spahn emerged as a star in 1947 when he contributed a 21–10 record and a league-leading 2.33 ERA. Over the next sixteen years, Spahn would often be the National League's best pitcher. Sain described Spahn's style: "Batters didn't mind hitting against Spahn because he couldn't throw sidearm and his delivery and rhythm were the same on every pitch, straight up and over every time. But he had uncanny control and painted the corners. Also, Spahn being left-handed, his ball moved naturally. He also had a very good pickoff move."

Besides building the team, the Braves worked hard to improve the experience of their fans. The team produced the first major league baseball yearbook, recorded a movie, and repainted much of the stadium. They also returned the outfield fences to more reasonable distances, and Braves Field again became the hardest park in the league to homer in.

Heading into the 1946 season, Perini and John Quinn were ready to take the next step to assemble a pennant winner. They had the manager they wanted, a great one-two pitching combination (although they probably did not yet realize it) and money to spend. The first two moves in early 1946 landed key contributors from Southworth's Cardinals. The team sent Eddie Joost and $40,000 for outfielder–first baseman Johnny Hopp and in a separate transaction paid $25,000 for Ray Sanders. A good wartime hitter, Sanders had his best season in 1944. That year *The Sporting News* named him to their major league all-star team, recognizing Sanders as baseball's top first baseman. Hopp, twenty-nine years old heading into the 1946 season, was a good hitter despite his lack of power.

Unfortunately, the Braves had little better luck with these two stars than they had with Cooper. Already off to a disappointing season, Sanders severely broke his arm in August in a collision at first base that effectively ended his career. Hopp suffered several injuries, including the effects of a beaning by New York Giants pitcher Monte Kennedy; fortunately, none of his mishaps had any long-term effect on his career.

Throughout 1946 the organization also spent heavily on minor league players. First, the Braves used $250,000 to acquire the Milwaukee club of the American Association. Additionally, the team paid $50,000 to acquire Earl "the Torch" Torgeson, the nonconformist first baseman from Seattle of the Pacific Coast League. The Braves also gave LSU–Marine Corps shortstop Alvin Dark a $45,000 bonus to sign.

After the 1946 season, the Pirates and the Reds were each in the market for a manager and both wanted Billy Herman, the Braves second baseman. Herman ended up in the Hall of Fame, but at this point he was well past his prime as a player. With the additional leverage provided by two competing bidders, Perini asked the Pirates for both Bob Elliott and Ralph Kiner, the latter soon to become the National League's premier home run hitter. Eventually, the Braves sent four players, including Herman, to the Pirates for third baseman Elliott and third-string catcher Hank Camelli. Elliott had been a good player during the war and became a star after it; he was almost certainly the National League's best third baseman during the 1940s. He never really got along with Pirate manager Frankie Frisch and moved his game up another notch under Southworth.

The final move the Braves made prior to the start of the 1947 season was the repurchase of hurler Red Barrett from the Cardinals. Southworth, who managed a career year out of Barrett in 1945, hoped for another couple of good seasons. In the event, Barrett pitched well enough, with records of 11–12 and 7–8 in 1947 and 1948 (respectively) and an ERA in the mid-threes both years.

Heading into the 1947 season, a good Braves team was taking shape. In the three years since Perini's group assumed full ownership, the club spent roughly $270,000 on major player acquisitions. The club now had an excellent manager, a deep and talented pitching staff, and several good position players: catcher Masi, first baseman Torgeson, second baseman Ryan, third baseman Elliot, and outfielders Hopp and Holmes.

The Braves continued to make excellent moves during the 1947 season. After Mort Cooper started slowly, Southworth and Quinn recognized that he had little left and traded him to the Giants for Big Bill Voiselle. In 1944 Voiselle had hurled one of the top rookie seasons of the era: a 21–16 record with a 3.02 ERA while leading the league in starts, innings pitched, and strikeouts. He had slipped in 1945 and 1946, compiling an aggregate record of 23–29. Off to a slow start in 1947, Voiselle turned it around with the Braves, pitching capably for several years.

The Braves also signed veteran first baseman Frank McCormick, who had been released by the Phillies. McCormick had been an all-star in every season since 1938 and a key member of the Cincinnati pennant winners in 1939 and 1940, winning the MVP award in 1940. Now thirty-six, he was obviously nearing the end of his career. With the Braves, however, he proved to have some useful baseball remaining. He hit .354 in 212 at-bats over the remainder of 1947 while platooning with Torgeson against left-handed pitchers.

The 1947 team advanced to third place with an 86–68 record. With the tremendous one-two combination of Spahn and Sain and the benefit of playing in Braves Field, the club's pitching ranked higher than its hitting. The team finished second in ERA but in the middle of the pack in runs scored. Among the position players, only third baseman Elliott had a particularly good season, good enough that he was named league MVP. In recognition of the team's improvement, the Braves rewarded manager Southworth with a five-year, $250,000 contract.

In evaluating their progress at the end of the 1947 season, one must give the Braves' management quite a bit of credit for recognizing the team's weaknesses and correcting them without hurting the rest of the club. Table 7.3 summarizes the offensive contributions of the 1947 Braves regulars.

The club still needed to upgrade its offense, particularly its power—only Torgeson and Elliott hit over ten home runs. To address this problem, Boston's management correctly identified the three weakest positions: second base, shortstop, and left field. The team then acquired significantly better players for these positions without losing any key starters or pitching depth.

To address the left-field situation, the club purchased outfielder Jeff Heath from the St. Louis Browns. Heath had his best year in 1938 as a twenty-two-year-old first-time regular, hitting .343 with twenty-one home runs and 112 RBI for the Indians. He never really lived up to the potential heralded by this season but he had been a fine player with a couple of All-Star Game appearances. In 1947 he had hit twenty-seven homers, and at thirty-two years old he could still play.

The Braves' other big off-season trade tackled the second base hole by landing Eddie Stanky from the Brooklyn Dodgers. Nicknamed "the Brat," Stanky often irritated both teammates and opponents with his hard-nosed, gung-ho style. Dodgers President Branch Rickey described Stanky this way: "He can't hit, he can't run, he can't field and he can't throw, but if there's a way to beat the other team, he'll find it." Of course, one of the ways Stanky could beat you was by constantly getting on base. Although he had a career batting average of .268, he walked enough that his career on-base percentage was .410. He led the league in bases on balls three times; his 148 walks in 1945 lasted as the National League record for over fifty years. He led the league in on-base percentage twice, and in his seven

Table 7.3 1947 Braves Regulars

		G	AVG	OBP	SLG	R	HR	RBI	SB	RC	WAAv	WAR
C	Phil Masi	126	.304	.377	.443	54	9	50	7	66	1.4	2.7
1B	Earl Torgeson	128	.281	.403	.481	73	16	78	11	79	2.9	4.2
2B	Connie Ryan/46*	143	.241	.317	.335	55	1	48	7	54	-0.6	1.0
2B	Connie Ryan/47	150	.265	.351	.371	60	5	69	5	72	0.0	1.9
3B	Bob Elliott	150	.317	.410	.517	93	22	113	3	111	4.4	6.2
SS	Dick Culler	77	.248	.309	.280	20	0	19	1	18	-1.1	-0.4
SS	Nanny Fernandez	83	.206	.281	.254	16	2	21	2	14	-1.6	-0.8
LF	Bama Rowell	113	.276	.310	.385	48	5	40	7	46	-0.4	0.9
CF	Johnny Hopp	134	.288	.376	.358	74	2	32	13	61	0.5	2.0
RF	Tommy Holmes	150	.309	.360	.416	90	9	53	3	89	1.2	3.2

RC = runs created   WAAv = wins above average   WAR = wins above replacement

*Two years of data are shown for Ryan to better illustrate the difference in value between him and Stanky (see table 7.4).

seasons with four hundred or more at-bats, he scored at least ninety runs in six of them.

Dodgers manager Durocher wanted to keep Stanky, but Rickey was ready to trade him, primarily because he wanted to move Jackie Robinson from first to second base, but also because Rickey liked making a buck. Rickey accepted first baseman Ray Sanders, outfielder Bama Rowell, and $40,000 and sent Stanky to Boston. One month later, the Braves bought Sanders back for $60,000. As Sanders was never able to come back from his broken arm, this repurchase offered little return.

To improve the shortstop position, the team promoted the highly regarded Alvin Dark. Dark was coming off an excellent year at Milwaukee in which he led the American Association in runs, doubles, and total bases. Although an average fielder, Dark was a strong enough hitter that

Table 7.4 1948 Braves Newcomers

		G	AVG	OBP	SLG	R	HR	RBI	SB	RC	WAAv	WAR
2B	Eddie Stanky/46*	144	.273	.436	.352	98	0	36	8	91	3.7	5.2
2B	Eddie Stanky/47	146	.252	.373	.329	97	3	53	3	79	.0	2.0
LF	Jeff Heath	141	.251	.366	.485	81	27	85	2	84	2.4	4.1
CF	Jim Russell	128	.253	.343	.381	68	8	51	7	64	-.2	1.5

RC = runs created   WAAv = wins above average   WAR = wins above replacement

*Two years of data are shown for Stanky to better illustrate the difference in value between him and Ryan (see table 7.3).

he was still playing shortstop regularly nine years later as a thirty-five-year-old. In 1948 Dark performed even better than expected, hitting .322 (his career high), and winning the Rookie of the Year award.

The only other interesting off-season trade was a swap of center fielders with the Pirates. The Braves traded Johnny Hopp and Danny Murtaugh for Jim Russell, reserve catcher Bill Salkeld, and pitcher Al Lyons. Russell was a good fielder who could get on base. Salkeld also proved valuable; in 1948 he batted nearly two hundred times subbing for Phil Masi and slugged .414.

To help understand the potential effects of these trades, table 7.4 summarizes the 1947 seasons of the new regulars brought in for 1948.

The team improved its pitching by promoting to the squad for 1948 two twenty-seven-year-old rookies, Bobby Hogue and Vern Bickford. Hogue would turn in a couple of good seasons in relief for Southworth, and in 1948 he posted a record of 8–2 and an ERA of 3.23 in forty games. As summarized in table 7.5, Bickford proved a valuable pitcher for several years. In 1951, he broke the ring finger on his pitching hand during a game of pepper in August, ending his string of successes.

◇ ◇ ◇

Entering the 1948 season, the Braves rightfully felt they had assembled one of the league's top teams. The club possessed a solid collection of front-line talent as well as a well-crafted bench. At catcher, Phil Masi was one of the league's best, and Bill Salkeld was a quality left-handed hitting

Table 7.5 Vern Bickford

	W	L	IP	ERA	Lg ERA
1948	11	5	146.0	3.27	3.95
1949	16	11	230.2	4.25	4.04
1950	19	14	311.2	3.47	4.14
1951	11	9	164.2	3.12	3.96

backup. The highly touted Torgeson, a left-handed hitter with both power and on-base ability, manned first base, backed up by veteran right-hander Frank McCormick. The club boasted Eddie Stanky at second base, Bob Elliott (the league's reigning MVP) at third, and Alvin Dark at shortstop. The infield reserves were Connie Ryan and Sibbi Sisti, each of whom was good enough to play over a thousand major league games.

The outfield was patrolled by Jeff Heath in left, Jim Russell in center, and Tommy Holmes, a consistent .300 hitter, in right. The fourth outfielder was Mike McCormick, who would hit .303 in 343 at-bats in 1948, his best year in the majors.

The Braves pitching staff is usually recalled as "Spahn and Sain, and pray for rain," and in 1948 the two lived up to this top billing. They finished first (Sain) and third (Spahn) in both games started and innings pitched. The overall mound staff, however, was the best and deepest in the league. In addition to the two stars, Bill Voiselle, Red Barrett, and rookie Vern Bickford were each quality starting pitchers in 1948. All five starters had ERAs well below the league average, and all but Barrett, who started only thirteen games, won at least eleven. The bullpen was deep, with rookie right-hander Hogue and the veteran lefty Clyde Shoun. At midseason the team signed Nelson Potter, a thirty-six-year-old righty who had just been released by the Philadelphia Athletics. Potter finished 5–2 with a 2.33 ERA in eighty-five innings.

The Braves did not have a particularly difficult time capturing the 1948 pennant. They jumped out to a comfortable lead by midsummer, before the Dodgers and Cardinals made a run. A strong stretch by the Braves just before Labor Day put the race out of reach. The team's depth proved crucial, first when Eddie Stanky broke an ankle in June, and then when Jim Russell had to be hospitalized with a heart ailment in August. The team was further crippled for the World Series when slugger Jeff Heath broke his ankle sliding into home on September 29.

After winning the first World Series game 1–0 behind Johnny Sain, the Braves lost four of the next five games to the Cleveland Indians. The

Braves were handicapped by their injuries, particularly in the outfield. To fill in for the hobbled Heath, journeyman Marv Rickert, a less-than-adequate replacement, was called up from Milwaukee. Mike McCormick had taken over for Russell, and although not as extreme a drop-off, this, too, hurt the team. The lack of outfielders also placed some limitations on Southworth's in-game strategic options. Furthermore, Eddie Stanky was far from 100 percent and basically hobbled through the series.

The Sporting News concluded that "the Braves lost because they played timid safety-first ball. At bat, in the first three games particularly, Boston players swung at first pitches—good or bad—as if they were afraid to let the Cleveland starters get a strike on them."

◇   ◇   ◇

Unfortunately for Boston Braves fans, the 1948 squad was the last pennant winner they would ever see. Following the heights of 1948, the team fell to three consecutive fourth-place finishes. The club would not return to the top until 1957, after it had been rebuilt in Milwaukee around Hank Aaron, Eddie Mathews, and the still-great Warren Spahn.

The decline of the 1948 Braves can be linked to three factors: the drop-off of several starting pitchers, the aging of the position players, and the emotional withdrawal of Billy Southworth. Table 7.6 compares the Braves' runs scored (RS) and runs allowed (RA) to the league average to emphasize that the pitching fell off much more drastically than the hitting.

For example, in 1948 the Braves scored 53 runs more than the league average team, the third highest total; they allowed 102 runs fewer than average, the fewest of any team. The pitching in 1949 relative to the league average degenerated by 115 runs (from 102 better than average to 13 worse). Much of this can be traced to an injury to Sain and to the sudden

Table 7.6 1946–1950 Braves Run Differentials

	RS +/-	Rank	RA +/-	Rank
1946	15	3	- 23	5
1947	-7	5	- 86	1
1948	53	4	-102	1
1949	0	4	13	5
1950	65	2	16	6

RS +/- = runs scored compared to league average

RA +/- = runs allowed compared to league average

loss of effectiveness of Barrett and Voiselle.

During spring training in 1949 Johnny Sain began to experience soreness in his shoulder, a discomfort that was to be chronic for the remainder of his career. After a subpar 1949 season, 10–17 with a 4.81 ERA, Sain learned to pitch with the injury but never again regained his postwar success. Barrett and Voiselle both had their best years during the war and, other than a brief renaissance under Southworth, pitched only adequately thereafter. For both, 1948 was essentially the end of the line. Over the remainder of their careers they combined for an 8–13 record and an ERA of 4.65 in only 265 innings pitched.

In part because of these struggles, the Braves never stopped looking for young pitchers. In 1948 they signed eighteen-year-old Johnny Antonelli for $52,000. Over the next couple of years, the team came up with Chet Nichols, who would lead the league in ERA in 1951, and Bob Buhl, who would win 166 games in his career. Unfortunately, none of the three could help immediately and all of them spent two years in military service during the Korean War. The team proved unable to uncover back-of-the-rotation starters like Barrett and Voiselle that Southworth had previously found success with.

The 1948 Braves were a veteran team: of the nine position players with at least 247 at-bats, six were older than thirty, and Russell, who was twenty-nine, had heart problems. The thirty-three-year-old Heath, one of the team's two power hitters, played only thirty-six games after his late 1948 injury. The Braves actually did a pretty good job of rebuilding their offense despite these obstacles, but it was not quite enough.

After the 1949 season, in one of baseball's most famous trades, the Braves dealt their keystone combination, Stanky and Dark, to the Giants for two power hitters, outfielder–third baseman Sid Gordon and outfielder Willard Marshall, plus shortstop Buddy Kerr and pitcher Red Webb. Since the Giants went on to win a pennant in 1951 and the Braves did not return to the top for eight years, this trade is usually viewed as a disaster for the Braves. Giants manager Leo Durocher, who loved Stanky's hard-nosed style, fed this perception by attributing much of the team's great 1951 comeback to him, later writing that "everybody was writing the next day that the Braves had got so much the best of the deal that they had put themselves right back into pennant contention. What happened was that it won us a couple of pennants and wrecked them so completely that they had to move the team out of Boston three years later."

Nevertheless, it is hard to find fault with this trade from the Braves' perspective, either in its design or its execution. First of all, they increased their record after the trade from 75–79 in 1949 to 83–71 in 1950. The Braves sorely lacked power after the loss of Jeff Heath; with Torgeson out for much of 1949 with a shoulder injury, only Bob Elliott hit more than eleven home runs. What's more, the Braves were loaded with options to play second base; in addition to Ryan and Sisti, they had spent $75,000 to acquire minor league star Roy Hartsfield, whom they were anxious to promote.

In the previous season, the thirty-one-year-old Gordon had hit .284 with twenty-six homers, and the twenty-eight-year-old Marshall had hit .307 with fourteen homers. Both also drew more than their share of walks. Kerr, the Giants' starting shortstop over the past several years, was only twenty-seven but not really a good enough hitter to be a major league regular.

On the defensive side, Dark for Kerr was a wash, and Stanky was only an adequate second baseman. Hartsfield turned out to be a disappointment; in 1950 he led the league in errors at second despite playing less than a hundred games, although the Braves actually turned more double plays in 1950 than in 1949.

Overall, the team probably overrated Hartsfield and Kerr, but Gordon and Marshall were solid major league regulars. With these new additions, plus Rookie of the Year Sam Jethroe, the 1950 Braves improved from fourth in the league in runs scored to second, and this in Braves Field, one of the toughest hitter's parks in the league.

Unlike Southworth's younger Cardinals, the 1948 Braves were largely seasoned and experienced men. Even those players with limited major league experience, like Bickford, Spahn, and Sain, were all older players who had seen a little of the world through their military service. Many of the Braves, most notably Stanky, held strong views as to how to run a baseball team. The consideration that Southworth showed to his players was often seen as a sign of weakness.

The team's troubles really began in the off-season after the 1948 pennant. In order to keep a veteran team with many personalities together, a manager must be willing to exert his will over the team. Southworth seemed to have lost the emotional energy necessary to control a team of strong personalities.

That Southworth was also often used as a foil in salary negotiations between management and players further added to the sense of distance between the players and their manager. A player might hear: "Southworth doesn't think you're worth any more than you're getting." Managers were often used this way in salary discussions—Durocher claims his big fallout with Stanky (before he got him back in 1950) was because of being forced to take management's side in a salary holdout. Furthermore, one cannot really know if Southworth said the things management attributed to him or if they were simply invoking Southworth's name as part of the negotiation process.

Both Stanky and Dark were moralistic men who disapproved of Southworth's heavy drinking. Stanky, a strong veteran personality, was also openly critical of Southworth's more patient and conciliatory managerial style, especially as compared to Durocher. The younger Dark, Stanky's constant companion and roommate until 1952, followed Stanky's lead in his dislike of Southworth. Dark, who twenty-five years later was willing to suffer almost any indignity as manager of the Oakland A's under domineering owner Charlie Finley, resented even the slightest appearance of a snub. Dark later related a story of Southworth calling Stanky and then Dark into his office to let them know he planned to give them a day off. Both objected so strongly that Southworth backed down.

One incident in 1949 further poisoned Stanky against Southworth. While in the batter's box, Stanky flashed the hit-and-run sign to Spahn, the base runner on first. Stanky hit a line drive, Spahn was doubled off of first, and the Braves ended up losing the game. When later asked whether he had given Stanky the hit-and-run sign, Southworth responded that he had not, and the press criticized Stanky for his "insubordination." In fact, Stanky believed that Southworth had given him the option to call for the hit-and-run whenever he thought it would help. Stanky later claimed that he lost all respect for Southworth after this incident for not backing him up.

The medical situation also contributed to the sense of chaos. In addition to Heath's injury at the end of the 1948 season, Torgeson separated his shoulder and Sain began experiencing shoulder pain en route to having a miserable year. When Torgeson began working out again in August, he suffered a further setback when he broke his thumb in a hotel-room fight involving Jim Russell and several soldiers.

As the season progressed, Southworth became more and more withdrawn, drinking heavily. On August 15, 1949, with a record of 55–54 and the team in disarray, Southworth, with Perini's blessing, took a leave of absence. Interim manager Johnny Cooney finished out the season. The players' discontent with Southworth can be seen from the fact that they voted him only a half share of their fourth-place World Series pool money.

Commissioner Happy Chandler reversed this decision, awarding South-worth a full share.

Southworth returned for the 1950 season, and with Stanky and Dark traded the atmosphere improved in the locker room. The team again finished fourth but improved its record by eight games. Nevertheless, South-worth never really regained his Midas touch with the pitching staff. In June 1951, with a record of 28–31, he was replaced by Tommy Holmes. Although officially Southworth resigned, Perini made no effort to retain him. Holmes had been sent down to manage the Hartford farm club that spring and was clearly being groomed for the spot. After his resignation, Southworth scouted for the Braves for another five years. Baseball historian David Voigt further suggests that Southworth's alienation from the team was partially due to his inability to curb the various sexual adventures of his players.

Billy Southworth was the best manager of the 1940s. Prior to his leave of absence for "ill health" at the end of the 1949 season, he had won four pennants with two different teams in the eight years in which he managed a full season. Southworth's .597 lifetime winning percentage places him fifth all-time among those who managed at least a thousand games and he is one of only a handful of managers to have won pennants with two different teams. From 1940 through 1948, Southworth likely managed at as high a level as any manager ever. With the help of Rickey's incredibly deep farm system he built a dominant team in St. Louis. Moving to the Braves after the war, he put together a pennant winner with the help of Perini's money in three years. Sadly, heartbreak in his personal life robbed him of the chance to have the extensive career he should have enjoyed.

◇   ◇   ◇

The rise of the Braves suggests several significant lessons. First, after a couple of unsuccessful ventures into the trade market, the Braves did not forsake this path as unprofitable. They continued to use trades as an important tool in building a champion.

Second, ownership hired knowledgeable and experienced baseball people. Perini and his ownership group retained Bob Quinn and later John Quinn, who had been groomed for the job. At least as important, they hired one of baseball's top managers, Billy Southworth. As the team brought in new talent, they had a skipper who knew how to use it.

Third, the team did not concentrate solely on major leaguers and ignore young talent. Team management showed its commitment to young players both by buying the Milwaukee American Association franchise and a number of minor league stars.

Fourth, whether by design or chance, the team assembled its talent in two stages. At first the club acquired a lot of quality players and let Southworth sort them out. After the 1947 season, the club sensed how close it was to winning, recognized its three weakest positions, and effectively addressed those areas without sacrificing any vital players.

For a brief moment during the huge upsurge of baseball attendance in postwar America, an ownership with deep pockets and a fair share of smart baseball men constructed a pennant winner out of one of the National League's weakest franchises. Their approach to building their team showed intelligence and patience. This forgotten winner represented a model for future owners with money to spend.

8

WHAT HAPPENED? THE VAGARIES OF HISTORY: THE POSTWAR BOSTON RED SOX

In 1949 Boston's left fielder fell short of his third Triple Crown by less than two-tenths of a batting average point. The team's shortstop drove in 159 runs, its second baseman drove in 118, its center fielder hit .307 with 96 walks, and its third baseman hit .306 with 100 walks. Meanwhile, the 1949 New York Yankees had no player drive in 100 runs, belt 30 home runs or hit .300. In fact, only two Yankees played as many as 120 games.

On the final day of the season, October 2, 1949, the New York Yankees defeated the Boston Red Sox, 5–3, to win the American League pennant. Since Boston had been heavily favored to triumph that year, fans and writers have debated this great race and its meaning for decades. The difference between the records of the two teams—one victory—is minuscule, but their reputations as ballplayers are vastly different.

Forty years later, David Halberstam wrote *Summer of '49*, a book about the season's American League pennant race largely devoted to unraveling the implausibility of this result. Explanations of the outcome of this pennant race, one of the most famous in baseball history, have become part of the game's conventional wisdom. The 1949 Red Sox failed to win the pennant because (pick one or more of the following): they had no pitching and poor defense; they had bad chemistry; they failed to do the necessary "little things"; they could not hit in the clutch; they could not win games when it mattered; their stars were selfish individuals; Casey Stengel outmanaged Joe McCarthy; the Red Sox overpaid their players, so they did not *need* the postseason money; and the Yankees had Joe Page and a dominant bullpen.

• • •

Many baseball historians have interpreted Boston's failure to win this great race as "proof" that some of their star hitters were frauds—their gaudy offensive statistics were only good enough for second place, so those statistics must have been inflated or illusory. Ted Williams and Vern Stephens, who combined for 318 RBI, have been painted as selfish players and no match for Joe DiMaggio and Phil Rizzuto, their "heroic" counterparts.

The problem with this line of reasoning, of course, is that the Red Sox finished 96–58. It seems inconceivable that a team with all of these flaws—a club with no pitching, defense, character, or managerial acumen—could win 62 percent of its games. On the contrary, the Red Sox must have had a few things going for them other than their offense.

The century-long rivalry between these two neighbors reached its zenith during the years immediately after World War II. The story of these postwar franchises has been well mined by baseball writers and analysts, enough so that it might seem pointless to bring it up. Because our understanding, or at least our perception, of these clubs is so strong, however, one can take a fresh look at several aspects without spending too much time introducing the teams. Accordingly, this chapter examines the years from 1946, when baseball's stars returned from the service, to 1950, Joe DiMaggio's last big season. Many of the various claims above cannot be proven or refuted—the character and leadership of the players on these team's cannot be objectively determined today, if they ever could have been. On the other hand, other issues might benefit from a closer look.

◇ ◇ ◇

By the late 1930s, Tom Yawkey and Eddie Collins had begun to find and develop their own young players. In 1936, Yawkey had hired Billy Evans to create and run a farm system, and the fruits of those efforts began to ripen by the end of the decade.

By far the Red Sox's most productive geographic area was the West Coast. Bobby Doerr of Los Angeles first spent three years with Hollywood and San Diego in the Pacific Coast League before coming to Boston as a nineteen-year-old second baseman in 1937. San Diego's Ted Williams spent two years with his hometown Padres (the first as a teammate of Doerr's) before the Red Sox signed him at the end of 1937. In 1938 the team sent Williams to its top farm club in Minneapolis, where he dominated the American Association (.366 with 43 home runs).

Dom DiMaggio, from San Francisco, starred for three years with the San Francisco Seals (hitting .360 in 1939) before taking over center field for Boston in 1940. Portland's Johnny Pesky spent two years in the Red Sox system (he was the International League's Player of the Year for Louisville in 1941) before arriving in Boston in 1942. Joe Cronin was impressed enough to finally step aside as the team's shortstop.

With these four players as a strong foundation, the 1942 Red Sox won ninety-three games, the most the club had won since 1915. Once again they finished well behind the Yankees, but the Red Sox were clearly making progress. Coming off of his legendary .406 season, the twenty-three-year-old Williams won the Triple Crown (36–137–.356) in 1942 and also led the league in runs, extra base hits, on-base percentage, slugging percentage, walks, and just about everything else. Pesky, a twenty-two-year-old rookie shortstop, batted .331 and led the AL in hits. Doerr, twenty-four, drove in 105 runs, and DiMaggio, twenty-five, scored 110. First baseman Tony Lupien and third baseman Jim Tabor were each only twenty-five years old and among the best in the league at their positions. Moreover, the pitching staff had the third-lowest ERA in the league. Tex Hughson (22–6), Charlie Wagner (14–11), and Joe Dobson (11–9) were all younger than thirty and seemed to have bright futures. Under ordinary circumstances, the Red Sox looked to have the makings of a dynasty.

But these were not ordinary circumstances. In 1943, most major league players went off to fight in World War II, if not there already. During the next three years, the careers of most baseball players were interrupted. General managers changed their plans and the game was played by players unsuitable for the military.

It would be a fool's errand to project what might have happened to the Red Sox had the war not interrupted their development. The 1942 Yankees had several older players in key roles—catcher Bill Dickey, infielders Frank Crosetti and Red Rolfe, and pitchers Red Ruffing, Spud Chandler, and Lefty Gomez. Had there been no war and had these two teams been left unattended, one can suppose that the Red Sox might have been superior during the 1943–1945 period; when the players returned in 1946, the Red Sox waltzed to the American League pennant. It is unlikely, however, that the Yankees would have been neglected. Yankee squads during this era usually found a way to plug their holes.

In 1946 the four Boston stars returned after missing significant parts of their baseball primes. Williams was now twenty-seven years old, Doerr twenty-eight, Pesky twenty-six, and Dom DiMaggio twenty-nine.

Williams did not win the Triple Crown—he finished second in each category (38–123–.342). Doerr drove in 116 runs, Pesky batted .335 and led the league with 208 base hits, and DiMaggio hit .316. This team could have contended by simply filling out the remainder of the club with average players.

The Red Sox felt they needed one more big bat prior to the 1946 season. Therefore they traded Eddie Lake, who had played shortstop while Pesky was in the Army, to Detroit for slugging first baseman Rudy York. Hitting behind Williams, York drove in 119 runs. The three remaining regulars were nothing special: catcher Hal Wagner hit .230, right fielder Catfish Metkovich batted .246, and third baseman Rip Russell managed only .208. By the World Series, the Red Sox generally used midseason acquisitions Wally Moses and Pinky Higgins in right field and third base, respectively.

The Red Sox also boasted an excellent pitching staff. Two twenty-game-winners, Dave "Boo" Ferris and Tex Hughson, were products of the farm system, as was seventeen-game-winner Mickey Harris. The Red Sox had acquired its fourth starter, Joe Dobson, in a trade with the Indians in 1940.

The Red Sox jumped out to a lead early in the season and were never threatened thereafter. The team won 104 games, the second highest total in Red Sox history, and won the pennant by 12 games. Favored to beat the St. Louis Cardinals, Boston lost in a seven-game World Series that came down to a classic final game.

This great team fell out of contention after just one year largely because their three best pitchers—Ferris, Hughson, and Harris—all came up with sore arms in the spring of 1947 and never regained their form. Ted Williams won another Triple Crown, but most of the other stars had off years. When Rudy York's production dropped dramatically, the Red Sox traded him in June to the White Sox for Jake Jones, who proved no better. Wagner also started slowly, and Boston dealt him to the Tigers for Birdie Tebbetts, who became the team's catcher through 1950.

The club's offense was concentrated heavily in its star players. When the rest of the team deteriorated, the core players alone could not make up the difference. The well-balanced 1947 Yankees won the American League easily, besting the Tigers by twelve games and the Red Sox by fourteen before defeating the Brooklyn Dodgers in a seven-game series.

The Red Sox underwent a dramatic makeover in the off-season of 1947–1948, starting at the top. Eddie Collins resigned after fifteen years as the team's general manager and Joe Cronin, the manager since 1935, moved into Collins's old job. For its new skipper, the club hired Joe Mc-Carthy, who had led the Yankees to eight pennants and seven World Series titles before stepping down in 1946. Yawkey later confided that this had been in the works for over a year.

On consecutive days in November 1947, the Red Sox made two deals with the St. Louis Browns that vaulted them back into contention. Boston sent seven players of no consequence—none would play or pitch regularly in 1948—and, most importantly, $375,000 to St. Louis for pitchers Jack Kramer and Ellis Kinder and infielders Vern "Junior" Stephens and Billy Hitchcock. Hitchcock was a valuable utility player and Kramer would win eighteen games for the 1948 Red Sox. Kinder was an excellent starter and reliever for the team over the next several years; he won twenty-three games in 1949 and saved twenty-seven in 1953. An All-Star shortstop both before and after the deal, Stephens took over at short and McCarthy shifted Pesky to third base.

These trades harkened back to the Yawkey acquisitions of the 1930s. In fact, the Red Sox had not made such a deal—trading nonentities and a lot of money for quality players—since the acquisitions of Doc Cramer and Eric McNair in 1936. The crucial difference in this instance was that the 1948 Red Sox were a team that could reasonably view these transactions as the final pieces of the puzzle. The core of the squad was still home-grown, but these two trades propelled the 1948–1950 teams back into contention.

Several other players came through the system over the next year or two. Billy Goodman took over first base in 1948 and won the batting title in 1950 as a multiposition regular. Mel Parnell, a rookie from New Orleans, bolstered the 1948 rotation and settled in as the club's ace for the next six years. A valuable hurler for several years, Chuck Stobbs came up as a nineteen-year-old rookie in 1949. Walt Dropo added a great rookie year in 1950, hitting thirty-four home runs and driving in 144.

The Red Sox enjoyed success in the late 1940s largely because their organization consistently produced quality players. Unfortunately, once Cronin replaced Collins as the team's general manager, the flow of talent slowed to a trickle. The system came up with only a handful of major league regulars in the 1950s and did not contend for another fifteen years. While the rest of baseball belatedly began signing black players, many of whom would soon be among the biggest stars in the game, the Red Sox would be the very last major league franchise to field a black player, Pumpsie Green in 1959.

◇ ◇ ◇

The New York Yankees organization did not sit idle while the Red Sox built their ball club. Like all great Yankee squads the team found and developed almost all of its own talent.

Joe DiMaggio first came to the Yankees in 1936, but he had been a great player for several years on the West Coast. DiMaggio hit .340, .341, and .398 for the Pacific Coast League's San Francisco Seals from 1933 to 1935, and although only twenty-one, he would have been a good player had he joined the Yankees a year or two sooner. The Seals sold him to the Yankees after the 1934 season on the condition that he stay one more year in San Francisco.

New York native Phil Rizzuto, signed and developed in the Yankee system, was the shortstop before the war and well into the 1950s. Other than he and DiMaggio, the Yankees turned the rest of their team over in the late 1940s. Thus, they were winning championships even while they seemed to be rebuilding.

The 1946 Yankees started several stars from their great prewar teams, including right fielder Charlie Keller, left fielder Tommy Henrich, second baseman Joe Gordon, and pitchers Spud Chandler and Red Ruffing. All but Ruffing were products of the Yankee farm system and all but Henrich contributed little after 1946. When these Yankees proved unable to compete with the Red Sox, New York quickly retooled.

After the 1946 season the Yankees traded Gordon to Cleveland for Allie Reynolds and shifted Snuffy Stirnweiss back to second base. They also acquired George McQuinn, recently released by the Athletics, to play first. McQuinn had spent seven years in the Yankee farm system and eight with the St. Louis Browns (including four as an All-Star) but was thirty-seven years old in 1947. Nonetheless, he hit .304 and kept the job for two years. The pitching staff, also in transition, included the likes of Bill Bevens, Bobo Newsom, and Specs Shea, all adequate short-term solutions.

The 1947 Yankees are a remarkable story. On paper they do not appear an outstanding team because many key players did not have impressive careers and did not contribute to the great Yankee clubs either before or after 1947. Nevertheless, they completely dominated the league.

During the late 1940s, the regular Yankees lineup was evolving. Beginning in 1947, Bobby Brown and Billy Johnson handled third base. Yogi Berra replaced Aaron Robinson at catcher in 1948. Henrich moved to first in 1949 until the Yankees acquired Johnnie Mize from the Giants in August. Jerry Coleman won the second base job in 1949. That same year Johnny Lindell, Gene Woodling, Hank Bauer, and Cliff Mapes shared the outfield corners. All these players were products of the Yankees system.

By 1948 the pitching rotation consisted of Allie Reynolds, Eddie Lopat, Vic Raschi, and Tommy Byrne; Whitey Ford joined them in 1950. Early relief ace Joe Page anchored an excellent bullpen. The Yankees acquired Reynolds and Lopat in trades, but the others came up through their minor leagues.

Considering their success, the Yankees went through a surprising number of managers in the late 1940s. Joe McCarthy lost his job in 1946, reportedly because he had trouble staying sober; Bill Dickey and Johnny Neun finished out the year. Bucky Harris was hired in 1947, but after winning the World Series in 1947 and another ninety-four games in 1948, the Yankees fired him. Casey Stengel took over, and his entertaining act played the Bronx for twelve years.

In 1948 the American League staged one of its best pennant races ever. The Red Sox, Yankees, and Indians were all tied with seven games remaining. The Indians won four straight to assume a two-game lead, and with two games remaining, they still held a one-game advantage on both rivals. The Indians lost their finale to Hal Newhouser in Detroit and Boston swept a two-game series against the Yankees in Boston to force a tie. The Indians then defeated the Red Sox in a one-game playoff to reach the World Series, where they defeated the Boston Braves.

Following this setback the 1949 Red Sox started sluggishly. On July 4 they found themselves in fourth place, twelve games behind the Yankees. Boston then went on a twelve-week tear and finally caught and passed the Yankees by beating them three straight times on the next-to-the-last weekend of the season. With only two games remaining, both against the Yankees, the Red Sox needed to win one of the two in New York to capture the pennant. They lost both, and the Yankees went on to defeat the Dodgers in the World Series.

In 1950 the Red Sox started slowly once again but caught fire and almost caught the Yankees and Tigers before finishing four games out. Boston was 32–30 in June when manager Joe McCarthy quit, but finished 62–30 under replacement Steve O'Neill. The Yankees swept the Phillies to win yet another World Series.

◇ ◇ ◇

Over the five-year period, from 1946 to 1950, the Red Sox and Yankees were evenly matched in both talent and regular season success. Table 8.1

Table 8.1 Aggregate Records, 1946–1950

	W	L	Pct
New York	473	297	.614
Boston	473	298	.613

shows the records of the two teams over the five-year period.

The Red Sox played one extra game—the 1948 playoff with the Indians—and lost it. Outside of that single contest the two ball clubs had identical records. Through 2001, this represents the greatest five-year stretch in Red Sox history—but the twenty-seventh best for the Yankees.

One of the wonderful things about baseball in this era was that each team played each other twenty-two times per year. As table 8.2 shows, the two clubs played to a draw during these years. A few Yankee blowouts account for the run differential.

The Yankees were obviously the more successful team; they won three World Series, while the Red Sox lost their only chance. But the difference on the field was razor thin.

◇　◇　◇

Most baseball writers and fans generally agreed that the Red Sox had great hitting and mediocre pitching while the Yankees were more balanced. When Red Sox teams fell short, most blamed their failure on a lack of quality pitching.

Observers have long recognized that the Red Sox's ballpark, Fenway Park, is quite favorable to batters, and writers have often correctly pointed out that many of their hitters benefited by playing there. The converse is also true, however: Red Sox pitchers have often pitched better than their statistics would otherwise indicate. In 1949 Mel Parnell finished 25–7 with a 2.77 ERA, the second lowest in the league, despite pitching half of his games in a hitter's park.

As explained in more detail in appendix 2, the characteristics of his home ballpark can dramatically affect a player's statistics. Over the five-

Table 8.2 Head to Head, 1946–1950

	W	L	Pct	RS	RA
New York	55	55	.500	557	521
Boston	55	55	.500	521	557

year period, the Red Sox and their opponents scored 19 percent more runs at Fenway Park than they did in Red Sox road games. That is, the Red Sox hitters operated under a 19 percent advantage, and their pitchers (and defense) at a 19 percent disadvantage, in one-half of their games. Yankee Stadium over this period decreased run scoring by 6 percent.

In order to judge the offensive and defensive contributions of the two teams and their players, one must account for these park effects. The Red Sox played one-half of their games in Fenway Park and one-half in the other seven American League stadiums. It cannot be known how many runs the clubs would have scored had they played somewhere else. However, adjustments can be made to account for the different environments. After making the necessary adjustments, Boston's offense was inflated about 7.5 percent by playing half their games in Fenway while Yankee Stadium decreased New York's offense by 3 percent.

Table 8.3 shows what happens when these adjustments are applied. The table illustrates that the Red Sox and Yankees actually had very similar balance. While the Red Sox scored fifty-two more runs per year and allowed seventy-six more runs per year than the Yankees, the adjusted numbers are very close. After adjusting for the ballparks, these formulas estimate that the Yankees would have scored thirty-five *more* runs than the Red Sox, but allowed only seven *fewer.*

The adjusted runs scored total (RS+) measures the strength of the team's offense. The adjusted runs allowed total (RA+), on the other hand, measures the strength of a club's pitching *and* defense. It is nearly impossible to apportion credit (or blame) between the pitchers and the other eight defenders for high or low run totals. A team with a low earned run average is typically assumed to have a good pitching staff, but it is possible that the team has an average staff and a great defense.

Our analysis suggests that the 1949 Red Sox actually had a slightly weaker offense than the Yankees but had basically equal pitching defense. These ball clubs were both strong and balanced, and the perception of the Red Sox as great hitters with mediocre pitching was an illusion caused by their home ballpark.

◇ ◇ ◇

One thing often said about teams like these Red Sox—squads with powerful offenses—is that they are apt to win a blowout one day but turn around and lose a low-scoring game the next. On the other hand, the reasoning continues, clubs with a balance of good hitting and pitching, like

Table 8.3 Park Effects, 1946–1950

	RS	RA	RS+	RA+
		New York		
1946	684	547	702	561
1947	794	568	815	583
1948	857	633	879	649
1949	829	637	851	654
1950	914	691	938	709
Total	4078	3076	4184	3156
Avg.	816	615	837	631
		Boston		
1946	792	594	732	549
1947	720	669	665	618
1948	907	720	838	665
1949	896	667	828	616
1950	1027	804	949	743
Total	4342	3454	4012	3191
Avg.	868	691	802	638

Note: The RS and RA columns show the actual number of runs scored and allowed by each team. The final two columns adjust these numbers by the park effect. (Note that the park effects were determined for the entire period rather than year by year.)

these Yankees, could better turn their runs into victories.

Baseball analysts have long observed that a team's won-loss record can be estimated from its runs scored and runs allowed totals. Applying the estimation formula adds insight into whether a club's record is a close reflection of its run totals. If a team wins fewer games than predicted, one might conclude that it either failed to efficiently distribute its runs or was simply unlucky. Additional detail and justification is provided in appendix 1.

Table 8.4 compares the estimated won-loss records for the Red Sox and Yankees for the 1946–1950 period along with their actual results. The final column is the difference between the two; a positive number indicates the team exceeded its expectation.

Table 8.4 Estimated Wins and Losses, 1946–1950

	Estimated	Actual	Difference
	New York		
1946	91–63	87–57	-4
1947	100–54	97–57	-3
1948	98–56	94–60	-4
1949	96–58	97–57	1
1950	98–56	98–56	0
Total	483–287	473–297	-10
	Boston		
1946	97–57	104–50	7
1947	82–72	83–71	1
1948	95–60	96–59	1
1949	98–56	96–58	-2
1950	96–58	94–60	-2
Total	468–303	473–298	5

The Yankees underperformed the estimate the first three years and totaled seventeen games under for the period. The Red Sox were much
more predictable, always finishing within two games of the formula after
1946.

If the Yankees and Red Sox had each won the predicted number of
games, Boston would have won the 1949 pennant by two games (rather
than losing by one). The 1948 Red Sox, however, would have finished
three games worse than the Yankees rather than beating them by two.
Since the personnel in these seasons was essentially the same, one cannot
really assume that these differences reflect on the character of the players.
In any case, the Yankees did not spread their runs more efficiently than
the Red Sox.

◇ ◇ ◇

In his book *Summer of '49*, David Halberstam repeatedly writes what is
probably conventional wisdom: one of the backbones of the Yankee
squads was their great defense. The Red Sox, he suggests, fielded great offensive players at the expense of their defense. The Yankees had the Great
DiMaggio in center field and Rizzuto at shortstop, so the pitchers could

safely throw the ball over the plate knowing that they had excellent defensive players behind them.

In contrast, in his excellent book on the 1948 American League pennant race, *Epic Season*, David Kaiser writes that the Red Sox defense was not only better than that of the Yankees, it was one of the best defensive teams ever.

There is no satisfactory way to determine the strength of a ball club's defense. The entire defense is best measured by how many runs it allows, but most of the blame or credit for runs lies with the pitcher. Determining the contribution of the other eight players remains an area of active baseball research.

The most traditional measure of fielding quality, fielding percentage, has severe limitations because it fails to differentiate between two surehanded players with vastly different range. A more modern fielding methodology is defensive efficiency record (DER), which measures the percentage of balls put in play that the defense turns into outs. The specific formula for DER is given in appendix 3.

Table 8.5 shows the fielding percentage and DER for the Red Sox and Yankees in this period and their rank in the American League for each category.

Both clubs were generally good in these measures, with the Yankees having a better DER and the Red Sox a better fielding percentage. In addition, the Red Sox DER was almost certainly negatively affected by their

Table 8.5 Team Defense, 1946–1950

	Pct	Rank	DER	Rank
	New York			
1946	.975	2	.713	1
1947	.981	2	.727	2
1948	.979	4	.714	2
1949	.977	4	.718	2
1950	.979	3	.708	3
	Boston			
1946	.977	1	.707	2
1947	.977	3	.703	5
1948	.981	2	.700	3
1949	.980	2	.702	6
1950	.981	1	.699	5

ballpark. Most teams defend fields of roughly similar dimensions, but Fenway has an extremely small foul territory. Foul pop-ups are beneficial to a ball club's DER since the formula does not penalize a team for not catching them. Further study is necessary in this area, but it seems likely that the Yankees caught significantly more foul flies than the Red Sox.

Additional insight may also be gained by comparing some of the individuals on the two squads. Joe DiMaggio might have been the best-looking outfielder ever, but available evidence suggests his brother Dominic was a better fielder. Joe played half his games in the largest outfield in the league, and stories are told that he caught everything hit anywhere near him, including balls that could have been more easily played by other outfielders. Dom, playing his home games in a park that restricted his range on two sides (with the wall in left center and the bullpen in right center), actually made quite a few more putouts per game than Joe every year.

Joe was also famous for his great arm, and he led the league is assists his rookie year, but Dom led in assists three times and recorded only six fewer career assists than Joe in 350 fewer games. Dom set an American League record with 503 putouts in 1948 that held up for thirty years, well after the schedule had expanded to 162 games. Dom led the league in plays (putouts plus assists) per game four times; Joe never did.

Indians center fielder Larry Doby told David Kaiser: "I think Dom DiMaggio was at least the equal of Joe as an outfielder. Of course, he did not have the New York media working for him." Red Sox catcher Matt Batts remembered, "I would take [Dom] over [Joe]. He was a super center fielder and I never saw anybody any better."

Bobby Doerr was the premier defensive second baseman of his time, regularly leading the league's second baseman in assists, putouts, double plays, and chances per game. His Yankee counterpart, Jerry Coleman, was no better than an average defensive player.

Vern Stephens led all league shortstops in assists from 1947 through 1949. Over their careers, Stephens and Phil Rizzuto recorded very similar chances per game statistics, although Rizzuto turned the double play better. The Red Sox also had Pesky, a good shortstop, playing third base and leading the league in plays per game in 1949 and 1950. It is risky to compare players by how many plays they make, since opportunities can vary between players for any number of reasons. In fact, the Yankees pitchers struck out more batters, lessening the number of fielding chances for their teammates. Even with this caveat, however, it is notable that the Red Sox had several players in both the infield and the outfield with excellent fielding statistics every year.

Comparing the defense of catchers is an exercise fraught with danger, but it bears mentioning that Yogi Berra was moved to right field in August of 1948 because Bucky Harris thought he was hurting the club behind the plate. Stengel put Berra back at catcher full time in 1949 but still played Tommy Henrich out of position at first base.

Despite Ted Williams's reputation as a mediocre fielder, many contemporary sources considered him a fine defensive player in the late 1940s. Due to the distinctive design of Fenway Park, left fielders have a very unique job to do, and almost always record fewer chances per game than other left fielders in the league. Williams's chances per game over his career are almost identical to Carl Yastrzemski's, although Williams had a lot fewer assists. Kaiser suggests that Williams was an outstanding defensive player in the late 1940s. Ed Rummill wrote in *Baseball Stars of 1950*: "He has made himself a fine defensive outfielder through constant practice." Johnny Pesky and Dom DiMaggio, speaking at the 2002 Society for American Baseball Research convention in Boston, repeatedly stressed that Williams was a good defensive player. Williams's fielding perception is likely shaped by his troubles early in his career and the injuries that slowed him down later. In 1949 he was in his prime as an athlete.

The Red Sox had a very good defensive team—one at least as strong as the Yankees. There is no reason to conclude that the Red Sox lost because of defensive inefficiencies.

◊   ◊   ◊

In the past generation, it has been shown that the number of runs that a team scores can be estimated from a complete set of the club's statistics. A number of baseball analysts have developed accurate formulas to properly balance each of the team's batting events. For our analysis, we use Bill James's runs created (RC) formula.

If a team scores many more runs than predicted by the formula, it is certainly possible that the ball club possesses some unique skill and does things that do not show up in the statistics: not getting thrown out on the bases, effectively taking the extra base, making productive outs (such as hitting a ground ball to second base to advance a runner), hitting well in the clutch, etc. It has been claimed, for example, that Joe DiMaggio was never thrown out going from first to third on a single. If the Yankees possessed special traits not captured by the statistics, we might expect them to score more runs than predicted by the formula.

Table 8.6 shows how the Red Sox and Yankee runs created compare to

Table 8.6 Runs vs. Runs Created, 1946–1950

	Runs	RC	Difference
		Yankees	
1946	684	690	-6
1947	794	775	19
1948	857	833	24
1949	829	785	44
1950	914	898	16
Total	4078	3980	98
		Red Sox	
1946	792	784	8
1947	720	730	-10
1948	907	863	44
1949	896	886	10
1950	1027	1009	18
Total	4342	4271	71

their actual runs scored. The last column compares the two; a positive number indicates that the team scored more runs than estimated by the formula; a negative number indicates the opposite.

In fact, both outfits consistently scored more runs than their offensive statistics would suggest. The two largest differences are the 1948 Red Sox and the 1949 Yankees, who each outperformed the formula by forty-four runs (about 5 percent). Typically, an additional ten runs in a season equates to about one win. Therefore, the 1949 Yankees may have won an additional four to five games because of a more efficient offensive.

For the most part, the Red Sox and Yankees teams of this era scored a lot of runs because they could hit. Each was also able to outperform its statistics overall, but the difference is slight (less than 2.5 percent), making it difficult to determine whether this was the result of a particular skill or random chance.

◇ ◇ ◇

As discussed earlier, the Red Sox hitters benefited from playing half their games in Fenway Park. The magnitude of the statistics of the star players, however, was such that they dwarfed any reasonable ballpark adjust-

Table 8.7 Individual Runs Created

Pos	Red Sox	RC	WAAv	Pos	Yankees	RC	WAAv
C	Tebbetts	56	-0.3	C	Berra	68	1.4
1B	Goodman	66	0.3	1B	Henrich	98	4.4
2B	Doerr	100	2.1	2B	Coleman	65	0.3
3B	Pesky	106	2.2	3B	Brown	53	0.7
SS	Stephens	128	4.1	SS	Rizzuto	87	0.0
LF	Williams	175	9.5	LF	Woodling	53	1.2
CF	D DiMaggio	110	2.6	CF	J DiMaggio	74	4.0
RF	Zarilla	71	0.3	RF	Bauer	49	0.7
	Total	811	20.9		Total	547	12.8
	Actual	896	19.0		Actual	829	20.0

ment. How could a team with all of these great statistics not wipe out the competition?

Table 8.7 shows a comparison of the Red Sox and Yankees lineups using the most common player at each position. Instead of displaying their traditional statistics, the table provides the number of runs the player created (RC) and the corresponding number of wins these runs were worth compared with an average hitter.

The scale of runs created is similar to that of runs or RBI. Williams' 175 runs created are like 175 runs or 175 RBI—an incredible performance, but not out of line with other Williams seasons. Stephens finished second in the league in runs created and the Red Sox had five of the top nine players.

The next-to-last row shows that the Red Sox starting lineup created 811 runs and hit well enough to take an otherwise average ball club to twenty-one games better than .500. Their Yankee counterparts created 547 runs and were thirteen wins above average. These values probably coincide with the perception that their traditional statistics create. The last row shows the actual number of runs scored and games over .500 for the two squads.

Boston's starting lineup created over 90 percent of their teams' runs, while New York's starters created only 66 percent of theirs. The Red Sox had a very stable lineup; all eight regulars played at least 120 games, and the five stars played at least 139 of the 154 games. Only one bench player, backup catcher Matt Batts, had more than ten RBI.

Two factors that led to the illusion that the Yankee offense was less than outstanding are that Joe DiMaggio played in only seventy-six games and, more important, Casey Stengel played so many different players that he did not allow a set lineup to pile up enough statistics to look impressive.

The Yankee third baseman was not really Bobby Brown—it was half Brown and half Billy Johnson (47 RC). When looked at this way, the Yankee third basemen created ninety-nine runs—fairly close to the production the Red Sox got from Johnny Pesky. A similar circumstance held true in the outfield, although Joe DiMaggio's injury complicated the situation. When healthy, DiMaggio played every game and Stengel alternated players in left and right fields. When DiMaggio was hurt, the outfielders changed daily.

The Yankee use of its entire roster helps create an illusion that the Red Sox lineup was vastly superior. Rather than dividing their statistics between eight players, the Yankees allocated them between fourteen. Stengel also found plenty of playing time for Cliff Mapes, Johnny Lindell, Dick Kryhoski, Snuffy Stirnweiss, Charlie Keller, and several others.

Because of the core of Red Sox stars, a perception developed that Williams and Stephens and their teammates could not have been as good as their individual statistics implied. It seems evident, however, that the Red Sox' best players really were superior, but New York's extraordinary depth made up for the disparity in star power.

◇   ◇   ◇

No individual player's reputation has been more adversely affected by the perception of the Red Sox as underachievers than that of Vern "Junior" Stephens. One of the better players in baseball while active, both by reputation and accomplishment, within a few years after retirement Stephens was remembered, if at all, as a plodding one-dimensional slugger.

Stephens was part of a special group of shortstops whose careers coincided in the 1940s. Lou Boudreau, Phil Rizzuto, and Marty Marion were born in 1917, Pee Wee Reese in 1918, Johnny Pesky in 1919, and Stephens in 1920. All played most of their prime years with contending teams; almost every World Series from the early 1940s through the middle 1950s featured one or two of these players at shortstop. Three of them were MVPs (Marion, Boudreau, and Rizzuto) and three are in the Hall of Fame (Boudreau, Reese, and Rizzuto).

During his career, Vern Stephens was considered to be as good or better than any of his illustrious peers. When he became eligible for the Hall of Fame in 1961, however, he did not receive a single vote. His story is illustrative of how reputations can be formed.

Stephens was born in October 1920 in McAlister, New Mexico, but grew up in Long Beach, California. He entered American Legion baseball at age thirteen and played shortstop on the 1936 Southern California champions. After graduating from high school at sixteen, he attended Long Beach Junior College for a year and hit .522 for the baseball team.

After his one college season, Stephens signed with the Browns for a $500 bonus. The Red Sox offered $5,000 and a four-year college scholarship a few days after he had signed. He played sparingly at two minor league stops in 1938. The next year he tore up the Kitty League, leading the circuit with 123 RBI and a .361 batting average while hitting thirty home runs. After another RBI title with San Antonio of the Texas League, manager Marty McManus called Stephens the "best shortstop prospect I have ever seen." Another excellent minor league season, with Toledo of the American Association, earned him a recall later in 1941 and the starting shortstop job for the Browns the next spring.

Predictions for his stardom were not unanimous. His Toledo manager, Fred Haney, told Browns skipper Luke Sewell that "Stephens will never play shortstop in the major leagues as long as he has a hole in his ass." Nonetheless, when John Beradino joined the Army Air Force in early 1942, Sewell gave the job to Stephens.

In his first year as a major league regular, Stephens hit .294 with fourteen home runs and ninety-two RBI, as the Browns achieved their best record in twenty years. Stephens finished fourth in the 1942 MVP balloting, one slot behind fellow rookie shortstop Johnny Pesky of Boston. He led the league with forty-two errors, but contemporary accounts make no mention of his defense being a problem. He was only twenty-one, and one of the bright young stars in baseball.

In early 1943, Stephens reaggravated a knee he had hurt in the minor leagues, causing him to flunk his army physical. The injury caused the Browns to consider moving him to the outfield, where they used him eleven times. At the plate he turned in another fine year—twenty-two home runs, ninety-one RBI, and a .289 average. The Browns slipped to seventh place, but Stephens still finished ninth in the MVP balloting. Later reclassified as 1-A, he again failed the exam in 1944 and remained one of the better players to play through the entire war.

In 1944 Stephens led his team to its first and only American League pennant, hitting .293 with twenty-two home runs and 109 RBI. He moved

Vern Stephens

up to third in the MVP vote behind Detroit pitchers Hal Newhouser and Dizzy Trout, who combined to win fifty-six games. In both 1943 and 1944 Stephens played all nine innings and batted fourth for the American League in the All-Star Game. He was the best player on the best team, and he was just turning twenty-four.

In William Mead's classic book on wartime baseball, *Even the Browns,* he quotes several Browns teammates who were seemingly in awe of Stephens. Mark Christman, the team's third baseman, considered Stephens to be as good a shortstop as Cardinals' star Marty Marion: "Not as good hands, but he covered as much ground, and he had an arm like a shotgun." Christman also marveled at Stephens's strength, noting that although he played at Sportsman's Park, a tough park for a right-handed hitter, Stephens would hit the ball the other way onto the pavilion roof in right center.

Stephens apparently enjoyed an adventurous nightlife during these years. Don Gutteridge, his roommate, marveled at "how he did it—go out like he did and then play as well as he did. He was superman."

In 1945 he had another carbon copy season—eighty-nine RBI, a .289 average and a league-leading twenty-four home runs. The Browns dropped to third place, but Stephens continued to impress the MVP voters, finishing sixth.

After the 1945 season, Stephens thought he deserved a decent raise. He asked for $17,500, while the Browns offered only $13,000. During the spring of 1946, Stephens jumped the Browns and accepted a five-year contract to play for the Veracruz Blues of the Mexican League. Jorge Pasqual, the president of the league, was defying the major leagues and attempting to sign several big stars. Though Pasqual made large offers to Ted Williams and Stan Musial, Stephens was the best player he was able to land. After only two games for Veracruz, Stephens decided he had made a big mistake. After sneaking out of Mexico with his father, he rejoined the Browns.

The Red Sox offered to deal Pesky, who had spent the last three seasons in the army, and cash to the Browns for Stephens. Manager Sewell vetoed the deal because "Stephens has a stronger arm. He'll throw out more men from the hole. I guess we'll hold on to him."

In 1946 all of the stars returned from the war, and many observers likely assumed that Stephens's star would dim. He missed thirty-nine games with assorted injuries that made his power (fourteen home runs and sixty-four RBI, both league highs for shortstops) look to have slipped, and he hit a career high .307. In 1947, he had another pretty good year with the bat (fifteen home runs, eighty-three RBI, and a .279 average). He turned twenty-seven that October and was rightly considered one of the best players—offensively and defensively—in baseball.

The Browns, on the other hand, had fallen into dire straits. In 1947 ownership spent $2 million buying and renovating Sportsman's Park in St. Louis as well as a new facility for their San Antonio farm club. After drawing only 320,000 fans and finishing last, the Browns had to sell off players to recover their huge losses. The demand for Stephens was high. The Cleveland Indians were prepared to trade Lou Boudreau and cash for Stephens, but when the story was leaked in the Cleveland papers, Indians fans picketed Cleveland Stadium. Newspapers printed ballots asking fans to vote on the trade of their beloved player-manager, and the result was a landslide for keeping Boudreau. Owner Bill Veeck had promised to abide by the will of the people, so the trade collapsed. With Cleveland out of the running, the Red Sox forked over eight players and $375,000 for Stephens, Ellis Kinder, Jack Kramer, and Billy Hitchcock.

The Red Sox, of course, already had an All-Star shortstop in Johnny Pesky, a lifetime .330 hitter who had surpassed two hundred hits in his each of his first three major league seasons. Which of the two shortstops would move to third base was the most interesting dilemma facing manager Joe McCarthy as he prepared for his first year in Boston. McCarthy did not announce his intentions until spring training in Sarasota, when he moved Pesky.

David Halberstam writes in *Summer of '49* that Pesky went to third because he had better hands and was quicker than Stephens. In Glenn Stout and Richard Johnson's team history, *Red Sox Century*, the authors theorize that McCarthy moved Pesky to spite the reporters, many of whom had written that Stephens would play third. Neither theory is plausible. McCarthy was one of the most successful managers ever, and it is presumptuous to contend that he would make the move unless he thought Stephens was a better shortstop.

In a June 1948 story in *Sport* magazine, Harold Kaese wrote of the great relationship between Stephens and his teammates, and that Stephens had "won the battle" for the position because he was one of the best fielding shortstops in baseball. Stephens's defensive statistics were generally better than Pesky's, and McCarthy was undoubtedly aware of Stephens's great range and arm.

In the same article, Bobby Doerr said, "[Stephens is] nice to work with like Pesky. They co-operate on pop flies in the sun, and work with you on other plays. Perhaps the best thing that impresses me about Vern is the speed with which he goes across the bag on double plays." In a story written just after Stephens passed away in 1968, Johnny Pesky said, "I always believed McCarthy did it because Stevie had such a great arm."

In 1948, playing in a friendlier park for his skills and hitting behind several great table setters, Stephens hit twenty-nine home runs and drove in 137 (second in the league to Joe DiMaggio). Though his batting average fell to a career low .269, he established a new high with seventy-seven walks. He finished fourth in the balloting for MVP, behind three great seasons from Boudreau, Joe DiMaggio, and Ted Williams. After several weeks of experimentation, McCarthy eventually settled on Stephens to hit cleanup behind Williams, where he would stay for the remainder of his years in Boston.

Bill James has written that anyone who had suggested after the 1948 season that Phil Rizzuto was destined for the Hall of Fame and Vern Stephens was not would have been laughed at. Stephens had been one of the best players in the league for several years and was the star shortstop for a marquee team. He had just turned twenty-eight years old.

In 1949 Stephens had his best year yet; he slugged a career-high thirty-nine home runs, a record for shortstops later broken by Ernie Banks, and drove in a surreal 159 runs, a total not surpassed by any player for fifty years. He also batted .290 and walked a career high 101 times. Despite this incredible contribution from their cleanup hitting shortstop, the Red Sox lost the pennant on the last day of the season to the Yankees.

When considering the great statistics of Stephens and several of his teammates, as opposed to the Red Sox losses on the last weekend in New York, it appears that the baseball world began to turn its collective back on Stephens. If the Red Sox could not win with all their impressive hitting, something must be missing, perhaps starting with their shortstop. Stephens received one first-place vote in the MVP balloting and finished seventh despite his historic year. Yankee shortstop Phil Rizzuto hit .275 with no power—he had ninety-four fewer RBI than Stephens—yet finished second to Williams in the voting.

Because of injuries and the whims of Casey Stengel, Rizzuto was the only Yankee who played more than 128 games in 1949. As the Yankees won the pennant, the writers concluded that Rizzuto must be the primary reason. In fact, the Yankees received more offense and defense from other positions where multiple players shared the job. Rizzuto was a fine player who had his typical year, but was not close to Junior Stephens in most seasons. In August 1949, Al Hirshberg suggested in *Sport* magazine that only Cleveland fans of Lou Boudreau would argue against Stephens as the most valuable shortstop in baseball. He did not even mention Rizzuto. Hirshberg also wrote that Stephens was the most popular player on the Red Sox with his teammates, the press, and the fans, an observation also made by other writers of the time.

In 1950 Rizzuto had a legitimately great year, a year that stands out in his career like a mountain in Kansas. He deserved and won the MVP award for his performance. Stephens hit thirty home runs, led the league with 144 RBI and hit .290. Nevertheless, he finished twenty-fifth in the MVP balloting, behind six of his teammates. It is hard to fathom how a good-fielding shortstop could lead the league in RBIs and be considered the seventh-best player on his own club.

One of the knocks on Stephens was that he was a good hitter who was fortunate to play in Fenway Park. While the park helped his statistics, they would have been among the best in any case. Table 8.8 provides Stephens's road totals for his first three seasons with the Red Sox.

A shortstop who can hit like this in half of his games, walk eighty times a year, play good defense, get along with his teammates and manager, and stay healthy has to be one of the best players in baseball. This was basically Stephens for ten years.

Halberstam writes of an encounter that supposedly occurred between Williams and Yankee pitcher Allie Reynolds at an All-Star Game. Williams

Table 8.8 Vern Stephens on the Road

	HR	RBI	BA
1948	13	76	.263
1949	18	63	.272
1950	13	61	.247

Source: Data courtesy of Pete Palmer

jokingly asked when Reynolds was going to start giving him some good pitches to hit. Reynolds countered with words to the effect of "not as long as Stephens is hitting behind you." Vic Raschi apparently told Halberstam that Stephens could be pitched to by throwing fastballs high and away, but that Doerr (who followed Stephens in the batting order) was as good a hitter as the Red Sox had and required extreme care.

This story is unconvincing. First, Stephens was a fairly patient hitter who walked 101 times in 1949, the base year for Halberstam's book. Second, Stephens drove in 159 runs, leaving one to question whether the pitchers knew what the heck they were doing.

In Ted Williams's fine autobiography, *My Turn at Bat,* he suggests that the best seasons he had driving in runs were the years he had Joe Cronin (1939) or Stephens (1949) hitting behind him. Pitchers, in Williams's view, would not pitch around him with Stephens coming up next. This may be true, but Williams never gave an inch to any pitcher, and actually walked 162 times in 1949. The top of the Red Sox lineup in the late 1940s (DiMaggio-Pesky-Williams-Stephens-Doerr) left the pitcher nowhere to hide. Whether the pitchers pitched around Williams to get to Stephens (Halberstam's position), or gave Williams pitches to hit because of the threat of Stephens (Williams's position), one thing is crystal clear— it did not work.

The 1949 Red Sox walked more times than any squad in history, just breaking the record set by the 1948 club. As table 8.9 shows, pitching staffs were very reluctant to throw strikes to this team.

The base on balls was a Joe McCarthy specialty. In his twenty-two full seasons as a big league manager, his clubs led their league in batters' walks fourteen times. In 1948, McCarthy's first year in Boston, the club improved from 666 to 823 free passes. Pesky and DiMaggio, the first two men in the Boston lineup, remember McCarthy telling them that their job was to get Williams up to bat—in other words, to get on base, to not make an out. In fact, the pair improved from 146 to 200 walks in their first year

Table 8.9 Most Walks, Team (All-Time)

	Year	Walks
Boston Red Sox	1949	835
Boston Red Sox	1948	823
Philadelphia Athletics	1949	783
St. Louis Browns	1941	775
New York Yankees	1932	766

under McCarthy, and sustained those levels as long as he remained the manager.

When pitchers were interviewed about Stephens at the time he was playing, they generally provided a glowing description. In an article in the fall 1951 issue of *Complete Baseball,* Ed Rummill quotes Ed Lopat on Stephens: "He's tough, real tough. . . . if you throw one to the outside corner, he's liable to hit it down the right field line for two or three bases." Ned Garver told the same writer: "That Stephens gives me as much trouble as the rest of the Red Sox combined." Jack Kramer was just as positive: "Stephens is as strong as Foxx ever was. I'm convinced of it."

In fact, the universal tone of articles written during his career is one of deep respect for Stephens as a power hitter, a shortstop, a teammate, and a man. Sometime in the ensuing generation, his star slipped substantially, and the reasons for it are not discernible.

Following the 1950 season, the Red Sox acquired yet another shortstop, their 1948 nemesis, Lou Boudreau. New manager Steve O'Neill moved Stephens to third and divided the time at shortstop between Pesky and Boudreau. Unfortunately, Stephens aggravated his old knee injury and played only ninety-one games in the field. In only 377 at bats, he hit .300 with seventeen home runs and seventy-eight RBI—production consistent with the previous three seasons.

He declined fairly rapidly thereafter. Following another injury-laden year in Boston, he moved on to the White Sox, the Browns, and the Orioles for three more mediocre seasons. He was finished in 1955, before his thirty-fifth birthday.

There are two theories about his sudden decline. One suggests that he was never able to recover from his knee injury, which disabled him in both 1951 and 1952. Fifty years ago a bad knee could be devastating to an infielder in his early thirties.

The other theory is that his drinking finally caught up with him. Although most of his old Browns teammates later marveled at his partying,

Boston roommate Johnny Pesky downplayed his reputation, suggesting that this was not going on while he was in Boston. Before the injury in 1951, Stephens was remarkably durable; he did not miss a single game in 1948 or 1949 and missed ten or fewer several other times.

Whatever happened to Stephens, it happened very suddenly. For his first ten seasons (1942–1951), Stephens was a very good, and often great, player. Over his last four, he was no better than average. Stephens worked for Hillerich and Bradsby for a while after his playing days, then as a sales representative for a construction equipment company. He was apparently robust and healthy in 1968 when he had a heart attack on a golf course. He died at age forty-eight.

◇ ◇ ◇

One can estimate that the 1949 Red Sox won about six more games than they would have with a replacement-level hitter playing shortstop. Table 8.10 shows the ten greatest offensive seasons (sorted by wins above replacement) turned in by the six shortstops cited earlier (Boudreau, Stephens, Rizzuto, Reese, Marion, and Pesky).

In 1948 Boudreau created 131 runs playing in the worst hitter's park in the league and had one of the best offensive seasons for a shortstop since Hans Wagner early in the twentieth century. When his great defense and the fact that he managed the world champions are also considered, it has to rank as one of the greatest seasons ever.

Stephens turned in four of the top ten offensive seasons of this group. Since these calculations adjust for the park, a few of his years with St. Louis actually rate higher than seasons in Boston, where he compiled more impressive numbers. If the list were expanded to include the top twenty-five, each of Stephens' nine full-time seasons would be included. Table 8.11 summarizes the career totals for each of these players.

Stephens, often remembered for a short career, actually played more games than all but Reese. He was the best hitter of the bunch and maintained his peak for a long time.

◇ ◇ ◇

Defensive value is much more difficult to measure than offensive value. Along with the traditional fielding percentage, most analysts believe that chances per game is the most telling statistic for a shortstop. As noted in a previous chapter, chances per game has a couple of weaknesses. To be

Table 8.10 Best Seasons by Select Shortstops (by WAR)

	Year	G	AVG	OBP	SLG	R	HR	RBI	BB	RC	WAAv	WAR
Lou Boudreau	1948	152	.355	.453	.534	116	18	106	98	131	6.2	8.0
Vern Stephens	1949	155	.290	.391	.539	113	39	159	101	128	4.1	6.1
Lou Boudreau	1944	150	.327	.406	.437	91	3	67	73	102	4.4	6.1
Phil Rizzuto	1950	155	.324	.418	.439	125	7	66	92	124	4.0	6.0
Vern Stephens	1944	145	.293	.365	.462	91	20	109	62	107	4.3	6.0
Johnny Pesky	1946	153	.335	.401	.427	115	2	55	65	110	4.0	5.9
Pee Wee Reese	1949	155	.279	.396	.410	132	16	73	116	119	3.7	5.8
Vern Stephens	1945	149	.289	.352	.473	90	24	89	55	98	3.6	5.3
Lou Boudreau	1947	150	.307	.388	.424	79	4	67	67	93	3.6	5.2
Vern Stephens	1943	137	.289	.357	.482	75	22	91	54	87	3.4	4.9

RC = runs created   WAAv = wins above average   WAR = wins above replacement

Table 8.11 Career Offense by Select Shortstops

	G	RC	WAAv	WAR
Vern Stephens	1720	1075	25	46
Lou Boudreau	1646	953	23	42
Pee Wee Reese	2166	1211	15	42
Johnny Pesky	1270	780	16	32
Phil Rizzuto	1661	804	5	25
Marty Marion	1572	624	-10	8

RC = runs created   WAAv = wins above average

WAR = wins above replacement

Table 8.12 Defense

	Years	A/G	PO/G	DP/G	Chances/G	Pct
Lou Boudreau	8	3.11	2.05	.77	5.31	.972
Marty Marion	9	3.18	1.95	.63	5.30	.968
Johnny Pesky	3	3.08	2.00	.65	5.26	.966
Vern Stephens	7	3.19	1.79	.67	5.16	.964
Pee Wee Reese	13	2.94	2.00	.62	5.13	.963
Phil Rizzuto	11	2.91	2.01	.76	5.08	.968

valid as a comparative measure, the players being evaluated need an equal opportunity to make plays, but differences in ballparks and pitching staffs make this assumption of equality unrealistic. Also, because it is based on games, the measure is only useful when comparing players that play entire games.

Table 8.12 shows the career defensive statistics for the six shortstops, sorted by chances per game. It includes only seasons in which the player had at least 125 games at shortstop.

In an interesting oddity, Stephens's assist totals were very high, yet his putout totals were the lowest. This could indicate that he did not get back on pop-ups very well. On the other hand, when we think of the range of a shortstop, we think largely of plays that result in an assist. Many putouts by infielders occur on pop-ups in the infield, which could often be caught by more than one player. Perhaps Stephens deferred more often to other infielders on these plays. In any case, his overall ability to make plays was consistently above average in a league with a lot of good-fielding shortstops.

◇ ◇ ◇

The histories of these two ball clubs are remarkably different: the Yankees have won twenty-six championships, all of them after the Red Sox last won in 1918. The teams have waged two very famous duels to the last game of the season—1949 and 1978; both resulted in Yankee victories. When the squads met in the American League Championship Series in 1999, many Red Sox fans tuned in to watch with a sense of dread.

Yet the Red Sox defeat on October 2, 1949, was not inevitable. When the teams squared off at the end of the 1949 season, much of this history remained to be written. The clubs had been in only two previous pennant races: the 1904 classic, when Boston beat New York on the next-to-last game of the year to clinch the flag, and 1948, when the Red Sox beat the Yankees on the final weekend.

The Yankees did not have a reputation for gutting out clutch victories at the end of the season; when they won, they tended to dominate the league so thoroughly that no such victories were needed. In the previous fifteen years New York had been in only two real pennant races, 1940 and 1948, and both times the Yankees finished third.

The Yankee ball club that beat the Red Sox in 1949 was a superb collection of players. New York had excellent starting pitching; the best relief pitcher in the game; a great, well-rounded offense; a very good bench; and an astute manager.

The Red Sox did not have Joe Page or much of a bench. The rest of the squad was outstanding: the best two hitters in the league, the best pitcher, and several other star quality players. Because the Red Sox lacked the depth of the Yankees, their loss on the final weekend in New York has blinded history to the quality of the team.

9

AN UNEXPECTED DROP-OFF:
THE 1960s MINNESOTA TWINS

After maintaining a stranglehold on the American League for the better part of fifteen years, the New York Yankees struggled to win the pennant in 1964. When the team collapsed suddenly in 1965, an opportunity arose for a team to step up and take its place for a while atop the league. As it happened, the Minnesota Twins dominated the AL in 1965 with a 102–60 record, finishing seven games ahead of the second-place Chicago White Sox. The club then lost a close seven-game World Series to the Los Angeles Dodgers. The Twins appeared poised to assume New York's mantle.

The 1965 Twins scored 774 runs in a year when no other team in the league scored more than 680. The offense was broad-based and well balanced. In Tony Oliva and Harmon Killebrew the Twins boasted two of the best five or six players in the league. A number of exceptional regulars supported these two stars. Shortstop Zoilo Versalles was named the league MVP and won the Gold Glove. Outfielders Jimmie Hall and Bob Allison were both excellent players, and Earl Battey was one of the league's best catchers.

This star-laden lineup had both power and speed. In 1963 and 1964 the club hit 225 and 221 home runs, the second- and third-highest single-season totals of all time up to that point. In 1965, manager Sam Mele and owner Calvin Griffith chose to emphasize the team's speed, so the Twins hit forty-two triples and stole ninety-two bases, the second- and fourth-highest marks in the league.

Despite playing in a ballpark that favored hitters, the pitching staff finished third in the league with an ERA of 3.14. This staff included one of the deepest collections of frontline starting pitchers put together in a long time. No pitcher who hurled more than seventy innings finished with an ERA above 3.40.

On the offensive side of the game, no member of the Twins' starting lineup was over thirty years old, and neither Versalles nor his MVP runner-up, Oliva, was older than twenty-five. The pitching staff was also fairly young; thirty-one-year-old Camilo Pascual was the oldest starter. These Twins were a great young team, and the future appeared extremely bright.

Unfortunately for the Twins and their fans, the club proved unable to sustain its success. Some poor decision-making, the emergence of a better team, and some unusually sudden career collapses spoiled the team's opportunity for a more extended run of greatness. That this club failed to win another pennant has to be viewed as both surprising and disappointing.

◇ ◇ ◇

As an eleven-year-old child, Calvin Griffith Robertson caught a big break when he and his sister Thelma left their subsistence lifestyle in Montreal and moved in with their uncle Clark in Washington, D.C. Clark Griffith, managing partner of the Washington Senators, introduced Robertson to a life in professional baseball. Although never formally adopted by Griffith, Robertson reversed his middle and last names so that his last name would be that of his new "father," Griffith. After a number of years working in the minors as both a manager and front-office executive to hone his craft, Calvin Griffith formally joined the Senator organization in 1942. When Clark passed away at age eighty-four after the 1955 season, Calvin assumed control of the club.

After nearly fifty years, baseball writers have a tendency to look back on the era of these owner-operators with a degree of nostalgia. In fact, these owners, who had no outside source of income, often ran their clubs on a shoestring budget and spent much less on scouting and minor league operations than the wealthier franchises. By the early 1950s, some of these teams were spectacularly unsuccessful. Connie Mack's Philadelphia Athletics only once finished as high as fourth in the twenty years from 1935 through 1954, the team's last year in Philadelphia, and finished last eleven times during that same period. While not quite as inept as the Athletics, the Senators rarely offered a competitive baseball product over their last twenty years in Washington. Setting aside the chaotic years of World War

II, the Senators never finished higher than fifth, while finding the cellar five times.

Joe Cambria was an ex–minor league player and longtime minor league owner who became a legendary scout for the Senators. Although he inked such players as Early Wynn and Mickey Vernon, he gained most of his fame for his efforts in Cuba, which led to the signing of over four hundred players. With the help of Cambria, the Senators' organization was at the forefront of signing Latin American—particularly Cuban— baseball players, a talent source that was especially attractive to the Griffiths because it was inexpensive. Cambria helped deliver several extremely talented Cubans to the franchise.

The Senators/Twins organization that Calvin Griffith directed evolved into an extended family operation. Brothers Sherry, Jimmy, and Billy Robertson and brother-in-law Joe Haynes all held down key executive positions within the system. In fairness, prior to Haynes's and Sherry's deaths (in 1967 and 1970) and the changing baseball economics of the 1970s, which Griffith never really understood, the Twins organization was one of the league's more successful, both on the field and in the stands.

◇ ◇ ◇

By the late 1950s the Washington Senators were finishing last in American League attendance every year, usually by quite a distance. When the Senators drew fewer than 450,000 fans in 1956, no other team was under 850,000. When Minnesota's Twin Cities of Minneapolis and St. Paul came calling on Griffith to entice him into a move, he was more than ready to listen, and the Senators moved to Bloomington, Minnesota, for the 1961 season.

While still in Washington, the team had acquired a number of the players who would later excel for the Twins by the typical method of the time: signing amateur Americans. During much of the 1950s, the rules required that a player receiving a signing bonus greater than $4,000 spend his first couple of years in the major leagues or be subject to the major league draft. This youngster, termed a "bonus baby," typically received little playing time in the majors before being sent to the minors for more active seasoning.

In 1954 the Washington Senators signed Harmon Killebrew for $30,000. Still only seventeen, Killebrew turned down a multisport scholarship to the University of Oregon. As a bonus baby, he played very little for the Senators before getting a chance to start his minor league apprenticeship in 1956. After an excellent year and a half in the minors, Killebrew hoped to make the team as a regular in 1958. Manager Cookie Lavagetto, however, preferred to stick with the veteran Eddie Yost. Despite the off-season trade of Yost in 1959, Lavagetto again seemed unwilling to make the slugging Killebrew his regular third baseman until Griffith forced the decision upon his manager in the spring. Killebrew responded with forty-two home runs.

The Senators signed three key members of their pennant-winning team for exactly $4,000 in the mid-1950s, effectively skirting the bonus rule. In 1955 outfielder Bob Allison signed with the Senators after his sophomore year at Kansas University. Jimmie Hall, the center fielder for the 1965 club, signed in 1956 after finishing high school in his native North Carolina. The team inked pitcher Jim Kaat in 1957 after his freshman year in college.

The Cuban connection also remained strong in the late 1950s. The team's top two starting pitchers during the Senators' final years in Washington, Camilo Pascual and Pedro Ramos, were both signed from Cuba. Reserve outfielder Sandy Valdespino came north in the mid-1950s. Cambria sent Zoilo Versalles to the United States in 1957.

Just before the start of the 1960 season, Griffith made a great trade with the 1959 pennant-winning Chicago White Sox. He dealt thirty-two-year-old outfielder–first baseman Roy Sievers for two young players who became starters on the 1965 team, Earl Battey and Don Mincher, plus $150,000. After graduating from Kent State, third baseman Rich Rollins joined the organization in 1960.

The club that Griffith moved had begun to show some improvement in its last year in Washington. After three consecutive last-place finishes, in 1960 the club moved up to fifth (of eight teams) and a record of 73–81.

In early 1961 the Twins added another Cuban, and this one would become one of the decade's best players. Pedro Oliva signed with Cambria in February and left for the United States six weeks later. Because he did not have a passport, he borrowed his bother Antonio's and thereafter adopted the name of "Tony."

After arriving in America, Oliva, along with twenty-one other Cubans, went straight to a tryout camp in Florida. The camp had only a few days remaining and Oliva was released after a four-game audition. Determined to get into organized baseball, Oliva received some help from Charlotte owner Phil Howser. Howser paid for Oliva's room and board,

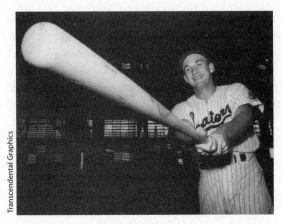

Transcendental Graphics

Harmon Killebrew

let him practice with the team, and then sent him to a rookie league in June. Fortunately for the Twins, Howser and his Charlotte club were part of their minor league organization. A man who was to become one of their greatest players had nearly slipped away.

While most of the key figures on the 1965 pennant winner were already in the organization by the time it moved to Minnesota, Griffith also made several astute deals in the early 1960s to round out the team. In 1963 the Twins acquired pitcher Jim Perry; the following year the team landed another pitcher, Jim "Mudcat" Grant. Griffith surrendered little in return (pitchers Jack Kralick and Lee Stange, and infielder-outfielder George Banks), and both new hurlers were soon stars on the Twins. At the winter meetings in 1964 the team obtained multiposition player Cesar Tovar for a promising lefty (Jerry Arrigo) who never really developed. Tovar would have a number of fine seasons with Minnesota.

When the team started slowly in 1961, Griffith replaced Lavagetto with Sam Mele in June. Sportswriter Max Nichols later called Mele's style the "Mele Method of Managing." Mele reprimanded and encouraged players in private, pointing out areas to work on, but did not provide a lot of instruction. As Nichols noted, players were expected to improve themselves.

The team responded well to Mele in 1962 and the Twins jumped all the way to 91 wins, the most by the franchise since 1933. The next year the Twins won 91 games again and expectations were high for this talented team. The Yankees were still the elite of the league, winning 104 games, but the Twins' youth, power hitting, and good pitching gave the team reasons for hope.

In 1964, the Twins fell all the way to sixth with a 79–83 record. Despite newcomer Tony Oliva's Rookie of the Year performance, this season was viewed as a bitter disappointment. Nichols wrote that the team had become renowned for its mental errors. After the 1964 season Griffith attempted to reduce Mele's salary by $6,000 after publicly saying Mele was "too nice a guy" and that the Twins needed to work on their fundamentals. Mele saved his job by agreeing to a $3,000 pay cut.

◇　◇　◇

The Twins broke through in 1965 behind an excellent and deep collection of talent. The club opened the season at home on April 12 by defeating the Yankees. The Twins jumped out to an early lead in the pennant race, but several other teams soon got hot. For the first two and a half months of the season an exciting five-team race seemed to be brewing. At the end of June the Twins stood at 43–28, one-half game behind the surprising Cleveland Indians. Chicago, Baltimore, and Detroit were also all within four games of first place.

At the start of July, the Twins quickly put an end to the pennant race by reeling off nine straight victories. They regained a share of the lead on July 4 and held on to the top spot thereafter. They finished 22–9 in July and expanded their lead to six games by the end of the month. The Twins continued to play well during August and held a seven-and-a-half-game lead over the second-place White Sox heading into September. With five games against the Twins in early September, Chicago had a chance to create a September pennant race. The Twins, however, won three of the five games, effectively ending any realistic threat to their pennant. At season's end, the Twins stood at 102–60, seven games ahead of the White Sox.

The World Series against the Los Angeles Dodgers opened in Minnesota on October 6. Dodger star Sandy Koufax was excused from the first game because it fell on the Jewish holiday of Yom Kippur, so Dodger manager Walter Alston started his other ace, Don Drysdale. The Twins went with their top pitcher, Mudcat Grant, who hurled a complete game to lead the Twins to an 8–2 victory. The Twins beat Koufax the next day, 2–1, receiving another complete game, this time from Kaat. After a travel day, the two teams played three straight games in Los Angeles. The Dodgers won all three handily. The Twins scored only two runs over the three games, and none of the three Twin starters, Pascual, Grant, and Kaat, pitched particularly well.

After another day off, the series resumed in Bloomington. Mele brought Grant back on only two days' rest, and the latter responded by surrendering only one run in a complete game victory. For the seventh and deciding game, both managers started their best available pitchers, Koufax for the Dodgers and Kaat for the Twins, on two days' rest. Unfortunately for Minnesota, Kaat gave up two runs in the third inning, which was enough for Koufax, who tossed a three-hit shutout. The Twins would have to wait another twenty-two years before they would capture a world championship.

In Harmon Killebrew and Tony Oliva, the Twins had two of the top hitters in the league. Table 9.1 provides summary support for this not-particularly-controversial contention. It lists the top players in the American League for 1964–1971, ranked by WAR per 150 games (minimum of 30 WAR).

Table 9.1 AL WAR/150 Leaders, 1964–1971

	G	AVG	OBP	SLG	R	HR	RBI	SB	RC	WAAv	WAR	WAR/ 150
Frank Robinson	827	.300	.405	.543	555	179	545	35	624	34	42	7.7
Harmon Killebrew	1162	.266	.399	.528	670	292	821	12	841	40	52	6.7
Frank Howard	1077	.279	.371	.513	516	237	670	4	709	34	45	6.3
Carl Yastrzemski	1233	.293	.399	.504	734	213	697	90	877	38	52	6.3
Tony Oliva	1179	.313	.363	.507	711	177	719	84	823	33	47	6.0
Al Kaline	1041	.288	.392	.478	584	151	553	36	666	29	40	5.7
Boog Powell	1131	.272	.373	.488	543	219	747	12	699	30	41	5.5
Norm Cash	1132	.266	.362	.475	565	201	611	17	654	24	36	4.8
Don Buford	1149	.270	.368	.390	663	88	391	191	646	21	34	4.4
Jim Fregosi	1206	.265	.344	.401	586	103	470	67	641	18	32	3.9
Brooks Robinson	1254	.273	.336	.437	631	169	720	11	690	17	32	3.8

WAR/150 = wins above replacement per 150 games

Harmon Killebrew was such a mild-mannered player that he was never thrown out of a game. One sportswriter felt that Lavagetto was reluctant to award Killebrew the third-base job in 1959 because he misinterpreted Killebrew's friendly and reserved personality as a lack of drive and courage.

Because of his low career batting average (.256), some historians seem to underappreciate Killebrew. He consistently drew a large number of walks, so his on-base percentage was consistently respectable. In fact, it is higher than several of his contemporaries who had significantly better batting averages, such as Pete Rose and Roberto Clemente.

Killebrew's claim to greatness, however, was his tremendous power. His career total of 573 home runs was for many years the fifth highest total of all time. Killebrew also proved remarkably consistent. He finished with a WAR above 5.0 in each of his twelve years as a regular except the injury-shortened 1968. Table 9.2 summarizes these first twelve seasons and includes Killebrew's performance in the MVP vote.

Contemporary writers recognized Killebrew's value. Six times he landed in the top four of his league's MVP voting. Bill James devised a method he calls "award shares" to quantify how a player performs in the MVP balloting. An award share is simply the percentage of the total available

Table 9.2 Harmon Killebrew, 1959–1970

	G	AVG	OBP	SLG	R	HR	RBI	BB	RC	WAAv	WAR	MVP
1959	153	.242	.356	.516	98	42	105	90	105	3.6	5.5	15
1960	124	.276	.377	.534	84	31	80	71	90	3.7	5.1	—
1961	150	.288	.409	.606	94	46	122	107	131	5.7	7.5	11
1962	155	.243	.369	.545	85	48	126	106	111	3.6	5.5	3
1963	142	.258	.353	.555	88	45	96	72	96	3.5	5.2	4
1964	158	.270	.379	.548	95	49	111	93	111	4.6	6.4	10
1965	113	.269	.386	.501	78	25	75	72	82	3.7	5.0	15
1966	162	.281	.393	.538	89	39	110	103	121	5.8	7.6	4
1967	163	.269	.413	.558	105	44	113	131	134	7.6	9.3	2
1968	100	.210	.365	.420	40	17	40	70	46	1.5	2.4	—
1969	162	.276	.430	.584	106	49	140	145	137	7.4	9.2	1
1970	157	.271	.416	.546	96	41	113	128	118	5.4	7.1	2

MVP = rank in MVP voting

Tony Oliva

voting points (the number of points a first-place vote is worth times the number of voters) that a player receives. For example, in 1969 Killebrew won the MVP Award with 294 points out of a total possible of 336 for .88 award shares. Summing award shares over a period of years gives a representation of how the writers felt about a player's value. For the decade of the 1960s (1961 through 1970), Killebrew totaled 3.17; no other American League player had more than 3.00. In fact, only Brooks Robinson (2.47) and Mickey Mantle (2.18) totaled more than 2.00.

After being the American League's best player for many years, Mickey Mantle saw his injuries finally catch up with him in the early 1960s. Frank Robinson arrived in Baltimore in a trade from Cincinnati in 1966 and promptly became the league's best player. Between the decline of Mantle and the arrival of Robinson, Twins right fielder Tony Oliva was probably the best player in the American League. In 1964 Oliva was the Rookie of the Year and finished fourth in the MVP voting; in 1965 he finished second in the voting, and *The Sporting News* named him AL player of the year. Table 9.3 ranks the top players by WAR for 1964 and 1965.

In the summer of 1961, the twenty-one-year-old Oliva, speaking no English, found himself in the Appalachian League. He had a terrific year at the plate, batting .410 and driving in eighty-one runs in only 249 at-

Table 9.3 AL WAR Leaders, 1964–1965

	AVG	OBP	SLG	R	HR	RBI	SB	RC	WAAv	WAR	WAR/150
Tony Oliva	.322	.372	.526	216	48	192	31	234	10	14	6.8
Mickey Mantle	.282	.406	.530	136	54	157	10	182	9	12	6.8
Rocky Colavito	.281	.378	.487	181	60	210	4	211	8	12	5.4
Harmon Killebrew	.270	.382	.529	173	74	186	0	193	8	11	6.3
Brooks Robinson	.307	.364	.485	163	46	198	4	204	8	11	5.5
Bob Allison	.261	.378	.502	161	55	164	20	183	8	11	5.7
Boog Powell	.268	.375	.501	128	56	171	1	174	8	10	5.6
Al Kaline	.288	.387	.470	149	35	140	10	175	8	10	5.7

WAR/150 = wins above replacement per 150 games

bats. As a defender, Oliva had a strong arm but was terrible at catching fly balls; his fielding percentage was an atrocious .854. In 1962 he moved up to Charlotte, hit .350, and lost the batting title by .0001.

At spring training in 1963, Oliva had little hope of making the major league squad. The Twins' corner outfielders were Killebrew and Bob Allison, who both finished in the top five in slugging percentage in 1962. While the Twins recognized that Oliva was an excellent prospect, they were unlikely to move an elite player to accommodate a rookie with just one and a half years of minor league experience. If the team could not play him regularly, it made sense to send him down for another minor league season.

After Oliva hit .304 with twenty-three home runs for Dallas–Fort Worth in 1963, the Twins realized they had to get Oliva into their lineup. The team elected to shift Bob Allison, one of the American League's top players, to first base to make room for Oliva. In 1963 Allison had finished second in the league in slugging percentage and fourth in on-base percentage.

Oliva responded to the Twins' show of confidence with one of the best rookie seasons ever. He led the league in batting average, runs, hits, doubles, and total bases. His 374 total bases were the most in the American League between Mickey Mantle in 1956 and Jim Rice in 1977. He turned

Table 9.4 Tony Oliva, 1964–1975

	Age	G	AVG	OBP	SLG	R	HR	RBI	SB	RC	WAAv	WAR
1964	23	161	.323	.361	.557	109	32	94	12	121	5.2	7.1
1965	24	149	.321	.384	.491	107	16	98	19	113	5.2	6.9
1966	25	159	.307	.356	.502	99	25	87	13	107	3.9	5.8
1967	26	146	.289	.350	.463	76	17	83	11	96	3.8	5.4
1968	27	128	.289	.360	.477	54	18	68	10	77	3.3	4.7
1969	28	153	.309	.358	.496	97	24	101	10	105	3.4	5.3
1970	29	157	.325	.366	.514	96	23	107	5	114	4.6	6.5
1971	30	126	.337	.372	.546	73	22	81	4	89	4.0	5.5
1972	31	10	.321	.367	.357	1	0	1	0	3	0.1	0.2
1973	32	146	.291	.347	.410	63	16	92	2	77	0.8	2.6
1974	33	127	.285	.328	.414	43	13	57	0	55	0.0	1.5
1975	34	131	.270	.348	.378	46	13	58	0	59	0.2	1.7

RC = runs created   WAAv = wins above average   WAR = wins above replacement

in a second excellent year in 1965, again winning the batting title. Oliva also worked extremely hard on his fielding and improved enough to win a Gold Glove in 1966.

Unfortunately for the Twins and Oliva, his right knee became a chronic problem, regularly locking up on him. Despite his two consecutive batting titles, Oliva elected to have surgery on his knee at the Mayo Clinic after the 1965 season. After the 1966 season Oliva required surgery on the same knee to clean up some bone chips. Other injuries plagued Oliva as well. He separated his shoulder diving for a fly ball on August 31, 1968, and missed the rest of the season. As table 9.4 shows, Oliva remained one of the league's best players over the latter half of the 1960s, but he never again dominated as he did during his first two years.

Oliva started using a new batting stance in 1971, and the results seemed encouraging. In late June, Oliva was hitting .377 and was well ahead in the batting race. Then disaster struck: he slipped while trying to make a catch and reinjured his bad knee. Oliva hobbled through the rest of the season, taking cortisone shots in the knee before finally having surgery in late September. His spectacular start allowed him to hang on for his third batting title.

Oliva hoped to be ready for the 1972 season, but his fragile right knee did not respond. In July 1972 he had another operation that ended his season early. The introduction of the designated hitter (DH) in 1973 prolonged Oliva's career for a couple more years, and Oliva even became the first DH to hit a home run. He played a few seasons as the DH for the Twins but never again approached his pre-1972 level. Oliva was only thirty when he suffered his career-altering knee injury in 1971. He was the best player in the league for his first two years and one of the best for the next six. Had Oliva been able to deliver another few seasons similar to those of the late 1960s, he would today be remembered as one of the era's greatest players.

◇   ◇   ◇

The team also had a strong offensive supporting cast outside of its two stars. Although any superlatives must be tempered slightly due to the hitter's bias of the Twins home park, Metropolitan Stadium, the team dominated the league's run scoring in 1965. Other than a hole at second base and a disappointing year from third baseman Rich Rollins, all regulars with at least three hundred at-bats accounted for more than two wins above what a league-average hitter would have produced, as shown in table 9.5.

Shortstop Zoilo Versalles led the league in total bases and runs scored, won the Gold Glove award, and was named the league's Most Valuable Player. Along with Versalles, *The Sporting News* named Oliva, Hall, and Battey to their year-end American League all-star team. Killebrew's elbow injury kept him from being the fifth Twin on the list.

The second-base hole existed because of an unfortunate injury in 1964 to twenty-five-year-old starter Bernie Allen. A starting quarterback at Purdue in 1960, Allen took over second base for the Twins in 1962. In June 1964 he severely tore ligaments in his knee on a play he remembers with some bitterness in Dean Urdahl's *Touching Base with Our Memories.*

> Don Zimmer came in and threw a cross-body block. That's the way the game was played back then. If you did it today, they'd throw you out of the game. But I don't blame him.
> My shortstop was hot doggin' a little bit and gave me a lollipop throw. I was waitin' on the throw. I wasn't even trying to make a double play, I was stretched out like a first baseman would. Zimmer came in. It was on a hit-and-run. Just one of those things.

It did not help matters that the Twins misdiagnosed the injury as

Table 9.5 1965 Twins

	Age	G	AVG	OBP	SLG	R	HR	RBI	SB	RC	WAAv	WAR
Earl Battey, C	30	131	.297	.379	.409	36	36	60	0	67	2.3	3.5
Don Mincher, 1B	27	128	.251	.348	.509	43	22	65	1	64	2.4	3.5
Harmon Killebrew, 1B/3B	29	113	.269	.386	.501	78	25	75	0	82	3.7	5.0
Jerry Kindall, 2B	30	125	.196	.278	.289	41	6	36	2	29	-1.7	-0.5
Rich Rollins, 3B	27	140	.249	.310	.333	59	5	32	4	50	-0.7	0.8
Zoilo Versalles, SS	25	160	.273	.322	.462	126	19	77	27	108	3.3	5.4
Bob Allison, LF	30	135	.233	.345	.445	71	23	78	10	76	2.4	3.9
Jimmie Hall, CF	27	148	.285	.350	.464	81	20	86	14	90	3.2	4.8
Tony Oliva, RF	24	149	.321	.384	.491	107	16	98	19	113	5.2	6.9

RC = runs created   WAAv = wins above average   WAR = wins above replacement

stretched ligaments. After receiving a second, independent opinion that provided a correct diagnosis, Allen had doctors outside of the Twins organization perform the surgery. After finally agreeing to pay for the operation, Griffith cut Allen's salary by the cost of the procedure.

The 1965 Twins team also boasted an excellent and deep pitching staff. Six pitchers started at least nine games; every one of them had an ERA below the league average despite pitching in one of the league's better hitter's parks. Additionally, between 1963 and 1970 every one of the six would win twenty games in a season at least once.

In 1965 the team hired controversial pitching coach Johnny Sain. Much of the hullabaloo surrounding Sain derived from his tendency to separate the pitchers from the position players. Many pitchers he coached were his ardent students, the Twins' Jim Kaat in particular. Sain believed in working his best pitchers, and the Twins' top two hurlers, Kaat and Jim "Mudcat" Grant, finished first and second in games started. In fact, the duo started half of the team's games.

With 283 lifetime wins, Kaat would not be a poor choice for the Hall of Fame. In 1965, he finished 18–11 while leading the league in complete games and innings pitched. The next year, Kaat jumped to 25–13 and surely would have won the Cy Young Award if it had been bestowed in both leagues; Sandy Koufax won the major league's only Cy Young Award that year with the last of his stellar years. It was not until 1967 that the writers began handing out separate awards for the two leagues. *The Sporting News* did name a pitcher of the year for each league, and it selected Kaat in 1966. In 1965 the award went to Grant for his 21–7 record and league-leading .750 winning percentage. Grant, acquired from Cleveland the year before after a number of fair years, broke through in 1965 to have his career-best season.

Curveball pitcher Camilo Pascual was the third Twin hurler with over twenty starts in 1965. Pascual led the league in strikeouts from 1961 to 1963 and finished second in 1964; he won at least twenty games in both 1962 and 1963. Unfortunately, after a great start to the 1965 season (winning his first eight decisions), Pascual tore a muscle in his back near his shoulder. He tried to pitch through it for a month before finally undergoing surgery in July. Although there was some concern he might be out for the rest of the year, Pascual made it back by early September but managed to win only one more game after his injury. He also started game three of the World Series, but with little success. Thirty-one at the time, Pascual never again regained his preinjury form, pitching more than 165 innings in a season only once more in his career.

The other three hurlers who started at least nine games were twenty-year-old Dave Boswell, twenty-one-year-old Jim Merritt, and swingman Jim Perry. In 1966 Boswell became a rotation regular with an ERA below 3.35 every year until he won twenty games in 1969. In game two of the 1969 American League Championship Series with the score still 0–0 in the tenth, Boswell felt something "let go" in his arm. He never pitched regularly again.

Merritt started at least twenty-eight games from 1966 through 1968; after the 1968 season the Twins traded him to Cincinnati for shortstop Leo Cardenas. Perry was an effective starter and reliever for many years who blossomed when finally given a chance for full-time duty in 1969. Al Worthington, with twenty-one (unofficial) saves and a 2.13 ERA, anchored a good bullpen.

That the Twins could put together such a strong season despite a number of injuries made its accomplishment all the more impressive. Besides the injury to Pascual, Killebrew's elbow injury caused him to miss nearly two months. Other, lesser injuries slowed several players as well. Bob Allison missed a portion of June with a fracture to his wrist, which may have continued to hinder him after his return. Dave Boswell missed a significant portion of the middle of the season with mononucleosis. Oliva suffered through an injury to the middle finger of his right hand that required surgery after the season. Battey missed a number of games due to miscellaneous injuries. The future appeared bright for a team that could overcome these injuries and still win 102 games.

◇ ◇ ◇

The 1966 Twins started slowly and found themselves just 35–43 on July 3. At this point Mele's job was in some jeopardy, but a two-year contract signed after the 1965 season and a 54–30 finish to the 1966 season to capture second place probably saved his position. Mudcat Grant, the reigning pitcher of the year, was only 5–12 at the All-Star break but 8–1 over the second half of the season.

Once again the Twins were bitten by the injury bug, but this time the club could not overcome the setbacks. Four of the previous year's regulars, Allison, Hall, Battey, and Versalles, played fewer than 136 games. The pitching also suffered several key injuries. Starter Camilo Pascual missed much of the summer with a sore arm and relief ace Al Worthington missed several weeks after getting his pitching hand caught in his garage door.

During the following off-season the team made two significant trades. In the first, the club sent Hall and Mincher to the California Angels for pitcher Dean Chance and shortstop Jackie Hernandez. The latter was a weak hitter who would play little in the coming year. Chance, notorious for enjoying the nightlife, was the key to the deal. He had won the Cy Young Award in 1964 but had fallen off since. In 1966, he finished just 12–17, although his ERA was still a respectable 3.08. In the other deal, the Twins acquired relief ace Ron Kline from the Washington Senators for Bernie Allen and Camilo Pascual. Kline led the league in saves in 1965 and sported an ERA below 2.65 in both 1965 and 1966.

For the 1967 season the Twins also added Rod Carew, a player from their own system they hoped would plug the persistent hole at second base. The trades, the addition of Carew, and the return to health of the

1966 regulars made the Twins favorites to win the pennant in a number of quarters.

The 1967 AL pennant race turned out to be one of the most famous of all time. In the end, the Boston Red Sox edged out Minnesota and Detroit by one game and Chicago by three. With the Twins at 25–25 on June 9, Griffith finally jettisoned Mele and surprised everyone by naming Triple-A Denver manager Cal Ermer to take charge. Ermer, whose major league experience consisted of one game at second base for the 1947 Senators and one year as a coach for the Orioles, had his hands full with a veteran team riven by several factions that had tasted success. Nevertheless, the team responded by finishing 66–46 under Ermer over the remainder of the 1967 season.

The Twins headed into the final weekend of the season in Boston with a one-game lead over the Red Sox and with Detroit's flag hopes also still alive; the club ultimately needed to win one of the two games against Boston to clinch the pennant. On Saturday the team started Jim Kaat, who had won seven consecutive games down the stretch. With the Twins leading 1–0 in the third, Kaat snapped a ligament in his elbow and the bullpen failed to hold the lead. Dean Chance started the final game of the season on Sunday. The Twins again jumped out front early and led 2–0 after five innings. Once again, however, the team could not hold on. The Red Sox won the game and the pennant. Griffith remembered that final weekend unhappily: "I was so sure going into Boston with Kaat and Dean Chance going in that we would win both games. And they both got hurt. . . . 'Course I'm still trying to figure out why Ermer put in that knuckleballer (Kline) in relief in that last game."

In his book on the 1967 season, *Down to the Wire,* Jeff Miller suggests that the Twins players were frustrated the club made no moves during the year to bolster the team while their competitors improved throughout the season. The Red Sox picked up Jerry Adair, Gary Bell, and Elston Howard, all quality veterans who played a large role in the team's pennant drive, and then signed Ken Harrelson in a reaction to Tony Conigliaro's eye injury. The White Sox acquired Don McMahon, Ken Boyer, and Rocky Colavito. The Tigers obtained veteran Eddie Mathews, who played a key role down the stretch at both third and first base. In contrast, the Twins made no major in-season moves. One regular commented: "We got a $35,000 bench."

The Twins had received excellent years from their newcomers. Carew won the Rookie of the Year award, and Chance won twenty and threw two no-hitters (one rain-shortened). One reason the team fell just short was because they had several positions from which they received basically no offensive production (see table 9.6).

The Twins received inadequate offensive performances from their third basemen, catchers, and shortstops. Versalles' WAR of -1.7 in 581 at-bats (he was nearly two games worse than a replacement-level hitter would have been) was especially harmful to the team's offense.

In 1968 the team slumped to seventh place with a record of 79–83. Kaat started the season on the disabled list as a result of his arm injury in Boston at the end of the previous season. Harmon Killebrew missed significant time after suffering a brutal hamstring injury, thought to be career threatening, in the All-Star Game. The team also failed to address satisfactorily any of their three offensively weak positions. During the off-season the club had traded Grant and Versalles to the Dodgers for catcher Johnny Roseboro and pitchers Bob Miller and Ron Perranoski. Roseboro was a slight improvement behind the plate, but the shortstop play was even worse than it had been in 1967.

At the end of the 1968 season the team fired manager Cal Ermer and promoted coach Billy Martin to the first of what would be his many managerial jobs. During the off-season the Twins also finally shored up the shortstop position by trading pitcher Jim Merritt to the Reds for Leo Cardenas.

In 1969 the American League divided into two six-team divisions; the Twins won ninety-seven games and the newly created AL West division. The team's offense rebounded and led the league in runs. Solving its third-base problem, Minnesota moved Killebrew across the diamond and played Rich Reese at first. Reese responded with what would be the best year of his career. Roseboro rebounded to hit .263, and the Twins lineup had no holes. Martin brought out the best in his pitching staff. Despite its ballpark, the team finished third in ERA, and Jim Perry and Dave Boswell both won twenty games.

Unfortunately the Twins failed to win the pennant as the Baltimore Orioles swept them in the American League Championship Series. A truly great team, the Orioles won 109 games, finished second to the Twins in runs scored, and dominated the league in pitching. The 1969 ALCS was actually closer than the sweep implies; the Twins lost the first two games by one run in the bottom of the ninth and tenth innings, respectively.

After the season Griffith caused a large commotion in the Twin Cities when he fired the popular Martin. Not surprisingly, Martin's and Griffith's personalities had not meshed. Griffith was also unhappy with Martin's decision to start Miller in the final ALCS game instead of Kaat, as well as

Table 9.6 1967 Twins

	G	AVG	OBP	SLG	R	HR	RBI	SB	RC	WAAv	WAR
Jerry Zimmerman, C	104	.167	.244	.192	13	1	12	0	7	-2.5	-1.7
Russ Nixon, C	74	.235	.309	.300	16	1	22	0	17	-0.4	0.2
Harmon Killebrew, 1B	163	.269	.413	.558	105	44	113	1	134	7.6	9.3
Rod Carew, 2B	137	.292	.342	.409	66	8	51	5	72	1.5	3.1
Rich Rollins, 3B	109	.245	.306	.342	31	6	39	1	36	-0.4	0.7
Zoilo Versalles, SS	160	.200	.250	.282	63	6	50	5	37	-3.7	-1.7
Bob Allison, LF	153	.258	.357	.470	73	24	75	6	92	3.8	5.3
Ted Uhlaender, CF	133	.258	.285	.381	41	6	49	4	47	0.0	1.3
Tony Oliva, RF	146	.289	.350	.463	76	17	83	11	96	3.8	5.4
Cesar Tovar, UT	164	.267	.328	.365	98	6	47	19	86	1.2	3.2

RC = runs created   WAAv = wins above average   WAR = wins above replacement

Martin's card and record playing on the flight home after the Baltimore losses. For the 1970 season Griffith brought in veteran manager Bill Rigney.

The team responded with another western division title and ninety-eight wins. The team that won the 1965 pennant, however, had now completely turned over beyond its stars. Only regulars Oliva and Killebrew and pitchers Jim Perry and Jim Kaat remained from the World Series team. All four had excellent years in 1970 and were the best players on the club that year. Unfortunately, the pitchers the Twins brought in behind the big two (with the notable exception of Bert Blyleven) did not develop. The Orioles again swept the Twins in the ALCS, and none of the games was particularly close.

The 1971 season brought the Twins' run to an end. The team slumped all the way to fifth in the division and a record of only 74–86. Killebrew was now thirty-five, and although he led the league in RBI, he was clearly on the decline. Oliva's knee injury ended his years as a great player. Perry was also thirty-five, and his 4.23 ERA did not portend well for the future. Other than Carew and Blyleven, the team had no stars coming in behind its greats from the 1960s.

◇   ◇   ◇

Why did the 1960s Minnesota Twins, blessed with excellent young front-line hitting talent and an extremely deep and strong pitching staff, fail to win another pennant? Below we take a look at several factors that conspired to prevent the Twins from capturing another title or two.

The Emergence of the Baltimore Orioles. The Orioles, who had finished eight games back in 1965, added three new regular position players for 1966. Most significantly, they acquired right fielder Frank Robinson, one of the top players in baseball, from the Cincinnati Reds. Upon his entrance into the American League, Robinson became the league's best player, winning the Triple Crown. In addition, the Orioles brought in two twenty-three-year-olds who would develop into pretty good ballplayers: catcher Andy Etchebarren and second baseman Davey Johnson. The Orioles also added a future Hall of Fame pitcher, Jim Palmer. Palmer first pitched regularly in 1966 but was essentially out of the majors for both the 1967 and 1968 seasons because of arm problems. He came back in 1969 and by 1970 was the best pitcher in the league.

Robinson and Palmer would anchor an Oriole club that by the end of the 1960s became one of the top minidynasties of the expansion era. In their book *Baseball Dynasties*, Rob Neyer and Eddie Epstein each rank baseball's greatest teams; the two ranked the 1970 Orioles as the second and third greatest team, respectively, of all time. From 1969 through 1971 Baltimore won three straight American League pennants and more than a hundred games every year. Losing two consecutive playoff series to the Orioles was no disgrace.

The Surprisingly Rapid Decline of Several Regulars. Baseball research has shown that most players (nonpitchers) typically peak in their late twenties, with the most common peak year being age twenty-seven. Star players typically retain much of their value into their thirties. Despite the relatively young age of the Twins' key offensive players, they all—other than the Oliva and Killebrew—declined quickly and dramatically. Although showing tables of statistics can often lead to more confusion than insight, the following career batting lines of several of the Twins illustrate this surprisingly rapid falloff:

- In the early 1960s, Jimmie Hall was not held in particularly high regard as a prospect. He spent six months in the army in 1961 and an-

Table 9.7 Jimmie Hall, 1963–1970

	Age	Team	G	AVG	OBP	SLG	R	HR	RBI	SB	RC	WAAv	WAR
1963	25	MIN	156	.260	.343	.521	88	33	80	3	87	2.8	4.4
1964	26	MIN	149	.282	.341	.480	61	25	75	5	77	2.0	3.6
1965	**27**	**MIN**	**148**	**.285**	**.350**	**.464**	**81**	**20**	**86**	**14**	**90**	**3.2**	**4.8**
1966	28	MIN	120	.239	.303	.449	52	20	47	1	46	0.2	1.4
1967	29	CAL	129	.249	.321	.404	54	16	55	4	53	1.4	2.6
1968	30	TOT	99	.207	.285	.262	19	2	16	2	17	-0.8	-0.1
1969	31	TOT	95	.224	.287	.337	23	3	27	9	25	-0.5	0.3
1970	32	TOT	67	.165	.224	.278	9	2	5	0	4	-0.8	-0.5

RC = runs created   WAAv = wins above average   WAR = wins above replacement

other ten months in 1962, retarding his development. He hit pretty well in very limited minor league duty in 1962 and extremely well in the Florida Instructional League after the season, where he edged out Oliva for the batting title. Hall made the Twins as a reserve outfielder in 1963 and received some playing time after an injury to Allison. Mele decided to keep Hall in the lineup, shifting him to center field and benching Lenny Green. Part of Hall's decline has been attributed to his never fully recovering from a beaning, but whatever the reason, he quickly turned mediocre after his stellar 1965 season. (See table 9.7.)

- In third baseman Rich Rollins's first year as a regular in 1962, he challenged for the batting title, hitting around .320 for much of the year before slumping to .298 and a tenth-place finish. That summer Rollins actually led all American League players in votes for the All-Star game. The next year Rollins hit .307 to finish third in the batting race. Still only twenty-five in 1963, Rollins never again put together seasons approaching his first two, although he remained a decent regular for a couple of years. (See table 9.8.)
- Opposing players often taunted Bob Allison by calling him "Mr. America." Exceptionally good-looking, Allison was a tremendous all-around athlete. He attended college on a football scholarship and claims he could have been a professional football player. Allison was known as an extremely competitive person, especially where money was concerned. A natural leader with a boyish charm, Allison became friendly with the Griffith family. Allison was already thirty,

Table 9.8 Rich Rollins, 1962–1970

	Age	Team	G	AVG	OBP	SLG	R	HR	RBI	SB	RC	WAAv	WAR
1962	24	MIN	159	.298	.379	.428	96	16	96	3	105	2.4	4.5
1963	25	MIN	136	.307	.360	.444	75	16	61	2	82	2.2	3.9
1964	26	MIN	148	.270	.335	.406	87	12	68	2	76	.6	2.5
1965	**27**	**MIN**	**140**	**.249**	**.310**	**.333**	**59**	**5**	**32**	**4**	**50**	**-0.7**	**0.8**
1966	28	MIN	90	.245	.290	.390	30	10	40	0	28	-0.5	0.4
1967	29	MIN	109	.245	.306	.342	31	6	39	1	36	-0.4	0.7
1968	30	MIN	93	.241	.287	.355	14	6	30	3	19	-0.3	0.4
1969	31	SEA	58	.225	.271	.326	15	4	21	2	16	-0.6	0.0
1970	32	TOT	56	.221	.284	.324	9	2	9	0	6	-0.2	0.0

RC = runs created   WAAv = wins above average   WAR = wins above replacement

Table 9.9 Bob Allison, 1959–1970

	Age	Team	G	AVG	OBP	SLG	R	HR	RBI	SB	RC	WAAv	WAR
1959	24	WAS	150	.261	.334	.482	83	30	85	13	90	1.6	3.6
1960	25	WAS	144	.251	.370	.413	79	15	69	11	80	1.5	3.2
1961	26	MIN	159	.245	.367	.450	83	29	105	2	93	1.1	3.1
1962	27	MIN	149	.266	.372	.511	102	29	102	8	101	3.2	4.9
1963	28	MIN	148	.271	.381	.533	99	35	91	6	107	4.8	6.5
1964	29	MIN	149	.287	.406	.553	90	32	86	10	106	5.4	6.9
1965	**30**	**MIN**	**135**	**.233**	**.345**	**.445**	**71**	**23**	**78**	**10**	**76**	**2.4**	**3.9**
1966	31	MIN	70	.220	.348	.411	34	8	19	6	28	0.8	1.3
1967	32	MIN	153	.258	.357	.470	73	24	75	6	92	3.8	5.3
1968	33	MIN	145	.247	.325	.456	63	22	52	9	66	1.7	3.2
1969	34	MIN	81	.228	.333	.418	18	8	27	2	24	-0.1	0.6
1970	35	MIN	47	.208	.345	.319	15	1	7	1	9	0.0	0.3

RC = runs created   WAAv = wins above average   WAR = wins above replacement

Table 9.10 Zoilo Versalles, 1961–1971

	Age	Team	G	AVG	OBP	SLG	R	HR	RBI	SB	RC	WAAv	WAR
1961	21	MIN	129	.280	.315	.390	65	7	53	16	62	-0.8	1.0
1962	22	MIN	160	.241	.290	.373	69	17	67	5	59	-2.0	0.0
1963	23	MIN	159	.261	.303	.401	74	10	54	7	73	-0.1	1.9
1964	24	MIN	160	.259	.312	.431	94	20	64	14	87	1.1	3.1
1965	**25**	**MIN**	**160**	**.273**	**.322**	**.462**	**126**	**19**	**77**	**27**	**108**	**3.3**	**5.4**
1966	26	MIN	137	.249	.308	.346	73	7	36	10	57	-1.0	0.8
1967	27	MIN	160	.200	.250	.282	63	6	50	5	37	-3.7	-1.7
1968	28	LA	122	.196	.245	.266	29	2	24	6	21	-2.2	-1.0
1969	29	TOT	103	.236	.301	.305	30	1	19	4	27	-1.0	0.0
1971	31	ATL	66	.191	.234	.325	21	5	22	2	12	-1.5	-0.8

RC = runs created   WAAv = wins above average   WAR = wins above replacement

and part of his 1966 decline can be attributed to a broken bone in his hand, but it is still surprising that Allison had only one really good season remaining. (See table 9.9.)

- Early in Zoilo Versalles' career he became known as a hot dog. These early years included a swagger and moodiness that masked the fears of a young man in a strange country. Coach Billy Martin took an individual interest in Versalles and the two became very close. By 1967, only two years removed from his MVP year, Versalles was one of the worst starting regulars in the league; both his on-base and slugging percentages fell below .285. (See table 9.10.)
- Along with Johnny Callison, John Romano, and Norm Cash, Earl Battey was one of four excellent young players traded away by the Chicago White Sox after their 1959 pennant when they tried to maintain their perch by acquiring veterans. Battey gained a reputation as an excellent defender and won three Gold Gloves. He was particularly known for a strong arm and soft hands. Battey was a thirty-year-old catcher who had been worked hard, so his decline is not as surprising as the others. Battey suffered from goiter and weight gain that along with chronically sore knees probably led to a premature end to his career. But the suddenness of his falling from one of the league's top catchers to being out of the league in two years would have surprised almost any team. (See table 9.11.)

Table 9.11 Earl Battey, 1957–1967

	Age	Team	G	AVG	OBP	SLG	R	HR	RBI	SB	RC	WAAv	WAR
1957	22	CHI	48	.174	.246	.322	12	3	6	0	7	-0.9	-0.5
1958	23	CHI	68	.226	.330	.417	24	8	26	1	24	0.3	0.9
1959	24	CHI	26	.219	.306	.391	9	2	7	0	8	0.0	0.2
1960	25	WAS	137	.270	.349	.427	49	15	60	4	68	0.9	2.5
1961	26	MIN	133	.302	.378	.470	70	17	55	3	78	1.5	3.1
1962	27	MIN	148	.280	.351	.393	58	11	57	0	71	0.1	1.9
1963	28	MIN	147	.285	.371	.476	64	26	84	0	86	2.8	4.3
1964	29	MIN	131	.272	.354	.407	33	12	52	1	51	0.1	1.5
1965	**30**	**MIN**	**131**	**.297**	**.379**	**.409**	**36**	**6**	**60**	**0**	**67**	**2.3**	**3.5**
1966	31	MIN	115	.255	.339	.327	30	4	34	4	41	-0.3	0.9
1967	32	MIN	48	.165	.254	.211	6	0	8	0	5	-1.0	-0.6

RC = runs created   WAAv = wins above average   WAR = wins above replacement

Obviously, knowing whether a dip in production is a one-time slip due to an injury or the start of a long-term slide requires a difficult judgment. The Twins' offense declined to between third and fifth in runs scored from 1966 through 1968 as they tried to respond to the falloff of more than half of their offense.

By 1969, the Twins had reacted to these problems. Ted Uhlaender and Cesar Tovar manned the outfield with Tony Oliva. The team had acquired veteran Leo Cardenas to hold down the shortstop position for 1969 after suffering through Jackie Hernandez and Ron Clark hitting .176 and .185 in 1968. Another veteran, Johnny Roseboro, was imported to catch in 1968. Unfortunately, these moves turned out to be too little, too late; by the 1969 season, the Baltimore Orioles had constructed the juggernaut that closed the window of opportunity for the rest of the American League.

Constant Position Shifts. The Twins had two players changing positions so often that it must have contributed to the difficulty of addressing the team's needs and slumping players. Although defensive versatility is valuable in the abstract, the Twins' continual changes inhibited making sound long-term decisions based on which positions needed improvement. As table 9.12 indicates, Harmon Killebrew changed positions be-

Table 9.12 Harmon Killebrew, Games by Position

	1B	3B	LF
1959	0	150	4
1960	71	65	0
1961	119	45	2
1962	4	0	151
1963	0	0	137
1964	0	0	157
1965	72	44	1
1966	42	107	18
1967	160	3	0
1968	77	11	0
1969	80	105	0
1970	28	138	0

tween first base, third base, and the outfield annually, depending on the Twins' personnel situation.

The Twins never really knew whether they needed a third baseman or a first baseman. In the spring of 1965, Killebrew moved from left field to first base. Over the first two months of the season he also shifted over to third several times. He then volunteered to move to third base full time to get Don Mincher's bat in the lineup on a regular basis. In 1967, after trading Don Mincher, the Twins moved Killebrew back to first. After Killebrew ruptured a muscle stretching for a throw in the 1968 All-Star Game, the Twins installed perennial prospect Rich Reese, now twenty-six years old, at first. Reese hit no more than adequately over the second half of the season, but the Twins kept Killebrew at third and Reese as the starting first baseman against right-handed pitching for 1969 (Killebrew still played in 80 games at first, Reese 117). Reese actually had a very strong 1969 season but never again hit above .261 or topped ten home runs.

Killebrew, while below average as a fielder at third, was not a critical liability. Manager Sam Mele noted in *Touching Base with Our Memories:* "Harmon was a better fielder than people think. He wasn't fast, but he was quick. His initial moves were good. His hands were quick. I had him for some games in the outfield, but he was better in the infield." This recollection is interesting because one of Griffith's criticisms of Mele involved his shifting Killebrew to the outfield.

Table 9.13 Cesar Tovar, Games by Position

	2B	3B	SS	OF
1966	76	0	31	24
1967	36	70	9	74
1968	18	75	35	78
1969	41	20	0	113
1970	8	4	0	151

As strange as Killebrew's odyssey around the diamond appears, that of Cesar Tovar was even more bizarre. Tovar first appeared regularly in 1966 as a candidate to fill the second-base hole, but played at least twenty games at third and in the outfield as well. Table 9.13 summarizes Tovar's first five years as a regular.

In 1967, Tovar led the league in at-bats while appearing at no defensive position more than seventy-four times. At the end of the season, one Minneapolis sportswriter cast a vote for Tovar as MVP, thus preventing Triple Crown winner Carl Yastrzemski from having a unanimous election. One year of Tovar-like versatility can be extremely valuable to a team filling in-season holes resulting from injuries or slumps, but when it shows up over an extended period of time, it more likely signifies a team unable or unwilling to make decisive player personnel decisions.

Mediocre Defense. The Twins never really exhibited the fielding prowess often demonstrated by top teams. Table 9.14 below summarizes the club's fielding percentage and defensive efficiency ratio, or DER (as discussed in chapter 2, the fraction of balls in play that the team turns into outs).

Over the three-year period 1966 through 1968, the Twins finished in the top half of the league in either statistic only once. In 1967, when they needed only one more victory, they may have been the worst defensive team in the American League. One cannot help but feel that the constant position shifts did not help this situation.

The Strange Case of Jim Perry. During the 1963 season the Twins made a great trade, landing Jim Perry from Cleveland for Jack Kralick, a good pitcher who had tossed a no-hitter a couple of years earlier. After a decent 1964 season, Kralick never again won more than five games. Perry currently holds the Twins career record for lowest ERA (minimum 750 IP) and finished with a career total of 215 wins.

Over Perry's first two years in the majors, 1959 and 1960, he won thir-

Table 9.14 Twins Fielding Statistics, 1964–1970

	Pct	Rank	DER	Rank
1964	.977	9	.708	7
1965	.973	10	.721	3
1966	.977	7	.720	2
1967	.978	6	.700	10
1968	.973	10	.712	8
1969	.977	8	.707	8
1970	.980	4	.712	6

ty games while leading the league in wins, winning percentage, starts, and shutouts in 1960. He slipped a little over the next couple of years, but with the help of new pitching coach Johnny Sain and a new curveball he rejuvenated his career with the Twins. For some reason, the Twins failed to put Perry into the rotation and persisted in keeping him as a swing-man during the four years from 1965 to 1968. Only once during those four years did Perry start more than twenty games, despite having an ERA better than that of any other rotation regular in three of the four years.

Perry again began the season in 1969 splitting his time between start-ing and relieving. Through the end of May he had started only five games. At that point, Martin moved Perry into the rotation, and he almost im-mediately became the rotation anchor. For the rest of the season Perry started almost exactly every fourth day. Perry pitched well after his inser-tion into the rotation and finished the season 20–6; the next year he won the Cy Young Award with a 24–12 record.

Team Turmoil. How dissension off the field affects team performance on the field has long been debated. The Oakland Athletics of the 1970s fought among themselves and with their management, but they won three straight World Series. On the other hand, many teams that have failed to capture a pennant have had their team chemistry, however defined, re-ceive much of the blame.

The turbulence on the Twins began in 1965, with a split in the coaching ranks pitting Billy Martin against pitching coach Johnny Sain and bullpen coach Hal Naragon. Both Sain and Martin had strong personalities and a desire to control their respective spheres on the team. In May, Sain asked Mele to ask Martin to refrain from criticizing the pitchers. After Martin again criticized a hurler in July, he and Sain clashed while Mele said nothing. When Sain later gave advice to nonpitchers, Martin felt Sain was caught doing the same thing he had been accused of.

During 1966 the working relationship between Sain, Martin, and Mele continued to deteriorate. When Griffith backed his manager by jettisoning Sain and Naragon after the season, Jim Kaat publicly lambasted the decision. Mele, who survived the team's slow start in 1966, would not survive another season.

The switch from Mele to Ermer in 1967 did not quell the Twins' disharmony and factionalism. The turbulence came to the fore during a contentious clubhouse meeting on September 29, with the pennant still in doubt, to determine the team's split of its World Series money. The team first voted against giving Mele a share. When the pro-Mele faction argued that Ermer should not be entitled to a share either, more havoc ensued. In the end, Mele would get nothing and Ermer would get a full share. The commissioner's office expressed displeasure at this outcome but took no action. Ermer would not survive the collapse to seventh place in 1968.

As he did throughout his career, Billy Martin while with the Twins found himself at the center of several controversies. In 1966, he became involved in an altercation with traveling secretary Howard Fox on a team plane trip. When the two arrived at the hotel, the dispute escalated into blows. Named manager for the 1969 season, Martin figured prominently in a brawl that season at a Detroit nightspot. Pitcher Dave Boswell confronted pitching coach Art Fowler outside the bar over a perceived injustice. When Bob Allison interceded, Boswell knocked him down, at which point some of the bar patrons joined in the fun. Boswell remembers Martin adding his licks during the brawl, after which Boswell required fifty stitches. Nevertheless, Boswell recalls Martin fondly as his best manager. Boswell was quick-tempered, wild, and a little bit flaky. He had grown up in gangs and liked guns. Carew noted that he slept wearing a motorcycle helmet, leather jacket, and dark glasses.

Racial Divisions. The Twins organization deserves a lot of credit for the racial and cultural makeup of the organization. One of the most integrated teams in the league, the club had quite a few African American and Latin American ballplayers. Unlike the St. Louis Cardinals, another of the more integrated teams of the era, however, the Twins often had less-than-harmonious racial relations.

In June 1967 in Detroit, a city steaming with racial tension, Boswell, who is white, was playing with his guns (unloaded) on the team bus. Oliva told him to put them away, and Boswell responded, "Well, you guys can play with guns in Cuba; why can't we play with guns here?" The situation escalated from there and a tense confrontation developed between several white and African American and Latin American players.

Ermer, new to the job and with little managerial experience, failed to address the issue to the satisfaction of some of the African American and Latin American players. Part of this perception stemmed from a team meeting at the hotel when Ermer encouraged the players to discuss the matter, and he failed to take a stand against several of the more egregious comments from a white player.

The racial divisions, however, should not be overemphasized; black-white tension was not unique to either baseball or the Twins. Nevertheless, the stress of the racial issues added to an already divided club. Mudcat Grant, for example, felt Killebrew and Allison received special treatment and was clearly unhappy with the attitude of some of the team's white players.

◇ ◇ ◇

The move from Washington in 1961 offered a fresh start for Griffith. During their first decade in Minnesota, the Twins actually led the American League in attendance. Griffith and his family organization proved astute judges of talent during the 1960s. Most of the club's trades during the period landed more talent than was surrendered and other personnel moves typically introduced capable players onto the roster. By 1965 the team's assembled club was both talented and deep, and the Twins cruised to a 102-win season and the American League pennant.

Unfortunately, a number of factors, some controllable by the club and some outside its influence, combined to thwart a second pennant over the last half of the decade. The Twins must have been surprised by the swift and widespread decline of a number of their supporting position players.

A peculiar organizational indecision over how to best use Killebrew, Tovar, and Perry added to the difficulty of filling the holes caused by the rapid falloff of some of the regulars. Turmoil both on and off the field may also have contributed to the difficulty of maintaining a pennant winner. In the end, the Twins could never quite take advantage of the three-year window between their first pennant at the end of the Yankee era and the emergence of the Orioles' minidynasty.

10

PLAYER GROWTH AND DECLINE: PATTERNS IN AGING

On December 9, 1965, Cincinnati Reds general manager Bill DeWitt pulled the trigger on one of the most infamous baseball deals ever made. By sending superstar Frank Robinson, described by the Red brain trust as "an old thirty," to the Baltimore Orioles for pitchers Milt Pappas and Jack Baldshun and outfielder Dick Simpson, DeWitt was forever linked to this oft-maligned trade. A lifelong baseball executive, DeWitt sported an otherwise strong track record as a baseball general manager: after taking over the Reds job in the fall of 1960 from Gabe Paul, he made a number of astute moves and Cincinnati won the 1961 pennant. Unfortunately, DeWitt added the Robinson trade to his legacy by misjudging Robinson's remaining productivity.

Understanding how ballplayers age is one of the key elements of team building. At what point does a player start to become less productive because of age or the accumulation of injuries? Many star players, like Hack Wilson in the 1930s and Jim Rice and Dale Murphy in the 1980s, tailed off fairly quickly upon reaching their early thirties. These three star players combined for just 2,501 at-bats after the season in which they turned thirty-three; Robinson alone had 2,461.

There is no surefire answer for determining how much production a particular player has remaining. Teams spend millions on scouting departments and front-office personnel to evaluate major league players, both their own and those on other teams for possible acquisition. Sometimes, however, additional insights can be gained from other disciplines.

In his fascinating book *Predictions: Society's Telltale Signature Reveals the Past and Forecasts the Future,* Dr. Theodore Modis, a physicist turned management science consultant, makes the case that the life cycle of a disparate assortment of phenomena, including the birthrate of women, the number of compositions by Brahms, and the lives claimed by the Red Brigades can be modeled by an S-curve.

An S-curve is a mathematical function that forms a line in the shape of an S when its data points are plotted on a graph. As will be apparent in the graphs in this chapter, the data plot typically looks like an S that has been straightened out. The formula has several constants (called coefficients), which are derived from the data to best fit the S-curve. Additional information on the mathematics of the function can be found in appendix 4.

Essentially, Modis's thesis boils down to two key observations. The first is that "many phenomenon go through a life cycle: birth, growth, maturity, decline, and death. . . . The element in common is the way in which the growth takes place; for example, things come to an end slowly and continuously, not unlike the way they came into existence. . . . The phases of natural growth proceed along S-curves, cascading from one to the next."

Modis's second realization concerns predictability: "There is a promise implicit in a process of natural growth, which is guaranteed by nature: The growth cycle will not stop halfway through. . . . If I have the first half as a given, I can predict the future; if I am faced with the second half, I can deduce the past."

To test whether the theory is valid for baseball players, we apply Modis's S-curve methodology to a number of major league ballplayers. The statistic used as a proxy for a player's output or contribution is his runs created (calculated using the most basic runs created formula).

To illustrate a baseball player's career, two curves based on the player's runs created are drawn on a graph. In one, career runs created are modeled by an S-curve. The S-curve "is derived from the law which states that the rate of growth is proportional to both the amount of growth already accomplished and the amount of growth remaining to be accomplished," Modis states. The terminology is taken from biology, where it refers, for example, to the changing height or weight of an animal at a given point in time. Growth in this instance is measured by career runs created.

In the other graph, a seasonal runs created curve representing the player's life cycle (defined as "coming into and out of existence" in major league baseball) is drawn. Often represented by a bell-shaped curve, the "concept of a life cycle has been borrowed by psychologists, historians,

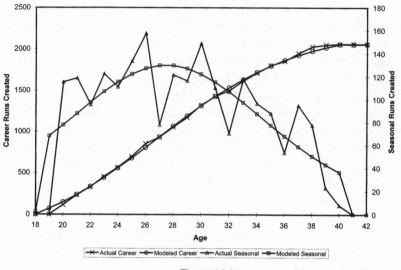

Figure 10.1

businessman and others to describe the growth of a process, a product, a company, a country, a planet, " Modis says.

The first question is whether or not Modis's first observation holds: does such a model fit the career of a baseball player? As an example, an S-curve and life cycle curve have been fitted to Frank Robinson's career in the graph in figure 10.1. The curves depict the shape of Robinson's career using his runs created.

Robinson's career appears well suited to description by an S-curve. Obviously there is some deviation from his exact career because of natural and injury-induced fluctuation. For example, Robinson had very strong rookie and sophomore seasons that the model underestimates. He also had a couple of down years in mid-career—particularly an off year in 1963 at age twenty-seven when he also suffered a thirty-stitch spike wound in early September—that the model cannot account for. Overall, however, the model captures the shape and output of Robinson's career quite well and correctly recognizes that his career ended at age forty.

To provide a more detailed numerical picture of the fit, table 10.1 presents the data points used to generate the graph. For each year of Robinson's career as a regular until its end, the first column gives his age and is followed by three columns with some standard statistics: at-bats, batting average, and home runs. The next two columns reflect his runs created that season as calculated from his actual statistics and the runs created as

Table 10.1 Frank Robinson's S-Curve Data Points

Age	AB	Avg	HR	RC	RC_M	RC_Car	RC_Car_M
18	0		0	0	3	0	3
19	0		0	0	68	0	71
20	572	.290	38	115	78	115	149
21	611	.322	29	119	88	234	236
22	554	.269	31	96	98	330	334
23	540	.311	36	123	107	452	441
24	464	.297	31	111	115	564	557
25	545	.323	37	134	122	697	679
26	609	.342	39	158	127	855	806
27	482	.259	21	78	130	933	936
28	568	.306	29	122	130	1054	1066
29	582	.296	33	117	127	1171	1193
30	576	.316	49	149	122	1320	1315
31	479	.311	30	110	115	1430	1430
32	421	.268	15	70	107	1500	1537
33	539	.308	32	118	97	1618	1635
34	471	.306	25	97	88	1715	1722
35	455	.281	28	88	78	1803	1800
36	342	.251	19	54	68	1857	1868
37	534	.266	30	95	59	1952	1927
38	457	.245	22	78	51	2029	1977
39	118	.237	9	23	43	2053	2057
40	67	.224	3	8	36	2061	2057

RC_M = seasonal runs created estimated by the model

RC_Car_M = cumulative career runs created estimated by the model

estimated by the model (RC_M). The last two columns show Robinson's career or cumulative runs created through the indicated season and the career total as estimated by the model (RC_Car_M).

As a reminder, runs created should be interpreted on the same scale as runs and RBI. A mental note should also be made for the run context of the era and any dramatic park effects. For example, in 1968 Willie McCovey led the NL in RBI with 108, while no one else exceeded 100; in 1999 Mark McGwire led the NL with 147 and five players had more than 130. Robinson had eleven seasons with over 100 runs created, many during the low-offense era of the 1960s. The S-curve estimates ten such seasons, eight

Transcendental Graphics

Frank Robinson

of which correspond to Robinson's actual 100 RC seasons.

As noted above, the S-curve methodology fits Robinson's career quite well. Like all players, Robinson shows some annual variation, but except for a few outlying seasons, the model usually captures his seasons within about ten to twenty runs created.

Although players exhibit considerable year-to-year variations, in outline they do follow Modis's idea of growth and decline fairly closely. To provide a further visualization of fitting S-curves to baseball players, graphs for a couple of additional players are presented in figures 10.2 and 10.3. The first, for Jim Rice (figure 10.2), is only a fair fit; the second, for Dick McAuliffe (figure 10.3), illustrates an excellent match.

Jim Rice played left field for the Red Sox during the 1970s and 1980s. He was one of the top players in the game in the late 1970s but declined fairly quickly thereafter.

Rice peaked in his mid-twenties and had several off years in his late twenties. The model tries to fit a smooth curve to his career and underestimates his early peak years and overestimates his down years. In his MVP season of 1978, when only twenty-five, Rice hit .315 with forty-six home runs and 139 RBI. Two years later Rice hit .294 with twenty-four home runs and 86 RBI. From age twenty-nine on, the model fits the second half or his career fairly closely.

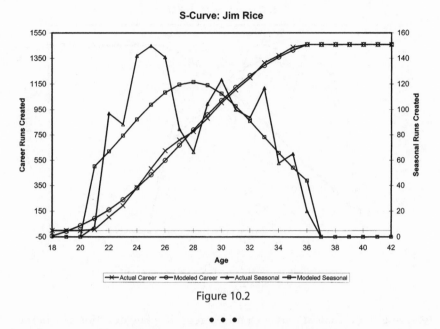

Figure 10.2

• • •

Dick McAuliffe started at shortstop and second base for the Detroit Tigers during the 1960s. He was the starting second baseman on the 1968 World Series champion team and one of the better-hitting infielders of the decade. McAuliffe did not hit for a high average but had decent power and could draw a walk.

Other than the drop in 1969, when he suffered a knee injury, the model corresponds to McAuliffe's career almost exactly. On the whole, the life cycle of most baseball players can be modeled quite accurately by an S-curve.

Like Rice and McAuliffe, many players will show negative modeled values at the beginning of their career. "The reason: better agreement between the curve and the data," Modis says. As with Modis's curve fitting to the cumulative number of Mozart's compositions, it is clear that many ballplayers have a theoretical ability to create runs before reaching the majors. (Mozart wrote his first composition when he was six.) In other words, a player is creating a minimal number of major league–equivalent runs, just not in the major leagues.

Of course it is often easy to appear right after the fact. To look back at a player's career and discern its shape and patterns may be interesting in the abstract, but it offers only limited help to front office personnel at-

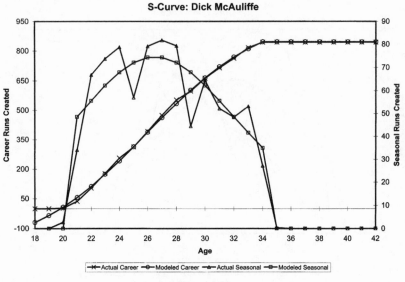

Figure 10.3

tempting to evaluate a player in mid-career. The key question is whether Modis's second observation regarding predictability holds: that one can predict a player's future from the first part of his baseball career. Could the S-curve methodology have helped Bill DeWitt realize that Frank Robinson still had many productive years remaining?

Robinson turned thirty late in the 1965 season, his tenth in major league baseball. What does the model predict for his future after fitting an S-curve to only these first ten years of data?

In table 10.1, we looked for the best fit to Robinson's data using his whole career. In table 10.2, the S-curve was modeled using only his runs created through age 29 (printed in bold in the table). To generate the projection for his career in table 10.2, we calculated the coefficients for the S-curve formula that best fit his career using only the data points through age twenty-nine. This formula is then applied to Robinson's seasons for age thirty and beyond. Figures 10.4 and 10.5 graphically illustrate Robinson's projection.

The model estimates the remaining productivity of Robinson's career fairly well. While the model misses the magnitude of his Triple Crown year (.316 batting average, 49 home runs, and 122 RBI), it still predicts his 112 runs created that year and forecasts his 1967 season almost exactly. The model slightly underestimates some of Robinson's years in his thirties, but what is important is that it does show him as productive into his late thirties.

Table 10.2 S-curve Using Data through Age 29

Age	RC	RC_M	RC_Car	RC_Car_M
18	0	0	0	-27
19	0	0	0	49
20	115	85	115	134
21	119	95	234	229
22	96	104	330	334
23	123	112	452	446
24	111	119	564	565
25	134	124	697	689
26	158	126	855	815
27	78	126	933	942
28	122	124	1054	1065
29	**117**	**119**	**1171**	**1185**
30	149	112	1320	1297
31	110	104	1430	1401
32	70	95	1500	1496
33	118	85	1618	1581
34	97	76	1715	1657
35	88	66	1803	1723
36	54	57	1857	1781
38	78	42	2023	1872
39	23	36	2029	1908
40	8	30	2053	1938
41	0	25	2061	1963
42	0	21	2061	1984

RC_M = seasonal runs created estimated by the model   RC_Car_M = cumulative career runs created estimated by the model

In summary, after the trade, Frank Robinson had eleven years and 890 runs created left in his career. Our model suggests that Frank Robinson had thirteen years and a total of 799 runs created remaining. Based solely on his career through age twenty-nine, the S-curve formula predicts within an accuracy of about 10 percent Frank Robinson's remaining offensive productivity. Armed with this information, Bill DeWitt may have hesitated to make his famous deal.

S-Curve Career Projection: Frank Robinson

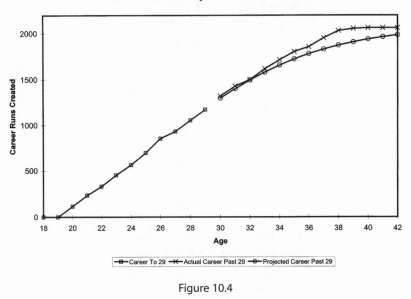

Figure 10.4

◇ ◇ ◇

One of the most fascinating trade controversies of the late 1960s involved three of the National League's expansion franchises and a first-year commissioner. The S-curve methodology will help illuminate some of the might-have-beens surrounding this eventful trade.

On January 22, 1969, the Houston Astros, run by general manager Spec Richardson, traded young outfield star Rusty Staub to the brand-new Montreal Expos for two pretty good players, outfielder Jesus Alou and first baseman Donn Clendenon. Although a free spirit, Staub was a very popular player in Houston, especially with the female fans. Not one to disappoint his admirers, Staub was rumored to reciprocate this affection. After the big trade, the Expos made their new star, dubbed "Le Grand Orange," the centerpiece of their preseason promotional marketing campaign.

Clendenon, who had not yet received the contract terms he was seeking, smartly discerned his negotiating leverage. On February 28, he announced his retirement, saying that he was taking an executive position with the Scripto pen company. Baseball's Rule 12-F stated that "a trade is nullified when one player retires within 31 days after the start of the season without having reported to the assigned club." Thus, with Clendenon apparently quitting, it looked as if the deal would be canceled, with Staub

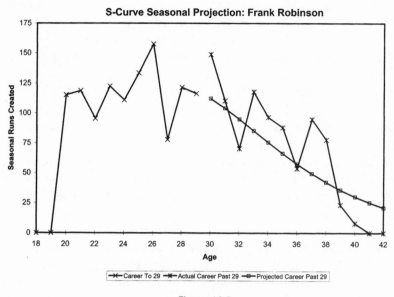

Figure 10.5

returning to Houston and Alou to Montreal.

After all the attention that had been lavished on Staub in Montreal, Expos management, including president John McHale and general manager Jim Fanning, lobbied hard against nullifying the deal. Staub now had a new contract and no desire to return to Houston. Adding to the confusion, Clendenon hinted on March 5 that he might still be willing to play and that his "door remains open to talk."

First-year baseball commissioner Bowie Kuhn, in a ruling that would be a harbinger of many decisions to come, claimed that the baseball commissioner had broad powers to override existing rules in the best interests of the game and declared the trade of Staub would stand. Staub belonged to the Expos, Alou to the Astros, Clendenon remained the property of the Expos, and the two clubs should restructure the compensation for Staub.

The Astros' management understandably reacted loudly and negatively. Richardson observed: "It's the worst decision handed down in the history of baseball. This thing ain't over yet." As an expansion club, the Expos were not overburdened with quality ballplayers, and Richardson claimed he couldn't find any other players he wanted and that the trade should be called off. On March 20, as the situation continued to unfold, Clendenon reiterated that he was retiring.

Judge Roy Hofheinz, an original owner of the Astros and the guiding

force behind the development of the Astrodome, was one of the more eccentric men ever associated with baseball. (When it was suggested to previous Astros General Manager Paul Richards that Hofheinz might be his
own worst enemy, Richards retorted: "Not while I'm alive he isn't.") Several days after Clendenon's confirmation of his retirement plans,
Hofheinz filed suit in U.S. District Court, ridiculed Kuhn as "Blewie," and
released a statement declaring, "This johnny-come-lately has done more
to destroy baseball in the last six weeks than all of its enemies have done
in the past one hundred years."

On April 3, Clendenon signed a contract for a nice salary increase with
Montreal, saying, "I feel I owe it to the game. I don't believe baseball deserves all this confusion. In the interests of baseball I feel I should come
back."

On April 8, the saga finally ended as Houston agreed to accept pitchers
Jack Billingham, Skip Guinn, and cash from Montreal to complete the
transaction. As a fitting finale, Montreal traded Clendenon again in June,
this time to the New York Mets for four players, including pitcher Steve
Renko. Although used only sparingly by the Expos over the first half of
the year, Clendenon had a pretty good second half and a stellar World Series against the Baltimore Orioles; he was named the series MVP.

Spec Richardson maintained afterward that the original trade of Staub
for Alou and Clendenon was a sound one, and that he wished it had gone
through. He had earlier turned down a trade for Joe Torre even-up for
Staub. In retrospect, it seems clear that Torre would have been a better
choice than Alou and Clendenon—after all, Torre went on to win the NL
MVP in 1971. But was this observable at the time? For that matter, Staub
went on to have a much more productive career than Alou and Clendenon. How detectable was that in early 1969?

Table 10.3 presents the projected remaining careers of each of the four
players in terms of runs created, along with their actual values. The projections are generated by fitting the S-curve model to each player's actual
runs created through the 1968 season.

The model estimates the remaining careers of the four players reasonably well and could have provided an indication that the deal, even in its
original form, shortchanged the Astros. The model suggests that Staub had
significantly more productive baseball left than the Alou-Clendenon combination. Furthermore, the model gives strong indications that Joe Torre
still had a number of good seasons ahead of him, and that if Houston felt
it imperative to trade Staub, Torre would have been a better choice.

The model projects the remainder of Staub's career fairly well; except

Table 10.3 Clendenon Trade: Actual and Projected Runs Created

	Rusty Staub		Donn Clendenon		Jesus Alou		Joe Torre	
	Act	Proj	Act	Proj	Act	Proj	Act	Proj
1969	121	119	43	40	42	50	97	92
1970	111	126	72	0	59	49	122	88
1971	112	126	33	0	47	47	148	83
1972	40	119	12	0	13	45	80	77
1973	88	106	0	0	17	41	77	70
1974	79	89	0	0	21	38	77	63
1975	94	72	0	0	9	0	40	56
1976	98	57	0	0	0	0	44	49
1977	95	43	0	0	0	0	3	42
1978	98	0	0	0	20	0	0	36
1979	45	0	0	0	5	0	0	0
1980	58	0	0	0	0	0	0	0
1981	30	0	0	0	0	0	0	0
1982	22	0	0	0	0	0	0	0
1983	18	0	0	0	0	0	0	0
1984	8	0	0	0	0	0	0	0
1985	7	0	0	0	0	0	0	0
Total	1126	856	159	40	233	270	689	657

for his injury-shortened 1972, the model captures his first half-dozen or so seasons almost exactly. Staub remained highly productive into the late 1970s, whereas the model estimates he would begin to tail off a couple of years sooner. Additionally, Staub played in a part-time role for a couple of years into the early 1980s, well beyond where the model forecasts his career would end. In any case, prior to the 1969 season, knowledge of Staub's final part-time seasons would have had only limited value.

For Clendenon, the model correctly perceives that his career was essentially over. It recognizes that he might still be of value in 1969, although it does miss that he still had the one productive season (1970) remaining. As for Alou, the model for all intents and purposes captures precisely his remaining career. Finally, other than missing the magnitude of Torre's MVP season and projecting a couple of part-time seasons in the late 1970s that did not happen, the model predicts the remainder of Joe Torre's career quite accurately.

● ● ●

Bill DeWitt was an intelligent baseball man who chose to trade a great player at his peak. Such a strategy can pay excellent dividends if a rapid decline is approaching. Or, as in the case of Frank Robinson, the strategy can lead to disaster if the player has either not yet reached his peak or has a number of outstanding seasons remaining. A high-risk strategy such as trying to time a player's peak requires excellent player evaluation skills. A model such as the S-curve approach provides an additional useful tool to aid in this assessment.

One can hardly overestimate the importance of perceiving a player's location along his career curve. Baseball organizations clearly understand this imperative and spend millions of dollars every year preparing scouting reports on major league players. This chapter outlined just two of an almost infinite number of misjudgments otherwise intelligent baseball organizations have made in trades or free agent signings. Of course, there is no foolproof way to predict the future of any human endeavor. Nevertheless, in conjunction with all the existing scouting methods, the S-curve model offers a unique and outside perspective on the growth and decline of the productivity of baseball players.

11

PLANS GONE AWRY:
THE 1971 CALIFORNIA ANGELS

After finishing second to the Minnesota Twins for two consecutive seasons, in 1971 the Oakland Athletics broke through to win the American League West by sixteen games. In retrospect, this emergence seems inevitable—Oakland was a team of good young players who had been steadily improving for several years. It is perhaps surprising, therefore, to recall that a significant portion of the public and the media expected the California Angels to be the team to beat in 1971.

In 1970 the Angels finished 86–76, an improvement of fifteen wins from 1969. The team had a number of promising young starting pitchers, including Clyde Wright (fresh off twenty-two victories), Andy Messersmith, and Rudy May. They had several solid infielders: shortstop Jim Fregosi, first baseman Jim Spencer, and second baseman Sandy Alomar. Left fielder Alex Johnson won the 1970 batting title in his first year in the American League. A young team, the Angels appeared to have a lot of upside.

Following their fine 1970 season, the Angels made several big trades and landed outfielder Tony Conigliaro, who had driven in 116 runs for the Red Sox; Ken Berry, a fine defensive center fielder; and Jim Maloney, one of the premier pitchers in the National League over the previous several years. Angels fans had every right to feel optimistic about the 1971 team.

Sports Illustrated, in its annual preview issue, picked the Angels to win the AL West. *Street and Smith's Baseball* picked the Angels to hold off the Twins. *True's Baseball Yearbook* concurred. In *Sports Quarterly Baseball*, Larry Borstein suggested the possibility of the first all-California World

Series between the Angels and the Dodgers. (Ironically, the two teams from northern California won their divisions that year.)

Unfortunately for the Angels and their fans, the season turned out to be a disaster. Not only did the Angels not win the division (they finished twenty-five-and-a-half games behind the Athletics), the team also faced a series of bizarre personnel crises that are still amazing to recount thirty years later. Dick Walsh, the Angels' general manager, would later say of 1971, "It's impossible to describe what it was like to live through." This chapter will flesh out the talented team that Walsh built and the events that brought it down before it ever got started.

◇ ◇ ◇

In 1960, as part of a plan to fight off the creation of a third major league, the two established leagues each decided to expand by two teams. The American League awarded its franchises to Los Angeles (where the Dodgers had enjoyed a monopoly for three years) and Washington (to replace an existing club that would move to Minnesota). The new AL teams, the Angels and Senators, were to begin play in 1961.

Gene Autry, one of the most successful and beloved entertainers in the country, owned several radio stations on the West Coast. One of them, KMPC in Los Angeles, broadcast the Los Angeles Dodger games. When the Dodgers decided to switch their flagship to KFI, Autry elected to pursue a broadcasting contract with the new Angels franchise in order to protect the interest of his station. Eventually, Autry was convinced to pursue the team itself, and the league selected his bid over one by Chicago insurance magnate Charles O. Finley.

In order to gain approval by the league, Autry was required to pay $350,000 to Walter O'Malley, whose Dodgers controlled the territory, and agree to a four-year lease to play as a tenant in the Dodgers' new stadium in Chavez Ravine. In 1965, the club changed its name to the California Angels, and it relocated to brand-new Anaheim Stadium the following year.

The 1962 Angels surprised the baseball world by landing in first place on July 4; the team ultimately won eighty-six games and finished third. The 1962 team will be forever notorious for the antics of pitchers Bo Belinsky and Dean Chance. Belinsky started his career 5–0, pitched a no-hitter, dated starlets, and partied all night; he finished his career with a 28–51 record, presumably having wasted whatever talent he was blessed with. Chance, a much better pitcher, tried to keep up with Belinsky off the field for a couple of years and ended up mixing some mediocre seasons with some brilliant ones.

This early success proved a fluke, but the Angels were different than a typical expansion team in that they did not suffer terrible seasons—mostly they were just mediocre. In their first seven seasons, they won eighty or more games four times. In contrast, of the other seven expansion teams from the 1960s, only the Kansas City Royals attained eighty wins in their first seven seasons.

Before the advent of the major league draft of amateurs in 1965, the Angels made a big splash with "bonus babies." In June 1964, Autry signed two of the most prized available players, Rick Reichardt, an outfielder from the University of Wisconsin, and Tom Egan, a catcher from nearby Whittier, California. Reichardt was a rising young star by 1966, but injuries limited his career. Egan had a career as a backup catcher.

The Angels' best player over their first ten seasons was Jim Fregosi, a six-time All-Star and almost certainly the top shortstop in the American League. Slick-fielding second baseman Bobby Knoop was the second-best player they developed in the 1960s. The rest of the club seemed to turn over every year. Veterans such as Leon Wagner, Dean Chance, and Don Mincher turned in solid seasons, but the club proved unable to develop much of its own talent.

Part of the problem was that the Angels never stuck to a plan for very long. In the expansion draft, manager Bill Rigney wanted to find young, unproven players, while general manager Fred Haney thought the team needed to create fan interest right away by picking established players. Over the next ten years and throughout the history of the Angels, the team's management constantly fought an internal philosophical battle between trying to win now and patiently building a team. The most common reason advanced in the early years for signing veteran players was that the local competition with the Dodgers did not allow a long-term outlook. Later, the team seemed most interested in winning before Gene Autry was too old to enjoy it.

The 1968 Angels finished tied for eighth in the ten-team league, and their 67–95 record was their worst yet. At the end of the season, the Angels hired Dick Walsh to be their new general manager and proclaimed a "new era." Commissioner of the North American Soccer League, Walsh had nevertheless paid his baseball dues as a Dodger executive for eighteen years. Walsh had left the Dodgers when he finally concluded that he would advance no further—the organization already included Peter Bavasi, the son of the general manager, and Peter O'Malley, the son of the owner.

Walsh was said to be a man of ability and intelligence, but his dictatorial and conspiratorial ways soon alienated everyone he dealt with. He fought with the city of Anaheim over the stadium, his players did not trust him, several members of the front office left because of his refusal to delegate responsibility, and he had abysmal rapport with his managers. He needed to be involved in every decision—he once complained to the players that they were using too many towels. Several Angels players went to Autry and team president Bob Reynolds asking to be traded, many referring to Walsh as the "Smiling Python."

When the Angels started poorly in 1969, Walsh fired popular Bill Rigney, up to that point the Angels' only manager, and replaced him with Walsh's good friend from the Dodgers, Lefty Phillips. Phillips was hired because he was a renowned student of pitching and fundamentals.

◇   ◇   ◇

After the Angels hit .230 and scored a league-low 528 runs in 1969, Walsh traded three pitchers, including Jim McGlothlin and Pedro Borbon, to the Reds for outfielder Alex Johnson and infielder Chico Ruiz. Having hit .312 and .315 the prior two years in Cincinnati, Johnson was considered one of the best young hitters in baseball. He was then twenty-seven.

A large man, Johnson was also one of the strongest players in the game and an incredible talent. While hitting against a pitching machine, Johnson often stood twenty or thirty feet in front of the plate and still hit line drives as his teammates watched in awe. Longtime manager Gene Mauch suggested he was the fastest right-handed hitter in baseball from home to first. In the field, he was a speedy outfielder with a powerful throwing arm.

Johnson also carried considerable baggage, however, and the Reds were the third team to deal him after two years. He had difficulties with each of his first three managers—Mauch in Philadelphia, Red Schoendienst in St. Louis, and Dave Bristol in Cincinnati—because of the perception that he gave less than his best effort as well as his unfriendly demeanor. After he had apparently turned a corner in 1969, Mauch, his former manager, said, "There is nothing Johnson cannot do in a baseball uniform that isn't major league. If a manager can find a way to do it, he's got a great player."

In 1970 Johnson provided the Angels with the desired offense—he hit .329 to win the league batting championship—but unfortunately he gave them a whole lot more. He displayed an alarming lack of hustle and re-

Alex Johnson

peatedly screamed obscenities at teammates and media members who tried to speak with him. Johnson's wife reportedly apologized to the other players' wives for the way Johnson was treating their husbands.

Johnson was fined several times for failing to run out ground balls and for lazy play in the outfield. In September, Phillips commented, "It's as if he doesn't consider it a hit unless the ball reaches the outfield. It's as if he has zones marked off in his mind, and unless the ball goes into one of these zones, he's just not going to run hard to first base."

When asked to compare Johnson with Richie Allen, the equally controversial National League star of the time, Phillips scoffed, "Once you get Richie Allen on the field, your problems are over. When Johnson gets to the field, your problems are just beginning." Phillips tried to discipline him further, but Walsh, who liked Johnson's bat and feared exacerbating the team's antiblack reputation, failed to back him up.

Perhaps the most frustrating thing about Johnson was that he seemed utterly unaffected by disciplinary actions. The players had a "kangaroo court," which held mock trials to fine players for offenses like not wearing a hat properly or being late for batting practice. Johnson, not wanting to be bothered with such nonsense, simply wrote a check for $500 and asked that it be applied to future abuses. One Angel player commented that "Alex wouldn't be good for us if he was hitting .400."

Nevertheless, Phillips believed that Johnson had begun to lighten up in the final weeks of the season and hoped the batting title, and its accompanying acclaim, would help Johnson see that the whole world was not aligned against him.

The 1970 season hinted at great promise for this developing team. On September 4, the Angels found themselves only three games behind the first-place Minnesota Twins and starting a three-game series against the Twins in Anaheim. Unfortunately, Minnesota won all three to take a six-game lead while the Angels' losing streak eventually reached nine. In the end the Angels won eighty-six games and finished in third place, twelve games out.

Despite the team's commendable season, Gene Autry was rumored to be unhappy with Phillips and reportedly wanted to install Jim Fregosi as player-manager. Nevertheless, prior to the end of the season, Phillips was rehired for 1971.

The team's improvement was fairly balanced between offense and defense. The team's offense increased by 103 runs, much of which was due to Johnson's stellar season and one of Fregosi's best years. The pitching improvement was less dramatic; the staff's ERA decreased from 3.55 to 3.49. This is actually a little more impressive than it first appears because the league ERA went up slightly. Furthermore, this improvement took place without the injured Andy Messersmith, who had been the team's best pitcher in 1969.

One of the major reasons for the pitching improvement was Phillips's handling of Clyde Wright. In 1969 Wright had finished only 1–8, and ex-manager Bill Rigney had believed that Wright did not have the stamina to be a starting pitcher. Phillips thought otherwise, moved the twenty-nine-year-old Wright into the starting rotation, and gave him thirty-nine starts. Wright responded with a record of 22–12, a no-hitter, and an ERA of 2.83, third best in the league.

One item of concern was the team's run differential. The Angels scored 631 runs and allowed 630, which typically leads to a record close to .500. That the Angels exceeded this expectation by five wins provided a pretty reliable indication that the team might not be quite as good as its record.

◇   ◇   ◇

To push the team over the top, Dick Walsh believed the Angels needed a cleanup hitter to hit behind Johnson. The team's two leading RBI men in 1970 were Johnson and Fregosi, and neither was a true power hitter. During the World Series, Walsh traded reliever Ken Tatum and two minor leaguers, Doug Griffin and Jarvis Tatum, to the Boston Red Sox for pitcher Ray Jarvis, catcher Jerry Moses, and slugging right fielder Tony Conigliaro.

It appeared to be a one-sided deal in the Angels' favor. Ken Tatum was only twenty-six and coming off of two very good years, but the Angels had no room for either Griffin or Jarvis Tatum. In 1967 Conigliaro had suffered a near-fatal beaning and missed the entire 1968 season because of impaired vision in his left eye. In 1969, however, he completed a heroic comeback, which he followed up with thirty-six home runs and 116 RBI, both career highs, in 1970. He was twenty-five years old at the time of the trade. Moreover, Moses was ready to compete for the starting catcher job.

A month later, Walsh made another six-player deal, this time with the Chicago White Sox. He gave up outfielder Jay Johnstone, catcher Tom Egan, and pitcher Tom Bradley for center fielder Ken Berry, third baseman Sid O'Brien, and pitcher Billy Wynne. The key pickup was Berry, a Gold Glove winner in 1970.

The previous August, Walsh had acquired Tony Gonzalez, a thirty-four-year-old outfielder who still hit well enough to be a useful player. The Angels also added Jim Maloney from the Reds for a minor leaguer. Maloney had been injured for almost all of 1970, but he was only thirty years old and had been an excellent pitcher (12–5, 2.77) in 1969. In the spring, Walsh acquired Jeff Torborg to help handle some of the catching duties.

Superficially, Walsh appeared to have done a fine job improving the team. Conigliaro and Berry filled the team's two most obvious needs—a cleanup hitter and a center fielder. Moses was a good young catcher who seemed an upgrade over the incumbent, Joe Azcue. Gonzalez and Maloney were veterans acquired at little cost for some depth.

The infield remained intact from 1970—Jim Spencer, Sandy Alomar, Jim Fregosi, and Ken McMullen. Fregosi was the team's best player and leader. Spencer, only twenty-two, had hit .274 with twelve home runs in 1970. Alomar was an overrated offensive player—he stole bases but did not get on base enough for a leadoff man—but he was a good fielder at second base. McMullen was also more of a defensive player, although he could supply occasional power. Johnson, Berry, and Conigliaro were set to patrol the outfield, backed up by Gonzalez.

In the rotation, Clyde Wright was coming off his excellent season. Andy Messersmith suffered from shoulder trouble and a rib injury in 1970, but he was only twenty-five and the injuries did not appear to have lingered. Tom Murphy was the same age and had won sixteen games in

1970. Maloney was just a year removed from stardom and Rudy May was a steady starter at the back of the rotation. They had traded their best reliever, Ken Tatum, but still had a couple of good ones in Eddie Fisher and Dave LaRoche.

Most prognosticators foresaw three main contenders for the American League West in 1971. The Minnesota Twins had won the past two titles and still had a core of outstanding players, including Harmon Killebrew, Tony Oliva, Rod Carew, Jim Perry, and Jim Kaat. The Oakland Athletics, led by stars like Reggie Jackson, Sal Bando, and Jim Hunter, were a young team that had been advancing over the past few years. After the Angels' high-profile off-season moves, many experts now believed the Angels could hold off the Athletics and Twins and win the division.

In retrospect, it is obvious that the Angels were trading players with more of a future than the ones they were receiving. Johnstone, Bradley, Borbon, and Aurelio Rodriguez (traded for Ken McMullen in 1970) in particular had more productivity left than the players they helped land. In fairness to Walsh, however, none of the players he traded would ever be a star. He believed that by filling a couple of specific needs, the team could compete for the division title.

With the passage of time, it is also clear that Walsh and most of the media overreacted to the Angels' surprising leap forward in 1970. The team scored just 631 runs, well below the league average, and it is easy to see why. Other than Johnson and Fregosi, Jim Spencer was the only Angel to have a batting average over .251 or drive in sixty-five or more runs. The acquisition of Conigliaro addressed the team's need for more offense, but Spencer, McMullen, Alomar, Berry, and Moses were average offensive players at best. It is difficult to envision a scenario where this team's offense would be much better than average.

One of the reasons for overrating the offense was the team's unusually poor on-base skills. Thirty years ago, Jim Spencer was considered an up-and-coming player, partly because no one noticed that his .274 batting average was backed up with just twenty-eight walks. Alex Johnson won the batting title but walked just thirty-five times in 614 at-bats. The Angels hit .251 as a team, which was higher than the league average, but they were last in the league in both walks and on-base percentage. The Angels and their enthusiasts did not recognize the severity of this problem and the team wrongly considered itself to be just a couple of players away from winning.

In addition, Conigliaro and Johnson were not superstars. Johnson had put together a few high-batting-average years but did not have many other offensive skills of note. Conigliaro was a fine slugger who was still young, but he was moving out of Fenway Park in Boston, a perfect setting for his skills, into Anaheim Stadium, a very difficult park for a right-handed power hitter. These two were fine players and the best two hitters on the Angels, but they were not capable of carrying a mediocre supporting cast.

◇ ◇ ◇

The Angels' harmony began unraveling in spring training. In a March 20 preseason game, Alex Johnson spent a hot day in left field staying within the shadow of a light tower rather than assuming his proper defensive position. When he failed to run out a ground ball in the first inning the next day, Phillips removed him from the game. Since it was only an exhibition game, the Angels hoped it was an isolated incident.

Instead, it proved the first in a bizarre series of conflicts between the team and its batting champion. Johnson was fined every few days for the next three months—a total of twenty-nine times by late June—and was benched five separate times. Phillips later said that he could have fined Johnson every day but began to look the other way to avoid confrontations. Phillips tried to suspend Johnson or get him traded but Walsh again refused to support his manager. Phillips told the press: "He did things differently last year. He gave about 65%. Now it's down to about 40%."

Johnson was completely unconnected with the rest of the team; he sat alone on the bench, not shaking anyone's hand or speaking to his teammates. Outfielder Bill Cowan reported, "We've had meetings, we've pleaded with him. We've asked if it's anything we've done. He doesn't say anything."

Johnson was benched on May 15 and again on May 21 for failing to hustle. Two days later, he jogged after a fly ball that landed in front of him and then did not run out a ground ball. Exasperated, Phillips finally called a clubhouse meeting without Johnson and told the team that Johnson would never play for the Angels again as long as Phillips was manager. The players applauded. Eddie Fisher told the press, "I won't make excuses or protect him any more. . . . The whole thing just leaves you disgusted."

In the meantime, Walsh talked to Johnson, defended him to the press, and asked Phillips to put him back in the lineup. Johnson was reinstated on May 26. Jim Fregosi later commented: "Lefty gained one player and lost the other 24 on that day." After playing well over the next week, on

June 4 Johnson failed to run out a ground ball and was benched for four more days.

The handling of Johnson severely undermined the morale of the team. During one heated exchange, Ken Berry charged after Johnson in the clubhouse. In another, Clyde Wright raised a stool at Johnson and had to be held back by his teammates. In response, Johnson let it be known he was willing to fight anyone who wanted a piece of him.

The players lost all respect for Phillips and Walsh. Backup catcher Jeff Torborg, who did not play much and was unhappy about it, claimed that he "no longer had any respect for the Angels' uniform." When Jerry Moses complained about his own lack of playing time, Phillips shot back, "He ain't exactly Gabby Hartnett." During one batting practice, the players reportedly spent considerable time trying to hit line drives at Walsh, who was standing with his back turned in foul territory down the left field line.

Chico Ruiz was a popular utility infielder for the Angels. He and Johnson had been great friends while teammates in Cincinnati and Ruiz was the godfather of Johnson's daughter. At some point during the previous twelve months, Johnson had begun to torment and abuse Ruiz, screaming vile profanities at him whenever they crossed paths. Ruiz and his teammates claimed complete ignorance as to what had caused the rift. Oddly, Dick Walsh thought Ruiz was good for Johnson: "If Ruiz were not there for him to kick around, I don't know what he'd do."

On June 13, Johnson accused Ruiz of pulling a gun on him in the clubhouse during a game. (Both players had been used as pinch hitters and removed from the contest.) According to Johnson, Ruiz had a gun in his locker and waved it threateningly. Ruiz denied the story and said he did not even own a gun. Nonetheless, a teammate was heard to comment, "If Chico did anything wrong, it was that he didn't pull the trigger."

The next day, Walsh held a press conference to let everyone know that he was still looking into the matter, but there was no evidence of a gun. Most of the press was skeptical. John Hall of the Los Angeles *Times* wrote, "The big A is an armed camp. . . . at least two other players have been seen carrying guns and several others are known to have knives stashed." It probably did not help that Gene Autry, the team owner and a world-famous cowboy, often gave his players guns as gifts.

When Johnson did not run out another ground ball on June 25, Phillips benched him again. Finally, perhaps even mercifully, on the following day the Angels suspended Johnson indefinitely without pay for "failure to give his best efforts to the winning of games." Most of his teammates thought that the suspension was long overdue. Jim Fregosi claimed, "He was given every opportunity." Conigliaro, who got along well with Johnson, nonetheless said, "He has inner hatreds so intense that he couldn't perform." Fred Koenig, a coach, was more direct: "I like Alex personally, but I despise him professionally."

In a rare interview, Johnson was blunt: "Hell, yes, I'm bitter. I've been bitter ever since I learned I was black. The society into which I was born and in which I grew up and in which I play ball today is anti-black."

Johnson blamed all of his problems on the insensitivity of his teammates, the "hypocrisy" of Walsh and Phillips, and Ruiz, who was the "cause of the dissension. . . . I never knew a man to be so determined in a negative way." When pressed to elaborate, he went no further. Johnson also claimed that he ran out ground balls the way he had his whole career. This may have been true.

Johnson also acknowledged the effect he had on his team: "The pitchers don't pitch well when I'm in there. . . . When I'm playing, the spirit is down." On the other hand, he had "justifiable reasons for not being in the spirit of playing properly. There was an indifference on the whole team in working together. I felt the game of baseball wasn't being played properly—so my taste wasn't there."

Johnson's suspension was indefinite and ultimately lasted for the remainder of the 1971 season. The Players' Association filed and won a grievance to recoup Johnson's pay for the balance of the 1971 season. The arbitrator ruled that Johnson was "emotionally incapacitated" and should have been placed on the disabled list. Two psychiatrists examined him, one each selected by the union and the Angels, and they agreed that Johnson had justifiable reasons for not being able to give his best efforts.

At the hearing, Walsh admitted for the first time that Ruiz actually did wave a gun at Johnson back in June. The general manager claimed that he covered for Ruiz, who was not an American citizen, to avoid problems with immigration officials. Walsh's deceit, which included calling up Johnson's wife to tell her that Johnson had become delusional, had resulted in three months of added ridicule for his disturbed player.

Marvin Miller, then head of the Players' Association, later wrote extensively of these events in his memoir *A Whole Different Ballgame.* Miller firmly believed that Johnson was emotionally disabled in 1971 and that an enlightened baseball establishment would have dealt with him much more humanely. Miller also felt that had Johnson been a white player the Angels would have treated him differently.

(In fact, baseball did witness another emotionally disabled player—who was white—just a year earlier: Tony Horton, the star first baseman for the Indians. Horton's case is much different, however. Well-liked by his teammates, and extremely hard working, Horton was apparently beset with an intense fear of failure. He hit twenty-seven home runs and drove in ninety-one for a poor Indians team in 1969 and was in the midst of another fine year in 1970, when he was just 25. He crawled to the dugout after a strikeout in Yankee Stadium, and a few weeks later manager Alvin Dark removed Horton from a game after he seemed to have gone into a trance at first base. Horton left the park and never returned to baseball. He has refused to discuss his baseball career in the more than thirty years since.)

Dick Allen, a teammate of Johnson's in Philadelphia when they were both breaking into the major leagues and a player with a reputation of his own for independence, wrote of Johnson in his 1989 autobiography, *Crash*: "Why don't you hear his name today? I'll tell you why. Because he called everyone dickhead. To Alex Johnson, baseball was a whole world of dickheads. Teammates, managers, general managers, owners . . . Alex would say, 'How ya doin' dickhead?' Just like that. The front office types would take it personally. But then again, maybe Alex hit a nerve."

◇ ◇ ◇

The trade to the Angels had been quite a jolt to Tony Conigliaro. After growing up a few minutes from Fenway Park, Conigliaro was treated like a rock star in Boston. In fact, he was a rock star—he had cut a few records and had his own lounge act. But before the trade to the Angels, he had not spent much time away from his family and friends.

The silver lining of the trade from Conigliaro's perspective was that he had "a chance to further my show business career." He auditioned for the role of Michael Corleone in *The Godfather*, a character eventually portrayed by Al Pacino. He lived in Newport Beach, right next door to Raquel Welch, which kept the gossip columnists busy for a while. Although Conigliaro apparently never met Welch, his move to the land of sunshine enhanced his image as a young, single, dashing playboy.

In fact, he proved to be a fish out of water. In Boston, Conigliaro was a civic treasure who played in front of passionate fans. In Southern California, he was just a baseball player in a place where such a person was nothing special. Conigliaro started in a slump and stayed in one, hitting in the low .200s with little power. The Big A was not as friendly as Fenway Park for a home run hitter. More important, he was unable to shake a series of nagging injuries (especially a hamstring pull and a pinched nerve in his back), which led to suspicion from his teammates.

On June 11, after Conigliaro had been out for a few games with his bad back, his teammates placed a stretcher in front of his locker with his uniform laid out, along with a pair of crutches and ketchup-stained feminine napkins. Conigliaro checked himself into the hospital and spent four days in traction. Subsequently an article in the Los Angeles *Times* quoted several of his teammates suggesting that he was a malingerer.

On July 9, the Friday before the All Star Game, the Angels hosted a game with Oakland, which they lost 1–0 in twenty innings. With a runner on first and one out in the eleventh, Conigliaro struck out. As the ball squirted away from the catcher, Conigliaro ran to first base before being called out by home plate umpire Merle Anthony (the dropped-strike rule does not apply when first base is occupied). Conigliaro had a heated disagreement with Anthony about it before retreating to the dugout.

In the bottom of the nineteenth, he got the bunt sign but missed two pitches. Though the sign was taken away, Conigliaro tried to bunt anyway and missed again for the third strike. When Anthony called him out, Conigliaro started screaming at him, following Anthony around the field gesturing wildly. He then threw his helmet in the air and hit it down the first base line with his bat. When first base umpire George Maloney ejected him from the game, Conigliaro hurled his bat over Maloney's head into right field. Phillips and a few of his teammates finally came out to get him off of the field. He had gone hitless in eight at-bats, with five strikeouts.

When the ball game ended, Conigliaro had already left the stadium. Whatever patience Phillips may have had a few weeks earlier was long gone: "He doesn't even know the rules of the game. He ran to first when he couldn't and then got into a big argument. Then he tried his favorite play, bunting with two strikes, the one that never works. He does a lot of things on his own. You never know what he's going to do. The man belongs in an institution."

A few hours later, Conigliaro rousted the media out of bed for a 5 a.m. news conference. He was retiring. "I almost lost my mind out on the field tonight. . . . I was saying good-bye to baseball." He revealed that he could not see the ball anymore. He also said that he had let his manager and his teammates down. He took the next flight back to Boston.

The press and talk shows, even in Boston, were very negative. Partly to combat this, Conigliaro had his left eye examined by his doctor, who released his report a few days later. Looking straight ahead, Conigliaro had 20–300 vision in the eye. There was a blind spot in the center of the eye that had grown 75 percent in the past year. Although this quieted the media down for a while, suspicion lingered that his failing eyesight was not the main reason that he had quit. His brother Billy, speaking twenty years later, suggested that if Tony had remained with the Red Sox, he might have battled through the eye problems.

In the years since, there has been speculation that the Red Sox's concern about the condition of Conigliaro's eye led to his being traded. Dick Walsh later suggested that the Angels should have demanded compensation from the Red Sox. Over the next few years, Conigliaro's eye improved enough for him to try another comeback in 1975, but he never regained the hand-eye coordination required to hit a baseball. After several years out of the game, Conigliaro suffered a debilitating stroke in 1982 that led to his death in 1990 at the age of forty-five.

◇ ◇ ◇

The Angels' nightmare 1971 season eventually came to a close, with California somehow winning seventy-six games and finishing in fourth place. The remains of the team, which seemed so well built and balanced in March, were quickly scattered to the winds after the season.

On October 5, Alex Johnson was traded to the Indians in a five-player deal that brought Vada Pinson to the Angels. Johnson played for eight teams in his thirteen-year career and was the only player in the twentieth century to play ten or more years but to play for no team for more than two seasons. He never hit .300 again and departed the game with a .288 lifetime average. After his career he worked in Detroit at his father's company, Johnson's Trucking Service, and took over the business upon his father's death.

On October 6, Walsh succumbed to the inevitable and fired Lefty Phillips. Phillips would only say, "Too much has been said already this year." Phillips was still out of work the following June 12 when he died of an asthma attack at age fifty-three. He was not the first of the 1971 cast to lose his life—Chico Ruiz died in a car accident in February 1972. Dick Walsh himself was fired on October 20. He never returned to baseball.

There is plenty of blame to go around for what befell the Angels in 1971. Dick Walsh is likely guilty of ignoring clubhouse harmony when putting his team together. The nuances of team chemistry are complicated and often overrated, but in this instance there were plenty of warning signs that his manager and players had difficulty playing with Alex Johnson. Johnson's troubles may have been emotional, but they were never completely corrected during his career, and he showed no signs of remorse twenty-five years later.

Conigliaro's problems were also complicated but mainly a direct result of his eye injury. Conigliaro may not have handled his physical problems in a professional manner, but he had been dealt a terrible setback when he was beaned in 1967 and his 1969 comeback from that injury was one of the greatest baseball stories of the day. Faced with such a situation today, Walsh would have insisted on an eye examination prior to the trade and, upon seeing the results, would likely have called it off.

Much of what befell the Angels in 1971 was just plain bad luck. The Johnson and Conigliaro issues devastated the team, not just because of the dissension the two players' problems caused but also because California desperately needed their bats in the lineup. Johnson hit .260 in 242 at-bats; Conigliaro hit .222 with four home runs in 262 at-bats. With this production from their two best hitters, the Angels scored just 511 runs, by far the lowest total in the league.

The Angels declined in 1971 by ten games, from 86–76 to 76–86. The drop-off was all offensive, as their runs scored fell from 631 to 511, while the pitching, led by Andy Messersmith, actually allowed just 576 runs, the third-lowest total in the league. Anaheim Stadium during these years depressed run production by about 5 percent but the offense scored 18 percent less than an average team.

The 1971 Angels were not as close to winning as many thought. Too many things had to go right and too many marginal players had to advance as offensive players in order for them to score enough runs to compete with the Athletics. With their good pitching, the Angels likely would have needed to score another fifty to seventy runs to finish .500. It is likely that a healthy Conigliaro and Johnson could have made up some, but not all, of that difference.

Finally, the team did not address its largest problem: its inability to put enough people on base. The Angels again finished last in walks and on-base percentage in 1971. Jim Fregosi hit .233 with five home runs. Ken Berry hit .221 with three home runs. Their most-used catcher, John Stephenson, hit .219. The Angels were a terrible offensive team.

In the end, Walsh's grand plan was defeated for three reasons: he overrated the quality of the 1970 team, especially his offense; he failed to address the disruptive influence of Alex Johnson during the off-season; and the team lost the services of its two best hitters in ways that could not have been anticipated.

Walsh dealt several young prospects to win a pennant that was very likely unwinnable. Although there was not nearly the media or analytical focus on the development chances of minor leaguers thirty years ago that there is today, the players that Walsh dealt—including Bradley, Egan, Johnstone, Ken Tatum, Rodriguez, and McGlothlin—were seen at the time as the best young players in the Angels system. Luckily for the Angels, none of the young players they dealt turned out to be star players, although both Johnstone and Rodriguez would have helped the teams of the mid-1970s. The distraction of Conigliaro's and Johnson's problems led many to miss the main lesson: the team was not going to win anyway.

During the winter meetings, new general manager Harry Dalton traded Jim Fregosi, the franchise's all-time best player, in a big swap to the Mets for a package of players that included young pitcher Nolan Ryan. This proved to be the best trade the Angels have ever made, though the holes in the rest of the team kept them from contending for several more years.

12

BRILLIANCE AND BOMBAST: THE 1970S OAKLAND ATHLETICS

*C*harles Oscar Finley owned and operated the Kansas City Athletics for seven years, from 1961 through 1967, at which point he packed up the team and moved it to Oakland. On the day after the departure was officially announced, Democratic senator Stuart Symington of Missouri condemned Finley on the floor of the United States Senate: "The loss of the A's is more than recompensed by the pleasure of getting rid of Mr. Finley. . . . He is one of the most disreputable characters ever to enter the American sports scene. . . . Oakland is the luckiest city since Hiroshima."

In one sense Senator Symington could not have been more wrong. All the while Mr. Finley was spending seven years aggravating the fine people of Kansas City he was also building a championship team right under their noses—an effort that paid off with three consecutive World Series titles in California. Seen in this light, the Athletics' on-field success out west might have been seen as adding insult to injury.

In another sense Symington was quite right. Oakland never warmed to Mr. Finley either, and, watching this success from half a continent away, the people of Kansas City always felt that they came out ahead. They received an expansion team in 1969 (the Royals) that won their hearts in a way that Finley's teams, win or lose, never did.

Charlie Finley is one of the most fascinating baseball personalities of the past fifty years. Nearly everyone, including fellow owners, players, the fans in the cities in which he operated, the media, and the baseball commissioner, disliked or even despised him. When losing, he blamed everyone but himself. When winning, he was apt to call the radio booth during the game if his name was not mentioned often enough. He was a self-made millionaire who, in the words of sportswriter Jim Murray, "worshipped his creator."

He also had more ideas and imagination than everyone else in baseball put together. He may have been tactless, rude, and vulgar, but he outworked everyone. In an age before cellular telephones, he spent countless hours on the phone, usually with someone who would rather have been doing anything other than talking to Finley. He was a professional salesman, and he worked his fellow owners by browbeating them until they finally gave in.

It is impossible to write about the 1970s Athletics without presenting Finley as the star of the show—the baseball team, even the games themselves, often seemed a sidelight to the real story. This is exactly how Finley wanted it. Ron Bergman, who covered the Athletics for the Oakland *Tribune*, once wrote, "Finley makes the games incidental. After the 1973 Series was over . . . I had to go back and read about the games to see what happened." Several books were written about the A's during their glory years and all presented the owner front and center.

Finley ran the entire operation to an extent that was startling. He not only made all the personnel decisions in Oakland—deciding whom to draft or sign, making trades, suggesting the lineup, advising on in-game strategy—he also wrote the copy for the yearbook, made out the song lists for the organist, decided the menu for the press room during the World Series, and designed the uniforms. Finley had to sign off on all injuries before a player could be put on the disabled list.

Finley was not a pleasant employer. He once approached a secretary who had been addressing envelopes, swept her finished stack into the wastebasket, dressed her down for all to see, and then showed her how to address the envelopes correctly. He went through office staffers at an alarming rate; employees eventually grew tired of being screamed at, humiliated, and treated, as one former employee put it, "worse than animals."

And yet he won. And what's more, Finley won almost entirely with players that his organization had signed and developed. The Athletics were built precisely the way a great team ought to be built: they signed or drafted dozens of quality players, sifted through them for a few years until several developed, made a couple of key trades to redistribute the talent, and provided depth with veteran role players. It worked splendidly, and likely would have continued to work splendidly had the game's labor system not changed. Once the players had to be treated on nearly equal ground with management, Finley's techniques were no longer successful. Then again, he probably did more to incite the player revolution than anyone else.

Finley built quite a team. If he had been anyone other than Finley, he might have received a book contract and spent his retirement years giving speeches on college campuses. Since he *was* Finley, people could hardly wait until he got out of baseball so that they could unplug their noses. It is impossible to imagine what the other owners must have felt watching this madman hoist the World Series trophy every year on national television.

◊   ◊   ◊

Charles O. Finley grew up poor outside of Birmingham, Alabama, and moved with his family to Gary, Indiana, at age fifteen. After graduating from high school, he worked in a steel mill for six years before becoming a life insurance salesman in 1942. He was an extraordinary salesman, setting company sales records that lasted for years. In the late 1940s, a severe bout of tuberculosis hospitalized him for two and a half years and nearly cost him his life. While recuperating, Finley developed a plan to sell life insurance to doctors and surgeons, and he was soon a multimillionaire. He started his own company, and it quickly became one of the largest insurance carriers in the country.

He was a lifelong baseball nut, playing semipro ball before his illness. Once he became wealthy, he spent ten years attempting to buy a major league team. He first tried to purchase the Philadelphia Athletics from the Mack family in 1953 and was later a spurned bidder for the Tigers, the White Sox, and the expansion Los Angeles Angels. Finally in December 1960 he bought a controlling interest in the Kansas City Athletics from the estate of Arnold Johnson, and within a few months he had bought out all of the other investors.

Finley immediately promised the good folks of Kansas City that he would relocate there any day now, a promise he also made to the people of Oakland in 1967. By the time he said it in Oakland, no one really believed anything that came out of his mouth. His business was in Chicago, and he would spend most of his time in his office there. For the next twenty years, he used the telephone to listen to most of his team's games and to scream at his manager or the commissioner or some other unlucky soul.

His first move was to hire "Trader" Frank Lane to run the team, a sure sign that Finley wanted a quick fix. Living up to his reputation and nickname, Lane started dealing right away. He made a six-player trade a few weeks after taking over and made several more multiple-player trades within a few months. Unfortunately, he had little talent on hand and was in no position to acquire much in exchange for what he did have, so the dealing did not amount to much. In the previous six years (1955–1960) only eight players who made their major league debut with the Athletics went on to play in the major leagues for ten or more years: Hector Lopez, George Brunet, Ken Johnson, Lou Klimchock, Howie Reed, Russ Snyder, Bob Johnson, and Dave Wickersham. These were the *successful* players in the system.

The Kansas City Athletics of the late 1950s were not just a poor team; they were a laughingstock. Under owner Arnold Johnson, the team was ridiculed for its habit of trading a succession of good players to the Yankees, including several who played vital roles for their World Series teams, such as Clete Boyer, Ryne Duren, Roger Maris, Ralph Terry, and Hector Lopez. Finley vowed to end this. He bought an old bus, symbolic of the "shuttle" between Kansas City and New York, and publicly burned it. Lane nonetheless announced that he would trade with the Yankees, or anyone else, if he thought it could help the team.

In June Lane traded Bud Daley, the Athletics' best pitcher, to the Yankees, which caused a firestorm of protest in Kansas City. Lane also quickly grew tired of Finley's promotional gimmickry, claiming that what the fans really needed was a good team. Early in the season, Finley overruled a few of Lane's moves, and it was soon apparent who was running the show. Lane did not make it through his first season despite the fact that he was working under an eight-year contract. He soon called Finley a liar and "an egotist," and later went to court to get some of the money Finley owed him. The man who "replaced" Lane was Pat Friday, who also worked for Finley in his insurance company. Within a few years, Finley's front office consisted mainly of his wife Shirley, his cousin Carl Finley, and his son, Charles Jr. The traveling secretary was apt to be a college intern.

Finley's insistence on controlling every aspect of his team was a constant from day one. His first manager was Joe Gordon, who once reportedly handed the home plate umpire a lineup card that was inscribed, "Approved by C.O.F." Gordon did not last as long as Lane. When Finley then decided to hire his right fielder as the new manager of the team, he instructed the public address announcer to call out: "Hank Bauer, your playing days are over. You have been named manager of the Kansas City A's." Bauer trotted in to the dugout, his playing days over, by declaration from on high.

In October, Red Smith wrote in the *New York Herald Tribune*, "It is not true that at the end of Charles Finley's first baseball season there was nobody left in the Kansas City office who knew first base from third, though if [assistant general manager] Bill Bergesch happened to be out to lunch there might have been hell to pay getting the infield fly rule defined." Bergesch soon left to run the Mets farm system.

Finley quickly concluded that he understood the game better than anyone else. One classic example involved promising outfielder Manny Jiminez. In July 1962, Jiminez, a twenty-two-year-old rookie, was hitting .337 with ten home runs. When asked about his rising star, Finley snapped, "I don't pay Jiminez to hit singles." He ordered manager Hank Bauer to get him to swing for the fences: "Get that smart Cuban in your office, and get another Cuban to interpret and bang your fist on the desk. We'll see what happens." What happened was that Jiminez, who was not Cuban at all but Dominican, hit .301, but with only one home run for the rest of year, and showed up in 1963 without a starting job.

◇   ◇   ◇

Finley spent an inordinate amount of his time complaining about the city and the ballpark and trying to move the team. In August 1961, only eight months after buying the Athletics, Finley visited Dallas looking for a new home. In May 1962 the American League tabled Finley's application for permission to move to Dallas–Fort Worth. He tried and failed again in September. On his return to Kansas City after the second attempt, he suggested that the locals "let bygones be bygones," and he asked the city council for a fifty-thousand-seat ballpark, reasoning, "I am convinced that without a new stadium, Kansas City cannot much longer have major league baseball."

By mid-1963 he was virtually at war with the city. Early that year the city lured an American Football League team from Dallas (renamed the Chiefs) by giving it an advantageous lease arrangement. Understandably, Finley wanted the same terms. In early April, he reached an agreement on an equivalent deal with a city council whose terms were just minutes from expiring. A few days later, the brand new city council invalidated Finley's lease and announced that negotiations had to start over. Finley was furious and soon began negotiating with Atlanta about a move there.

At the league meetings during the All-Star break, he disclosed that he was interested in moving his team to Oakland, claiming that he had lost $1.4 million in two years. He approached Horace Stoneham, the owner of the San Francisco Giants, about sharing Candlestick Park until a new stadium in Oakland was ready. Stoneham rejected this overture, saying that he had been assured that he would have the San Francisco market to himself.

The American League was known to be interested in getting a team into Oakland—scheduling had proven difficult with only one team (the Los Angeles Angels) on the West Coast, and Joe Cronin, the league president, was an Oakland native. The city had begun work on a new forty-eight-thousand-seat stadium and offered to temporarily expand Youell Stadium (the twenty-thousand-seat home of the AFL Raiders) until the new park was ready.

The mid-1960s were replete with rumors of major league baseball teams uprooting themselves to head off to new locales. Several cities were actively trying to lure a team, including Oakland, Atlanta, San Diego, Indianapolis, Dallas, Toronto, and Seattle. At least three teams were looking to move: the Milwaukee Braves, the Kansas City Athletics, and the Cleveland Indians. (William R. Daley's purchase of the Indians in August 1966 prevented that franchise from moving to Oakland in 1967.) Many other teams were threatening to relocate unless new ballparks were built for them.

In December 1963, Finley announced that the team was moving its offices out of Municipal Stadium. In January, Finley signed a lease with the state of Kentucky to use Fairgrounds Stadium in Louisville. Unfortunately, Finley made the tactical error of failing to notify the American League. Ten days later, the league voted nine to one against the shift, and gave Finley until February 1 to conclude a lease in Kansas City.

Finley remained undeterred. He flew to Oakland, signed a letter of intent to move his team there, and told the league he would sign no more than a two-year lease in Kansas City. In an emergency league meeting, the owners voted nine to one that the lease being offered by Kansas City was "fair and reasonable" and called another meeting to consider expelling Finley from the league. He finally gave in and signed an ironclad four-year lease to keep the Athletics in Kansas City through 1967.

◇ ◇ ◇

When he first acquired the team, Finley tried anything and everything to interest people in his team: cow-milking contests, greased-pig contests, a sheep pasture (with a shepherd) beyond right field, a zoo beyond left. He installed a mechanical rabbit named "Harvey" behind home plate to pop up and hand the umpire new baseballs. He had "Little Blowhard," a compressed air device in home plate that blew dirt away. He hired Miss USA to be the batgirl. He installed a yellow cab to bring in pitchers from the bullpen. He released helium balloons with A's tickets throughout the countryside. He installed lights in the dugout so that the fans could see the manager and players discussing strategy. He shot off fireworks in the park, but the neighbors complained and the city made him desist. In response, Finley sued the city.

Manager Gordon once tried sitting up in the press box to see if he could better manage from where he could see the whole field. Finley requested permission to install a telephone line between Gordon and the umpire so that the manager could continue to dispute the umpires' calls from on high. Permission was denied, and Gordon quickly gave up the experiment.

During Finley's early tenure in Kansas City, the team received a lot of attention for its uniforms, for which the owner himself, of course, selected the design. Finley first introduced the sleeveless top to the American League in 1962, and the following year he shocked the baseball traditionalist by dressing his team head to toe in yellow with green trim. The Athletics' lone All-Star Game representative in 1963, Norm Seibern, did not play in the game, reportedly because manager Ralph Houk thought that the Athletics' uniform was a disgrace to the American League. In 1966, the team added "kangaroo white" shoes to its ensemble.

In 1965 Finley introduced the baseball world to his new mascot, a Missouri mule, predictably named Charlie O. Not only did the mule have its own pen just outside the park, it also went on a few road trips and stayed in the team's hotel. In Yankee Stadium, Finley got Ken Harrelson to ride Charlie O., and the frightened mule ran around trying to buck him off. Only the Chicago White Sox did not let Charlie O. on the field, so Finley arranged a protest rally across the street from Comiskey Park with pretty models and a six-piece band, which played appropriate tunes like "Mule Train." One afternoon in Kansas City, he led the mule onto the field through the center field fence before realizing that the game had already started.

In late 1965, he signed the fifty-nine-year-old Satchel Paige to start a game against the Red Sox in Kansas City. Allowing only a single to Carl Yastrzemski, Paige threw three shutout innings. Soon thereafter, Bert Campaneris played all nine positions in a game before finally leaving in the ninth inning, when, while playing catcher, he was involved in a colli-sion at home plate. After the season, coach Whitey Herzog had seen enough: "This is nothing more than a damned sideshow. Winning over here is a joke."

Despite all of these early efforts at promotion, the Athletics had miser-able attendance throughout Finley's years in Kansas City. In 1960, the year before Finley bought the team, the Athletics drew 774,944 fans. This was a modest total, even for the time, but it was more than Finley ever at-tracted in any of his seven years in Kansas City. In 1965, the team attract-ed only 528,344 admissions. In their first season in 1969, the Kansas City Royals easily surpassed Finley's highest attendance figure.

Finley was also full of bright ideas to improve the game. He wanted interleague play and realignment to promote geographic rivalries. He pushed for World Series and All-Star games at night. He wanted the sea-son shortened. He cajoled for the adoption of a designated hitter for the pitcher. He proposed a designated runner, who could freely pinch-run for a player any time he got on without replacing him in the lineup. He tried to get the owners to adopt a three-ball walk and actually used the rule in one preseason game in 1971. (There were nineteen walks in the game, and it was not tried again.) He pushed to have active players eli-gible for the Hall of Fame. He installed a clock in the scoreboard to en-force a long-ignored rule that mandated no more than twenty seconds between pitches.

Finley continually tried to add elements of color to the game. His first year in Kansas City, he painted the box seats and the outfield fences citrus yellow and the foul poles fluorescent pink. At the league meetings in 1970, Finley proposed colored bases and colored foul lines, and the A's received permission to use gold bases for their home opener. A few years later, he pushed for orange baseballs, which he carried with him everywhere he went. He even received permission to use the balls in a spring training game. About this time most tennis organizations began using a yellow ball, and one cannot help but think that the orange baseball might have caught on if Finley had not been the author of the idea.

Finley once offered the following advice to a hypothetical man think-ing of becoming a baseball owner: "Do not go into any league meeting looking alert and awake; slump down like you've been out all night and keep your eyes half closed, and when it is your turn to vote you ask to pass. Then you wait and see how the others vote, and you vote the same way. Suggest no innovations. Make no efforts at change. That way you will be very popular with your fellow owners."

◇ ◇ ◇

After being forced to sign his lease in early 1964, Finley essentially stopped trying to promote the team. Ernie Mehl wrote in the *Kansas City Star*, "Had the ownership made a deliberate attempt to sabotage a baseball organization, it could not have succeeded as well. . . . It is somewhat the sensation one has in walking through a hall of mirrors designed to distort, where nothing is normal, where everything appears out of focus." Finley responded by staging Ernie Mehl Appreciation Day and planned to present Mehl with a poison pen. When Mehl did not attend, Finley arranged to have a truck circle the park with a caricature of Mehl dipping his pen in poison ink.

Mehl later wrote a letter to the American League offices claiming, "Finley has done nothing to promote the season ticket sale. He has never had one salesman on the street. The A's do not have a ticket outlet outside of Greater Kansas City." He ignored booster clubs. He gave no support to local groups that organized ticket-buying programs. He made only cursory attempts to sell radio and TV rights. He decided that the city did not care about him so, by God, he was not going to care about the city.

Despite Finley's lack of interest in the city, in mid-1965 the Kansas City Sports Commission began to consider a $66.5 million complex with a domed stadium for baseball and football. The commission eventually built a two-stadium complex, but by that time Finley was long gone.

Finley constantly fiddled with the dimensions of his ballpark until it reached the point of absurdity. His first year he thought the Kansas City pitchers needed help, so he moved the left field fence back forty feet. By 1964 he had determined that the Yankees won every year not because of their great talent but because of the dimensions of their ballpark: deep in most of left and center fields with a short distance in right. Finley decided to make his right field configuration identical to that of Yankee Stadium.

Unfortunately, as of 1958 the rules decreed a minimum distance of 325 feet down the foul lines with the exception of those parks already with shorter dimensions. Never one to be put off by something as silly as the rules of the game, Finley ordered his fence to conform to the Yankee Stadium dimensions from center field to right field until it reached a point five feet from the foul line and 296 feet from home plate (the Yankee Stadium distance). From there, the fence angled sharply back out so that it was exactly 325 feet away when it reached the foul line. He thus neatly skirted the regulation, which stipulated the distances only on the foul line, not the distance five feet from the line. He painted "KC pennant porch" on the new fence (which was forty-four inches high like it was in New York).

After two exhibition games, Commissioner Ford Frick and American League President Joe Cronin told Finley that *all* of the fence must be at least 325 feet from the plate. Finley moved the fence back to 325, changed the sign to say "One-Half Pennant Porch" and painted a line on the field that represented the Yankee Stadium dimensions. He then ordered the public address announcer to call out, "That would have been a home run at Yankee Stadium" for every fly ball that went past this line.

This was no joke to Finley. He was apoplectic about the Yankees and believed the rules were deliberately stacked so that they won the pennant every year. Before its reconstruction in 1974–1975, Yankee Stadium had monuments for Miller Huggins, Lou Gehrig, and Babe Ruth in deep left center field. Finley threatened to put a statue of Connie Mack right in the middle of center field, saying, "They let the Yankees have their monuments out in the playing area, but if I put one up they'll probably run me out of baseball."

In the meantime, Finley traded for Rocky Colavito and Jim Gentile to hit home runs over his new fences. This strategy sort of worked, in that the team finished third in the league with 166 home runs, including 34 by Colavito and 28 by Gentile. Unfortunately, Kansas City pitchers allowed 220 home runs, a major league record that lasted until 1987. The 1964 Athletics finished last with a record of 57–105.

The next year, Finley moved the fences back, put a forty-foot screen above them, and got rid of Colavito and Gentile. These actions suggest a management that does not have any idea what it is doing. Just as the pitchers and hitters begin to figure out how best to deal with the dimensions of the park, the next year they come back and have to learn all over again. In 1965, the Athletics remained in last place, with a record of 59–103. The screen stayed, and Municipal Stadium remained a pitcher's park as long as the A's stayed there.

◇   ◇   ◇

One should understand that Finley accelerated the building of his great team just as he started to cut back on this nonsense. He likely never relinquished the idea of leaving Kansas City once his four-year lease expired, but there was nothing much for him to do about it in the meantime. He could now concentrate all of his considerable energies on a different task—signing players for his team.

Dick Green was the only player Finley inherited who moved with the team to Oakland. Green signed with the Athletics in 1960 out of San Diego and had taken over the second base job by 1964. The first expensive free agent amateur Finley acquired was Lew Krausse Jr., the son of the scout (and former Athletics player) who signed him for $120,000. That same year the team signed Ted Kubiak, a high schooler from New Jersey.

In 1962, A's scout Felix Delgado inked Cuban catcher Bert Campaneris for $500. Campy played every position in Cuba and in the minors, and he could pitch with either hand. The A's brought him up to play shortstop in 1964, and he hit two home runs off Jim Kaat in his first major league game. In 1963, the Athletics signed a couple of college pitchers, Jim Nash from the University of Georgia and Paul Lindblad from the nearby University of Kansas. Both were in the majors by 1966.

In a late 1964 meeting that led to the institution of the amateur draft, Finley claimed that he had spent $634,000 during the past year for eighty players. The team spent $65,000 on Dave Duncan, an eighteen-year-old catcher from San Diego. Finley purchased Chuck Dobson of the University of Kansas for $25,000. He signed Joe Rudi for $25,000.

Finley personally flew to North Carolina to retain eighteen-year-old pitcher Jim Hunter for $75,000. He went to Macon, Georgia, to attend John Odom's graduation and afterward showed up at Odom's house with a carload full of food. He inked Odom for $75,000 and christened his new prodigy "Blue Moon." In December, Rollie Fingers signed with the A's because he saw a faster path to the majors with them than with his other suitor, the Dodgers.

Naturally, most of the eighty players Finley signed did not end up helping the A's win their championships. The Athletics had high hopes that Tony LaRussa ($25,000 in 1962) would be their long-term shortstop, but Campaneris earned that role. For a few years the team expected John Donaldson to beat out Dick Green, but Donaldson proved unable to hold the job. George Lauzerique was a great minor league pitcher who could not make the next step. Dobson, Nash, and Krausse sputtered after promising starts, but Hunter and Odom did not. From the sheer volume of talent, somebody was bound to come forward.

In 1965 the major leagues instituted a free agent draft for amateurs, and the A's hit the jackpot there as well. With the very first pick in the first draft they selected Rick Monday from the NCAA champion Arizona State Sun Devils, signing him for $100,000 and a new car. Finley went to the College World Series himself to look at Monday and while there also became enamored of his teammate, third baseman Sal Bando. He ordered the selection of Bando in the second round and signed him for $30,000.

Later in the same draft, the Athletics took Gene Tenace, a high school prospect from Ohio.

In 1966 Kansas City drafted Reggie Jackson, also from Arizona State, with the second overall pick. Jackson, a great all-around athlete from Pennsylvania, had gone to Arizona State on a football scholarship but hit fifteen home runs in his one season on the baseball team. Scout Bob Zuk signed him for $95,000.

While fortunate to have high picks in these first two drafts, the Athletics were also smart enough to pick the right players. The Mets effectively had the same opportunity: the second pick in 1965 (after the A's) and the first pick in 1966 (before the A's). The Mets wound up with Les Rohr and Steve Chilcott. Finley and his scouts deserve a great deal of credit for their draft selections.

The A's cut back dramatically on their scouting and signing activities at this point and in fact received only limited contributions from players signed after 1966. In these three signing years, from 1964 to 1966, Finley invested perhaps $2 million in two hundred players. This group included three future members of the Baseball Hall of Fame (Hunter, Fingers, and Jackson) and several other future all-stars (Monday, Rudi, Tenace, Odom, and Bando).

The development program first began to pay off in the minor leagues. The better prospects quickly raced through the system, and many of them (like Jackson and Monday) skipped Triple-A entirely. Nonetheless, the Athletics had some great minor league teams in the mid-1960s.

The 1965 Lewiston (Idaho) Broncs of the Northwest League, led by Monday, Duncan, and Odom, won the league championship by five games. The next year Monday and Odom advanced to Mobile of the Southern League, where LaRussa and Bando joined them. Mobile rolled to the championship by nine and a half games.

Just behind this group, Jackson, Duncan, Rudi, and Fingers helped the 1966 Modesto Reds win the California League title by eleven games. The next year, this same crop moved up to Birmingham, where Jackson was player of the year and the team won the Southern League by three and a half games. By 1968 most of this group was in the major leagues, at which time the Athletics' minor league teams stopped winning pennants.

One at a time the prospects began to arrive in Kansas City. By 1964, Dick Green had taken over at second base. Bert Campaneris became his middle infield partner one year later. Jim Hunter skipped the minor leagues entirely and joined the Athletics' rotation by mid-1965. Jim Nash came up in 1966 and posted a record of 12–1 with a 2.06 ERA.

The baseball world began to notice. The 1966 team won 74 games, the most by an A's team since 1952. In a March 12, 1967, *Sports Illustrated* cover story entitled "Dark's Outlook is Young and Bright," William Leggett suggested that the Kansas City team (managed by Alvin Dark) might be as few as two years away from a pennant. The key to their high hopes, wrote Leggett, was the young starting rotation of Jim Nash (22 years old), Chuck Dobson (23), Lew Krausse (23), Catfish Hunter (20), and Blue Moon Odom (21), each of whom had been signed by Finley's scouts. The hitting appeared less impressive, but Rick Monday was ready to play center field and Reggie Jackson looked a half-season away. It seemed to be only a matter of time.

It *was* only a matter of time, but the 1967 season turned out to be a setback on the road to glory. The A's won only sixty-two games, and a bizarre player revolt in August marred the season.

◇ ◇ ◇

On August 3, 1967, the Athletics returned home from Boston on TWA Flight 85, a commercial flight that stopped in both Baltimore and St. Louis. According to most witnesses, the flight was not especially unusual—the players who tended to drink and carry on were drinking and carrying on. A couple of weeks later word got back to Finley, who was not on the plane, that there had been some excessive rowdiness and that some improper language might have been used in front of some of the female passengers. On August 18, Charlie Finley called Lew Krausse Jr. at his hotel room to talk about the flight and, after an exchange of angry words, suspended Krausse indefinitely and fined him $500. He also wrote out a lecture to the players (released to the press) about their deplorable behavior and banned alcohol from all future team flights.

Krausse was known as something of a drinker and was certainly in the middle of whatever happened, but according to his teammates there was no particular reason for singling him out. He had been fined earlier in the year for curfew violations and, just a month before, had apparently shot off a hand gun from a window of his hotel room in Kansas City. Earlier in the season, he had kicked down a hotel room door in Anaheim. The players backed Krausse and issued their own statement to suggest that the event had been blown out of proportion, blaming the whole episode on Finley's "go betweens."

Finley did not like back talk, especially from the hired help. Things deteriorated quickly. He first demanded that the players publicly retract their statement, which they refused to do. Inevitably, Finley fired Alvin Dark, who knew about the players' statement and had failed to forewarn his boss about it. Dark issued his own statement suggesting that the players were "courageous" for sticking up for their teammate and denying any duplicity on his own part.

Ken Harrelson was quoted referring to Finley as a "menace to baseball." Finley responded by giving Harrelson, one of the better players on the team, his unconditional release. "The Hawk" turned his freedom into a $75,000 contract with the pennant-bound Red Sox. The ramifications of Harrelson's free agency so disturbed major league owners that they amended the rules to provide that, in the future, a released player had to pass through waivers before becoming a free agent.

The surviving players sought and received a hearing with Commissioner William Eckert, causing Finley to threaten retribution against those who planned to participate. The players contacted Marvin Miller, the new head of the Major League Players Association, who subsequently filed an unfair labor practice charge with the National Labor Relations Board (NLRB).

On September 11, at a fourteen-hour meeting with the commissioner and players' representatives, Finley agreed to back down in exchange for the players dropping the charge to the NLRB. It eventually all blew over, but this proved to be a watershed event in baseball labor relations. From this point forward, each time the major league players got a little more power, Charles O. Finley would be at the barricades.

A very forgettable season ended with the Athletics, so full of promise in March, back in their familiar position of last place. The ending of the 1967 season also marked the expiration of Finley's four-year lease at Municipal Stadium. This time Finley had laid the groundwork for his escape by quietly gathering the votes of his fellow American League owners. On October 18, the league formally approved his move to Oakland as part of a package deal that included the league expanding to two cities, including Kansas City, in 1971.

Thinking that he had achieved a workable compromise, league president Joe Cronin called Kansas City mayor Ilus Davis and Senator Stuart Symington to give them the good news. Neither was amused. Davis threatened to block the move in court and Symington told Cronin he would hold hearings to reconsider major league baseball's antitrust exemption. Suitably alarmed, Cronin quickly reconvened the meeting and the league agreed to accelerate their expansion plans to 1969, only one season away. The following day, Symington blasted Finley in the U. S. Senate chamber. The seven-year nightmare was over for Kansas City.

◇   ◇   ◇

Finley likely chose Oakland over other possibilities because it had a brand new ballpark ready to go. The city of Oakland, cognizant of whom they were dealing with, drew up a strict twenty-year lease with no option for moving. Finley signed, but was talking with Toronto by 1970.

Finley got right to work. On October 20, 1967, he introduced a new manager, Bob Kennedy. Two days later, Finley announced Joe DiMaggio as his new vice president and coach, a move that landed Finley a lot of press and goodwill for a time. Working mostly with the hitters, DiMaggio seemed to enjoy himself during his two years in Oakland, although the Yankee legend looked a little less regal in green and gold than he had in pinstripes.

In 1968, Reggie Jackson and Sal Bando entered the lineup, Jim Hunter won thirteen games (one of them perfect), Blue Moon Odom won sixteen, and the A's took their great leap forward, winning eighty-two games. It was an extraordinarily young team. The oldest pitcher to start even a single game was twenty-five-year-old Lew Krausse. No position player older than twenty-eight made any significant contribution. The future looked bright indeed.

Of course, the team was embroiled in what would become known as its usual mayhem. In midseason, Finley told Reggie Jackson, his best player and obviously a future star, that he had to play despite a severely bruised left hand. Jackson told the reporters, and Finley flew in to demand that Jackson publicly retract his statements. Jackson did as he was told, though the reporters knew better. Predictably, Finley fired Bob Kennedy, manager of the best A's team since 1952, immediately after the season.

The organization added one last great prospect to its system in 1968. Vida Blue was a football star (thirty-five touchdown passes his senior year) at DeSoto High in Mansfield, Louisiana. He had signed a letter of intent to play football at the University of Houston, but the sudden death of his father that year made it necessary that Blue help support his family. After he threw three no-hitters his senior year, the A's selected him in the second round of the June draft. When scout Connie Ryan tried to sign him cheaply, Blue kicked him out of his house. Finley fired Ryan, called up Blue himself, and inked him for $25,000.

The A's took another step forward in 1969, winning eighty-eight games to trail only the Twins in the brand new American League West. Reggie Jackson, who reached forty home runs by the end of July, became the big story early in the season by appearing to threaten Roger Maris' single-season home run record. Jackson faded in August and September, but he was still a twenty-three-year-old who had hit forty-seven home runs. The young Reggie Jackson was a wonderful all-around ballplayer: he had great speed and a fine throwing arm and he could hit the ball a mile. Bright, talkative, and funny, he obviously enjoyed baseball and stardom. Jackson was a national celebrity—the biggest story in baseball prior to the New York Mets' late-season rush to the pennant.

The following winter Jackson made the mistake of asking Finley for more money and did not sign his contract until just prior to the start of the 1970 season. During the ugly negotiations, Finley was highly critical of Jackson in the press.

Without the benefit of spring training, Jackson started the season in a slump and was given little opportunity to shake it. Finley first ordered Jackson benched against left-handers, then benched against everyone, and finally told reporters that he was considering sending his star to the minor leagues. Eventually manager John McNamara asked Jackson to consent to being sent to Des Moines for a few weeks. Commissioner Bowie Kuhn stepped in to forbid the demotion, saying that the dispute was "motivated by personal reasons unrelated to Jackson's ability."

Kuhn also said that the incident "played right into the hands of the critics of the reserve system by suggesting that club owners held complete power over their players and that such power could be exercised arbitrarily or capriciously." Of course, they *did* hold such power and it *could* be exercised this way, but Finley had the temerity to be indiscreet about it.

None of this was very helpful to Jackson. He was not a terrible player that season (.237 with twenty-three home runs), but a star having a lost year. His teammates believed that he was not allowed to get hot, that Finley ordered him to the bench as soon as he had two good games in a row but insisted he play while struggling. On September 5, Jackson pinch-hit a grand slam, then gestured to Finley in his owner's box as he crossed home plate. Finley ordered Jackson to sign an apology, which the outfielder did, in tears, in front of McNamara, Bando, Finley, and all the coaches.

Though outspoken and brash, Jackson was an extremely fragile and sensitive young man who likely needed nothing more than words of encouragement and a few pats on the back. Instead, Finley publicly humiliated him. One can only wonder whether Jackson might have had an even better career had he been dealt with more humanely in 1970. As one

Reggie Jackson

of the best and most important players in baseball, Jackson was naïve enough to think he could deal with Finley man-to-man, as an equal. Finley burned him badly, and Jackson never again played with the joy he showed in 1969.

The funny thing about Finley, or rather, *another* funny thing about Finley, is that he could be very generous with his players. He was reprimanded or fined several times for giving impromptu performance bonuses (which were and continue to be forbidden) to players for pitching a no-hitter, hitting a game-winning home run, or some other such thing. For many years he offered to invest the money of players in the stock market risk-free—Finley gave the player all gains and assumed all losses. At contract time, on the other hand, he considered it a personal insult if a player was not satisfied with his offer.

He was often called "Massa Charlie" in the press, not so much for his racism as for his paternalism. When Vida Blue commented that Finley treated his black players like "field niggers," Dave Duncan pointed out that he treated his white players the same way. He might give a player the occasional gift, even a new car, but he made it very clear that the relationship was between a master and a servant. As he told writer Bill Libby, "We have not won a pennant, but we will win one, we will win more than one with these players who are like my own sons, and I am only sad when they will not accept my counsel, the counsel of a man who is older and wiser than they."

During that same season of 1970, Finley found himself in a strange financial situation with Jim Hunter. Finley had lent his pitcher $150,000 to buy a farm near Hunter's parents' home in North Carolina. By midseason, as Finley was preparing to buy the Oakland Seals of the National Hockey League and the Memphis Sounds of the American Basketball Association, Finley called Hunter and told him he needed the money to be repaid immediately. Hunter was taken aback, since he did not have the money—he had a farm. Finley continued to pester Hunter every few days until he finally forced his ace to go home and sell four hundred acres, nearly the entire farm.

At the end of the tumultuous season, during which the A's won eighty-nine games and again finished second, catcher Dave Duncan told reporters that the team had but one manager—Charles O. Finley—and "we'll never win so long as he manages it. We had the team to win it, but because of the atmosphere he creates, there's no spirit." Finley reacted predictably by firing the titular manager, McNamara, reasoning that he had lost control of the players. Of course, everyone had always assumed that McNamara would not be back—Finley fired his manager every year. Billy Martin, out of work at the time, claimed that Finley had offered him the manager's job as early as July.

During the press conference to announce the firing, Finley even took a shot at Duncan's living situation, saying, "One day I found out that Duncan was sleeping with [coach] Charlie Lau. [Pause.] By that I mean that they were rooming together, sharing expenses." Finley fired Lau for fraternizing with the players.

For his next manager, Finley hired Dick Williams, a no-nonsense disciplinarian who had won the pennant in 1967 with the Red Sox. Williams turned out to be one of Finley's best signings, and he proved adept, at least for a while, at walking the tightrope between listening to Finley and keeping the respect of his players.

In 1971 the A's were again blessed with the most sensational player in the land, this time the twenty-two-year-old left-handed pitcher Vida Blue. Blue had given the baseball world a taste of his talent the previous September when he threw a one-hitter and a no-hitter in successive starts after his recall from Des Moines. In 1971, he continued in the same vein. Despite a second-half slump, Blue finished with twenty-four wins, a 1.82 ERA, and 301 strikeouts. Like Jackson, he became a national celebrity, and he appeared on the cover of *Time* magazine. He was called, by no less a

Vida Blue

figure than President Richard Nixon, "the most underpaid superstar in sports." One can only imagine how Finley felt hearing that.

Not only was Blue an undeniably great pitcher; he was also extremely likable and movie-star handsome. He was smart and well-spoken, although not an extrovert like Jackson. He ran on and off the mound. Obviously shy, he nonetheless grew increasingly comfortable with himself and his fame. He was self-deprecating and funny. During an A's visit to the White House, he taught President Nixon his "power shake," explaining, "This is how *we* do it." When told that he reminded Dick Williams of Sandy Koufax, Blue responded, "Funny, I don't look Jewish." Finley had offered him a bonus to legally change his name to "True" Blue. When asked about this, Blue retorted, "Why doesn't he change his name to 'True' O. Finley?" The baseball world was in love with Vida Blue.

When it came time to sign a contract for 1972, Blue wanted the average salary of the top ten pitchers in baseball, which he calculated to be $115,000, a hefty raise from the fifteen grand that he made in 1970. He lowered his demand to $92,000 and went public with it. Among the statistics that Blue was able to cite were these: Forty-three percent of the A's home attendance came when Blue was pitching, and one of every twelve tickets sold in the league in 1971 was for a game pitched by Blue. When one Blue start was rained out, Finley admitted that the postponement cost him $30,000.

As long as Blue was willing to play the grateful field hand, Finley loved the kid. Once Blue asked for more money, Finley set out to crush him. Flush with his earlier "success" with Jackson—if that is what you call turning a happy, confident young star into a confused and moody wreck—Finley was not going to give an inch to his latest "malcontent." He offered $50,000 and never moved.

Blue eventually announced his "retirement" and took a job as the vice president for public relations of Durasteel Products, a manufacturer of medicine cabinets. On April 27, Commissioner Kuhn summoned the two parties to Chicago, an action that Finley did not appreciate. After numerous snafus and breakdowns, Blue received a $5,000 bonus, some money for college tuition (which he never used), and Finley's original $50,000 proposal. Finley had won; the last holdup in the negotiations was Finley's insistence on announcing the terms of the contract. He needed to provide that one last bit of humiliation for his young star.

Blue understandably emerged from this holdout a disillusioned young man. He won only six games in 1972, and the smiles and witty quips from the sunny man with the lyrical name dried up. Blue had a fine career and was a key member of the Athletics staff for their run of division titles. Although he went on to win 209 games in his career, he battled drug addiction in the 1980s and was never again the delightful young player about whom so much was written in 1971. One cannot help but wonder what kind of career, and what kind of life, Vida Blue might have had on a different team.

As part of the settlement from the 1972 players' strike, the basic player agreement was amended to allow any player the right to submit his salary demands to arbitration. This was not good for Finley, who underpaid his players and now had the best team in baseball. During the first three years of the arbitration system, fifteen of the forty-six cases heard involved Oakland players. Finley won his share, but most of his "victories" involved substantial raises for the player. Going to arbitration, he could no longer offer ridiculous salaries and wait for the player to cave in. Even as his great team was about to dominate the baseball world, bells warning of Finley's eventual undoing were tolling.

◇ ◇ ◇

The mother lode of prospects continued to arrive: relief pitcher Rollie Fingers in 1969, left fielder Joe Rudi in 1970, and Vida Blue and catcher Dave Duncan in 1971. The team that finally broke through to the division title in 1971 was still young—thirty-year-old Dick Green was the oldest of the nucleus. Led by Blue, the A's won 101 games and captured the division by 16 games. The team fell short in the playoffs, losing three straight games to the Baltimore Orioles.

The core of this team remained intact for five straight division titles. Bando, Campaneris, Green, Jackson, and Rudi held down five of the eight regular lineup spots. Hunter (for four years), Blue, and Fingers starred on the pitcher's mound.

Finley made two great trades that solidified the dynasty. He believed that Rick Monday was not going to be the star everyone predicted and that prospect Angel Mangual was ready to take over in center field. Therefore, after the 1971 season, Finley traded Monday to the Chicago Cubs for left-handed pitcher Ken Holtzman. Mangual never amounted to much, but Holtzman proved to be the third excellent starter who was critical in the postseasons ahead. After the 1972 season, realizing that he now needed a center fielder, Finley traded Bob Locker to the Cubs for Billy North. North anchored the outfield for the A's for the next several seasons.

With his great young ball club in place, Finley constantly tinkered with the depth of his team, making trade after trade, either to fill in the gaps or because he liked making deals. Finley acquired a huge number of veterans to play a role during the five-year string of division titles, including Don Mincher, Mike Epstein, Tommy Davis, Larry Brown, Felipe Alou, Darold Knowles, Mudcat Grant, Matty Alou, Mike Hegan, Ollie Brown, Dal Maxvill, Curt Blefary, Orlando Cepeda, Denny McLain, Joe Horlen, Ray Fosse, Deron Johnson, Billy Conigliaro, Jesus Alou, Vic Davalillo, Jay Johnstone, Mike Andrews, Rico Carty, Larry Haney, Jim Holt, Billy Williams, Tommy Harper, Cesar Tovar, Billy Grabarkewitz, Dick Bosman, Stan Bahnsen, Sonny Siebert, and Jim Perry.

Some of these moves worked very well, but most landed players who just passed through. Epstein started at first base in 1971 and 1972. Fosse, acquired for Dave Duncan, caught for a while until he hurt himself trying to break up a fight between Jackson and North in 1974. Deron Johnson was the DH for two years, Billy Williams for one.

Finley tried everything. He outworked the other general managers during most of his twenty-year career, but he pushed himself even harder once he realized how good his team had become. In 1972 alone he made nineteen trades, many of them during the season. Dick Williams later claimed that he found out about trades by seeing who was in the clubhouse when he showed up for work.

For spring training of 1972, Reggie Jackson showed up with a mustache. After first privately trying to get Jackson to shave it off, Finley reacted to this display of individuality by making it his idea. He staged a Mustache Night, let mustachioed patrons in for a reduced price, and gave each player a small bonus if he wore a mustache for that night's game. All players and coaches obliged and most kept their mustaches all season. A few even sported beards. The team, dubbed the Mustache Gang in the press, won its division by six games over the surprising White Sox, beat the Tigers in the American League Championship Series, and (without the injured Jackson) edged the Reds in the World Series.

In 1972, *The Sporting News* named Finley its "Man of the Year," and Finley was ecstatic. Jackson and Blue, each once the biggest star in all of baseball, were now back in their rightful place as mere players. The only star on the team was Finley. In case anyone had missed it, he reprinted his cover photo from *The Sporting News* in the 1973 team yearbook.

The next season followed a similar pattern, only this time the A's fought off the Royals to win the division, the Orioles to win the playoffs, and the Mets to take the World Series. Reggie Jackson (32 home runs and 117 runs batted in) was once again the best player in the league and was named MVP. Hunter, Blue and Holtzman each won at least twenty games.

◇   ◇   ◇

The 1973 World Series will be forever remembered for Finley's tyrannical behavior. His antics finally turned him into a national pariah, an identity he never shed.

Game two took place in Oakland on October 14, and the Mets defeated the A's 10–7, scoring four runs in the twelfth inning. Oakland second baseman Mike Andrews aided the Mets' cause immeasurably by committing two errors in the twelfth, the first on a ground ball that went through his legs, the second on a throw that pulled Gene Tenace off of the bag at first.

After the game, Finley conferred with the team doctor and decided to make a change. He forced Andrews to sign a statement acknowledging that his shoulder was injured and that he could no longer play. Finley then added Manny Trillo to the roster to replace Andrews, who left the team and flew home. The players, in the middle of a deadlocked series, rallied around Andrews. Sal Bando said, "That's a joke. I've seen some bush things on this club, but this is going too far." Reggie Jackson added, "All that non-baseball stuff takes the little boy out of you." The whole team seemed defeated and uninterested in playing.

On the October 16, before the third game at Shea Stadium, manager

Dick Williams told the players that he had decided to resign at the end of the series, a decision he followed through on. The A's players showed up for the game with Andrews's number on their sleeves.

Commissioner Kuhn, meanwhile, refused to allow the promotion of Trillo and ordered Finley to reinstate Andrews. The infielder reached New York in time for the fourth game the next night and pinch hit in the eighth inning. He received a prolonged standing ovation from the New York crowd—Finley did not stand—before grounding out off Jon Matlack.

One A's employee expressed the general feeling: "Although it hurt Andrews, a lot of people were glad it happened because for the first time it directed attention at the way Finley treated people, even if it was far from the first time he'd treated them that way. All of a sudden he was not just a quaint old guy, a fellow who did funny things, but a man who could hurt people and did." The A's released Andrews at the end of the season, and he never again played in the major leagues.

The aftermath of the Athletics' seventh game victory was eerie. The Oakland locker room was subdued, as if everyone just wanted to get out and go home. Yogi Berra, the manager of the defeated Mets, walked in and commented, "This doesn't look like a winning dressing room to me." Williams announced that he was quitting and Jackson said, "I wish I could get out with him." When a writer suggested to Jackson that Finley deserved credit for getting the team riled up, the star responded, "Please don't give that man credit. . . . It would have been the easiest thing in the world for this team to lie down because of what that man did. He spoiled what should have been a beautiful thing."

At this point in the story, Reggie Jackson's star finally rose up and replaced Finley's. He was voted the World Series MVP, not only for his play on the field but for the way he conducted himself as a sincere, intelligent man in the face of what was finally recognized as nearly intolerable working conditions. Finley had spent years trying to be the center of the team, and he had succeeded even after his team had acquired so many star players. Finley's childlike behavior in 1973 challenged his players to step forward, and Jackson did.

Although Jackson is often remembered as a slugging outfielder and designated hitter for the Yankees teams of the late 1970s, he was a magnificent and complete player when he was in his athletic prime with the Athletics. An excellent base runner, he stole twenty bases a year and caused havoc on middle infielders breaking up double plays. A fine defensive outfielder with a strong throwing arm, Jackson often played center field (in 1972 he was the A's regular there). He was also the best power hitter in the league during most of his career. He rarely hit for a high average, but this is largely a reflection of playing half of his games in an extreme pitcher's park. In 1973, he hit .321 on the road but .259 in the Oakland Coliseum.

The departure of Williams resulted in yet another long circus, as Finley first publicly supported Williams's decision but later refused to let him out of his contract. No one quit on Finley. Williams signed to manage the Yankees, a move the American League blocked. Finley demanded compensation, which the Yankees refused to give, preventing Williams from getting the job. Williams remained out of work until midsummer, when he signed to manage the lowly California Angels. The A's lingered without a manager until late February when Finley finally hired old friend Alvin Dark for 1974.

Finley showed Dark, whom he had fired dramatically in 1967, no respect at all. When the A's were in a mild slump early in the 1974 season, he stormed into the clubhouse and, with players and reporters listening in, shouted, "If you don't start playing aggressive baseball, I'll kick your [expletive deleted] ass!" (The expletive was deleted by *Time* magazine, in its June 3, 1974 issue.) He phoned Dark in the dugout and at home. While Finley's intrusion into his manager's job had been joked about for years, Dark now openly asked for the boss's approval of lineups right in front of reporters.

By 1974, much of the fun was gone. Whereas Finley had flown in to get retractions from players for the occasional criticism in years past, by now the pretense of kissing up to the boss was ancient history. Captain Sal Bando claimed, "I would say all but a few of our players hate him. It binds us together."

The team struggled to hold off the surprising Texas Rangers and won only ninety games. Once the postseason bell rang, the A's beat Baltimore in four games and the Los Angeles Dodgers in five to capture their third straight world championship. Inevitably, yet another player relations nightmare dominated the 1974 post-season. This time it involved not a backup infielder but the contract of a twenty-five-game winner, Jim "Catfish" Hunter.

In January 1974, Hunter signed a two-year contract for a salary of $100,000 per year. The arrangement included a wrinkle: half his salary was to be paid into a life insurance fund as a form of deferred payment. On the day before the World Series began in Los Angeles, the story broke that Finley had not paid the mandated $50,000 to the insurance company, even after receiving written notice in mid-September. Hunter reportedly planned to ask for his release from his contract as soon as the World Series was over. Finley, obviously more worried than he admitted, went into the clubhouse with American League President Lee McPhail to present Hunter with a check for the amount due. Hunter refused to accept the check and told Finley that they would discuss it after the series was over.

After a month of rumors in the press, a hearing was held on November 26 in New York in front of arbitrator Peter Seitz. On December 13 Seitz found for Hunter and declared him a free agent. The baseball world went berserk—never before had a player of Hunter's caliber been available to the highest bidder at the height of his career.

Commissioner Kuhn initially ordered all clubs to refrain from negotiating with Hunter but soon thought better of it and backed off. A three-week bidding war ensued among nearly every team in baseball. The Yankees landed him with a five-year deal totaling $3.75 million, about three times the going rate for the top stars in the game. As with Ken Harrelson seven years earlier, the players were given a glimpse of what a free market might do to their wage scale. They noticed.

◇ ◇ ◇

Without Hunter the A's were a good team, but they had clearly lost some of their swagger. The World Series championship teams featured three excellent starters; Hunter, Blue, and Holtzman had started all twenty-one post-season games the previous two seasons. Now there were but two.

The 1975 Athletics won ninety-eight games, their highest victory total since 1971, but the Boston Red Sox swept them in the American League Championship Series. Blue and Holtzman combined to win forty games, and Finley provided manager Dark with a boatload of veteran pitchers throughout the year to fill out the rotation. None of them could replace Hunter.

The Athletics dynasty, already showing signs of decay, effectively died on December 12, 1975, when arbitrator Seitz dropped another bombshell. This time he declared Dodgers pitcher Andy Messersmith and Expos pitcher Dave McNally free agents after they had played out the season without signing contracts. This decision ultimately put an end to baseball's reserve clause, which bound a player to his team in perpetuity. The agreement negotiated the following summer allowed for a player with six years' service to become a free agent at the end of his contract.

Massa Charlie was finished. Once Finley had to bargain with players as equals, once he had to look an agent in the eye and come to terms, he just was not capable of competing. Charlie Finley did not, and could not, operate in this manner. The whole team hated him and had seen their teammate Hunter go on to happiness and wealth in another city, leaving little doubt about what they were going to do. Finley traded Jackson and Holtzman during spring training in 1976. Bando, Tenace, Campaneris, Fingers, and Rudi (along with Jackson, now an Oriole) became free agents that fall.

In June 1976, Finley attempted to make the best of a bad situation by selling Blue to the Yankees and Fingers and Rudi to the Red Sox for a total of $3.5 million. Because he was about to lose all three at the end of the year anyway, it seemed like a wise idea. Bowie Kuhn voided the sales, claiming they were not "in the best interests of baseball."

Even with the passage of time, it is difficult not to conclude that Kuhn intended only to destroy Finley. Finley had proven to everyone, time and time again, that he could stay one step ahead of the other owners. But this time Kuhn bested his longtime nemesis. The decision ended whatever chance Finley had to survive in Oakland. His farm system, long neglected, could not replenish the heavy losses.

Despite the loss of Jackson and Holtzman and the circus-like atmosphere surrounding the attempted player sale, the team actually held up fairly well in 1976 under new manager Chuck Tanner. The team won eighty-seven games and finished second, only two and a half games behind the Kansas City Royals. After the season Finley traded manager Tanner to the Pittsburgh Pirates for catcher Manny Sanguillen and $100,000.

In 1977, with nearly all of their stars having departed through free agency, the Athletics quickly fell out of contention. They fell to a record of 63–98 and last place, behind even the Seattle Mariners, a first-year expansion team.

It is tempting to conclude that the A's of the 1970s rose to great heights in part because of a common dislike of their owner. Tempting, but unsatisfying. More likely the team excelled *despite* its problems with Finley. Reggie Jackson was not helped by the way he was treated in 1970—he was a twenty-three-year-old star who was set back for a few years and never completely recovered. Vida Blue looked like one of the best pitchers ever when he was twenty-one. He enjoyed a healthy and productive career but was never again the same pitcher. Of the big stars, only the affable Hunter came through relatively scar-free, in the end earning riches and more glory in New York.

Finley's other silly ideas, his designated pinch runners and revolving second basemen (four second baseman share the game and are pinch hit for every time up) were no help either. The team did not need a new manager every year. The Andrews imbroglio could just as easily have cost the team the 1973 World Series.

Charles O. Finley deserves credit for the way he built this team. In a textbook on how to construct a baseball champion, his team could be the centerpiece. But his actions along the way created many unnecessary obstacles. His great team deserves the credit for rising above his foolishness and pettiness. As time passes, one hopes that the owner's giant persona fades into the background and that this team will be remembered for the wonderful things it did on the field.

13

THE NEW SPECIALIST:
THE FIREMAN VS. THE CLOSER

*B*eginning *with the realization that the starter could not finish every game, the* importance of the relief pitcher has continually increased over the past 130 years. In the last generation the evolution of the bullpen has become particularly rapid. As first discussed in chapter 5, the decade of the 1970s introduced the first group of star relievers: the "firemen," who were given large workloads and were recognized and rewarded for their efforts.

By the end of the 1980s, the fireman profile was extinct. In its place teams now employ a "closer," an extreme specialist who pitches fewer innings but in presumably more important ninth-inning situations. This new role for the relief ace was adopted quickly and universally. In this chapter we bring the story of the relief pitcher, begun in chapter 5, up to the present, explore why the closer role was created, and discuss its effectiveness.

◇ ◇ ◇

Figure 13.1 shows the average number of innings a relief ace has worked per season since 1975, the first year of the current save rule. (The numbers have been adjusted for a 162-game season.) The pitchers used in this analysis are those who recorded at least ten saves, led their team in saves, and started no more than three games. The definition is arbitrary, but the trend would be similar with other appropriate criteria.

A typical relief ace threw one hundred innings per year through 1982, when his workload went into a free fall. By 1988 the star closer was pitching only seventy-four innings, a total that has remained relatively steady

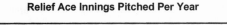

Figure 13.1

since. Explaining and justifying the change has proven a challenge for baseball analysts.

The importance of the entire bullpen has obviously increased along with its workload. The percentage of the game that has been pitched by the relief staff, however, has grown only slightly in the past thirty-five years. Figure 13.2 shows the percentage of the game worked by the bullpen in the recent past. (Tom Ruane, using data from Retrosheet, Project Scoresheet and Total Sports, provided the information for this table.) There is a line in the graph for each league because the AL data is available back to 1963, the NL to 1974.

The cumulative work performed by the bullpen has changed very little of late. A dip in the early seventies was the result of a short-lived increase in complete games and the introduction of the designated hitter rule in the AL in 1973.

A typical bullpen has consistently pitched about 450 to 500 innings per season over the past thirty-five years. Obviously, one of a baseball manager's most important jobs is to divide those innings among his relief pitchers. A manager in the 1970s fortunate enough to have a quality fireman often gave him 120 or more innings and tried to use him at the most important points in the game.

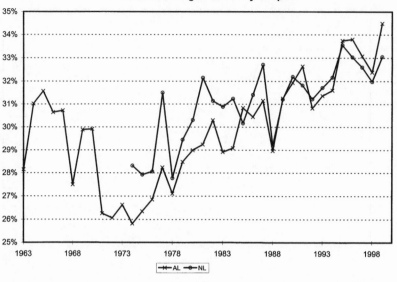

Figure 13.2

Chuck Tanner, manager of the 1977 Pittsburgh Pirates, assigned 133 innings to Rich Gossage, 103 to Kent Tekulve, and no more than about 50 to anyone else. Tanner tried to use Gossage in the most important situations and Tekulve whenever Goose was unavailable or being saved for later in the game.

Tony LaRussa, with a star reliever of his own on the 1988 Oakland Athletics, gave only 73 innings to Dennis Eckersley, 112 to Gene Nelson (including one start), 78 to Greg Cadaret, and 80 to Rick Honeycutt. In choosing to entrust many important innings to his less-talented pitchers, LaRussa obviously felt he was saving Eckersley for the most important situations and also from overwork.

To better show the changing use of relief pitchers over the past forty years, figure 13.3 graphs the number of relief pitchers used per game since 1963 (an earlier graph in chapter 5 shows the trend for all of baseball history). Between roughly 1980 and 1995, while the number of innings pitched by the bullpen remained steady, the number of relief pitchers used per game by each team grew from one and a half to two and a half. The rise in offense levels in the mid-1990s did not cause an increase in pitchers used—the increase actually predated the jump in run scoring. One could, in fact, argue the reverse—that transferring innings away from

Relief Pitchers Used Per Game Per Team

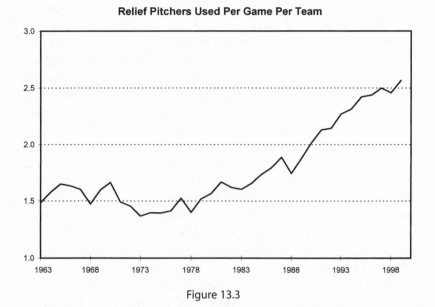

Figure 13.3

the team's best relief pitcher and giving them to the eleventh and twelfth men on the pitching staff helped create the offensive explosion.

As pointed out in chapter 5, there has been a corresponding need to employ more pitchers on each team. A typical club in 1980 used about four relief pitchers (defined as twenty or more games and fewer than five starts); by 1999 this number had jumped to six and a half.

During the 1980s, the fireman role evolved into the modern closer role. A closer enters the game at precisely those times defined in the definition of the save rule, usually at the start of the ninth inning with a one-, two-, or three-run lead. If the lead is more than three, the ace comes in only if the tying run is on deck—for example, with a four-run lead and two runners on. In the seventh inning of the 1978 AL East playoff game, the Yankees used Rich Gossage to get out of a tight jam. Faced with a similar situation, the 1988 Oakland Athletics would likely have brought in Greg Cadaret to try to stem the Red Sox rally, turned to Gene Nelson and/or Rich Honeycutt to pitch the eighth, and finally summoned Eckersley in the ninth (if his teammates had managed to maintain the lead).

Lee Smith is a prime example of a good pitcher who was a relief ace during the transition. Smith pitched 103 innings and recorded a league-leading 29 saves for the 1983 Cubs. Twelve years later, he required only 49 innings to pick up 37 saves for the Angels. The intervening years were a smooth progression between these two seasons. A quality pitcher for many years, Smith had a record 478 saves that were largely due to his ability to continue getting the closer's job over a long career. This also applies to Jeff Reardon, who held the record briefly before Smith blew by him.

Dennis Eckersley, the best reliever of the modern era, was a throwback in that he was an ex-starter. An excellent pitcher for several years with the Indians and Red Sox, he appeared washed up when he arrived in Oakland at age thirty-two in 1987. When manager Tony LaRussa turned Eckersley into a reliever, a star was reborn. In his first year out of the bullpen, Eckersley was mostly a long reliever before LaRussa made him the closer in midyear.

It has become fashionable to credit, or blame, Tony LaRussa for causing the drop in the star reliever's workload, but the data does not support this assertion. Prior to 1988, Eckersley's first year as a closer, the average workload for the ace reliever was already dropping very quickly and was down to seventy-four innings for the 1988 season. A 1999 relief ace averaged seventy innings, not much different from a typical total in Eckersley's first big year.

LaRussa's role in the evolution was to use his number one reliever exclusively in save situations. He did not ask Eckersley to warm up in the bullpen unless he planned to use him, and he always gave his star sufficient time to throw before bringing him into the game. LaRussa's policy precluded using Eckersley as a fireman, who might need to get up and ready in a hurry. For the next five years, 1988 through 1992, Eckersley was a dominant pitcher for an Athletics team that won four division titles and the 1989 World Series. In 1992, he was rewarded with the Cy Young and MVP awards for his fifty-one saves and 1.91 ERA.

This philosophy was quickly extended to the rest of the team's relievers, who were also soon assigned set roles. If Eckersley was most effective when he knew that he could prepare to pitch in a certain situation, then the same might hold true for Greg Cadaret and Rick Honeycutt. LaRussa did not warm up a pitcher in the sixth, sit him down when the starter got out of the jam, warm him up again in the seventh, and bring him in to pitch the eighth. With well-defined roles, a reliever warmed up to pitch at a particular time in the game. If that time of the game passed without the pitcher being needed, his day was likely over.

Soon after Eckersley's emergence, all relief aces pitched almost exclusively in save situations. After several decades of experimentation, clubs began to look for one relief star who could work seventy innings a year, mostly to protect ninth-inning leads, and the rest of the bullpen was organized to "set up" for him. This closer recorded nearly all of the saves, and therefore received most of the credit and the higher salary that went with it.

Saves Per Game

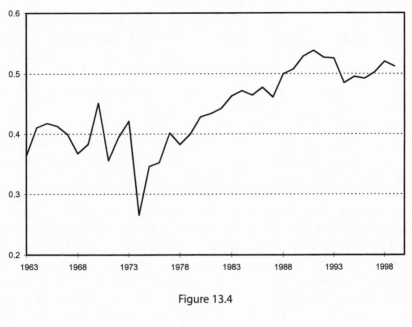

Figure 13.4

◇   ◇   ◇

One possible advantage of the modern closer role over the fireman is that, by usually pitching only one inning, the closer may be available to pitch more often. But the best of the modern closers—Eckersley, Trevor Hoffman, Mariano Rivera—do not pitch any more games than Gossage and Fingers did. They may be available more often, but the benefits of the role are not obvious.

The post-Eckersley closers receive more saves than the firemen for three principal reasons. First, as figure 13.4 shows, more saves are available in the current era than in the 1960s and 1970s. The increase is larger than can be accounted for by the drop in complete games, which suggests that many saves now come when a closer relieves another reliever who is credited with the win.

Twenty years ago an ace reliever might come in to pitch in a tie game in the eighth inning and subsequently receive the win and finish the game. In this instance, no save would be awarded. Many great relievers had very high won and lost totals in the 1970s and early 1980s. Today, a reliever other than the closer would come into this game in the eighth and, if his team seized the lead, the closer would take over in the ninth.

The first reliever would receive the win, the closer the save. Figure 13.4 summarizes this increase in saves per game.

Second, the modern closer also receives a higher percentage of his team's saves than the 1970s fireman. During the Oakland A's World Series run from 1972 to 1974, relief star Rollie Fingers earned 61 of the Athletics' 112 team saves. His managers, Dick Williams and Alvin Dark, likely believed that some of the save situations were not important enough for their ace.

On the other hand, Eckersley received fifty-one of the A's fifty-eight saves in 1992. This reflects a profound difference in Fingers's and Eckersley's use. Fingers might have been brought in to pitch the eighth inning of a tie game on Saturday and would either win or lose or turn the tie game over to someone else. Eckersley would only very rarely enter a game in this situation. In the event of a save opportunity on Sunday, Eckersley would have been available while Fingers would not. The trade-off is that the hypothetical situation on Saturday might have been more significant than the save opportunity on Sunday. Of Eckersley's fifty-one saves in 1992, he entered the game with the tying run on base or at bat on only twelve occasions. It is likely that Eckersley could have had more of an impact by pitching in games other than the ones in which he recorded his other thirty-nine saves.

Finally, modern managers believe that an ace reliever is more effective knowing that he can gear himself up for pitching at a certain time every day. Data on how often a fireman such as Lyle or Gossage or Fingers was asked to warm up and then sit down is not available. Our recollections, and the recollections of the pitchers involved, indicate that this was quite common. One might assume that the progress made in this area in the last generation has been positive for the relief pitchers and the team.

In an article in the fourth edition of *Total Baseball*, Bill Felber explores whether teams were performing better in the late innings since the advent of the closer. Using box scores for every game played in the 1952, 1972, and 1992 seasons, he determines the probability of victory starting from six common save situations. Felber concludes that the probability of winning from each of the six save situations was essentially the same for the three years he examined.

If the main goal of the change in the role of the relief ace from fireman to closer was to win games, these numbers suggest that the change has not worked. The revised strategy has produced no discernible effect on the likelihood of winning in typical save situations.

◇ ◇ ◇

A problem inherent in determining the value of relief pitchers is that the best relievers pitch a disproportionately large percentage of their innings in important situations. If a team's closer and long reliever each produces the same raw statistics, the closer has probably been more valuable because most of his appearances have come in close games.

To properly measure situational value, we introduce a statistic called win probability added (WPA). A player's WPA estimates how a player's plate appearances (for batters) or batters faced (for pitchers) affected his team's probability of winning the game. A detailed explanation of WPA can be found in appendix 5.

The method is based on establishing the probability of a team winning from every possible game situation. Suppose the home team is ahead by one run in the bottom of the fifth with runners on first and third and two outs. What is the probability the home team will win the game? Using the 1980 through 1983 Retrosheet play-by-play files as a base, we generated tables that provide the likelihood of victory given any particular game situation. In the example just posed, the probability of winning was 74 percent. The tables were calculated using every game played in these four seasons for all major league teams. In a particular season or ballpark where run scoring was significantly higher or lower than the major league average of the early 1980s, the tables may require adjustment.

Once these tables are generated, one can evaluate the effect an individual has on his team's chances of winning over a large number of games. If a player comes to bat in the situation mentioned above (home team ahead by one run in the bottom of the fifth with runners on first and third and two outs) and singles, scoring one runner and moving the other to second, he has increased his team's chances of winning from .740 to .838. For this plate appearance, the batter's WPA is .098. For the pitcher, the result is the opposite, and his WPA is -.098 (negative .098).

Summing a player's WPA over an entire season, using each discrete at-bat or batter faced, provides an interesting way to measure his value. If two batters have identical statistics but one has hit better in more important situations, that player could have a much higher WPA. Similarly, pitchers who are used only at the most important moments in a game have an opportunity to record a higher WPA than other pitchers with similar statistics. Win probability added estimates the total wins a player adds to a team above a .500 record. The 1983 Minnesota Twins had a won-loss record of 70 and 92; summing the WPA of all the Twins' events—both

Table 13.1 Top Ten Pitchers, 1969

	Team	W	L	S	ERA	IP	Events	WPA
Bob Gibson	SLN	20	13	0	2.18	314.0	1308	9.09
Denny McLain	DET	24	9	0	2.80	325.0	1344	7.82
Juan Marichal	SFN	21	11	0	2.10	299.7	1214	7.60
Larry Dierker	HOU	20	13	0	2.33	305.3	1238	7.40
Tom Seaver	NYN	25	7	0	2.21	273.3	1115	7.36
Jerry Koosman	NYN	17	9	0	2.28	241.0	979	7.14
Tug McGraw	NYN	9	3	12	2.24	100.3	439	6.07
Bill Singer	LAN	20	12	1	2.34	315.7	1291	5.32
Ken Tatum	CAL	7	2	22	1.36	86.3	355	5.30
Mike Cuellar	BAL	23	11	0	2.38	290.7	1155	5.12

WPA = win probability added

offensive and defensive—results in a value of -11 (70 minus 81).

One can apply the WPA calculation and other game information to take a more detailed look at the use and value of relief pitchers over the years for which Retrosheet play-by-play data are available. Tables 13.1–13.3 list the top ten pitchers in WPA for the 1969, 1978, and 1988 seasons.

No contextual adjustments have been made for either the era in which the pitcher was pitching or the pitcher's home park. Over these three sample years, no relief pitcher was able to rank with the most effective starting pitchers.

A pitcher's WPA considers all events that occur when he is pitching or,

Table 13.2 Top Ten Pitchers, 1978

	Team	W	L	S	ERA	IP	Events	WPA
Mike Caldwell	MIL	22	9	1	2.36	293.3	1205	6.94
Ron Guidry	NYA	25	3	0	1.74	273.7	1091	5.79
Bob Knepper	SFN	17	11	0	2.63	260.0	1094	5.29
Craig Swan	NYN	9	6	0	2.43	207.3	850	5.01
Jim Palmer	BAL	21	12	0	2.46	296.0	1234	4.90
Steve Rogers	MON	13	10	1	2.47	219.0	897	4.52
Gaylord Perry	SDN	21	6	0	2.73	260.7	1099	4.42
Burt Hooten	LAN	19	10	0	2.71	236.0	978	4.37
Rich Gossage	NYA	10	11	27	2.01	134.3	561	4.32
Doug Bair	CIN	7	6	28	1.97	100.3	419	4.28

WPA = win probability added

Table 13.3 Top Ten Pitchers, 1988

	Team	W	L	S	ERA	IP	Events	WPA
Orel Hershiser	LAN	23	8	1	2.26	267.0	1102	8.47
Danny Jackson	CIN	23	8	0	2.73	260.7	1065	5.40
Frank Viola	MIN	24	7	0	2.64	255.3	1056	5.25
Teddy Higuera	MIL	16	9	0	2.45	227.3	918	5.24
Randy Myers	NYN	7	3	26	1.72	68.0	270	5.20
David Cone	NYN	20	3	0	2.22	231.3	996	5.15
Doug Jones	CLE	3	4	37	2.27	83.3	345	4.74
Mike Scott	HOU	14	8	0	2.92	218.7	912	4.57
Greg Maddux	CHN	18	8	0	3.18	249.0	1082	4.48
John Franco	CIN	6	6	39	1.57	86.0	345	4.47

WPA = win probability added

in other words, when the pitcher's team is in the field. Obviously fielding and defending the running game play a role in defense, but for simplicity we do not unscramble the pitching from the fielding component; all events are used, including ones that result in an error or stolen base. (A similar problem exists in comparing pitchers' ERAs.) Thus some of WPA shown in these tables should rightfully be extrapolated to the other fielders. Because our analysis here involves comparing pitchers to each other, this should not materially upset any conclusions.

The timing of runs is very important in this measure. If a pitcher gets ahead 7–0 quickly and then gives up three runs, these runs will count very little against him because with a four-run lead his team still has only a small chance of losing. On the other hand, if a pitcher gives up three early runs in a zero-zero game, the pitcher will accumulate a large negative WPA: his team's win probability will drop from about 50 percent to well under 30 percent.

WPA can help assess the ramifications of the transition from fireman to closer. The following study examines the use and value of seven relief pitchers approximately ten years apart: Darold Knowles and Hoyt Wilhelm in 1967; Rollie Fingers and Rich Gossage in 1978; and Dennis Eckersley, Jeff Reardon, and Randy Myers in 1988. These pitchers were chosen because they were quality pitchers whose usage patterns best fit the strategy of their era. Table 13.4 summarizes each of the seven pitchers' seasonal statistics, along with his WPA.

The probability of the visiting team winning heading into the bottom of the ninth with a one-run lead—the classic closer situation—is 80.7 per-

Table 13.4 Sample Relievers' Raw Statistics with WPA

	Year	W	L	S	G	GS	ERA	IP	WPA
Knowles	1967	6	8	14	61	1	2.70	113.3	4.23
Wilhelm	1967	8	3	12	49	0	1.31	89.0	5.12
Fingers	1978	6	13	37	67	0	2.52	107.3	3.07
Gossage	1978	10	11	27	63	0	2.01	134.3	4.32
Eckersley	1988	4	3	45	60	0	2.35	72.7	3.06
Reardon	1988	2	4	42	63	0	2.47	73.0	1.86
Myers	1988	7	3	26	55	0	1.72	68.0	5.20

WPA = win probability added

cent. A relief pitcher who closes out this game (moving the win probability to 1.0) earns .193 (1 - .807) WPA. If he blows the lead and the game without being relieved (moving the win probability to 0), his WPA for the outing is a dismal -.807 (0 - .807).

On the other hand, if a reliever comes in to the top of the seventh with runners on second and third and nobody out ahead by one run—a fireman situation—the probability of his team winning is 43.5 percent. If the pitcher gets out of the inning unscathed, the win probability jumps to 80 percent (home team ahead by one heading into the bottom of the seventh), and the pitcher has added .365 WPA to his ledger. If the reliever allows only one of the base runners to score, the win probability still grows to 60.9 percent (game tied heading into the bottom of the seventh), and his WPA is increased by .174.

Read the above examples closely. According to WPA, a reliever who comes in to the tight jam described in the second example and allows only

Table 13.5 Games Pitched by Inning on Entering Game

Inning	Knowles	Wilhelm	Fingers	Gossage	Eckersley	Reardon	Myers
1–5	6	0	0	4	0	0	0
6	7	5	1	5	0	0	1
7	10	16	13	16	0	1	2
8	21	13	36	13	22	23	25
9	11	12	12	23	31	37	19
10+	6	2	5	2	7	2	8
Total	61	49	67	63	60	63	55

WPA = win probability added

Table 13.6 Games Pitched by Score Differential on Entering Game

Delta	Knowles	Wilhelm	Fingers	Gossage	Eckersley	Reardon	Myers
-3+	10	5	1	2	1	3	2
-2	2	1	1	4	0	0	2
-1	9	9	8	3	0	1	6
0	19	14	9	9	2	3	11
1	12	11	22	14	22	21	13
2	2	4	18	14	13	16	9
3+	7	4	8	17	22	19	12
Total	61	49	67	63	60	63	55

one of the runners to score has actually helped his team approximately as much as the pitcher who comes in to start the ninth with a one-run lead and closes the door. This conclusion is contrary to current baseball thinking.

The Retrosheet files also provide concrete evidence as to how our seven pitchers were used. Table 13.5 indicates the innings that the pitchers were brought in to the game.

One can see the drastic changes with Eckersley and Reardon, who were used exclusively from the eighth inning on. In fact, less than 40 percent of the two closers' appearances occurred before the ninth, while only ten years earlier, 75 percent of Fingers's appearances occurred prior to the ninth inning.

Table 13.6 shows the score of the game when the star reliever was brought in. The first row represents situations where the team was trailing by three or more runs, the second row shows cases where the team was trailing by two runs, etc.

The majority (56 percent) of Eckersley's and Reardon's appearances came with the team ahead by at least two runs. In contrast only 16 percent of Wilhelm's appearances occurred in these situations. Myers, who assumed the role of primary relief ace during the season, did not have nearly the regular pattern that his contemporaries did.

In *The New Bill James Historical Abstract*, James explains a computer simulation he created in order to, among other things, discover in which situations a relief ace would have the largest impact. Based on the study, he concludes that a reliever has the most effect when brought in to a tie game, followed by a one-run lead. No other situation even approaches the same potential benefit. Assuming James is right, the 1967 relievers were used in the most highly leveraged situations, followed by the 1978 fireman.

Table 13.7 Games Pitched by Win Probability on Entering Game

Prob.	Knowles	Wilhelm	Fingers	Gossage	Eckersley	Reardon	Myers
0–.3	21	15	10	12	1	4	11
.3–.5	16	11	11	9	2	4	9
.5–.7	5	9	6	8	0	5	9
.7–.8	5	4	13	6	10	5	6
.8–.9	7	6	17	8	20	15	8
.9–1.0	7	3	10	20	27	30	12
Total	61	49	67	63	60	63	55

WPA = win probability added

By 1988, bringing a star reliever in to a tie game was a rare occurrence. Randy Myers pitched fewer innings than Eckersley and Reardon but was brought in to more close games. Myers had a higher WPA than the other two pitchers combined, a result consistent with James's conclusions.

Finally, table 13.7 shows the team's probability of winning at the time the star reliever enters the game.

The modern closer (typified by Eckersley and Reardon) generally enters the game when the probability of winning is greater than 80 percent. The 1960s and 1970s relievers were much more likely to be used in situations where the result of the game remained in doubt.

Using pitchers as fireman instead of closers will likely offer higher WPA to the team. A counterbalancing argument is that the earlier relief aces may have been more susceptible to injury, a theory we discuss below. Randy Myers, who had the reduced workload consistent with a modern closer but was used in many more tight games, was an exception. Employing a modern bullpen has likely reduced the number of difficult in-game decisions that a manager must make. Whether the team has benefited is debatable.

◇   ◇   ◇

The principal reason advanced for the reduction in the star reliever's workload is that the fireman role placed too much strain on his arm. A few high-profile relief aces from the 1970s blew out their arms after one or more great years with a high workload and never recovered.

Bill Campbell worked 167 innings for the 1976 Twins, recorded a 17–5 record and twenty saves, and signed a lucrative free agent contract with the Red Sox that fall. The next year in Boston he pitched 140 more innings

(13–9, 31 saves). Unfortunately, he suffered an elbow injury in 1978; he had a mediocre career thereafter.

Jim Kern had two very good seasons with the Indians in 1977 and 1978 before posting one of the best relief seasons ever for the 1979 Rangers: a 13–5 record, twenty-nine saves, and a 1.57 ERA in 143 innings. *Total Baseball*'s formulas rank him the best player in baseball that year. Kern hurt his elbow in 1980 and was never again better than an average pitcher.

Over the next several years, most likely in order to reduce these breakdowns, the high workloads were abandoned. Are relief pitchers less likely to get injured now? This is a difficult problem to study because pitchers have always gotten hurt, and we do not really know why they get hurt. Do today's closers get hurt any less than their predecessors?

One way to study the issue is to make a list of all pitchers who might have lost effectiveness prematurely after being the team's ace reliever and look for conclusions that can be drawn. We determined the list of pitchers using the following criteria.

1. Identify all relievers (since 1974) who saved twenty or more games at least once through age thirty but never did so again.
2. Remove several pitchers who did not really lose effectiveness, but just changed roles (e.g., Charlie Hough, Greg McMichael, Mike Stanton).
3. Remove several pitchers who are still active.

This process resulted in a list of thirty-seven pitchers, which can be categorized chronologically.

- 1970s firemen (eleven): Tom Murphy, Rawly Eastwick, Bill Campbell, Lerrin LaGrow, Terry Forster, Al Hrabosky, Dave LaRoche, Skip Lockwood, Jim Kern, Joe Sambito, Don Stanhouse.

  Only nineteen pitchers saved at least twenty games in a season through the age of thirty in these years, and eleven (or 58 percent) might have "broken down." Most had one or more years of high-workload, high-quality seasons but were much less effective after age thirty. In particular, Kern, Campbell, Murphy, and Eastwick were quality pitchers who got hurt or burned out prematurely.

- 1980s hybrids (eleven): Doug Corbett, Ed Farmer, Tim Stoddard, Salome Barojas, Dan Spillner, Ron Davis, Frank Dipino, Pete Ladd, Bill Caudill, Bob James, Mark Davis.

These eleven pitchers who appeared to prematurely lose effectiveness came out of a pool of forty-seven qualifiers. This is only 23 percent, a huge drop from the 1970s. Corbett (136 innings) and Spillner (133 innings) each had a heavy workload in their one big season, although Corbett was a twenty-seven-year-old rookie and Spillner was not really an effective pitcher before his breakout season in 1982. Mark Davis won the Cy Young Award in 1989 for his one great season (92 innings) but was injured the next year and never again effective. Bill Caudill had his last big save year in 1984 (96 innings), a very good season in a different role for the Blue Jays in 1985 (69 innings), and then developed a shoulder injury.

- 1990s closers (fifteen): Mike Schooler, Rob Dibble, Doug Henry, Bobby Thigpen, Gene Harris, Bryan Harvey, Darren Holmes, Duane Ward, Mel Rojas, Mark Wohlers, Rich Loiselle, Ricky Bottalico, Rod Beck, Joe Grahe, Kerry Lightenberg.

The 1990s saw fifty-four pitchers save twenty games in a season through age thirty, and at least fifteen (28 percent) could be considered to have lost effectiveness soon thereafter. (Other candidates to join the washout list for the 1990s include Tom Gordon and John Rocker.) Thigpen broke down after pitching a bit more than the typical closer of the era (80–90 innings). Ward had five great hundred-plus-inning seasons as Tom Henke's setup man but (ironically) got hurt after one great season as the full-time closer (71 innings) in 1993. Dibble also lost effectiveness only after having success in a reduced closer role. Schooler, Harvey, and Beck, among others, were high-quality closers who suffered injuries.

These results suggest that 1970s firemen may have been overworked but that the 1980s hybrids probably worked at sustainable levels. This study does not specify, however, whether the 1970s pitchers hurled too many innings, had an inappropriate pattern of usage, or some combination of the two. With regard to starting pitchers, many have concluded that the limiting factor is not the total number of innings pitched but the number of pitches thrown in a game. For relief pitchers, perhaps more attention should be paid to pitch counts and providing appropriate rest between long outings. In addition, improved surgical procedures are likely affecting the data. Whether, for example, Bill Campbell could have recovered from his 1978 elbow injury with today's medical advances cannot be known.

• • •

During the 1980s, managers and pitching coaches deliberately reduced the role of their best relief pitchers. As we have seen in this chapter, the modern closer pitches many fewer innings than the firemen, but also works in less-critical situations. In fact, the closer, generally considered the best pitcher in the bullpen, often pitches fewer innings than one or more other relievers on his team. Modern managers now rely on their tenth, eleventh, and twelfth pitchers to handle innings that used to be pitched by their best relievers.

To balance this, managers must believe that either their team is more successful in the late innings or their best relief pitchers will be less susceptible to injury with a reduced workload. The available evidence suggests that the former is not happening. The injury situation, however, is more complicated.

Based on the number of pitchers who developed arm injuries or lost effectiveness at a relatively young age, the 1970s firemen were probably asked to pitch more than they could handle. Managers reacted to this by dramatically curtailing the workload of their star relievers and, by the late 1980s, severely limiting the situations in which they appeared. The injury problem, however, seems to have abated prior to the adoption of the rigid closer role.

We believe that relief aces could pitch more innings than they do today, perhaps as many as 100 or 110. Managers would also benefit by using their best relief pitcher in more highly leveraged situations, especially tie games. A usage pattern similar to the hybrid of the 1980s (such as Randy Myers's 1988 season) where the ace is not reserved exclusively for save situations and is occasionally allowed to pitch multiple innings would likely enhance his value without increasing his injury risk.

If a manager used his star reliever this way, he might record fifteen wins and twenty saves rather than three wins and forty saves, but increase both his value and the team's record. Because ace relievers today are judged and paid based on their save totals, top closers would naturally show some resistance to a different usage pattern. All interested parties—the closer, the manager, and the general manager—would have to agree on the strategy and its effect on compensation.

14

UNFULFILLED PROMISE:
THE EARLY 1980S MONTREAL EXPOS

With the recent discussion regarding Montreal's viability as a major league
baseball town and the controversy surrounding the contraction of
its franchise, one might easily forget the excitement that engulfed the
Expos twenty years ago, when the team was widely hailed as the team of
the eighties. In an era when drawing over two million fans in a season
was still uncommon, the Expos exceeded that every year from 1979 to
1983 (except for the strike-shortened 1981). In 1980, Steve Wulf wrote in
Sports Illustrated, "The team is almost as beloved as *les Canadiens*."

The Expos built a strong foundation throughout the mid- to late 1970s.
Between 1973 and 1981, five different Expos finished first or second in the
NL Rookie of the Year voting. Even more impressive, four players who
debuted as Expos in this period—Andre Dawson, Tim Raines, Gary
Carter, and Tim Wallach—had careers of more than 2,200 games, something only ninety-seven players managed to do in the twentieth century.
Another four players with careers of more than 1,000 games also broke in
with Montreal during these years. Furthermore, the Expos introduced
three pitchers—Steve Rogers, Bill Gullickson, and Scott Sanderson—who
pitched more than 2,500 innings in the major leagues.

From the Expos' inception as an expansion franchise in 1969, the team's
management, led by owner Charles Bronfman and president and chief executive officer John McHale, created strong scouting and baseball development organizations. During the early 1970s the Expos had used the amateur draft to great effect, and by the end of the decade the club had a
formidable young talent base. The Expos drafted all seven players men-

tioned above, plus others such as Warren Cromartie and Ellis Valentine.

In the end, this fine young group never fulfilled the high expectations the baseball world had for it. The team narrowly produced the best cumulative record in the NL over the years 1979 through 1983 (the team won 413 and lost 341, a .547 winning percentage over the five year period; Philadelphia finished 413–342 and the Dodgers 413–346) and won one division title in the strike-jumbled 1981, but never advanced to the World Series. After outlining the Expos' seasons through 1984, this chapter will explore some potential explanations for the team falling short.

◇ ◇ ◇

After finishing 55–107 during a dismal 1976 season, the Expos hired manager Dick Williams to turn the club around. Although caustic and occasionally abusive, Williams was the perfect choice for this young team. Williams had his flaws, but breaking in and developing young ballplayers was not one of them. In 1967, Williams led the extremely young Boston Red Sox to a completely unexpected pennant, and later he won two consecutive World Series titles at the helm of the youthful Oakland A's.

Williams immediately began to redesign his team. In 1977, his first year in charge, he made twenty-three-year-old Gary Carter the regular catcher after he had split time between catcher and the outfield in 1976. Williams handed outfield jobs to Warren Cromartie (twenty-three) and Andre Dawson (twenty-two); Dawson responded by winning the Rookie of the Year award. The rifle-armed Ellis Valentine, just twenty-two, solidified his starting role in right field. Larry Parrish, a twenty-three-year-old third baseman, already had two years of major league starting experience. The other incumbent infielders in 1976 were mediocre at best. Consequently, the Expos acquired veterans Tony Perez, thirty-five, and Dave Cash, twenty-seven, to play first and second in 1977. In April, Williams and general manager Charlie Fox acquired twenty-seven-year-old shortstop Chris Speier, who had been an all-star for San Francisco in his early twenties. They had built a solid top-to-bottom line-up, and the team improved its record by twenty games, finishing 75–87.

The pitching staff, however, included staff ace Steve Rogers and little else. Rogers had finished second in the 1973 Rookie of the Year balloting but had improved only modestly since. He pitched better in his first couple of years under Williams, but the two hated each other. Williams considered Rogers "weak-kneed" and selfish, and Rogers once called

Williams a "worthless human being." In his autobiography, *No More Mr. Nice Guy,* Williams almost gleefully tells a 1978 story in which Charlie Fox, one day before a game, told Speier to "swing that damn bat, would you. Get the damn bat off your shoulders." After thinking Fox had left, Speier replied: "F— you, Charlie." Fox overheard the comment, grabbed Speier and expressed his displeasure. Rogers, the team's union representative, pushed Fox away and told him to leave Speier alone. Fox, to the surprise of everyone, probably including himself, slugged Rogers in the jaw. This incident likely contributed to Fox losing his general manager title (which was mostly nominal anyway) after the season.

For 1978 the team added two left-handed starting pitchers, free agent Ross Grimsley and trade acquisition Rudy May. Grimsley won twenty games, but May battled injuries and pitched only 144 innings. Dan Schatzeder, the first of Montreal's crop of young starting pitchers, pitched semiregularly in 1978. Despite the pitching additions, the team improved by only one game because of a slight regression by several offensive performers.

Heading into the 1979 season, the Expos had assembled a good ball club. Because the team had never finished higher than fourth, expectations were still modest. *Sports Illustrated,* for example, forecast a third-place finish for the Expos. In the off-season the club traded with the Cubs for second baseman Rodney Scott, who soon became one of Williams's favorite young players. Although not much of a hitter, Scott could draw a walk and steal bases. Scott had not accomplished much prior to his acquisition by the Expos, and Williams surprised the team when he chose Scott, partly in an effort to shake things up, as his starting second baseman over the popular Cash.

The other key acquisition for 1979 was left-handed pitcher Bill "Spaceman" Lee, obtained from the Red Sox for reserve infielder Stan Papi. This deal proved a steal, as Lee finished 16–10. Lee joined a rotation of Rogers, Grimsley, and two young hurlers, Scott Sanderson and Dan Schatzeder. Another youngster, twenty-one-year-old David Palmer, moved into the rotation in midyear and finished 10–2. The right-handed Elias Sosa (eighteen saves, 1.96 ERA) and the ageless left-hander Woody Fryman (ten saves, 2.79 ERA) ably anchored a strong bullpen. The staff led the league in earned run average.

The Expos used a stable set of regulars in 1979. Other than Cash, who spelled Scott at second base several times, no reserve received more than 140 at-bats. Twenty-five-year-old Gary Carter was now recognized as a star at catcher and was selected to his second All-Star Game. At third base,

Parrish had developed into an excellent slugger. On the other hand, veteran first baseman Perez was now thirty-seven and well past his productive years, and Speier had plateaued at a mediocre level.

By spring 1979 the outfield was widely viewed as the best young group in baseball. Left fielder Warren Cromartie was only twenty-five and in his third year as a starter; although regarded as a coming star, he had yet to hit more than ten home runs or have a slugging percentage over .420. In center field, twenty-four-year-old Andre Dawson had slumped to .253 in his sophomore season in 1978 but was still considered a future prize. Another twenty-four-year-old, right fielder Ellis Valentine, was probably the most highly regarded of the three: he had played in the 1977 All-Star Game and won a Gold Glove in 1978.

With excellent pitching and a few offensive stars, the Expos improved by twenty games and finished 95–65, only two games behind the eventual world champion Pittsburgh Pirates. In fact, the Expos remained alive in the pennant race until the last weekend of the season. Despite the fine reputation of their offensive players, the Expos owed most of their success to their pitching staff. The team led the league in fewest runs allowed but finished only sixth in runs scored.

The team was extremely young—only two starting position players, Perez and Speier, were older than twenty-five—but tested: by 1979 most of the regulars had started for several years. Not surprisingly, the Expos' strong season created high expectations for the following year, particularly after McHale acquired speed merchant Ron LeFlore from the Detroit Tigers during the off-season for Schatzeder.

The lineup for 1980 changed very little. LeFlore became the starter in left field and Cromartie shifted to first base. Perez left for the Red Sox as a free agent and Williams released Grimsley now that it was clear he had little left. Bill Gullickson, only twenty-one, joined the starting rotation, and another young pitcher, twenty-three-year-old Charlie Lea, started nineteen games. Gullickson pitched extremely well (10–5, 3.00), struck out eighteen batters in a game against the Cubs, and finished second in the Rookie of the Year vote.

The 1980 Expos battled the Phillies all season, setting up a showdown for the Eastern Division title on the last weekend of the season. With both clubs 89–70, the Phillies came into Montreal for the final three games of the season. The Phillies won the first two and clinched the division title. For the second straight season, the team that edged out the Expos at the end of the season went on to win the World Series. The addition of LeFlore helped the offense a bit as the Expos moved up to fourth in runs scored. A falloff on the defensive side to third in runs allowed offset some of the offensive gains.

Dick Williams blamed the failure to win the division title on poor pitching down the stretch (read: Williams believed Rogers could not handle pressure situations) and inexperience. The team also suffered a surprising number of injuries that year. Ellis Valentine's cheek was shattered in late May when he was beaned by Roy Thomas of the Cardinals. Valentine missed a month and a half, then suffered a hip injury in August. Larry Parrish was hit on the wrist with a pitch in early May and regressed from his outstanding 1979. Ron LeFlore fractured his wrist September 11 and was limited to pinch running for the remainder of the season (he still managed to steal ninety-seven bases). David Palmer was injured much of the season, pitching only 130 innings.

Bill Lee suffered the most bizarre injury of the season, hurting himself by falling off a building onto an iron fence and severely injuring his hip. Lee's version is that he was out jogging one morning and happened by a friend's apartment. He wanted to say hello without waking her up and decided to climb up the building to her window. Williams's version is that Lee had to make a quick escape from a girlfriend's apartment in the middle of the night when her husband came home. Lee fell to 4–8 in only 118 innings after pitching 222 innings in 1979.

Lofty expectations surrounded the team again in 1981, although a perceived lack of team chemistry created some uncertainty. *Inside Sports* suggested: "To know them is not to like them. The Expos may have less feeling than any club in baseball." Once again, Montreal made only a couple of material transactions. In one, the team allowed LeFlore, the man *Inside Sports* called "the worst of the lot," to leave via free agency. Williams complained that LeFlore was a "rabble-rouser" in the clubhouse and wrote of his "late night forays into strange parts of town which wouldn't have been so bad if he hadn't taken the team's younger players with him."

The Expos' player development system remained in high gear, however, and the club promoted Tim Raines to replace LeFlore in left field. Raines excelled immediately en route to becoming one of the greatest leadoff men ever. In the other move of note, the club signed journeyman hurler Ray Burris to round out the rotation behind the big three of Rogers, Gullickson, and Sanderson. Lea had a tender elbow much of the second half of the season, and Palmer's elbow kept him out basically the entire year.

In 1981 the long summer players' strike created a split season and an additional round of playoffs, with the winners of each division's first half squaring off against the winners of the second half to determine the division champ. Early in the season the Expos traded the slumping Valentine to the Mets for relief pitcher Jeff Reardon to bolster the bullpen. At the time of the strike, Montreal was 30–25, four games back.

On September 8, with the team 14–12 in the second half, McHale fired Williams, who had worn out his welcome. Several years earlier he had successfully integrated a number of young ballplayers into a 107-loss team and transformed it into a winner. But after nearly five years, his aggressive in-your-face style began to lose a little of its effectiveness, and the players became more ambivalent towards him. Dan Turner, in his excellent book *The Expos Inside Out*, further suggests that some players and the front office began to resent the fact that Scott, Valentine, and LeFlore had been allowed to set their own rules. In a long and successful managerial career with six teams, Williams had his longest stint in Montreal.

McHale replaced Williams with the team's vice president of player development, Jim Fanning. The team played 16–11 under Fanning to finish the second half 30–23, good enough for the second-half title. Andre Dawson was the big offensive star for the Expos: he finished second in the MVP balloting, and *The Sporting News* named him NL Player of the Year.

The Expos next faced off with Philadelphia in a best-of-five series to determine the Eastern Division champion. Steve Rogers pitched great in the division playoffs. In two starts he threw 17 2/3 innings and gave up only one run; he won the fifth and deciding game by throwing a shutout.

The best-of-five 1981 NLCS came to down to a dramatic fifth game in Montreal against the Dodgers. In the ninth inning of a 1–1 game, Fanning bypassed his regular bullpen and brought in Rogers for his first relief appearance since 1978. Rogers had continued to pitch well during the NLCS, winning the third game with a one-run complete game. This time, with two out in the ninth, Rick Monday hit a home run to give the Dodgers a one-run lead. When the Expos failed to score in the bottom of the inning, the Dodgers had won the pennant. Chris Speier recently told Jeff Blair in *Baseball America*, "The thing is, after that game none of us had any doubt that we were going back." Unfortunately for the Expos and their fans, the team would never make it back to the playoffs, much less the World Series.

Once the Expos broke through to their first division flag, expectations were higher than ever for 1982. Dan Turner summarized a number of the preseason publications; nearly all favored the Expos to repeat as division champions. Part of the reason for the optimistic outlook was the expected

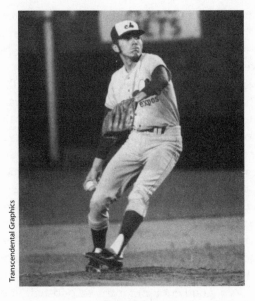

Steve Rogers

improvement of the offense. Announcer Duke Snider maintained that the Expos needed a "big left-hander with hair on his butt." At the end of spring training the team traded Larry Parrish to the Texas Rangers for veteran slugger Al Oliver. Oliver was big and left-handed; we cannot attest to the rest.

Oliver took over at first base and Cromartie moved to right field for the now-departed Ellis Valentine. At third base the Expos had another future star, twenty-four-year-old Tim Wallach. The bulk of the pitching starts went to Rogers, Gullickson, Lea, and Sanderson. Now free of his managerial nemesis, Rogers turned in the best season of his career: a 19–8 record, a league-leading 2.40 ERA, and a second-place finish in the Cy Young Award balloting. Oliver, too, enjoyed a terrific year and led the league in batting average and RBI. But despite these fine individual performances, 1982 proved to be an extremely disappointing year for the Expos.

Jim Fanning had returned as manager, but he never earned the respect of the players. Lee described the atmosphere shortly after Fanning assumed the helm near the end of the 1981 season:

[T]he players realized that we had to get our act together because Gentleman Jim didn't have a clue as to what was going on out on the field. It would have been tolerable if he had been a nonmanager, someone who just made out the lineup card and allowed us to play. But he was like a hyperactive kid, running up and down in the dugout, panicking as soon as we got behind in a ball game. His ideas on strategy were vague if not nonexistent. He also held the most disorganized team meetings that I could remember.

Fanning had been a backup catcher for four years with the Cubs in the 1950s. He treated his players with patience, but as Turner noted, he seemed to resent the fact that he could not discipline the players as had been done in his day.

Early in the season Fanning released second baseman Rodney Scott, described by Turner as a "spoiled brat, a bad-apple, a sulker." A favorite of Williams, Scott was not a great player, but the Expos had no one else to play second. The player Fanning championed for the position, Wallace Johnson, was unable to handle it defensively. The eccentric Lee caused some commotion after the dismissal of Scott and was released as well.

The problems brought on by the revolving door at second base can hardly be exaggerated. Leaving aside any intangible effects, the lack of hitting from the position imposed a large burden on the rest of the offense. The situation became so bad that the team moved left fielder Tim Raines, who had played second base in the minors, back to the keystone for thirty-six games. Late in the season, the Expos acquired Doug Flynn from Texas for $40,000 to solidify the position. Flynn was nothing special offensively, but he was still an improvement over his predecessors. Table 14.1 provides the season statistics for the players who spent time at second (excluding Raines).

The right end of the table quantifies the obvious: With no home runs and a .216 batting average, the Expos' second basemen were two games worse than a replacement-level batter and three and a half worse than an average hitter.

To make matters worse, in December 1980 the team had traded twenty-four-year-old second baseman Tony Bernazard, with just 213 at-bats behind him and many ahead, to the Chicago White Sox. Bernazard went on to a pretty good major league career; the Expos would have found him very useful in 1982.

The final column of table 14.1 shows each player's win probability added (WPA), a measure introduced in the last chapter. By examining each plate appearance, WPA estimates the effect the player's offense had on the Expos' likelihood of winning games. WPA supports the contention that this group offered no offense.

Table 14.1 1982 Expos Second Basemen

	AB	AVG	OBP	SLG	R	HR	RBI	SB	RC	WAAv	WAR	WPA
Frank Taveras	87	.161	.223	.241	9	0	4	4	4	-0.8	-0.5	-0.7
Rodney Scott	25	.200	.286	.200	2	0	1	5	2	-0.1	0.0	-0.2
Mike Phillips	8	.125	.125	.125	0	0	1	0	0	-0.1	-0.1	-0.1
Bryan Little	42	.214	.283	.214	6	0	3	2	2	-0.3	-0.2	-0.2
Wallace Johnson	57	.193	.258	.263	5	0	2	4	4	-0.3	-0.1	-0.7
Mike Gates	121	.231	.285	.298	16	0	8	0	10	-0.5	-0.1	-0.6
Doug Flynn	193	.244	.259	.295	13	0	20	0	11	-1.4	-0.7	-1.5
Total	533	.216	.260	.270	51	0	39	15	33	-3.5	-1.7	-4.0

WPA = win probability added

The rest of the lineup could not overcome the terrible offensive performance of the second basemen. As table 14.2 indicates, Oliver hit much better than anyone could have anticipated and Carter and Dawson had their typical strong seasons. On the other hand, Raines had his worst season in Montreal, Cromartie and Wallach hit little above the league average, and Speier provided a second drag on the offense.

Over the second half of the 1982 season, Montreal was never more than peripherally involved in the division race. The team finished 86–76, in third place, six games behind the St. Louis Cardinals. On the final day of the season, Fanning resigned.

Despite only the one division title, the pundits showed a healthy respect for the Expos' talent. *Sport* magazine anticipated a first-place finish in 1983, while *Sports Illustrated* predicted second place behind the 1982 world champion Cardinals. The returning team changed very little from the 1982 version. The starting eight, with Flynn at second for the entire year, was unchanged. The top four starting pitchers remained the same. Fryman was finally showing his age in the bullpen, so Reardon assumed the bulk of the closer's role.

The Expos hired veteran manager Bill Virdon for 1983. A two-time winner of *The Sporting News* Manager of the Year award, Virdon was much more of a disciplinarian than the easy-going Fanning. Although Virdon had never brought a team to the World Series, his teams had twice lost the deciding game of the NLCS after taking a lead late into the game.

In 1983, the Expos' offense basically consisted of three stars, one aging

Table 14.2 1982 Regular Lineup Excluding Second Base

	AB	AVG	OBP	SLG	R	HR	RBI	SB	RC	WAAv	WAR
Gary Carter, C	557	.293	.385	.510	91	29	97	2	100	3.6	5.3
Al Oliver, 1B	617	.331	.394	.514	90	22	109	5	114	5.0	6.8
Tim Wallach, 3B	596	.268	.314	.471	89	28	97	6	80	1.0	2.9
Chris Speier, SS	530	.257	.318	.360	41	7	60	1	54	-1.0	0.7
Tim Raines, LF	647	.277	.354	.369	90	4	43	78	94	1.8	3.9
Andre Dawson, CF	608	.301	.346	.498	107	23	83	39	101	3.3	5.1
Warren Cromartie, RF	497	.254	.348	.398	59	14	62	3	68	0.9	2.5

veteran, one developing youngster, and three terrible hitters. Dawson, Carter, and Raines were three of the league's best players but received little help from the other five regulars. Oliver, now thirty-six, made the All-Star team one final time in 1983, but 1982 was actually his last productive season. Twenty-five-year-old Tim Wallach was generally viewed as a rising star but slumped to nineteen home runs and a .269 batting average in 1983. Flynn, Speier, and Cromartie provided little help on offense.

The NL East race was four-team affair until mid-September, but the Phillies finished 23–8 to capture the division. The Expos ended up only 82–80 and in third place, eight games back. On the bright side, the big three pitchers, Rogers, Gullickson, and Lea, won fifty games between them—the most of any NL trio. Dawson had another great season (.299 average, 32 HR, 113 RBI) and came in second in the MVP voting.

Virdon returned for 1984 but the team was deteriorating rapidly. The front office signed forty-one-year-old Pete Rose and hoped his winning aura would help turn the club around. Looking for his four-thousandth hit, Rose had played regularly (hitting .245 with no home runs) the previous year for the pennant-winning Phillies. After a heated competition for his services, the Expos signed Rose to a one-year contract for $700,000, well above the major league average of $330,000. Several years earlier this might have been an interesting experiment, but by 1984 the Expos' talent level had fallen too far—whether or not Rose's hustle and enthusiasm was contagious was by this time a moot point.

After the trade of the rapidly slipping Oliver at the end of spring training and the loss of Cromartie to Japan, only Raines, Carter, Dawson, and

Wallach remained from the previous year's key regulars. The Expos sup-
plemented these stars with barely adequate players. Dawson moved to
right field because of his sore knees and slumped to one of his worst seasons. Overall the team scored only 593 runs, eleventh in the twelve-team
NL. In August, with the club below .500, the Expos fired Virdon and
brought Fanning back down from the front office to finish the season.
Fanning fared no better and the team finished the season 78–83, eighteen
games behind the Cubs.

The 1984 season essentially concluded a run of quality seasons begun
by the Expos in 1979. Rogers reported to camp in 1984 with a sore shoulder and never came around. He finished 6–15 in his last year as a regular.
After the season the club traded Carter to the Mets, where he finally won
a World Series two years later. By 1985 little remained of what many predicted would be the team of the eighties.

◇   ◇   ◇

Why were these Expos unable to win more than one division title? The
next several pages will explore several general conclusions regarding this
enigmatic franchise.

Bad Luck or Bad Chemistry? As discussed throughout this book, the
number of games a team is likely to win can be estimated fairly accurately from its runs scored and runs allowed totals. Any deviation from
the win expectation suggests that a team may have played either better
or worse than its actual won-loss record. Table 14.3 summarizes the
Expos' actual record and their expected record for the seasons 1978
through 1984.

The last column is the deviation from the expected win total and indicates that after the firing of Dick Williams in September 1981, the Expos
underperformed their expectations for the next three years. Much of the
difference between 1981 and 1982 can be explained by the team's record
in one-run games. In 1981, the Expos finished with a winning percentage
of .600 (24–16) in games decided by only one run. The next year the club
declined to .433 (26–34) in this category.

Usually when a team falls sort of its expected wins it simply implies a
little bad luck, but in the Expos' case, one is tempted to attribute it at least
partially to the team's chemistry or mental approach to the game. For
three years in a row, the team seemed to underperform its talent, at least
in the area of converting its runs into wins. Al Oliver believed that "men-

Table 14.3 Actual Wins vs. Expected Wins, 1978–1984

	GB	W	L	Pct	Runs	OppR	ePct	eWins	dW
1978	14	76	86	.469	633	611	.515	83	-7
1979	2	95	65	.594	701	581	.580	93	2
1980	1	90	72	.556	694	629	.542	88	2
1981	—	60	48	.556	443	394	.549	59	1
1982	6	86	76	.531	697	616	.553	90	-4
1983	8	82	80	.506	677	646	.520	84	-2
1984	18	78	83	.484	593	585	.505	81	-3

ePct = expected winning percentage based on runs scored and allowed

eWins = expected wins based on runs scored and allowed

dW = difference between actual wins and expected wins

tally, we didn't come to the park ready to play every day. Physically, we had the talent, but if you don't come to the yard prepared mentally, you're not going to win. And we didn't." Gary Carter wrote several years later, "Several players continued to add some bitterness to the Expos' pot of resentment. Not that we needed any more foul ingredients in our already strange brew. We had all sorts of ugly stuff floating around in there."

A team's runs can also be calculated quite accurately from its component statistics (e.g., home runs, doubles, walks). Like the estimation of wins, deviations from the calculation of runs (dR) are typically due to chance variation—everything does not even out over only 162 games. Table 14.4 provides the data for the Expos.

Once again, the Expos consistently underperformed their expectation after the loss of Williams. Whether because of a run of bad luck or something inherent in the use of their hits and outs, the Expos fell thirty to forty runs below expectation from 1982 to 1984.

Given that every ten runs over the course of a season equates to approximately one additional win, one can guess at the impact of these twin deficits. In 1982, the Expos scored thirty-one runs below their run calculation, implying a shortfall of about three wins. That year the team also finished with four wins fewer than their expectation based on runs scored and allowed. The two combined statistics suggest the team lost about seven wins to a failure to turn hits into runs and runs into wins. As the team finished only six games back, turning this around might have been enough to capture the division. It would not have been sufficient, however, in either 1983 or 1984.

**Table 14.4 Actual Runs vs.
Expected Runs, 1978–1984**

	Runs	RC	dR
1978	633	628	5
1979	701	701	0
1980	694	714	-20
1981	443	438	5
1982	697	728	-31
1983	677	719	-42
1984	593	632	-39

RC = runs created

dR = runs minus runs created

Drugs. Modern readers may have forgotten the size and scope of baseball's drug problem, particularly with respect to cocaine, in the late 1970s and early 1980s. In 1985 several drug trials in Pittsburgh contained player testimony that shocked the baseball community, and commissioner Peter Ueberroth called drug use the number one problem in baseball. The *New York Times* reported: "A government source familiar with the Pittsburgh case said that some of the players interviewed by the Federal Bureau of Investigation said that '40 to 50 percent of all players use drugs.'" At the other end of the spectrum, player agent Ron Shapiro told the same newspaper that he believed the number of addicted players was closer to 8 percent.

Bill Lee estimated that "fifteen percent of major league ballplayers have a serious addiction, forty-five percent are occasional heavy partyers [sic], and the remaining forty percent play golf." Even 15 percent suggests about four seriously addicted players per team. The *Times* noted that even the Pirate mascot was involved as a go-between for a drug dealer and players.

Montreal President John McHale told the *Times* that he believed cocaine caused his team to fall short in 1982:

> I don't think there's any doubt in '82 that whole scenario cost us a chance to win. We felt we should've won in '82. When we all woke up to what was going on, we found there were at least eight players on our club who were into this thing. There's no question in my mind and Jim Fanning's mind— he was managing the club that year—that cost us a chance to win.

Expos star Tim Raines, who entered a treatment center after the 1982 season, acknowledged both his and the team's problems. He confirmed to the *Times* that he "used the drug with 'eight or nine' players, mostly teammates but also some players from other teams." Raines admitted that the use of cocaine hurt his performance, and his 1982 season was statistically worse than the surrounding seasons. McHale estimated, "Raines probably cost us six, eight, ten games doing things we couldn't believe he was doing." One thing he was doing was sliding headfirst to protect the vial of cocaine in his back pocket.

Expo reserve John Milner, another player who admitted to using cocaine, testified at the 1985 drug trial of Curtis Strong and named another Expo reserve, outfielder Rowland Office, as a fellow user. Dick Williams wrote in his autobiography that he suspected Ellis Valentine, although he never saw him take any drugs; Valentine later denied it.

Williams also tells the story of finding evidence of ongoing marijuana use by the players in a secluded area under the box seats, an area the players called "the launching pad." He further notes that the Expos would buy and sell drugs from opposing players in the parking lot.

There is little doubt that drugs were a problem on the Expos, but it would be easy to exaggerate the effect for two reasons. First, as John Schuerholz, general manager of the Kansas City Royals, another team beset with drug use, told the *New York Times:*

> It's so hard to isolate the effect the problem had on the club. We didn't win the pennant [in 1982]. We did have a drug problem. But that's not to say we could've won if we hadn't had the problem. I don't know if we would have won without the problem. But we've always challenged for titles.

Second, other teams with drug problems were winning championships during that time. The world champion 1979 Pittsburgh Pirates had three players testify in the Strong trial. Milner, in 1979 a semiregular for the Pirates, told the court he purchased cocaine from Strong in the Pirates locker room in 1980. Dave Parker, a Pirates star and the 1978 NL MVP, testified he used cocaine off and on from 1976 through 1982, and "with some consistency in 1979." The *Times* reported that Parker "claimed to have used cocaine with six current and former members of the Pirates." Reserve shortstop Dale Berra also testified to cocaine use in 1979.

Like McHale's Expos, the St. Louis Cardinals had drug problems in 1982, but they went on to win the World Series. Manager Whitey Herzog told the *Times* that his Cardinals had "an even bigger drug problem than the Expos when he took over in 1980." Two of the team's biggest stars, Keith Hernandez and Lonnie Smith, testified at Strong's trial that they were involved with cocaine during 1982, and both identified teammate and fifteen-game-winner Joaquin Andujar as a fellow user.

An Overrated Offense. In 1983 *Sport* magazine ran a story entitled "The Best Player in Baseball." In the article, author Glen Waggoner utilizes several statistical techniques, including those by Bill James and Thomas Boswell. Waggoner concludes that the four best players in the major leagues (excluding pitchers) were Gary Carter, Andre Dawson, Mike Schmidt, and Robin Yount; in the end he named Schmidt number one.

After a subpar 1979 in which he hit only .275 with twenty-five home runs and a .311 on-base percentage, Dawson rebounded to become one of the National League's top hitters over the next several years. Mike Schmidt was clearly the league's best hitter, but Dawson belonged in a group right behind him.

While much of Gary Carter's value was defensive, his offense was well above that of any other catcher. In 1982, when Carter recorded an on-base percentage of .385, no other regular catcher in baseball (minimum 400 AB) even managed .350. That same year Carter slugged .510; only two other starting catchers exceeded .455 (Detroit's Lance Parrish and San Diego's Terry Kennedy).

The hitting ability of players at positions with a high defensive requirement (e. g., catcher or shortstop) is typically below that of a corner outfielder or infielder. When building a strong offense, having a hitter significantly above the norm for a position offers an excellent head start. The Expos received excellent offense at both catcher and center field. Their inability to find better hitters at the less demanding defensive positions prevented the team from developing a top offense.

Table 14.5 lists the top batters in the National League from 1980 through 1983. The table ranks the batters by wins above average over the four-year period. Dawson ranks third and Carter eleventh; no other Expo is at the top of the list (although Raines would be, with a lower games-played threshold). We included win probability added (WPA) in table 14-5 for comparison and a check of the macro statistics. WPA, which is generated from the play-by-play data, does not lead to any materially different conclusions.

To the degree these Expos are remembered, however, it is mostly for their star-studded offense. In addition to Carter and Dawson, most fans recall Valentine, Cromartie, Wallach, LeFlore, and Oliver as big bats in the

Table 14.5 Top NL Hitters, 1980–1983 (min 500 G, 8 WAAv)

	G	AVG	OBP	SLG	R	HR	RBI	SB	RC	WAAv	WAR	WPA
Mike Schmidt	554	.282	.406	.580	394	154	408	45	449	23	29	17
Keith Hernandez	572	.306	.404	.450	332	43	304	54	389	16	23	9
Andre Dawson	561	.302	.355	.518	378	96	347	124	388	15	22	9
Dale Murphy	584	.281	.368	.496	385	118	369	76	395	15	21	13
Jack Clark	518	.273	.370	.475	309	86	304	14	320	11	17	10
Darrell Evans	539	.265	.367	.444	278	78	269	30	320	11	17	6
George Hendrick	531	.298	.353	.482	278	80	371	16	321	10	16	6
Dusty Baker	552	.292	.356	.452	279	76	307	46	319	9	16	8
Jose Cruz	582	.293	.358	.423	279	47	306	92	314	9	16	5
Bill Madlock	503	.312	.377	.453	257	47	261	55	290	9	14	8
Gary Carter	553	.271	.348	.474	278	91	345	7	312	8	14	4

WPA = win probability added

lineup. In fact, the Expos never led the league in runs scored, finishing between third and sixth every year from 1979 through 1983.

The run-scoring totals were not a product of their venue, Olympic Stadium. From its opening in 1977 through 1984 the park decreased offense by about 3 percent. Since teams play half their games on the road, the Expos' offense was handicapped only half of that, or 1.5 percent overall. If the 1984 season is pulled out of the calculation, the park played essentially neutral.

Valentine and Cromartie each hit well at a young age and were thought to have an excellent chance to develop into superstars. Valentine played semiregularly at twenty-one and as a twenty-two-year-old in 1977 hit .293 with twenty-five home runs and a slugging percentage over .500. He plateaued over the next couple of years and never exceeded his highs from 1977. In 1980 a pitch shattered Valentine's cheek, an injury Bill Lee believed led to his decline. On the other hand, Dick Williams described him as man "who stole from his own ability because of his lack of motivation and his unreliability." Whatever the reason, Valentine never exceeded 350 at-bats in a season after 1979.

In 1977, twenty-three-year-old Warren Cromartie hit .282 with forty-one doubles. Like Valentine, he failed to develop as hoped, although he was probably slightly overrated to begin with. Twenty-three is not especially young to become a regular, and he failed to hit for power either that year or in the minors. In the end, he improved very little and spent the next few years as an average offensive player. Both Carter and Williams claimed he was a constant complainer and Carter blamed Cromartie for poisoning Dawson against him.

Other than Oliver's excellent 1982, the Expos' first basemen did not hit much. From the aging Tony Perez to a couple years with the overrated Cromartie to Oliver to a collection of several players in 1984, the Expos never generated the level of offense needed from the position.

Their third basemen provided good but not great production. Larry Parrish played excellently in 1979 but slumped in 1980 because of his injured wrist and was traded for Oliver. In 1981 the team introduced the twenty-three-year-old Wallach to third base. Wallach would remain the Expo regular until 1992 and play in five All-Star Games, but he never became a great player. Prior to 1987 Wallach never hit above .270, slugged thirty home runs, or had an on-base percentage over .340; four times he supplied a slugging average below .400.

Finally, the offense from the middle infield positions was consistently meager. Even after the acquisition of the weak-hitting Doug Flynn, second base remained a problem. Aging shortstop Chris Speier was a liability on offense as well; he typically hit around .250 with little power or speed.

By 1983, Tim Raines was on his way to becoming a great offensive player, but it was a little too late to save the Expo offense. Teams with great players often make the mistake of assuming that they can carry weak players at other positions. Carter and Dawson were both elite players, but the two plus Raines were not enough to overcome a number of average-and-below hitters.

Good Young Pitching, but No New Ace. After leading the league in ERA in 1979, the Expos finished between second and fifth over the next five years. During these years the team introduced a number of very good and very young pitchers. Dan Schatzeder became a regular (loosely defined) at twenty-three in 1978; David Palmer and Scott Sanderson in 1979 at twenty-one and twenty-three, respectively; and Bill Gullickson and Charlie Lea in 1980 at twenty-one and twenty-three, respectively.

All of these hurlers pitched very well as youngsters. But while several had long and noteworthy careers, none developed into a staff ace, and a couple could never overcome injury problems. Steve Rogers was an excellent number-one pitcher through the end of 1983, although a notch below the best in the league. The young hurlers all had a number of very good seasons but none became the dominant starter the Expos needed to take the next step.

One of the supposed deficiencies on the Expos was poor fielding. Dan Turner wrote that this weakness was a key reason for the Expos' failure to achieve expectations. For 1982 he cited first baseman Oliver and the pre-Flynn second basemen and shortstop Speier as the main culprits. On the other hand, Montreal also had Gold Glovers behind the plate (Carter) and in center field (Dawson).

While measuring team fielding remains problematic, it can best be evaluated by examining defensive efficiency record (DER), the percentage of balls in play that the defense converts into outs, and fielding percentage. Table 14.6 reviews the Expos' data and rank from 1978 to 1984.

The Expos may not have been a great defensive team, but the team was usually quite good. Other than in 1980, Montreal consistently finished in the top half of the league and often in the top three.

It is exceedingly rare for a baseball organization to turn out the quality and quantity of young talent delivered by the Montreal farm system in the mid-1970s. The club hired Dick Williams, an excellent manager for a young team, to integrate them and help them develop. In just three years the team improved from fifty-five to ninety-five wins. Unfortunately for the Expos and their fans, over the next five years the team could only produce one division title and no pennants.

The organization correctly recognized its window of opportunity and worked hard to capitalize on the young talent and win a title. When the

Table 14.6 Fielding Summary, 1978–1984

	DER	Rank	Pct	Rank
1978	.716	1	.979	3
1979	.707	2	.979	6
1980	.694	9	.977	8
1981	.712	3	.980	3
1982	.704	4	.980	3
1983	.703	5	.981	3
1984	.707	2	.978	7

Expos thought they needed a speedy left fielder, they acquired Ron LeFlore; when a power-hitting left-handed hitter seemed necessary, they traded for Al Oliver; when second base became the obvious weak spot, they landed Doug Flynn. The fine-tuning of the talent base, however, could not push them over the top.

A number of factors conspired to prevent the Expos from realizing their promise. An inability to win as many games as their statistics suggested, plus a widespread drug problem, added to the already challenging task. In addition, the team overrated some of its offensive talent, which left the club with too many average and below-average hitters at a number of positions. That none of the young pitchers ever developed into elite players further magnified the offensive shortcomings.

The city of Montreal showed tremendous support for these Expo teams. In both 1982 and 1983 the team finished fourth in the entire major leagues in attendance. One can only hope that the excitement surrounding these competitive teams that never lived up to their promise will be remembered when chronicling Montreal's baseball story.

15

A CHANGE OF PLANS:
THE 1997 FLORIDA MARLINS

In 1996, the Florida Marlins completed their fourth season, the most successful in their history. The club won nearly half of its games and included a nucleus of several very good players who were in or entering their prime baseball years. If left unattended, the team would probably have improved further in 1997. The team was not left unattended, because H. Wayne Huizenga, the Marlins' billionaire owner, was not happy.

In their inaugural 1993 season, the team attracted over three million people, the seventh-best attendance in baseball, and finished with a winning percentage of .395. Over the next three years, the Marlins improved each season, but their attendance steadily declined. By 1996, after a work stoppage had shut down the game for eight months and parts of two seasons, Florida's 1.7 million admissions ranked only eighteenth among the twenty-eight major league teams. While there is ample reason to be skeptical of the team's bookkeeping, Huizenga claimed that the team lost $20 million in 1996 alone.

His solution to the team's financial woes was simple and predictable: he wanted a new stadium and he wanted the public to build it for him. According to Huizenga, the team's current venue, Pro Player Stadium, was unsuitable for baseball, especially since it did not offer fans protection from the daily South Florida rains.

One of the most successful businessmen in the United States, dubbed "Midas" in the business press, Huizenga could easily have come up with $300 million to fund a new stadium himself. After building Waste Management Inc. from a one-truck operation into the world's largest garbage company, he turned a seventeen-store video chain into Blockbuster Entertainment, which merged with Viacom in 1994. The chairman of several other huge companies, Huizenga was also the sole owner of the Florida Panthers hockey team, the Miami Dolphins football team, and Pro Player Stadium (formerly Joe Robbie Stadium), the home of the Dolphins and Marlins.

In order to make money on the Marlins, Huizenga believed that he had two options. The simplest was to lower the annual payroll from $32 million to $15 million and thereby reduce expenses to equal the team's reported revenues. Such a payroll reduction would almost certainly have condemned the Marlins to field a perennially lousy team, driving people from the ballpark and shrinking their fan base further. Huizenga saw no point in owning a bad baseball team that was breaking even.

His second option was to spend *more* money, which would (hopefully) lead to a better baseball team, more fans, and, most important, enough political goodwill to secure financing for a new state-of-the-art baseball field with a retractable roof. Without the stadium, Huizenga no longer had any interest in owning the Marlins.

Huizenga had reason to believe that this strategy could work. A year earlier, in September 1995, he had claimed that his hockey team was losing $1.2 million every month because of a bad lease at Miami Arena. After he threatened to move the Panthers, politicians in Broward County came up with the money to fund a new rink that would open in 1998. During the legislative process for the arena proposal, the Panthers' extraordinary success on the ice surely contributed to the bill's approval; the team ultimately reached the Stanley Cup finals in only its third year as a franchise.

In September 1996, Dave Dombrowski, the Marlins' general manager, and Don Smiley, the president, informed Huizenga that to create a contender for 1997 would necessitate increasing the team's payroll from $32 million to $47 million. When Huizenga asked how many tickets the team would sell and how much money he would lose, Smiley told his boss to expect an average attendance of 29,500 per game and a $30 million loss.

Armed with this information, Huizenga gave his management team the green light to improve the ball club and take one last crack at winning over the fans and politicians of South Florida. If the spending did not work, he was prepared to sell the team, even if it might lead to Miami losing its franchise.

◇ ◇ ◇

Six years earlier, in December 1990, the National League unveiled a list of six candidate locations to receive two new expansion franchises. The league chose three Florida sites—South Florida, Tampa-St. Petersburg, and Orlando—along with Denver, Buffalo, and Washington. Wayne Huizenga, then a minority owner of the Miami Dolphins and half-owner of Joe Robbie Stadium, was selected from three competing South Florida groups to present his case.

With the help of enormous tax breaks, Joe Robbie, the Dolphins' owner, built Joe Robbie Stadium, a football facility that opened in 1987. The first baseball games were played at the site during spring training in 1988, with a 30-foot fence constructed to partially compensate for the 272-foot left field foul line.

In February 1991, after renovations had begun to transform Joe Robbie Stadium into a suitable baseball venue, the National League Expansion Committee toured the facility. On March 30 and 31, the park played host to two exhibition games between the New York Yankees and Baltimore Orioles, and a combined total of 125,013 fans were in attendance. The crowd on the first night, 67,654, was the largest ever to watch a spring training game.

In July, commissioner Fay Vincent announced that baseball had awarded Denver and Miami the two new franchises and that they would begin play in 1993. This was somewhat of a surprise, as St. Petersburg had a new domed baseball stadium and had almost lured the White Sox out of Chicago two years before. Nonetheless, Miami represented a larger market than St. Petersburg, and Huizenga's assurance that Joe Robbie Stadium was an adequate baseball facility was a strong factor in Miami's favor. Huizenga also downplayed concerns that the region's notorious late afternoon rains would hurt attendance.

Dave Dombrowski, the general manager of the Montreal Expos, was hired to run the Marlins in September 1991, nineteen months before Florida's first game. He set to work building up the club's organization immediately. Several low-level minor league affiliates fielded teams in 1992, and the Marlins participated in the 1992 amateur draft. Their first draft selection was the University of Miami's catcher, Charles Johnson.

The expansion draft for Florida and Colorado was held on November 17, 1992. The Marlins drafted thirty-six players. Most were not destined for significant major league careers. Bryan Harvey, a star relief pitcher for the Angels, was the best player the club acquired. With hindsight, the best of the rest were Trevor Hoffman, acquired from Cincinnati; Carl Everett from the Yankees; and Jeff Conine from the Royals. All three had All-Star seasons ahead of them, although only Conine would have one in Miami.

The Marlins drafted several other established players for the sole purpose of trading them. For example, the club dealt draftee Greg Hibbard to the Cubs for infielders Gary Scott and Alex Arias. The Marlins also swapped Danny Jackson to the Phillies for pitchers Joel Adamson and Matt Whisenant.

Like the Athletics of the mid-1960s, the Marlins collected prospects by the dozen and were prepared to wait to see who developed. Most, quite naturally, did not. Later, once the team figured out where its holes were, the Marlins would trade a number of these prospects for established players. In the meantime, Dombrowski signed veteran free agents such as pitcher Charlie Hough, catcher Benito Santiago, and infielder Dave Magadan so that the Marlins could field a team. Orestes Destrade, a Cuban who had played the last few years in Japan, was imported to play first base and was the Marlins' best hitter in 1993.

Conventional speculation was that Harvey, out for much of the 1992 season with an elbow injury, was drafted so that he could be traded in midseason to a contender—an established closer seemed an unnecessary luxury for an expansion team. The Marlins ended up holding onto him, and Harvey saved forty-five of their sixty-four victories in 1993.

The big move the Marlins did make (in June) was to deal relief pitchers Jesus Martinez and Trevor Hoffman (their second and fourth expansion draft picks) to the San Diego Padres for third baseman Gary Sheffield. A big-time star, Sheffield was coming off a 1992 season in which he had hit thirty-three home runs, driven in a hundred runs, and batted a league-leading .330. A few years later these figures would not sound as impressive, but in 1992 this was an outstanding season. Still only twenty-four-years old, Sheffield was easily the best player ever to play for a first-year expansion team.

The loss of Hoffman, who went on to stardom with the Padres, was counterbalanced when the Marlins traded pitching prospect Chris Carpenter to the Rangers for Kurt Miller, a highly regarded twenty-year-old hurler, and twenty-three-year-old pitcher Robb Nen as a throw-in. Nen initially pitched horribly (7.02 ERA in fifteen appearances), but better days lay ahead.

The first-year Marlins finished at 64–98 but looked to be on the right track. The major league team boasted several good young position players in addition to Sheffield. Bret Barberie, a twenty-five-year-old second baseman, hit .277. Conine, just twenty-seven, played every game in left field and hit .292. Chuck Carr, a twenty-five-year-old center fielder, led the league with fifty-eight stolen bases. Since most of the team's investment was playing in the minor leagues, it was a decent beginning.

Before the players' strike ended the 1994 season in early August, the Marlins had climbed to a record of 51–64, despite some bad luck. Their best player, Sheffield (who had been moved to right field), missed twenty-eight games with a bad shoulder but still hit twenty-seven home runs and slugged .584. Harvey, the team's other star, blew out his elbow early in the year, effectively ending his career. Greg Colbrunn, a promising rookie first baseman, injured his knee and managed only 155 at bats.

Other developments were more promising. Robb Nen flourished as Harvey's replacement. Left fielder Jeff Conine stepped forward and hit .319 with power. Their best starting pitcher was not forty-six-year-old Charlie Hough, the 1993 staff anchor, but twenty-six-year-old Pat Rapp, who had a fine 3.85 ERA in his 133 innings. Catcher Charles Johnson, the first product of the Marlins farm system, joined the team just before the strike, went five for eleven, and gave the fans another star to look forward to when the game resumed.

The 1994–1995 off-season was brief. The ongoing players' strike precluded all transactions, and when the impasse ended in April, the teams had only a few weeks to prepare for the season. The Marlins hastily signed some pitchers that few other teams wanted—Mark Gardner, Terry Mathews, and Randy Veres—and two big names well past their primes, Andre Dawson and Terry Pendleton. The work stoppage did not impair the Marlins' organizational plan, which consisted mainly of waiting for their young players to develop.

Once again some things went wrong for the Marlins in 1995. Sheffield was disabled with a finger injury for most of the season. Chuck Carr, who had seemed like an essential piece of their future in 1993, dropped to .227 and was finished as a regular player.

Nevertheless, the progress continued. Johnson became the regular catcher, showed some promise with the bat, and fielded like a Gold Glover. Quilvio Veras (acquired from the Mets for Carl Everett) took over second base and hit .261 with a league-leading fifty-six steals. Young shortstop Kurt Abbott belted seventeen home runs. Conine drove in 105 runs in just 133 games and hit a home run in the All-Star Game. Rapp finished 14–7 with a 3.44 ERA. Nen saved twenty-three games. All of these players were still in their twenties.

The Marlins' three-year performance could not be faulted. The team had not placed an unreasonable burden on any of its young players and therefore was not derailed when one or two of them regressed. Collecting several young players of ability maximized the team's chances of development without identifying any one player as a savior. The 1995 Marlins finished 67–76, although the team scored and allowed an equal number of runs (673), suggesting they were an average team. The Marlins were making steady progress.

By 1995 several of the Marlins' young players had developed to the point that Dombrowski was able to gauge the strengths and weaknesses of his team. The club was fifth (of fourteen) in the league in runs scored, with center fielder Carr the weakest link. Accordingly, in November the team signed thirty-three-year-old Devon White, a huge upgrade, especially on defense, where he was one of the best in the game. Good defense in center was especially important for this team, as neither Conine nor Sheffield was considered a good outfielder.

Dombrowski realized that the team's pitching was not as far along as its hitting, so in December he signed two quality starters, the Orioles' Kevin Brown and the Blue Jays' Al Leiter. Neither pitcher came to Florida as an established ace. In 1995, the thirty-year-old Brown had finished 10–9 with an ERA of 3.60. Leiter, twenty-nine, was prone to injury and wildness. Healthy in 1995, he had pitched fairly well but had led the league in both walks and wild pitches. Nevertheless, Dombrowski had landed two pitchers who could throw quality innings and take some of the burden off his youngsters.

The 1996 Marlins were half of a great team, but were weighed down by several substandard players. The core of their club, the best pitchers and hitters, was as good as any in baseball. When the team found itself at 39–47 at mid-season, Dombrowski fired Rene Lachemann, the team's first and only manager. This dismissal was the first sign of Dombrowski's impatience with the team's progress. Florida finished strong under John Boles and improved its final record to 80–82.

The two new moundsmen were a smashing success and formed the league's best starting pitching tandem outside of Atlanta. Kevin Brown was the best pitcher in the National League (17–11 and a league-leading 1.89 ERA), and Al Leiter won sixteen games and posted a 2.93 ERA despite again leading the league in walks. Closer Robb Nen had a great season out of the bullpen.

The Marlins could also boast the league's best hitter in Gary Sheffield:

forty-two home runs, 120 RBI, a .314 average, 142 walks, a league-leading .469 on-base percentage (the best by an NL right-handed hitter since Rogers Hornsby), and a .624 slugging percentage. Sheffield often flirted with this type of season, both before and since, but has had difficulty staying healthy. In this remarkable season he missed just one game.

The Marlins also introduced a star rookie, twenty-year-old shortstop Edgar Renteria, who hit .309 in 431 at-bats. Inexplicably, the Rookie of the Year Award went to the Dodgers' Todd Hollandsworth, a left fielder who hit twelve home runs. Ray Knight, the Reds' manager, considered Renteria "a franchise type player."

In August, with hopes of a capturing a playoff spot fading, Dombrowski made a few trades that indicated that he was looking ahead. Over a span of several weeks, he dealt away John Burkett, his third-most reliable starter; Terry Pendleton, the 1991 NL MVP but no longer an effective player; and a couple of relief pitchers, Terry Mathews and David Weathers. None of these players was either providing much help or figuring to be a major component of the team's future plans.

Gary Sheffield blew his stack. On August 16, he blasted Dombrowski about the team's lack of progress: "I could go back and count on two hands the number of things he's lied about to me. I just never said anything in public. I've forgiven and forgiven. But he's gotten his last forgiveness." Upon elaboration, Sheffield's main complaint was that the team had passed on free agents he thought they needed, specifically Ron Gant, Darryl Strawberry, and Dwight Gooden (Sheffield's uncle). Dombrowski kept his cool. Sheffield was bound to pop off now and then, and Dombrowski most likely did not take his personnel advice seriously.

For the next several weeks, it was widely assumed that Sheffield would be traded, that his "baggage" could no longer be tolerated. During the previous eight months he had received a restraining order for allegedly threatening the mother of his son, was kicked out of several games, and blasted his general manager in the press. He was also shot in the shoulder during an apparent carjacking attempt. Since Sheffield hit like Rogers Hornsby, Dombrowski decided he could live with the rest.

The Marlins' progress at this point illustrates a valuable lesson in team construction. In trying to improve a mediocre team (as indicated by their 80–82 record), it is preferable to have clear, identifiable weaknesses. The Marlins were not a team filled with average players—they had a lot of great players mixed with a lot of bad players. Below-average or replacement-level players are generally easier and less expensive to upgrade.

The 1996 Marlins had a team ERA of just 3.95, but the quality was concentrated: only three pitchers who pitched at least fifteen games—Brown, Leiter, and Nen—had an ERA lower than 4.30. Pat Rapp, the erstwhile ace of the previous two years, finished 8–16 with a 5.10 ERA. Chris Hammond, tried as the fifth starter, sported an ERA of 6.56.

The club had a very good outfield but also had a third baseman (Terry Pendleton) who was thirty-five and could no longer hit or field and a first baseman (Greg Colbrunn) who did not have the power or plate discipline required from the position in the 1990s. Quilvio Veras, a good 1995 rookie, lost his job to Luis Castillo and was sent down to Charlotte.

Dombrowski had continually sought veteran players who could fill holes temporarily while the young talent matured. In 1996, some of the young talent experienced growing pains (specifically Quilvio Veras and Charles Johnson) and many of the veteran players were no longer adequate major leaguers (Pendleton and Dawson).

◇   ◇   ◇

Once Huizenga gave Dombrowski the green light to raise the payroll by $15 million, the tenor of the 1996–1997 off-season changed dramatically. The Marlins had steadily improved for four years and, still a young team, were in a good position to continue. Huizenga was effectively telling his management team, "Throw away the plan, we need to win *right now*." Dombrowski was not simply *allowed* to increase payroll, he was *ordered* to do so. The team had obvious holes, and Dombrowski now looked to fill them not with young prospects or temporary veterans but with quality regulars.

Dombrowski felt the Marlins' most pressing need was a slugging outfielder to hit behind Sheffield and allow Conine to move to first base. Sheffield had grown increasingly frustrated at his lack of good pitches to hit and complained about it all season. The team also needed another dependable starting pitcher, a third baseman, and depth for the bullpen and bench. Living the dream of many young fans, Dombrowski went to work.

His first order of business was to hire a new manager. When Jim Leyland, the longtime skipper of the Pittsburgh Pirates, resigned his position on September 25, it was immediately assumed he would wind up with Florida. One veteran Marlins employee began referring to Boles, the team's interim manager, as "Dead Man Walking." Leyland hankered to manage a team that would spend money to compete and therefore chose Florida over several other suitors, including Boston, California, and the Chicago White Sox.

Early in the off-season Dombrowski targeted the best player in baseball, Barry Bonds, then having a spat with the Giants over the team's firing of his father Bobby as hitting coach. It was reported that Bonds might be available in exchange for Renteria, Leiter, and a few prospects, but, even if true, the Marlins were not interested at this price. The Giants and Bonds soon settled their differences. A more attainable prize, free-agent slugger Albert Belle of the Indians, was thought to be demanding close to $10 million per year, the largest contract in history. The Marlins had the money and many considered them the favorite to sign him.

The off-season plans of all major league teams were complicated by the ongoing labor negotiations. The players had ended an eight-month strike in April 1995, but a year and a half later the owners had still not ratified the agreement that their negotiators had reached with the union. The owners were dissatisfied that the new deal granted the players credit for service time missed while on strike. If ratified, several star players, including White Sox sixteen-game winner Alex Fernandez, would become free agents. The Marlins coveted Fernandez, a Cuban-American from Miami who had starred at the University of Miami and Miami-Dade South Community College.

Dombrowski was reluctant to spend his money only to see a new batch of players become available. As he told *Baseball Weekly* in early November, "You really have trouble zeroing in on many things because of the uncertainty. A club's philosophy is going to keep changing, depending on who is a free agent and who is not, who might be available because of arbitration and who is not. And right now everything is in limbo." On November 6, the owners voted 18–12 against the deal, with the Marlins joining the majority.

The catalyst to end the impasse with the players came from an unexpected source: Chicago White Sox owner Jerry Reinsdorf, the leader of a hard-line faction that had helped force the strike and was now preventing an agreement. Shocking the baseball world, Reinsdorf on November 18 announced the signing of Albert Belle for five years and $55 million, significantly more than anyone had anticipated. A stunning signing under any circumstances, it was doubly so because the White Sox had been at the forefront of the antilabor position. Additionally, it was the Marlins, another hard-line pro-small-market team, that helped drive Belle's price up so high. Reinsdorf's faction soon crumbled, and on November 27 the owners overwhelmingly approved the identical pact they had rejected three weeks earlier. The battle over, the new pact guaranteed labor peace for at least five years.

Denied the biggest fish in the pond, the Marlins reaped the benefits of the new order that the Belle signing had helped create. The Marlins turned their attention to two of the best of the newly available free agents, Fernandez and Moises Alou, and landed both within a couple of weeks. Alou, also coveted by the Red Sox, was a good left fielder who had driven in ninety-six runs for the Expos in 1996.

The third big-name free agent Dombrowski landed was Bobby Bonilla. Bonilla had driven in 116 runs for the Orioles but feuded with manager Davey Johnson because he disliked being used as the designated hitter. Bonilla, never known for his glove, was signed as a third baseman, a position he had played occasionally and adequately over the previous few years.

The Marlins also signed the two best reserve outfielders available: Jim Eisenreich, who hit .361 in 338 at bats for the Phillies in 1996; and John Cangelosi, who hit .263 for the Astros. Finally, the team addressed its bullpen problems by signing Dennis Cook, a serviceable veteran left-hander.

The total haul—Bonilla, Alou, Fernandez, Cook, Eisenreich, and Cangelosi—signed contracts totaling $89 million spread over the next several years. The team also spent $6 million to tie up Leyland, and re-signed Nen for $17.6 million over four years. Just prior to the start of the 1997 season, Dombrowski inked Sheffield to a six-year, $61 million contract extension.

Table 15.1 shows the turnover of the lineup, starters, and bullpen, from 1996 to the beginning of 1997. In addition to the free-agent acquisitions, the team improved at first base, where Conine replaced the departed Colbrunn, and second base, where Castillo became the regular at the end of 1996.

Jim Leyland had left Pittsburgh, where he was happy and beloved, because he wanted to manage someplace where he could compete for championships. "We're fortunate here. We've got a great organization and we've done a lot of things this off-season to help this club. But it's not going to mean a thing unless we get the job done."

In the spring, the team posted a record of 26–5, reportedly the best record in Grapefruit League history. In its opening-day issue, *Baseball Weekly* printed its initial power rankings, which deemed the Marlins the third-best team in baseball (after Atlanta and Seattle). This quick start boosted the Marlins' already high expectations from the free-agent signings.

◇ ◇ ◇

Despite all the favorable press surrounding his baseball team, April 1997 was not good to Wayne Huizenga. Early that month, the state legislature

Table 15.1 1996–1997 Marlins

	1996	1997
C	Charles Johnson	Charles Johnson
1B	Greg Colbrunn	Jeff Conine
2B	Quilvio Veras	Luis Castillo
3B	Terry Pendleton	Bobby Bonilla
SS	Edgar Renteria	Edgar Renteria
LF	Jeff Conine	Moises Alou
CF	Devon White	Devon White
RF	Gary Sheffield	Gary Sheffield
P	Kevin Brown	Kevin Brown
P	Al Leiter	Al Leiter
P	John Burkett	Alex Fernandez
P	Pat Rapp	Pat Rapp
RP	Robb Nen	Robb Nen

debated a bill to give Huizenga a $60 million tax rebate on Pro Player Stadium to match one he had received in 1991. The bill was at first considered a sure thing, but legislators were soon bombarded with angry phone calls from constituents who were tired of giving tax breaks to billionaires. Amid the loud and angry public outcry, the bill failed on April 28. After years of receiving subsidies and tax breaks from governments for his sports teams and facilities, Huizenga sensed that the tide had turned against him. He now realized that his new baseball park was out of reach and the off-season spending, from his point of view, was already a failure.

For the rest of the Marlins family, everything appeared to be moving ahead splendidly. On June 26, the team was two and a half games behind the Braves, attendance had increased 35 percent from 1996, and the Marlins' revenues were in line with Don Smiley's projections. Both the front office and the team knew that the franchise might be at stake, and that this was a do-or-die season. Everyone associated with the Marlins assumed they were on the road to survival.

On that day, Huizenga shocked his organization by announcing he was selling the team: "We had just changed our minds about being willing to accept higher losses." The Marlins had met all of their goals except the unstated one: they had not helped Huizenga get his $60 million tax rebate and could not entice the taxpayers to build him a new stadium. When asked if his $30 million loss estimate for the Marlins considered revenue generated from his stadium, particularly the luxury boxes, Huizenga admitted that it did not.

This was a devastating turn of events for the players, the manager, the front office, and the fans. In their first pennant race, the team's employees no longer knew where they would be in six months. Their lives would be in limbo while their owner looked for someone willing to take the team off his hands.

In the meantime, as the Marlins fought for a playoff spot, they continued to fine-tune their ball club. After Luis Castillo proved incapable of hitting the ball out of the infield on a regular basis, he was demoted to Charlotte. As a replacement, the Marlins traded for Colorado minor leaguer Craig Counsell, who ended up hitting .299.

Jeff Conine, the original and dependable Marlin, stayed in a hitting slump nearly the whole season. Dombrowski responded by dealing for Darren Daulton to platoon with Conine at first base. Daulton was a three-time All-Star catcher for the Phillies, but nine knee operations had reduced his contributions to hustle, inspiration, emotional clubhouse speeches, a lot of bases on balls, and an occasional key hit.

The most important roster move was promoting Livan Hernandez from the Marlins' minor league team in Charlotte. A twenty-year-old pitching star for the Cuban national team, Hernandez had defected two years earlier while on a trip with his team to Monterrey, Mexico. After spending the winter auditioning for several major league teams while pitching in the Dominican Republic, he signed with the Marlins in January 1996 for $4.5 million. He spent the next year and a half in the minor leagues, winning seven games.

After watching several pitchers struggle to fill out the rotation after his three main starters, Leyland turned to Hernandez. He pitched spectacularly, won his first nine decisions, and finished 9–3 in seventeen starts with a 3.18 ERA.

The pennant race produced little drama. In the divisional race, Florida moved within a few games of the Braves a couple of times, but Atlanta pulled away and won by nine. The Marlins led the wild card race virtually wire to wire, pulled away from the Mets in August, and coasted to a 92–70 record.

In the postseason, the Marlins swept the Giants in the divisional series and then bested the Braves in six games in the NLCS. In the World Series the team defeated the Indians in seven games, winning the final game in the last of the eleventh inning. In the process the Marlins became the first wild card team to win baseball's biggest prize.

Livan Hernandez, forced into a postseason starting role by a torn rotator cuff suffered by Alex Fernandez in the second game of the NLCS, was the October hero. Leyland probably bears some responsibility for Fernandez's breakdown in that the pitcher lost effectiveness down the stretch after throwing over four hundred pitches in a nine-day span in August. The injury would sideline Fernandez for eighteen months. Hernandez won two games in relief before receiving his first start against the Braves and Greg Maddux in the fifth game of the NLCS. Hernandez responded with a controversial three-hit 2-1 victory, partly due to home-plate umpire Eric Gregg's outlandishly wide strike zone. He then won two games against the Indians in the World Series without pitching particularly well. For his efforts, Hernandez was named the MVP of both the NLCS and the World Series.

Many of the players the Marlins were depending on in 1997 actually had disappointing seasons. Gary Sheffield hit just .250 with twenty-one home runs, though he still walked 121 times. Devon White was injured for half of the season and ineffective (.245) for the other half. Conine and Castillo both had poor years offensively. Al Leiter, who had apparently turned the corner in 1996, was no better than an average starter.

Whereas the 1996 team consisted of a few excellent players carrying a number of inadequate players, the 1997 version was deep enough to have a different hero every night. Charles Johnson recovered from his off year to provide some offense (.250 with 19 home runs). Bonilla (.297, 96 RBI) and Alou (.292, 115 RBI) came through with big years. Renteria played a solid shortstop and hit .277. The supporting cast, including Daulton, Counsell, Cangelosi, Eisenreich, and Kurt Abbott, made valuable contributions.

The pitching followed the same pattern. Although he slipped slightly from his phenomenal 1996 season, Brown was once again one of the best pitchers in the league (16–8, 2.69). Alex Fernandez lived up to his free-agent contract with a strong season (17–12, 3.59). Behind the efforts of Nen (35 saves), Cook, Jay Powell, and Felix Heredia, the bullpen bounced back from an awful 1996. The primary improvement was in the depth of the staff rather than in the stars.

In considering the startling rise of the Florida Marlins, a fifth-year expansion team, from the disappointment of 1996 to World Series champs the very next year, one should appreciate that the team improved its record by only twelve games (from 80 to 92 wins). This level of improvement is not particularly unusual; several teams improved their records by more than twelve games in 1997. The New York Mets, whom the Marlins held off for the wild card, improved from 71 to 88 wins. The San Francisco Giants, whom Florida defeated in the Division Series, rose from 68 to 90 wins. Put another way, the Marlins were twelve games better than the Giants in 1996, but only two games better in 1997.

One can see the origin of the historical consensus that 1997 Marlins came out of nowhere to the top of the baseball world. On a superficial level, a team that had never even competed for a playoff spot signed a number of free agents and won the World Series. This is an oversimplification, and a misleading one. Also-rans are inevitably relegated to the dustbin of history, but the Marlins had made steady improvement in their first four years and were a very promising team before the buying frenzy that helped take them the last few steps. In terms of quality, the 1996 team was much closer to a championship contender than to a first-year expansion team.

The 1997 Marlins were not a great team but they were strong enough to overcome off-years from a couple of their key regulars and still reach the playoffs. The structure of the modern baseball playoff system allows a good team, such as the Marlins, to squeeze into the playoffs, have a few hot weeks, and win it all. They played a great NLCS against the Braves to get to the World Series, where they met the Indians, also not a great team (they had the fifth-best record in the American League). By scoring a run in the bottom of the eleventh inning of the seventh game, the Marlins became the 1997 champs.

◇　◇　◇

In the aftermath of his team's great achievement, Wayne Huizenga stuck to his claim of a $30 million loss despite the fact that his team had drawn 400,000 fans, paying premium prices, during the post season. Where did the money from the post-season go? Later, Huizenga claimed that his loss was actually $34 million.

Although the team was supposedly bleeding money, Don Smiley, the president of the Marlins and presumably someone with access to the team's financial records, declared that he was interested in buying the Marlins. Huizenga, who paid $95 million for the team in 1991, set his asking price at $165 million, and called the latter figure "fair . . . on the low side."

A year later, in a *New York Times Magazine* article, sports economist Andrew Zimbalist concluded that the 1997 Marlins actually made a *profit* of

$13.8 million. The major discrepancies Zimbalist reported were $38 million dollars in revenue generated by the stadium (owned by Huizenga) that was fairly attributable to the Marlins and a local cable television deal (with a company also owned by Huizenga) that was deliberately set well below market value.

If the rise of the Marlins was steady and unrelenting, the fall was startlingly swift. In the wake of his team's great World Series victory, Huizenga gave Dombrowski the reverse order of the one he had given twelve months earlier: drastically reduce payroll to make the team more salable. Dombrowski, as he had done so ably the previous winter, got right to work.

By Thanksgiving, he had traded Moises Alou, Devon White, Robb Nen, and Jeff Conine. By New Year's Day, Kevin Brown, Dennis Cook, and Kurt Abbott were also ex-Marlins. By August 1998, the team's payroll had been reduced to $13 million, of which $7 million was for Alex Fernandez. (Fernandez's injury made him untradable, and it is likely that most of his contract was covered by insurance.) The 1998 team, the defending world champions, finished 54–108, one of the worst records of the past thirty years.

Several Marlin season ticket holders filed suit against the team for fraud. WQAM, the team's flagship radio station, also sued the team, claiming that the current Marlins team was much less marketable than the one with which they signed their broadcasting contract.

After months spent trying to put together a group of investors to meet Wayne Huizenga's asking price, Don Smiley could not pull off the purchase. Huizenga eventually sold the team to John Henry, a commodities trader from Boca Raton. The deal almost fell through when Huizenga insisted that Henry assume the remaining twenty-seven years of the deliberately below-market television contract with SportsChannel Florida, which Huizenga owned. They ended up settling on a ten-year deal. After destroying his team, Huizenga would continue to profit from it for many years. The team remained severely hampered by bad television and stadium deals, and H. Wayne Huizenga remained the beneficiary of both.

Henry, more connected and liked in South Florida than Huizenga, immediately began lobbying for a new stadium. He was willing to put up some of his own money, and came tantalizingly close a few times, but was ultimately unsuccessful.

In the first few years under John Henry, the team made positive strides toward the future by collecting hordes of young talent, much as a well-run expansion team. The Marlins climbed from fifty-four wins in 1998 to seventy-six three years later. The team was extraordinarily young, and could boast the emergence of several good young pitchers, such as Brad Penny, Ryan Dempster, A. J. Burnett, and Josh Beckett. By 2001, Henry had allowed the payroll to creep up to $35 million, still one of the lowest figures in baseball.

At the conclusion of the 2001 season, with the teams' future in doubt, Dave Dombrowski left the Marlins to become president of the Detroit Tigers. He had built the Marlins organization brilliantly in the early years and created a team that was both good and young. When given the authority in 1996 to spend the money necessary to create a contender, he spent it well and filled the largest holes on the team with players who all contributed in their championship year. When told to dismantle the team, he was able to extract a fair return from teams despite his lack of leverage. Heading into the 2002 season, the low-payroll Marlins were again one of the more interesting young teams in baseball. Dombrowski excelled at his ever-changing job for ten years.

In early 2002, John Henry sold the Marlins to Jeff Loria, the outgoing owner of the Expos, and Henry led a group that acquired the Boston Red Sox. The 2002 Marlins had a new owner, the most promising young pitching staff in baseball, some young hitting talent, and aspirations for the playoffs. They still played in Pro Player Stadium.

16

TRANSLATING MINOR LEAGUE ABILITY: AN OUTSIDE VIEW

Heading into the 1999 season, the Kansas City Royals had severe payroll lim- itations and a lack of anything resembling adequate power. Among the main culprits for their power shortage were their designated hitters in 1998, primarily post-prime players such as Hal Morris and Terry Pendleton. No expectations for a pennant existed, but additional hitting would be necessary just to be competitive.

Although only twenty-five at the beginning of the season, Royals catcher Mike Sweeney already appeared to be at the crossroads of his career. The primary backstop in 1998, he was not a favorite of the field staff because of perceived defensive limitations, and his status for the upcoming season remained uncertain. After his promotion from the minors, Sweeney first appeared regularly in 1996 and was nominally the regular catcher, but he had recorded only 687 major league at-bats through 1998. Sweeney had hit adequately for a catcher: a .258 batting average, nineteen home runs, and ninety RBI. By themselves, these numbers do nothing to suggest the type of slugging required for a hitter's position, such as DH or first base.

Whether the Royals recognized some latent ability or simply because of a lack of alternatives, the team made Sweeney their designated hitter prior to the 1999 season. Later moved to first base, Sweeney had the breakout year highlighted in table 16.1 and was viewed as one of the most improved players in the league.

The last statistic in table 16.1, offensive winning percentage (OWpct), was developed by Bill James twenty-five years ago to measure the contribution of a player's batting statistics within the context of the game. Of-

311

Table 16.1 Mike Sweeney, 1999

G	AB	R	H	2/3B	HR	RBI	BB	AVG	RC	OWpct
150	575	101	185	46	22	102	54	.322	115	.679

OWpct = offensive winning percentage

fensive winning percentage attempts to estimate the winning percentage of a team with eight other hitters of equal ability and league-average pitching and fielding. For a left fielder or first baseman, an offensive winning percentage of .500 might be inadequate; a shortstop or catcher could make a valuable contribution with a .400 offensive winning percentage. We use offensive winning percentage as the player-valuation statistic in this chapter (see appendix 6 for additional detail).

Evaluating players like Mike Sweeney while in the minor leagues against the backdrop of a number of questions is crucial in building a solid major league team. Teams must consider which of the organization's young position players will be good enough to replace the aging veteran who's slipping, which players in a different organization should be targeted if trading a veteran at midseason, which players in one's own system might be overvalued by others and thus good trade bait, which positions within the organization are the deepest, etc.

The importance of the ability to acquire, develop, and evaluate minor league talent, of course, is no secret to major league teams. Teams invest vast resources in preparing for each year's amateur draft and developing their players. Procurement, development, and evaluation are tightly intertwined, and a truly first-class organization requires excellence in each area. Acquisition of quality players is largely a function of a correct evaluation of both one's own players and those of other organizations.

The development of ballplayers requires a large and knowledgeable minor league coaching staff. Other than some analysis of the influence of pitch counts on young pitchers, there has been little research outside of the professional baseball community on such things as methods for developing a young hitter's power or how to teach a young pitcher to gain better command of his breaking ball.

One developmental issue we can stress, however, is the importance of a consistent organizational philosophy. The Oakland A's over the past several years have emphasized throughout their entire system the importance of getting on base. Although the virtues of this approach seem clear, even at this point it has not been universally accepted. It may be argued, however, that the merits of any particular philosophy are not as important as simply communicating a consistent message throughout the system.

For example, if a major league team stresses a particular batting style, this style should be emphasized throughout the organization. The pressure on a young player to succeed upon arriving in the majors is great enough without the player also feeling he has to learn something new. The Minnesota Twins have done a remarkable job developing a nucleus of good young players over the past several years, but even they have experienced some difficulties in this regard. Outfielder Torii Hunter first appeared semiregularly for the Twins in 1999 after spending six years in the Twins' minor league system. Almost immediately manager Tom Kelly and the team's major league field staff attempted to shorten Hunter's swing. Although he eventually turned into one of the league's top outfielders, Hunter struggled that first year as a twenty-three-year-old. He hit only .255 with nine home runs and thirty-five RBI while striking out seventy-four times in 384 at-bats. The next year saw only limited improvement: a .280 batting average with five home runs and forty-four RBI to go with sixty-eight strikeouts and only eighteen walks. We do not know who was right regarding his swing, but we can say that it is inordinately difficult to maintain a productive minor league system without a consistent philosophy between those running the farm system and the major league field staff.

◇　◇　◇

Organizations spend millions of dollars and employ many knowledgeable scouts to evaluate baseball talent, the third leg of the stool of necessary organizational skills. Baseball personnel typically evaluate players based on their "tools." By observing players, scouts try to predict a minor league player's major league ability by judging things such as his ability to hit for average and power, his running speed, and his throwing arm. Having scouts who are superior judges of talent can offer an enormous benefit in building a ball club. The remainder of this chapter, however, will focus on a fresh methodology for evaluating minor league baseball players outside of what can be learned by direct observation.

Were there clues in Sweeney's minor league performance to suggest he might develop into a quality hitter? Yes. In fact, strong evidence of Sweeney's potential for this breakout year can be found in his minor league batting statistics. Bill James first introduced the concept of minor league equivalencies in the *1985 Baseball Abstract.* He demonstrated that minor league batting statistics are meaningful and could be translated into major league equivalents.

The key to making sense of minor league statistics, as with many of baseball's other statistical issues, is understanding their context. The three contextual items that one must consider in minor league player evaluation are:

1. The player's age—younger players have more time for improvement
2. The level of the league (i.e., AAA, AA, A, etc.)—the higher the classification, the closer it is to major league caliber
3. The run context the team plays in, including the average runs scored per game in the league and effect of the team's home park

For our analysis of minor league players we use a player's statistics and the context factors listed above to predict what the player's offensive winning percentage at the major league level will be at age twenty-five. Applying this projection for all players provides a common evaluation point at an age by which most quality players have made their major league debut. (For a detailed discussion of the application of the context factors to minor league statistics, see appendix 7).

Let us continue with Mike Sweeney. Sweeney's last two seasons in the minors consisted of a year in High-A at Wilmington in the Carolina League, one of the lowest-scoring venues in the minors, and a year split between Double-A and Triple-A. (See table 16.2.)

The last column is a projection of what Mike Sweeney's major league OWpct would be at age twenty-five given only the knowledge of that single batting line, his age, his league, and his home park. Sweeney's excellent statistics in a very difficult offensive environment in 1995 indicated fine future.

Averaging the two seasons (weighted by at-bats) gives a projected OWpct at age twenty-five of .701, a value very close to Sweeney's actual

Table 16.2 Mike Sweeney, 1995–1996

	Level	Age	AB	HR	RBI	AVG	RC	OW25
1995	A+	21	332	18	53	.310	78	.786
1996	AA	22	235	14	51	.319	56	.692
1996	AAA	22	101	3	16	.257	13	.444

OW25 = projected offensive winning percentage at age 25

Table 16.3 Todd Walker, 1996

	Age	AB	HR	RBI	AVG	RC
1996	23	551	28	111	.339	136

OWpct at age twenty-five of .679. It should be noted that Sweeney was not a particularly highly regarded prospect. A tenth-round draft choice in 1991, prior to his stellar 1995 season he was not one of the Royals' top ten prospects as listed by *Baseball America*, the best source for information on minor league ballplayers, as well as the best reflection of who the teams themselves identify as their best prospects. *Baseball America* gathers a tremendous amount of information from the teams and their scouts in compiling its lists, which typically reflect a traditional perspective on player evaluation. After his great 1995 season, Sweeney was still regarded as only the sixth-best prospect for the Royals.

At the end of the 1996 season, twenty-three-year-old Todd Walker had just completed a monster season (outlined in table 16.3) at Salt Lake City in the Triple-A Pacific Coast League. Playing primarily third base but prized mostly for his hitting talent, Walker was named Triple-A Player of the Year and generally viewed as one of the top prospects in baseball. Prior to the 1997 season *Baseball America* ranked this former top ten draft pick as the seventh-best prospect in baseball and first in the Minnesota Twins farm system.

As a comparison, in 1996 Sean Casey, as shown in table 16.4, had a pretty good year at Kinston in the High-A Carolina League. Casey was regarded as a decent prospect but not in Walker's class. Drafted in the second round in 1995, Casey was not ranked in *Baseball America*'s top one hundred prospects overall; the publication did, however, place Casey eighth in the Cleveland Indians organization.

By the raw statistics shown in tables 16.3 and 16.4, the evaluation of Walker as the better prospect appears correct. After making the three key contextual adjustments to the statistics, however, one can conclude that, at least in terms of their 1996 seasons, Casey was as strong a hitting prospect as Walker:

Table 16.4 Sean Casey, 1996

	Age	AB	HR	RBI	AVG	RC
1996	21	344	12	57	.331	75

Table 16.5 Walker and Casey's Projections

	Age Factor	Level Factor	Run Context	OW25
T. Walker	1.10	.78	5.74	.662
S. Casey	1.24	.65	4.35	.700

OW25 = projected offensive winning percentage at age 25

For the age and level factors, higher values lead to a higher OW25. The run context assesses how many runs score in the team's games; if this number is low, fewer runs are needed to win and each run is more valuable. Thus, applying the context factors in the present case, (1) the twenty-three-year-old Walker is assumed to have less growth potential than the twenty-one-year-old Casey; (2) Walker's AAA level is closer to the majors than Casey's high-A, so he takes less of a reduction relative to his league level; and (3) the run context factor dramatically adjusts Casey's value upwards. Only 75 percent as many runs were scored in Kinston's games as in Salt Lake's, highlighting the additional value of each run created in Kinston's games.

Todd Walker first became a regular in 1998 with the Minnesota Twins, the same year as Casey first played regularly for the Cincinnati Reds. Walker evolved into an unspectacular second baseman: after an excellent first year as a starter he slumped slightly in 1999 and drastically in 2000, so much so that he was demoted to the minors before being traded to the Colorado Rockies in midseason. Casey, traded by the Cleveland Indians to the Reds for Dave Burba just prior to the 1998 season, emerged as one of the top young first baseman in the National League. He missed the first month and a half of his 1998 season after being struck just below the eye with a baseball. After returning, Casey started slowly but soon began to hit and by 1999 was an All-Star.

Calculating Walker's and Casey's OW25 for their first two years in the majors helps convey the value of their respective major league seasons

Table 16.6 Todd Walker, 1998–1999

	Team	Age	AB	HR	RBI	AVG	RC	OW25
1998	MIN	25	528	12	62	.316	95	.631
1999	MIN	26	531	6	46	.279	73	.434

OW25 = projected offensive winning percentage at age 25

Table 16.7 Sean Casey, 1998–1999

	Team	Age	AB	HR	RBI	AVG	RC	OW25
1998	CIN	23	302	7	52	.272	46	.610
1999	CIN	24	594	25	99	.332	126	.741

OW25 = projected offensive winning percentage at age 25

(from a batting perspective only).

Casey's 1996 OW25 of .700 based on his minor league statistics fits in well with his first two major league seasons. In 1996 Walker's minor league statistics projected to an OW25 of .662; this compares closely to his actual 1998 season. One must, of course, be careful when basing conclusions on only one year of data. Obviously injuries, personal problems, or simply the random fluctuations in a career can cause any single year to be unrepresentative of a player's true potential.

As a more systematic test of the predictive value of minor league statistics, all players who had at least five hundred at-bats in both the minor and major leagues between 1996 and 1999 were analyzed. Only seasons in which a player was twenty-eight years old or younger were used, and results from any year in which a player had less than two hundred at-bats in either the majors or the minors were excluded for that level. These criteria provided us with thirty-seven qualifiers.

Tables 16.8 and 16.9 show the results for a couple of players, Todd Helton and Miguel Cairo, whom the projections fit fairly well.

On the other hand, the model overprojected outfielder Karim Garcia, a disappointment through 2001 (see table 16.10). The Cleveland Indians signed Garcia after he was released by the woeful Baltimore Orioles in October 2000, and he spent most of 2001 back in the minors. In early August 2002, the Indians recalled Garcia from the minors and inserted him into

Table 16.8 Todd Helton, 1996–1999

	Status	Age	AB	OW25
1996	Minor	22	390	.742
1997	Minor	23	392	.635
1998	Major	24	530	.668
1999	Major	25	578	.741
Total	Minor			.688
Total	Major			.706

Table 16.9 Miguel Cairo, 1996–1999

	Status	Age	AB	OW25
1996	Minor	22	465	.366
1997	Minor	23	569	.409
1998	Major	24	515	.369
1999	Major	25	465	.421
Total	Minor			.390
Total	Major			.394

the starting lineup. He responded with an outstanding two months: a .297 batting average, sixteen home runs, and fifty-two RBI in only 202 at-bats. Whether this signifies a new major-league level of ability or simply a two-month anomaly remains to be seen.

Examples can be interesting, but it is almost impossible to substantiate a statistical claim with them. The bottom two rows of tables 16.8 through 16.10 show a weighted average of both the players' minor and major league data. As a test of the predictive value of minor league statistics, a correlation coefficient can be used to measure the level of association between the minor league and the major league estimate of OW25 for our thirty-seven players. If the major league OW25 perfectly follows the minor league OW25, then the correlation coefficient would be 1; if the major and minor league values are completely unrelated, then the correlation is 0. A value between 0 and 1 indicates some positive level of association.

The correlation coefficient for the major and minor league OW25 data is .59, indicating a fairly strong positive association between a player's minor league results and his major league performance. The graphical representation in figure 16.1 may help illustrate the relationship between minor and major league OW25 results.

Table 16.10 Karim Garcia, 1996–1999

	Status	Age	AB	OW25
1996	Min	20	456	.599
1997	Min	21	262	.668
1998	Maj	22	333	.390
1999	Maj	23	288	.428
Total	Min			.624
Total	Maj			.408

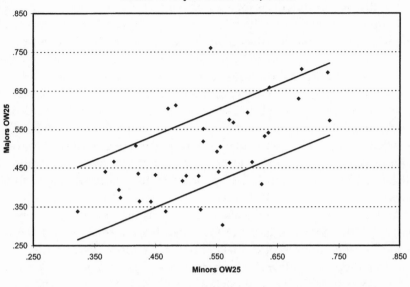

Figure 16.1

For those interested in the statistics, the two trend lines in figure 16.1 represent one standard deviation above and below the predicted value. By statistical theory, about two-thirds of the data points will fall between the two lines. In our example, this implies that in approximately two-thirds of the cases, a player with a minor league OW25 of .450 will exhibit a major league OW25 between .350 and .550. As for a couple of further statistical insights, one can be 90 percent confident that a minor leaguer with a .660 OW25 will produce at least a .500 OWpct in the majors; as to the opposite, one can be 90 percent confident that a player with a .340 OW25 in the minors will not reach a .500 OW25 as a major leaguer.

The same correlation test was run on a different set of players based solely on their major league statistics. Using the same criteria as above, fifty-two players were found who totaled at least five hundred major league at-bats in 1996 and 1997 combined and another five hundred between 1998 and 1999. The weighted average of their 1996–1997 OW25 was correlated to the weighted average of their 1998–1999 OW25. The majors-to-majors comparison resulted in a correlation coefficient of .78, a result that makes intuitive sense, as one would expect major league performance to show a tighter relationship to future major league performance no matter how judicious the adjustments to minor league data.

• • •

The discussion above has focused on only 60 percent or so of the base-ball population. Projecting the major league proficiency of pitchers based on their minor league statistics is much more problematic. Success or fail-ure is determined so strongly by the pitching arm that even small injuries can lead to significant short-term or long-term changes in ability and sta-tistics. The theme of this chapter, that a systematic analysis of minor league data can lead to an increased confidence in minor league statistics, needs quite a bit of refinement before it can be applied to pitchers. The best that can be said today is that certain statistics (e.g., strikeout to walk ratio, strikeouts per inning, and hits per inning) can give a indication of pitcher quality. Beyond this, few specific quantitative conclusions can be drawn.

An important caveat in the above analysis is that it is based solely on statistics. No allowance is made for subjective information and the re-vealing observations scouts make from watching a player. Also, the growth patterns of a player's ability vary. Some players peak earlier than others. Some never learn to hit pitching above the high-A level. The whole gamut of human differences makes projecting future abilities an uncertain endeavor at best.

Another important reason for caution lies in the need to estimate the relative competition of the four league levels. Although the adjustment factors appear fairly accurate based on our analysis, this area needs more research, especially for the single-A leagues. Additionally, the projections are based solely on batting. Fielding ability is obviously critical in the analysis of minor leaguers; a shortstop is a prospect at a much lower of-fensive level than a first baseman or DH.

Despite these caveats, minor league hitting statistics, when properly adjusted, can offer substantial insight into the major league potential of a minor league hitter. Systematically applying the three contextual factors of age, level, and run context can turn minor league performance into a quality indicator of a player's major league future.

17

UNHERALDED DYNASTY:
THE 1990s ATLANTA BRAVES

On October 4, 1955, the Brooklyn Dodgers defeated the New York Yankees, 2–0, in the seventh game of the World Series, to capture their first and only championship. The Dodgers of this era were a consistently fine team, winning six National League pennants between 1947 and 1956, but their legacy would be vastly different had they not won this single contest. Sports fans remember the winners, and these great Dodger teams, with Jackie Robinson, Duke Snider, Roy Campanella, and others, narrowly avoided being cast as a valiant loser or, even worse, a team that could not handle the pressure of big games.

The Atlanta Braves won five National League pennants between 1991 and 1999 and fielded excellent teams for twelve straight years through 2002. It will be interesting to see how history judges this great team that, like the Dodgers, has only been able to win a single World Series. Most stories written about the Braves in the last few years have considered them a disappointment because of their postseason failures. Although their record of success has been at least as impressive as that of the great Dodger teams of the 1950s, most contemporary writers have overlooked the Braves' achievements in favor of their October disappointments.

Atlanta transformed itself from a very bad team to a very good one during its amazing 1991 season. The team's sudden breakthrough was a great accomplishment, but more impressive is what followed: a sustained run of excellence for more than a decade while continually turning over its roster. That the Braves have encountered difficulty navigating through extended postseasons should not detract from what they accomplished over a decade of success.

◇   ◇   ◇

In 1973 Ted Turner owned and operated WTCG, a small UHF station in Atlanta that broadcast old movies and *Leave it to Beaver* reruns and could not be received clearly in all parts of the city. Eager for original programming, Turner offered the Atlanta Braves $3 million to televise sixty baseball games per year for five years. The Braves management team had never heard of Turner and was concerned about the amateurish quality of his operation. Nonetheless, the team desperately needed money and accepted his offer.

By 1975 the Braves had become one of the worst franchises in baseball. Henry Aaron had set the all-time home run record while with the Braves in April 1974, but the team then sold him to the Milwaukee Brewers to finish his career, removing one of the last remaining reasons to attend a Braves game. The team finished 67–94, its worst record since 1942, when it played in Boston, and drew only 534,672 fans. Rumors abounded that the owners might sell to investors interested in moving the team to Denver or Toronto.

Ted Turner, already dreaming of making it big in cable television (a nascent technology in 1975), could ill afford to lose the Braves, the only original programming he offered. If the Braves left town, his operation would take a step backward. Largely for these reasons, he made an offer to buy the team, which was accepted in January 1976.

Turner knew very little about baseball but was enthusiastic about his new concern. He even appeared in TV commercials, inviting people to call him up if they had any questions or suggestions.

As Bill Veeck and Charlie Finley had done before him while owning poor teams, Turner turned to silly promotions to generate interest. The team staged motorized bathtub races, ostrich races, mattress stacking (with college fraternities and sororities competing to see how many people they could stack on a bed), and Wishbone Salad Dressing Night (when fans searched for keys to a new car inside a giant bowl of salad greens). Whenever possible, Turner himself participated in these events. A few in which he did not participate included a wet T-shirt contest, Karl Wallenda walking a high wire over the stadium, and Wedlock and Headlock Night (thirty-four weddings before the game and a wrestling match afterwards).

In the Braves' 1976 home opener, Turner ran out on the field to congratulate Ken Henderson at home plate after a home run. His enthusiasm and promotions may have paid off. Despite finishing in last place for the first time since 1935, the Braves' attendance reached 800,000 in 1976, up more than 50 percent from the previous year.

On the field, the ball club was a failure in Turner's early years, finishing in last place in each of his first four seasons. In 1977, Turner was suspended for "tampering" with Giants outfielder Gary Mathews while successfully wooing him as a free agent. He also caused himself some trouble when, after asking manager Dave Bristol to take a few days off, he suited up and ran the team himself.

Looking for a spark, Turner brought in Bobby Cox to manage in 1978. Cox had spent nearly a decade in the minors before becoming the Yankees' third baseman in 1968, but bad knees forced his retirement in 1971. Over the next several years he managed in the Yankees system and spent a year as a Yankees coach. The Braves improved steadily under Cox, and by 1980 they were a .500 team.

Led by the strong hitting of Dale Murphy, Bob Horner, and Gary Mathews and the able pitching of Phil Niekro and Doyle Alexander, the Braves followed up an 81–80 year with a 50–56 record in the strike-marred 1981 season. Though they were obviously going in the right direction, Turner made what he later described as the biggest mistake of his tenure as owner. To appease the television executives at his growing empire, he fired Bobby Cox and replaced him with Joe Torre. Unlike Cox, Torre was talkative and comfortable with the media and their cameras.

The Braves won a division title in 1982 but quickly slipped back into mediocrity. Turner had launched CNN, the first all-news cable station, in 1980, and soon relinquished control of the team to his baseball staff. After a third-place 80–82 finish in 1984 cost Torre his job, the Braves finished last or next-to-last for the next six years under Eddie Haas, Chuck Tanner, and Russ Nixon.

By the mid-1980s, talented players were flowing into the Braves' organization under the tutelage of longtime farm director Paul Snyder. The Braves drafted Ron Gant and Mark Lemke in 1983, Tom Glavine and Jeff Blauser in 1984, and David Justice in 1985. In 1986 the Braves rehired Cox, this time as general manager. Under Cox, the team continued to stock pitching prospects: Kent Mercker in 1986, Mike Stanton in 1987, and Steve Avery in 1988. Cox also made one great midseason deal, trading Doyle Alexander to the Tigers in 1987 for twenty-year-old minor leaguer John Smoltz.

Although there were some talented prospects in the system when he returned, Cox and his organization patiently allowed them to develop. After years of being active in the free agent market, the Braves signed just one high-profile player during Cox's five years as general manager. By the time he stepped down to return to managing in 1990, the system was loaded with young prospects.

The lone free agent Cox signed did not pan out. After Nick Esasky drove in 108 runs for the Boston Red Sox in 1989, the Georgia native accepted less money to sign with the Braves. Unfortunately, in his first nine games Esasky struck out fourteen times in thirty-five at-bats and committed five errors. Suffering from extreme dizziness, Esasky was found to have an ear infection that had caused him to develop vertigo. Esasky experimented with many solutions over the next few years but would never again play in the major leagues.

The 1990 Braves finished with a record of 65–97, the second-worst record in baseball—two games better than the New York Yankees—but the Braves clearly had some young talent. Their two best position players, David Justice and Ron Gant, were twenty-four and twenty-five years old. Their two best pitchers, Tom Glavine and John Smoltz, were twenty-four and twenty-three. The team promoted Steve Avery, a nineteen-year-old left-handed pitching phenom too early (3-11, 5.64), but he was still considered one of the best young pitching prospects in baseball. Many other players on the team were young and promising, and the farm system appeared well stocked.

On June 22, 1990, Cox returned to the dugout, replacing Russ Nixon as the Atlanta skipper. In October, Cox dropped his general manager's duties and embarked on one of the best decades ever enjoyed by one baseball manager.

To replace Cox, the Braves hired John Schuerholz, who had run the Kansas City Royals for the previous ten years. A Baltimore native, Schuerholz had left his junior high school teaching position to join the Orioles' front office in 1966. Two years later he became an administrative assistant with the expansion Royals and worked his way up to farm director in 1975, vice president of player personnel in 1979, and executive vice president and general manager in 1981. During his tenure in Kansas City, the organization was a model for baseball player development, and its success culminated in a World Series title in 1985.

During the 1980s the Royals organization was beset with an inability to either develop or acquire good offensive players. The best hitters the system produced during Schuerholz's ten-year reign were Kevin Seitzer, Mike MacFarlane, and Don Slaught. By the end of the 1980s, the team consistently had one of the better pitching staffs in the league, but the offense had lost its punch.

◇ ◇ ◇

Schuerholz and Cox went right to work to improve the Braves. The pitching staff (with Smoltz, Glavine, Avery, and the veteran Charlie Liebrandt) was left alone to develop, but Schuerholz signed three free agents and made one trade in order to broaden the offense. At the time, these moves did not appear particularly significant.

To replace Nick Esasky, the Braves signed Sid Bream, an adequate-hitting, good-fielding first baseman, from the Pirates. To shore up the infield defense, Schuerholz inked Pittsburgh shortstop Rafael Belliard. To play third base, the team lured Terry Pendleton, an excellent defensive player but one of the worst hitters in baseball in 1990 (a .230 average with just thirty walks and six home runs), from the Cardinals. Just prior to the start of the season, the Braves acquired Otis Nixon, a good outfielder whose offensive skills were limited to his speed, from the Expos.

The rest of the offense remained intact. Lonnie Smith, Ron Gant, and David Justice, joined by Nixon, patrolled the outfield. Mark Lemke, Jeff Treadway, and Jeff Blauser were adequate young middle infielders. After spending ten seasons in the minor leagues, Greg Olson became the starting catcher in 1990. Bobby Cox had young outfielders Deion Sanders and Brian Hunter on the bench.

Because of their young pitching, hopes ran high that the Braves could approach .500. Most preseason prognosticators, however, anticipated another year in the cellar, mainly because it was hard to envision any improvement of the offense. All four acquisitions were glove men and unlikely to provide much punch. Justice and Gant appeared to be the only good hitters on the team. The Braves seemed to be placing an awful lot of pressure on their young pitching arms.

The 1991 Braves exceeded even the most optimistic expectations and finished 94–68. After trailing by nine and a half games at the All Star break, Atlanta embarked on a remarkable second-half tear to pass the Los Angeles Dodgers in the last week and clinch on the next-to-last day of the season. The Braves won eight games in a row from September 27 through October 5 to take their first division title since 1982. They defeated the Pirates in a dramatic seven-game National League Championship Series and then lost an even more exciting World Series to the Minnesota Twins.

The Braves' pitching was magnificent. Their team ERA of 3.49, third in the league, did not fully reflect the quality of the staff because of an extreme park effect: their ERA was 3.81 in Atlanta but only 3.17 on the road. Tom Glavine finished 20–11 with a 2.55 ERA and won the Cy Young Award. Steve Avery supplied an 18–8 record and a 3.38 ERA. John Smoltz went 14–13 with an ERA of 3.80. The bullpen was excellent and deep. Juan Berenguer was the principal late-inning reliever until he hurt his arm in August, at which point Schuerholz acquired Alejandro Pena, who saved eleven games in the season's final five weeks.

The Braves were second in the league in runs scored, though their home park overstates the case somewhat. Nonetheless, the offense exceeded nearly everyone's expectation. The team's depth allowed it to deal with injuries to David Justice and Sid Bream, who each missed a third of the season, and the loss of Otis Nixon, suspended through the postseason in September for violating baseball's drug policy.

Terry Pendleton was the big surprise and the major reason for the improvement in the team's hitting. He hit .319, an advance of eighty-nine points in one year, and belted twenty-two home runs. He won the batting title and the MVP award for his efforts. The rest of the offense was solid but unspectacular.

Many analysts had been raving about the Braves' young pitchers for a few years, although no one envisioned the simultaneous breakthrough of Glavine, Smoltz, and Avery in 1991. Looking ahead, however, the offense still looked to need upgrading. Other than Justice and Gant, the lineup was mainly filled with journeyman players, none of whom seemed likely to improve.

◇ ◇ ◇

The Braves could not have maintained their success for a decade without a continual influx of talent. The team that won the World Series in 1995 was much different than the one that had lost four years earlier; five of the eight position players, two starting pitchers, most of the bench, and all of the bullpen had turned over. When the Braves lost the World Series in 1999, five of the eight position players, two starters, and all of the bench and bullpen were different from the champions of 1995. The following paragraphs will briefly outline their great run, emphasizing the important changes to their personnel.

In March 1992, John Schuerholz agreed to a trade with Pittsburgh general manager Ted Simmons that would send reliever Alejandro Pena and young outfielder Keith Mitchell to the Pirates for Barry Bonds. The two

John Schuerholz

then arranged to speak the next day to formalize the details. Unfortunately for the Braves, Pirates manager Jim Leyland talked Simmons out of the deal. Bonds left the Pirates at the end of the season as a free agent.

With a team unchanged from 1991, the Braves cruised to the 1992 division title and repeated as National League champions. The team again employed the league's best pitching staff and enough offense from a flexible and deep group with a couple of stars. Once again they defeated the Pirates in the playoffs, but this time lost a six-game World Series to the Toronto Blue Jays.

Prior to the 1993 season, the Braves shocked the baseball world by signing free agent Greg Maddux, the twenty-six-year-old ace of the Chicago Cubs, to bolster a pitching staff that was already the envy of the league. Maddux responded with the second of what would be four straight Cy Young awards, and Glavine, Avery, and Smoltz won twenty, eighteen, and fifteen games, respectively.

On July 18, with the team struggling to stay with the Giants in the division race, Schuerholz traded three minor leaguers, none of whom ever became a quality player, to San Diego for first baseman Fred McGriff. McGriff hit .310 with nineteen home runs and 55 RBI in his sixty-eight games with the Braves. Justice (forty home runs, 120 RBI) and Gant (thirty-six home runs, 117 RBI) helped out the improved offense.

The Braves finished 51–17 after the McGriff deal. They made up nine and a half games after August 7 and clinched the division on the season's final day. Heavily favored to reach the World Series again and finally win, the Braves outscored the Phillies 33–23 in the NLCS but lost in six games.

In February 1994, the Braves resigned the twenty-seven-year-old Gant, who had finished fifth in the 1993 MVP voting, to a one-year, $5.5 million contract. A week later, Gant broke his right leg in a dirt bike accident, causing him to miss the entire 1994 season. The Braves elected to terminate Gant's contract, a move that cost them just one-sixth of his annual salary. Gant's career would continue in 1995, but he would never again play for Atlanta.

Chipper Jones, the number one pick in the 1990 amateur draft, streaked through the Braves system and appeared to have won Gant's old left field job in the spring of 1994. Unfortunately, Jones tore up his knee in late March and missed the entire season. The left field role was mainly given to another rookie, Ryan Klesko, who proved adequate with seventeen home runs and seventy-eight RBI. Javy Lopez, another first-year player, became the principal starting catcher.

When the player strike hit in August the Braves were poised for another postseason. They were in second place, six games behind the Montreal Expos, but had the second-best record in the National League. With the introduction of the wild card that season, plus the Braves' penchant for late-season runs, Atlanta was as good a bet as anyone to reach the 1994 World Series. The work stoppage shut down the rest of the season and lasted into early 1995.

Once labor peace was finally restored, teams had just a few weeks to prepare their rosters for the 1995 season. In April, the Braves traded for Expos center fielder Marquis Grissom, a Gold Glove outfielder. Recovered from his injury, Chipper Jones won the third-base job and responded with twenty-three home runs and eighty-six RBI.

The Braves actually fielded a below-average offense in 1995. Shortstop Jeff Blauser, second baseman Mark Lemke, and center fielder Grissom had puny slugging averages of .341, .356, and .376, respectively, and the bench proved unproductive. Lopez and Klesko were fine young hitters but both players shared their positions with players (Charlie O'Brien and Dwight Smith) who provided no offense.

Greg Maddux produced a season for the ages, finishing 19–2 with a 1.63 ERA, in a league with an ERA of 4.63. Glavine went 16–7 and Smoltz 12–7, both with ERAs in the low threes. The bullpen was solid and deep. After winning their division by twenty-one games, the Braves won eleven of fourteen postseason games to cruise to their first World Series title in Atlanta.

The team quieted, if only temporarily, the notion that it was missing the guts and heart necessary to win a championship. This idea seems ridiculous for a team that had provided so many late-season heroics. The 1991 team was below .500 in midseason but caught the Dodgers with a marvelous final two months. Down three games to two to the Pirates in the NLCS, the Braves pitched back-to-back shutouts in Pittsburgh to advance. The 1991 World Series was one of the most evenly matched classics ever played. The 1992 club defeated the Pirates in the playoffs by staging a come-from-behind rally in the final inning of game seven. The 1993 Braves enjoyed another of the most dramatic second halves in baseball history. Their record in big games was outstanding.

Up to this point in the story, Schuerholz's performance with the Braves had been nearly flawless. After inheriting a team filled with young talent, he acquired several inexpensive veterans for depth, one of whom (Terry Pendleton) won the MVP award. The team signed only one significant free agent in this period, Greg Maddux, and he merely became one of the best pitchers who has ever lived. Fred McGriff added needed offense for little cost. The organization had produced Klesko, Lopez, and Jones, three of the better young position players in the league.

For the second time in the Schuerholz era, the Braves went into the 1996 season with no major changes from the previous year. The offense improved, mainly because youngsters Lopez, Klesko, and Jones continued to develop. Grissom bounced back to hit .300 and McGriff, by now only an average-hitting first baseman, contributed his typical 107 RBI.

On the other hand, Justice hurt his shoulder, missing most of the season and all of the post-season. The Braves replaced him with Jermaine Dye, a twenty-two-year-old who showed flashes of power but little strike zone judgment. In late August the Braves recalled nineteen-year-old wunderkind Andruw Jones, who displayed flashes of brilliance on offense and defense, especially in the World Series. To gain a little more pop in the lineup, Schuerholz reacquired Terry Pendleton from the Marlins in August, put him at third, and moved Chipper Jones to shortstop. Pendleton was several years removed from his productive seasons, and his lifeless hitting was no help.

Smoltz won twenty-four games and the Cy Young Award; he, Glavine, and Maddux posted three of the best five ERAs in the league. Seemingly never satisfied with his pitching, in August Schuerholz traded pitching prospect Jason Schmidt to the Pirates for twenty-seven-year-old left-hander Denny Neagle, who had a record of 14–6 at the time of the deal.

The team again cruised to the division title and beat the Dodgers and Cardinals in the playoffs but fell to the Yankees in a six-game World Series. Since Atlanta had won the first two games in New York before losing four straight and had outscored the Yankees 26–17 over the six games, the team once again faced the criticism that it had underachieved in the post-season.

With David Justice recovered for 1997, the Braves had a glut of capable outfielders: Justice, Klesko, Grissom, Dye, and Andruw Jones. In March Schuerholz reacted by dealing Justice and Grissom to the Indians for Kenny Lofton, a Gold Glove center fielder who typically hit well over .300 with a fair share of walks and had led the American League in steals for the past five years. Lofton hit .333 for Atlanta but his defense and base stealing were hampered by various leg ailments. Thinking he still had one starting outfielder too many, Schuerholz also dealt Dye to the Royals for outfielder Michael Tucker and second baseman Keith Lockhart. Tucker platooned with Andruw Jones in left field and Lockhart shared second base with Mark Lemke.

Once again, the 1997 Braves dominated the league's pitching: Neagle finished 20–5 with a 2.97 ERA; Maddux was 19–4, 2.20; and Glavine and Smoltz won fourteen and fifteen games, respectively. The Braves cruised to the best record in the league, but again the team fell short when the Florida Marlins toppled them in the NLCS.

Kenny Lofton and Jeff Blauser left as free agents after the 1997 season, the latter after turning in a surprisingly good offensive year in 1997. The team sold McGriff to the new expansion team in Tampa Bay. To partly re-place these players, Schuerholz signed thirty-four-year-old shortstop Walt Weiss and thirty-seven-year-old first baseman Andres Galarraga.

These deals represented an important crossroads for John Schuerholz and the Braves. The 1997–1998 off-season was the first time during their great run that the team brought in old players to fill holes. Up until this point, the team kept winning while bringing in younger players to replace declining veterans, a remarkable accomplishment. Discarding Blauser and McGriff, players with very little future, was consistent with their phi-losophy. Picking up Weiss and Galarraga, each older than the man he re-placed, was not. This marked the first time during the Schuerholz era that a player older than thirty had been acquired to play regularly.

Defying the baseball analysts, who believed his great statistics over the previous five years were the result of playing in the thin air of Colorado, Galarraga responded with forty-four home runs in his first year in Turn-er Field. Weiss struggled after a hot start, so the Braves brought in Ozzie Guillen, an even older and weaker hitter. Nonetheless, the Braves had their best offensive team of the 1990s, powered by thirty-homer seasons from Galarraga, Lopez, Chipper Jones, and Andruw Jones.

Unbelievably, the team boasted yet another fine starting pitcher with the emergence of twenty-three-year-old Kevin Millwood, the first starter the Braves had developed since Steve Avery in 1990. Glavine won twenty games and the Cy Young Award, and Maddux, Smoltz, Millwood, and Neagle each won between sixteen and eighteen games. This was the first pitching staff with five sixteen-game winners since the 1902 Pirates. Unfortunately, the team lost the NLCS to the Padres.

As the Braves' reputation for postseason failure grew, Schuerholz finally decided to trade some of his plentiful starting pitching for some position players. He dealt Denny Neagle, Michael Tucker, and pitching prospect Rob Bell to Cincinnati for thirty-year-old second baseman Bret Boone plus a thirty-three-year-old relief pitcher, Mike Remlinger. Boone fielded well and showed midrange power but walked infrequently and had not hit over .270 or had an on-base percentage over .330 in four years. The Braves also signed free agent outfielder Brian Jordan from the Cardinals. Both Boone and Jordan had experienced up-and-down careers and Schuerholz hoped for a couple of good seasons with the Braves.

Neither newcomer was a star but each was an upgrade over the player he replaced in the lineup, Keith Lockhart and Michael Tucker. In 1999 the Braves increased their run scoring slightly despite losing Andres Galarraga for the season to skin cancer and Javier Lopez for most of the season with a knee injury. Chipper Jones had a monster season, with forty-five home runs, 110 RBI, and a .319 average. He was a unanimous MVP selection.

The pitching was again dominant. Glavine had an off year, but Maddux and Millwood were among the best hurlers in the league and John Smoltz pitched better than his 11–9 record. The Braves beat the Astros and Mets in the playoffs to reach the World Series, where the Yankees defeated them once again.

In December 1999, Schuerholz consummated another big trade, dealing Boone and Klesko to the Padres for outfielder Reggie Sanders, second baseman Quilvio Veras, and first baseman Wally Joyner. The principal reason for the trade was to upgrade the top of the order, which had been dismal in 1999. Veras and his .368 on-base percentage would lead off; Sanders would hit second.

In July 2000, Veras was batting .309 with a .413 on-base percentage as the team's best leadoff man in some time when he blew out his anterior cruciate ligament and missed the rest of the season. Sanders, also hurt a lot, hit just .232 with eleven home runs. Rafael Furcal, believed to be nineteen but actually twenty-one, won the shortstop job in the spring, hit .295

with a .394 on-base percentage, and was named Rookie of the Year. Chipper Jones, Andruw Jones, and comebacks from Lopez and Galarraga kept the offense above average. A midseason trade of marginal prospects to the Orioles for left fielder B. J. Surhoff provided little help.

The pitching staff suffered a major blow when John Smoltz required surgery on his elbow and missed the entire 2000 season. This marked the first time Smoltz, Glavine, or Maddux had been set back by an injury after seven years in the rotation together. Faced with an unusual shortage of starting pitching, Schuerholz signed thirty-five-year-old John Burkett and thirty-seven-year-old Terry Mulholland, each of whom provided league average innings. Maddux and Glavine reversed slight slides and won forty games between them, but Kevin Millwood slumped. At the midseason trading deadline, the Braves dealt pitching prospect Bruce Chen to the Phillies for veteran moundsman Andy Ashby, who won eight games for Atlanta. The staff was still one of the best but no longer dominated as it had for so long.

In 2001, the Braves again began to address their aging offense with internal solutions as opposed to aging veterans. After losing in the division series for the first time in 2000, the Braves let Galarraga and Sanders leave as free agents. Having introduced Furcal in 2000, the Braves promoted first baseman Wes Helms and second baseman Marcus Giles the next year. The former was only a marginal prospect but Giles was a promising hitter; the jury is still out on his ability to handle the defensive responsibilities of second base. The team returned to the NLCS before falling to the Diamondbacks in five games.

In January 2002, Schuerholz made his biggest trade in years, dealing pitcher Brian Jordan and pitcher Odalis Perez to the Dodgers for right fielder Gary Sheffield. Although thirty-three at the time, Sheffield was a great hitter, and the Braves offense had become somewhat poor (thirteenth in the league in runs in 2001). Cox also moved Chipper Jones to left field to make room for free agent acquisition Vinny Castilla, and shifted John Smoltz, recovered from his elbow injury, to closer.

The Braves won their division by nineteen games and finished with a league-best 101 wins. Led again by a dominant pitching staff, with Maddux, Glavine, Millwood, and a deep bullpen all having excellent years, the Braves were able to hide an offense with huge holes. Castilla, Lockhart, Lopez, and the entire bench were inadequate. Giles and Furcal both regressed from their promising starts. The team lost the division series in five games to the Giants. Once again, the great pitching was not enough.

Table 17.1 summarizes the Braves' success over the twelve-year period.

Table 17.1 Atlanta Braves, 1991–2001

	W–L	Pct.	Finish	Postseason	W–L
1991	94–68	.580	1	Lost World Series	7–7
1992	98–64	.605	1	Lost World Series	6–7
1993	104–58	.642	1	Lost NLCS	2–4
1994	68–46	.596	2	Strike	
1995	90–54	.625	1	Won World Series	11–3
1996	96–66	.593	1	Lost World Series	9–7
1997	101–61	.623	1	Lost NLCS	5–4
1998	106–56	.654	1	Lost NLCS	5–4
1999	103–59	.636	1	Lost World Series	7–6
2000	95–67	.586	1	Lost Division Series	0–3
2001	88–74	.543	1	Lost NLCS	4–4
2002	101–59	.631	1	Lost Division Series	2–3

Four times in this period the Braves recorded the best record in all of baseball (1992, 1993, 1997, and 1999). In four additional years they posted the best record in the National League (1995, 1996, 1998, and 2002). The last column is their won-loss record in the postseason and illustrates how difficult it is to win three playoff series. Atlanta's aggregate record in the eleven postseasons was 58–52, but only once were they able to grab the brass ring.

A further comparison to the Brooklyn Dodgers might be helpful. The 1946–1956 Dodgers compiled a fine winning percentage of .604, won six pennants, and twice lost titles in a best-of-three playoff series. The 1991–2002 Braves played .611 baseball, compiled the league's best record (in a much larger league) eight times, and won five flags. Both were excellent teams that won only a single World Series.

In 110 playoff games in this period the Braves scored 471 runs and allowed 379. According to Bill James's Pythagorean method, these results would lead, on average, to a record of 67–43, nine wins better than the Braves actually achieved. In two series in particular—the 1983 NLCS loss to the Phillies and the 1996 World Series defeat to the Yankees—the Braves decisively outscored seemingly inferior teams but came up short in victories. Some have speculated that the Braves have had a tendency to lose close postseason games and underperform their win expectations because of an inconsistent bullpen and, especially, an inadequate bench. This limited sample of games, spread over twelve years, is too small to allow any such conclusion to be drawn. The Braves *have* lost a number of close October games, but it is not obvious that this is anything other than a string of bad luck.

◇ ◇ ◇

A modern major league organization looking to add talent has essentially three avenues available. It can draft or sign an amateur player, nurture him through the minor leagues, and reap the benefit if he becomes a quality player. A ball club can make trades, which typically requires having attractive talent in the system for exchange. Finally, a team can sign a veteran major league player who has attained his free agency. The Braves of the 1990s used all three methods, and the remainder of this chapter will examine how well the Braves utilized each.

The most remarkable part of the Braves' twelve-year run, the best in baseball history by a non-Yankee team, is the way they were able to turn over their personnel while continuing to win. Table 17.2 shows the significant players from their minor-league organization who were given large roles on the team after it had first tasted success in 1991.

This list of players represents a large influx of talent. Good teams are often reluctant to give significant roles to untested players. The Braves of the early 1990s had several veteran journeymen who needed replacing within a few years. The key to the longevity of their dynasty was the seamless integration of four young players into the lineup, all of whom worked out splendidly, within a three-year period.

A comparison to the Cleveland Indians of the 1990s under general manager John Hart is instructive. Hart built a great team in Cleveland that blossomed in 1994–1996, but as holes emerged he was reluctant to fill them from within the organization. Over the next few years he dealt such

Table 17.2 Players from Within

Player	Position	Year	Player	Position	Year
Mike Stanton	RP	1991	Kevin Millwood	SP	1998
Mark Wohlers	RP	1993	Kerry Ligtenberg	RP	1998
Ryan Klesko	OF	1994	John Rocker	RP	1998
Javy Lopez	C	1994	Rafael Furcal	SS	2000
Greg McMichael	RP	1994	Marcus Giles	2B	2001
Chipper Jones	3B	1995	Jason Marquis	SP	2001
Andruw Jones	OF	1996	Damian Moss	SP	2002

players as Sean Casey, Danny Graves, Jeromy Burnitz, Albie Lopez, Brian Giles, and Richie Sexon, often in order to acquire a veteran player who proved less productive than the internal solution he discounted. On the other hand, the 1994 Braves were the best team in baseball and handed starting jobs to two rookies, Klesko and Javy Lopez. Within a couple more years, Chipper and Andruw Jones also claimed key roles on the team and later Rafael Furcal did as well.

The club also produced a steady supply of useful relief pitchers. Although they seemed to have spent the entire decade looking for a star closer, the Braves generally employed a deep and effective homegrown bullpen. The only starting pitcher added before 2001 was Kevin Millwood, partly because no openings existed during much of the period.

Table 17.3 shows the significant free agents signed by the Braves during the Schuerholz era, the year they first played with the team, and their age in that year.

Although the Braves are one of the wealthiest teams in baseball, they have not made a habit of signing top-level free agents. Schuerholz signed a few veterans to fill out the roster in 1991, and one of them, Pendleton, was the best position player on the first two World Series teams.

The signings of Weiss and Galarraga provided the first indication that the Braves might be shifting away from their successful reliance on solving problems from within the organization. Galarraga had a surprisingly good year in 1997, but neither he nor Weiss was an effective player at the end of his contract. Jordan was also a disappointment.

Along with the Giants' signing of Barry Bonds, Greg Maddux was one of the two greatest free agent acquisitions in baseball history. No one could have predicted how terrific he eventually became, but he had a

Table 17.3 Free Agent Signings

	Position	Year	Age
Terry Pendleton	3B	1991	30
Sid Bream	1B	1991	30
Rafael Belliard	SS	1991	29
Juan Berenguer	RP	1991	36
Greg Maddux	SP	1993	27
Walt Weiss	SS	1997	34
Andres Galarraga	1B	1997	37
Brian Jordan	OF	1999	32

much higher ceiling than virtually any other free agent because (a) he was already a great player, and (b) he was young.

Since the advent of player free agency in the late 1970s, many free agents have been disappointments to their new teams. Some fans and writers have suggested that such players simply stopped trying, losing their hunger once they received the big salaries. The more likely explanation is much simpler and less sinister. Under the terms of the collective bargaining agreement, players can elect to become free agents when they have played at least six full seasons in the major leagues. Most good players stick in the majors between age twenty-two and twenty-five, and teams often sign these players to contracts that push their free agency off for a few years. It is therefore unusual for a quality player to be available on the open market before the age of thirty.

As discussed in chapter 10, it is imperative that ball clubs understand how players age. Since position players, on average, peak in their late twenties, nearly all free agents have already had their best years and are in their decline phase by the time they become available. Pitchers don't have such a regular aging pattern but their injury risk makes them even less inviting as midcareer signings.

In table 17.4 we attempt to identify all free agents who were considered stars at the time they switched teams and were not yet thirty years old in their first season with their new team. The list excludes those who had just one good year prior to hitting the open market (e.g., Wayne Garland and Darryl Kile).

The list is necessarily subjective, but we are confident that other observers would come up with virtually the same group. Of these players, just two were disappointments: Mark Davis, who wasn't really a star, but is included because he was coming off a singularly great relief season that earned him the Cy Young award; and Darryl Strawberry, whose career was eaten away by injuries and personal problems. The jury is still out on the 2001 signings (though Mike Hampton is off to a terrible start in his two seasons with the Rockies), but the rest retained their stardom for several years after signing their big contracts.

Much like their restraint in the free agent market, the Braves were not active traders during the first several years of their run. Table 17.5 lists the most interesting trades made by Schuerholz during his first twelve years with the Braves. (In a few cases, inconsequential players in the deal are omitted for simplicity.)

During the first five years of the Braves' dynasty (1991–1995), most At-

Table 17.4 Best Free Agents under Thirty

	Year	Old Team	New Team	Age
Rich Gossage	1978	Pirates	Yankees	26
Dave Winfield	1981	Padres	Yankees	29
Mark Davis	1990	Padres	Royals	29
Darryl Strawberry	1991	Mets	Dodgers	29
Greg Maddux	1993	Cubs	Braves	27
Barry Bonds	1993	Pirates	Giants	28
Rafael Palmeiro	1994	Rangers	Orioles	29
Larry Walker	1995	Expos	Rockies	28
Roberto Alomar	1996	Blue Jays	Orioles	28
Mike Hampton	2001	Mets	Rockies	28
Manny Ramirez	2001	Indians	Red Sox	29
Alex Rodriguez	2001	Mariners	Rangers	25

lanta deals (not listed) were minor ones to acquire depth in the bullpen or bench. Schuerholz acquired Nixon just prior to the 1991 season and he played a major role in their first two pennants. When the Braves lost closer Juan Berenguer that August they acquired Pena, and he pitched well down the stretch.

The McGriff deal was a marvelous one. The Braves' offense was struggling, McGriff was one of the best and most dependable hitters in baseball, and none of the prospects sent to the Padres ever amounted to anything. The team caught fire after the trade and ran down the Giants in one of baseball's best pennant races. The Braves also acquired Grissom for little cost and he was an important part of their great teams in 1995 and 1996.

Beginning with the acquisition of Pendleton in 1996, Schuerholz's record as dealmaker diminished, indicating a new reluctance to trust the players in his system. Pendleton was thirty-five and no longer a good player when reacquired, but he was handed a job in the lineup over Jeff Blauser, a better player. The Neagle acquisition worked out well for the Braves, mostly because Schmidt has never shaken arm problems. It would have been interesting to see how Schmidt might have developed under Cox and pitching coach Leo Mazzone.

The Braves traded Dye because they had a surplus in the outfield and needed help in the infield. Considered a decent fourth outfielder, Dye eventually became a topflight hitter. Neagle was 36–16 in his two full years with the Braves, but they received little for him. The Braves discarded Klesko too cheaply as well—they seemed to focus on what he

Table 17.5 Significant Trades

Date	Team	Traded	Acquired
April 1991	Expos	Minor leaguers	Otis Nixon
Aug. 1991	Mets	Tony Castillo	Alejandro Pena
July 1993	Padres	Minor leaguers	Fred McGriff
April 1995	Expos	Roberto Kelly	Marquis Grissom
Aug. 1996	Marlins	Roosevelt Brown	Terry Pendleton
Aug. 1996	Pirates	Jason Schmidt	Denny Neagle
March 1997	Indians	David Justice Marquis Grissom	Kenny Lofton Alan Embree
March 1997	Royals	Jermaine Dye	Michael Tucker Keith Lockhart
Nov. 1998	Reds	Denny Neagle Michael Tucker Rob Bell	Bret Boone Mike Remlinger
Dec. 1999	Padres	Ryan Klesko Reggie Sanders	Bret Boone Quilvio Veras Wally Joyner
July 2000	Phillies	Bruce Chen	Alan Ashby
Jan. 2002	Dodgers	Brian Jordan Odalis Perez	Gary Sheffield

could not do (play good defense or hit lefties) and lose sight of the fact that he was an excellent offensive player. By the end of the decade, he and Dye were better hitters than any outfielder on the Braves.

Importantly and significantly, in the last few years nearly all of the new, useful players were brought up from the minor leagues. For the most part, the players acquired from other organizations, many on the downside of their careers, were disappointments.

◇ ◇ ◇

The Atlanta Braves of the 1990s stand as a model for how to create and maintain a contending team. Although all organizations make decisions that work out and decisions that do not, the Braves have been right often enough that much can be learned from their story.

Several lessons stand out. The most important step to creating a team capable of contending for multiple pennants is the development of a strong farm system that can produce a steady stream of talent. The organization built by Paul Snyder and Bobby Cox produced several quality players before the 1991 breakthrough. After the Braves achieved their pennant, the talent flow did not stop, and the team successfully integrated the likes of Javy Lopez, Chipper Jones, Ryan Klesko, and Andruw Jones. Most prospects, even first-round draft picks, do not become major league regulars, but the Braves system was deep enough to withstand the inevitable disappointments.

A team needs to be careful when acquiring veteran players in the decline phase of their career unless they are projected to fill a short-term vacancy at reasonable cost. Sid Bream, Marquis Grissom, and others were replaced as soon as better long-term solutions became available. Teams that regularly sign older players to long-term contracts inevitably end up with players they feel obligated to play. The Braves rarely faced this problem.

What has set the Braves apart from other great teams of the past generation is their willingness to give regular roles to the jewels of their farm system. When Gregg Olson or Terry Pendleton or Ron Gant needed replacing, Schuerholz did not trade his young talent for veteran solutions. In the mid-1990s, the Braves turned over half their lineup with quality rookies from their great system.

It is quite unusual for a star player in his prime to be available, either as a free agent or via a trade. When such players have been available, the Braves have recognized the benefit of pursuing them. The Braves signed Greg Maddux, one of the greatest pitchers of the past fifty years, though they already had the best staff in baseball. Schuerholz made a great trade for Fred McGriff that catapulted the Braves to the 1993 division title.

The key to the Braves' success over the past decade has obviously been the greatness and endurance of their pitching staff, under the expert tutelage of pitching coach Leo Mazzone. Maddux and Glavine, with five Cy Young Awards between them as members of the Braves, are headed for the Hall of Fame. John Smoltz was one of the top ten pitchers in baseball for a decade. Other topflight hurlers, including Steve Avery, Denny Neagle, and Kevin Millwood, contributed for several seasons.

Besides the obvious benefits of having a great pitcher on the mound 80 percent of the time, the Braves' quality staff allowed them to devote most of their energy and resources toward finding and acquiring position play-ers. Pitchers are generally so fragile that teams, even good ones, need to find new starting pitchers every year; the Braves escaped this burden.

The Atlanta Braves of the 1990s and beyond have enjoyed one of the most impressive runs of success by a team in baseball history. The team has been underrated because it navigated through the postseason un-scathed only once, but the philosophy that led to their success is worth emulating. John Schuerholz and Bobby Cox, the two principal architects of this dynasty, will likely be honored for their efforts with induction into baseball's Hall of Fame.

CONCLUSION

*T*o *paint a complete picture of how championship teams are constructed, this* book would need more than a hundred chapters. Every baseball club in history has operated in a unique time and place, and the problems and opportunities each has faced are different from those of any other team. Nonetheless, several general lessons can be derived from the survey presented here.

Unlike the Florida Marlins' Dave Dombrowski, most general managers are not commanded to contend for a championship in a single year. Because of the high risk of injuries and bad luck and the possibility of a better team emerging, the chances of winning a championship or two are greatly enhanced by building a strong organization that can contend repeatedly over a period of years.

Teams that compete for multiple titles are those with the most talent. The Brooklyn Superbas inherited their talent by merging with a team of stars and then absorbing its best players. This strategy was half-successful—Brooklyn won on the field but the league's fans thought their dominance disreputable and grew tired of the team.

The Philadelphia Phillies of the 1910s acquired two of the best players in the National League—Pete Alexander and Gavvy Cravath—from independent minor leagues and were able to fill in the holes of their team in one very successful winter. The Chicago White Sox of the same era, on the other hand, acquired their two superstars—Eddie Collins and Joe Jackson—from teams that could not afford them or would not pay them what they were worth.

One cannot really generalize from Charles Comiskey's path with the White Sox because players the caliber of Jackson and Collins are rarely available at any price. Even in today's world of free agency, nearly all players on either the free-agent or trade market are past their prime and declining quickly. If a team chooses to wait for the next Greg Maddux or Barry Bonds, it may need to wait a long time.

Clark Griffith's Washington Senators are an excellent example of a team that patiently added quality players one at a time, not to win a particular pennant but in the hope that enough good players having quality seasons together would result in a title. Griffith was able to find long-term solutions at several positions, resulting in less turnover and requiring fewer new players to keep the team going. The Senators of 1924 and 1925 were loaded with fine players having typical years and needed only a couple of big seasons and a few short-term solutions to put them over the top. They represent a fine recipe for success in any era.

A team must be able to evaluate the talent available and soundly judge how that talent is likely to evolve. Good organizations have employed professional scouts for many years, but modern performance analysis can also help. We know, for example, that hitters, as a group, have their best years in their late twenties and all but the best slip steadily after reaching thirty. Pitchers are less predictable, which makes most of them high-risk acquisitions. We also know that environmental factors—a player's era and home ballpark—can dramatically affect his statistics. A team in the 1990s needed to understand that a first baseman who hit twenty-five home runs and drove in a hundred runs was likely an average player; the same statistics in the 1960s might have earned MVP consideration.

While taking advantage of the unusual availability of a few star players, the 1930s Red Sox filled out their roster with rapidly aging mediocrities. Since several of the acquisitions had achieved some past success, the team and the media failed to recognize the team's weaknesses. Most historians continue to misjudge this team by not considering the effect that the high run scoring of the era had on everyone's statistics. Most of all, this team underscores the folly of trying to acquire veteran players (likely on the decline) in lieu of creating a farm system that keeps young talent flowing into the organization.

After the failures of the 1930s, the Red Sox changed course and built a developmental program, highlighted by the signing of several young players from the West Coast. This path worked splendidly, a fact lost to history because the team narrowly missed out on a World Series title and two additional league pennants. These Red Sox are an interesting example of a team whose home ballpark causes us to misread the nature of their talent. Moreover, their losses in crucial games at the end of the 1948 and 1949 seasons have obscured the quality of their ball club.

The 1948 Boston Braves are a forgotten example of a team that had more money than their competition and spent it intelligently. They hired a sound management team that used astute trades and minor league acquisitions to acquire precisely what the team needed. The team's philosophy led to short-term success, but the resultant team included several players who needed replacement after a couple of years. The Braves also invested in creating a minor league system, but the fruits of that effort were not evident until after they moved to Milwaukee in 1953.

Calvin Griffith, like his uncle before him, had only a small budget for players. The Senators, who later became the Twins, were the first team to consistently mine talent in Latin America, which provided them with a few stars and several other useful players. Unfortunately, the 1960s Twins stand as an example of the role that luck can play in the building of a team. The club produced a lot of talent, both pitching and hitting, and made several intelligent trades, but the unexpected decline of a few of their better players caused the team to be a player or two short in a couple of seasons.

When the Twins receded in 1971, many predicted that the California Angels would step up to replace them as the American League West champions. Instead, the Oakland Athletics blew away the division and proceeded to win five straight titles. We are confident that modern analysis, applied in 1971, would have prevented the Angels from misreading their chances so greatly. The Angels had some bad luck, but the hopes for their offense seem unrealistic today. The A's were younger and much more talented, with high upside at several positions. With today's more advanced methods for evaluating the expected growth of young players, their breakthrough in 1971 does not seem surprising. Although Oakland's bombastic owner had spent the past ten years antagonizing everyone he dealt with, he also brilliantly built a dynasty.

Like the A's, the Expos of the late 1970s and early 1980s were built completely from within. The system produced a steady stream of young talent and a fine string of successful teams. The talent was just a hair short of being able to run off a few pennants.

More relevant, perhaps, to the general manager of the immediate future are the stories of the Florida Marlins and the Atlanta Braves. The 1997 Marlins are considered a tarnished champion because of the huge spending spree that preceded their success. They also seem like a fluke because they won only ninety-two games (the only time they have ever finished over .500) but captured the wild card and won three somewhat sloppily played postseason series. On the other hand, Dave Dombrowski deserves a great deal of credit for the steady progress he made in creating a fine organization and for the brilliant way he spent the money available to him. Many teams have spent a lot of money in order to win "now"; the fact that the Marlins succeeded is to their credit.

It is to the Braves, however, that we turn for our modern model. In order to win consistently a team needs a steady supply of talent, and the best way to insure its availability is through a strong developmental system. The twelve-year (as of this writing) run of success that the Braves have enjoyed is largely due to players they developed themselves. John Schuerholz made a few good trades and also several bad ones. He signed a couple of free agents who worked out very well (especially Greg Maddux) and several who did not.

The Braves' sustained success has been the result of both their ability and their willingness to patch holes from within. Their best years, 1995 and 1996, followed the influx of a group of regulars from their minor league system. When the pipeline slowed in the late 1990s, the team slipped a bit.

Players available on the open market, either as free agents or trade acquisitions, tend to be in their declining years. Inevitably, such players are expensive risks, especially when given long-term contracts. The Braves exemplify a team that found success with front line talent on the open market—specifically Greg Maddux and Fred McGriff—but has been regularly disappointed by their more recent second-tier free agents and veteran trade acquisitions.

◇   ◇   ◇

To conclude, here are a number of lessons for building and maintaining a quality major league team.

1. The most efficient method for acquiring talent is through a strong developmental system that can produce major league players on a regular basis and stars on occasion. Talent obtained from a farm system is much less expensive, and therefore lower risk, than bringing in veterans.
2. To fill in the inevitable gaps, it is important to use all avenues available to find good players.
3. It is critical to understand where the team is in the development cycle. In the rebuilding phase, one needs to look for players with a

high upside. To take a team that is near championship quality to the next level, filling in with quality veterans is acceptable for the short term. For a team already at the championship level, the necessary retooling and replacing of players should be handled from within the organization if possible.

4. Teams should avoid multiyear contracts with players unlikely to still be productive at the end of the contract unless a significant short-term benefit is expected.

5. Teams need to recognize players that are likely to improve or retain their value. Younger players, especially those in their early to mid-twenties, have much more potential for improvement than older players. Players in their thirties are declining but are often paid to duplicate their peak years. Additionally, finding long-term solutions reduces the cost and uncertainty of frequently needing to replace players.

6. Clubs need to understand how to evaluate talent. Most successful teams employ a group of scouts who perform an invaluable role in the organization. In addition, teams need to be able to determine the value of players in terms of their contribution to wins and losses while recognizing the distorting effects of environmental factors.

The above list, of course, is not exhaustive. Many other insights and ideas can be gleaned from the stories in this book and those of other successful franchises. Neither are these recommendations universally applicable. Some teams have won while violating or ignoring the above guidelines, while others have fallen short while generally paying heed to them.

Nevertheless, the development and maintenance of good baseball teams is not random. While luck clearly plays a part in some clubs' level of achievement, many different decisions play an influential role in the process. The team that recognizes its environment, understands the principles of team construction, and makes good decisions, can compete at the highest level for many years.

APPENDIX 1

PLAYER VALUATION METHODOLOGY

A *ny attempt to evaluate the process and success of team building requires* some objective method for valuing players. Trades, free agent acquisitions, and player purchases cannot be analyzed without reference to the ability of the players involved. Baseball statistics offer an understandable and recognizable approach to this issue. Of course, the problem is which statistics should be used. For hitters, batting average remains a popular frame of reference, but it fails to capture a number of critical offensive characteristics, particularly power and the ability to draw walks.

An obvious point needs to be made: baseball teams win by scoring runs and outscoring their opponents. Accordingly, what we really want to know when we judge a hitter is how many runs his accomplishments are worth to his team and how many wins those runs are worth. Thus, a statistic derived to quantify a player's overall value needs to be expressed in runs or wins. The problem with simply using a player's runs scored or RBI for the run portion of this analysis is that those two statistics are too team and situation dependent. Where one bats in the order and the strength of the rest of the team has a huge influence on these statistics.

Help appeared more than twenty years ago as several baseball analysts, most prominently Bill James and Pete Palmer, recognized and expanded upon two essential quantitative relationships in baseball statistics: the number of runs a team scores in a season can be estimated very closely from the team's component offensive statistics—its hits, home runs, stolen bases, etc.; and a team's seasonal won-loss record can be estimated from the number of runs a team scores and allows. Quantifying this second relationship allows us to establish context for a team's or player's run value. For example, it allows us to estimate the additional value of each run in an environment where, on average, only four runs are needed to win a game, versus an environment where a team needs to score six.

Elsewhere in the book we discuss the mid-1960s Minnesota Twins. To show the accuracy of the above concepts, table 1 summarizes for each major league team in the 1967 season (1) the actual number of runs the team scored and the estimate calculated using the team's component statistics, and (2) the team's actual win-loss record and the predicted record based on the number of runs the team scored and allowed.

The column titled "RC" is the estimate of runs scored using the runs created formula outlined at the end of this appendix. The column "dRuns" shows how close the estimate is to the actual runs scored (that is, the difference between the two). The column headed "OR" is runs allowed by the team (or, alternatively, opponents' runs scored). The three columns whose headers begin with an e (eW, eL, and ePCT) represent an estimate of the team wins, losses, and winning percentage using Pete Palmer's runs-per-win formula outlined at the end of this appendix. The column "dW" indicates the accuracy of the win total calculation.

The calculated run total usually comes within twenty or so of the number the team actually scored. This is remarkable, especially as the formula contains no information on "little things" like hitting behind the runner or the timeliness of hits or outs. Similarly, the formula generally predicts the team's won-loss record within a few wins. (The one outlier in this table is the defending champion Baltimore Orioles, who won only seventy-six games despite outscoring their opponents by sixty-two runs.)

The crucial step for player evaluation is that both of the preceding two relationships can be taken from the team level and applied to individual players. For our estimation of player offensive value we combine the two relationships. We first estimate the number of runs a player generated for his team, then how many wins those runs provided.

Therefore, we can apply the formula derived at the team level to a player's batting statistics to estimate the number of runs he contributed to his team's offense. Bill James calls this runs created (RC); Pete Palmer calls it batting runs. Whatever the result is called, we can calculate an excellent estimate of the number of runs a player is "worth" to his team. Conceptually, too, the result is simple. On a seasonal basis RC can be viewed on the same scale as runs and RBI; on a per-game basis, it can be viewed on the same scale as earned run average.

Since the introduction of these two techniques, other analysts have refined the original formulas and introduced numerous new metrics to try to improve the accuracy of the estimates. Today several quite accurate for-

Table 1 Major League Teams, 1967

	Runs	RC	dRuns	OR	W	L	PCT	eW	eL	ePCT	dW
				American League							
BAL	654	637	17	592	76	85	.472	87	74	.542	-11
BOS	722	692	30	614	92	70	.568	92	70	.570	0
CAL	567	550	17	587	84	77	.522	78	83	.486	6
CHI	531	505	26	491	89	73	.549	86	76	.530	3
CLE	559	561	-2	613	75	87	.463	75	87	.463	0
DET	683	680	3	587	91	71	.562	91	71	.563	0
KC	533	539	-6	660	62	99	.385	67	94	.414	-5
MIN	671	623	48	590	91	71	.562	90	72	.554	1
NY	522	520	2	621	72	90	.444	70	92	.430	2
WAS	550	510	40	637	76	85	.472	71	90	.440	5
				National League							
ATL	631	613	18	640	77	85	.475	80	82	.494	-3
CHI	702	653	49	624	87	74	.540	89	72	.551	-2
CIN	604	590	14	563	87	75	.537	86	76	.528	1
HOU	626	639	-13	742	69	93	.426	69	93	.426	0
LA	519	539	-20	595	73	89	.451	72	90	.446	1
NY	498	497	1	672	61	101	.377	62	100	.381	-1
PHI	612	603	9	581	82	80	.506	84	78	.521	-2
PIT	679	691	-12	693	81	81	.500	80	82	.491	1
SF	652	638	14	551	91	71	.562	92	70	.569	-1
STL	695	676	19	557	101	60	.627	95	66	.593	6

Note: An "e" prefix indicates an estimate of the value; a "d" prefix indicates the difference between the actual value and the estimated value.

mulas exist for both relationships. For our run estimate we have elected to use Bill James's most recent RC derivation (as revised in the *STATS All-Time Major League Handbook*) with a couple of adjustments noted below. Most of the various formulas to determine a player's run value do not produce materially different results. We chose James's version because it is well established, has multiple versions to cover many eras throughout baseball history, and can generally be reproduced.

After determining a player's worth to his team in terms of runs, the next step is to translate those runs into wins. One of the key components in this calculation is the team's run context, essentially the number of runs scored in a typical game. Applying the runs-to-wins formula to a player's runs created puts his contribution to the team in terms of its most basic element: wins.

To make this calculation meaningful, an appropriate baseline is needed. Baseball analysts have yet to agree on which one to use. Should the base be zero? In other words, should we compare the player to an imaginary batter who creates no runs? If a player creates one hundred runs, which, for the sake of argument, corresponds to ten wins, should we value this player as worth ten wins? After some reflection, this seems counterintuitive; after all, a team can always pick up somebody who can hit a little—perhaps an ex–major leaguer toiling in Triple-A while he waits for another shot.

Some analysts use the league average hitter as the baseline. To continue the example, assume the league average is eighty runs created. Should the player be valued based on the twenty runs he creates above the league average and thus be valued at two wins?

Significant problems also exist using an "average" baseline. First of all, the league average does not represent the midpoint, or median, hitting ability. There are far more players of below-average ability than above-average. The league's total is the sum of all players' total contributions, but because better players play more, they raise the overall average. The average is further skewed because batting statistics have a floor of zero and no theoretical maximum. If the universe of hitters consisted of five players who hit two, five, eight, fifteen, and fifty home runs, the average player would have hit sixteen. Thus four of the five players appear below average and below the baseline value.

The league average does not represent the median, but even if it did the average would not be the correct base because players just below the median have value. A player can be below average but still be a valuable member of the team; after all, league-average players are not readily available at zero cost. History is littered with teams that would have won the pennant had they been able to fill several positions with even average players.

Probably the most widespread and popular single number for valuing a player is total player rating (TPR) as presented in *Total Baseball*. We do not use this value because it measures a player's value relative to the league average. In addition, we often want to use a measure that evaluates only a player's offense; TPR includes a fielding rating and positional adjustment that complicate it as a straightforward gauge of offensive ability.

Many baseball analysts believe that a baseline exists between zero (no value) and the average player. This theoretical baseline corresponds to the value of a player who is readily available if a team needs to fill a hole. For analytical purposes a player of this ability is often referred to as a "replacement player." These hypothetical players might be found in an expansion draft—good minor league veterans, often with some major league experience, looking to get back to the majors. We estimate a team of such players would attain a winning percentage of .355. We do not claim any particular precision to this value. It may be anywhere between .325 and .375, but our research suggests .355 is a reasonable estimate.

We subscribe to the theory that the replacement level is the correct baseline, and, therefore, our calculation of a player's offensive value measures his difference from a replacement player. In looking at a player's worth over a number of seasons, the replacement level gives a player credit for his value in being "average." The lower the baseline, the more of an impact the quantity of playing time has as opposed to the quality; replacement level strikes the correct balance between the two.

We need to emphasize that by estimating the replacement level at .355, we do not mean to imply that potentially average major league players are not currently toiling in the minor leagues. Some players will always be overlooked for any number of reasons. Furthermore, the replacement level has historically been subject to a number of anomalies. Prior to 1947, potential stars were shut out of the major leagues because of their skin color. In the early days of the major leagues players were often overlooked because of the haphazard and informal scouting methods then employed. Additionally, until the farm system developed, the established minor leagues were not designed as feeders for major league teams, and major league–caliber players often played either for long stretches or entire careers in these leagues. The key, however, is that players in the general talent pool from which a typical team searched for talent would be freely available above the replacement level only on the most sporadic basis.

In his new win shares methodology, Bill James introduces a new baseline for converting runs created into wins. He effectively uses a baseline that equates to a winning percentage around .210 to .220. We feel that this baseline is too low, and that a team could easily find many players above this level to fill holes.

Our preferred presentation of a player's offensive value is in the form of wins above replacement level (WAR). This formula attempts to estimate how many additional games a player's team will win as a result of his offensive performance. Our objective in creating WAR is not to introduce an additional statistic to the mix but simply to combine established

SPECIFIC WAR METHODOLOGY

Our specific methodology for estimating the offensive run value of players is outlined below.

1. Calculate the player's runs created (RC) using the method summarized in the STATS All-time Major League Handbook. Note that our RC calculation may vary by up to 2 percent because James seems to round his calculation at various stages and our calculation carries through all the decimal places. Also, from 1988 forward James includes two situational statistics in the calculation: home runs with runners on base and batting average with runners in scoring position. Our RC calculation does not.

Technical note: in the derivation of the new RC calculation, James now places "each player in a theoretical team context consisting of players with average skills and eight times as many plate appearances as the subject." This creates RC values that differ little for most players from the previous way of doing things; the major difference lies in a slight reduction in runs created for the very best players.

James has a whole set of formulas for calculating runs created during different eras throughout baseball history to adjust for the changing availability of various statistics. For reference, the formula we use for the seasons 1955 through the present is shown below:

Afactor = H + BB + HBP - CS - GDP

Bfactor = (TB + (BB - IBB + HBP) x 0.29 + SB x 0.64 + (SH + SF) x 0.53 - 0.03 x K)

Cfactor = (AB + BB + HBP + SH + SF)

For teams the three are combined as:

Runs Created = (Afactor x Bfactor / Cfactor)

For individuals, to put the player within a theoretical team concept, the factors are combined as:

Runs Created = ((Afactor + 2.4 x Cfactor) x (Bfactor + 3 x Cfactor)/(9 x Cfactor) - (0.9 x Cfactor)

One additional note on James's runs created calculation: to the degree that a team scores more or fewer runs than estimated by the formula, the excess or shortfall of runs is allocated back to the players so that the sum of the players' RC equals the actual runs scored by the team.

2. Convert RC to a per game factor using James's method:

RC/G = RC x LgOutsPerGame/PlayerOuts
    x LgOutsPerGameFactor

Where:

LgOutsPerGame = LeagueIP x 3/LeagueGames

LgOutsPerGameFactor = LgOutsAccountedFor/LeagueIP x 3

LgOutsAccountedFor = (AB − H + SH + SF + CS + GDP)

An additional note on our method: as discussed in this appendix, we believe some sort of additional numerical analysis beyond RC/G is necessary to evaluate a player's contribution based on both playing time and efficiency. The *STATS All-Time Major League Handbook*, however, makes no effort to numerically compare these run statistics or place them in context beyond simply presenting the league average RC/G next to the player's RC/G. With his previous RC methodology from the mid-1980s, James placed hitters into context by calculating a player's offensive won/lost percentage (OW%), effectively a calculation of a team's winning percentage if the subject player batted in all nine positions and the team had an average defense (pitching and fielding). Under his new RC derivation, which puts a player in a theoretical team setting, a calculation of OW% has some limitations when applied to a player's RC/G.

3. Calculate the seasonal run context by adjusting the league RC/G (LgRC/G) by the park factor (PF). The park factor is derived from the ratio of runs scored in the subject team's home park by both the home and road teams to the runs scored on the road by both the subject team and its opponents in games at the opponents' parks. This ratio is then added to one and divided by two (because the team plays only half its games at home) and helped by minor adjustments.

4. Generate the number of runs the player creates above replacement (RCAR) by calculating the difference between the player's RC and how many runs a replacement player would create using the same number of outs as the subject player (RCR).

RCR = LgRCpGAdjByPF x .7419 x (Outs/LgOutsPerGame)/
LgOutsPerGameFactor

RCAR = RC - RCR

Where

.7419 represents the adjustment for replacement level

The .7419 is derived from James's formula for calculating a team's offensive winning percentage from its runs created per game as a percentage of the league average ("x" in the formula below) assuming a league average defense (pitching and fielding):

OWPct = x^2/(1 + x^2)

If we plug in .355 for the OWpct and solve for x, x equals .7419.

5. Put the number of runs into the context of the era and park by calculating how many wins above replacement (WAR) a player is worth by using Pete Palmer's runs-per-win methodology (RpW). This is the final step in which the number of wins the player adds based on his offensive statistics versus a league replacement hitter is calculated.

WAR = RCAR/RpW

Where:

RpW = 10 x Sqrt(LgRCpGAdjByPF x 2/9)

This logic behind the runs-per-win formula can also be used to estimate winning percentage from a team's runs scored and allowed. The following formula is the one used in table 1 of this appendix.

Expected Winning Percentage = 0.5 + ((R - OR)/
(10 x Sqrt((R + OR)/IP)))/Games

Note on baseline: steps 4 and 5 can also be calculated using the league average as the baseline as opposed to a replacement player. Our methodology defines the replacement level to be a .355 ballplayer. For comparison, under our methodology an average player would be a .500 ballplayer.

Table 2 Minnesota Twins, 1965

	AB	AVG	OBP	SLG	R	HR	RBI	SB	RC	WAAv	WAR
Bob Allison	438	.233	.345	.445	71	23	78	10	76	2.4	3.9
Earl Battey	394	.297	.379	.409	36	6	60	0	67	2.3	3.5
Jimmie Hall	522	.285	.350	.464	81	20	86	14	90	3.2	4.8
Harmon Killebrew	401	.269	.386	.501	78	25	75	0	82	3.7	5.0
Jerry Kindall	342	.196	.278	.289	41	6	36	2	29	-1.7	-0.5
Don Mincher	346	.251	.348	.509	43	22	65	1	64	2.4	3.5
Joe Nossek	170	.218	.253	.306	19	2	16	2	12	-1.0	-0.4
Tony Oliva	576	.321	.384	.491	107	16	98	19	113	5.2	6.9
Frank Quilici	149	.208	.280	.255	16	0	7	1	10	-0.9	-0.4
Rich Rollins	469	.249	.310	.333	59	5	32	4	50	-0.7	0.8
Sandy Valdespino	245	.261	.322	.322	38	1	22	7	27	-0.3	0.5
Zoilo Versalles	666	.273	.322	.462	126	19	77	27	108	3.3	5.4
Jerry Zimmerman	154	.214	.275	.253	8	1	11	0	10	-1.1	-0.6

RC = runs created   WAAv = wins above average   WAR = wins above replacement

methods in a way we feel most correctly captures a player's value to his team. Note that in several instances we also provide wins above average (WAAv) in tables for comparison. One final reminder: these calculations solely evaluate the player's offensive contribution; the defensive value component is not addressed.

Table 2 presents the WAR for the pennant-winning 1965 Minnesota Twins along with some more conventional statistics for comparison.

One example will illustrate how this table should be read. The line for Tony Oliva provides his traditional offensive statistics and three columns of sabermetric data. These show that (a) Oliva created an estimated 113 runs for the Twins, (b) these runs permitted the Twins to win 5.2 more games than they would have with an average American League hitter in his place, and (c) these runs permitted the Twins to win 6.9 more games than they would have with a replacement player in his stead.

A look at the whole table helps us understand how the Twins scored their runs. Several players made a large contribution, but the at-bats given to Kindall, Nossek, and Zimmerman produced little. This type of distribution is fairly typical. It is very unusual for a team to avoid giving at-bats to below-average hitters. Players who can hit at the major league average are not readily available.

In looking at a player's effect on his team over a single season, we often use wins above average. Describing a hitter such as Oliva as adding 5.2 wins to an average team allows us to estimate that he would turn a 81–81 team into a 86–76 team if he replaced a league-average hitter. This is much more intuitive and easier to understand than looking at a replacement level.

APPENDIX 2

MEASURING PARK EFFECTS

*F*ans and analysts have long debated the impact of a player's home park on his value and statistics. The recent introduction of major league baseball to Colorado and the offensive explosion in the 1990s have brought renewed interest in the issue. How should the nature of a player's home park influence our evaluation of his abilities and accomplishments? Do ballparks affect the context of the game? Can they materially increase or decrease offense? If so, how should we adjust our perceptions of a player based on the nature of his home park?

There is little doubt that a park can affect the nature of the baseball played there. In 1995 in Denver's Coors Field, the Rockies and their opponents scored 975 runs in 72 games (485 by the Rockies and 490 by the opposition), 13.5 runs per game. In contrast, in their 72 away games that year, 593 runs were scored (300 by the Rockies and 293 by their opponents), 8.2 runs per game. Put another way, 64 percent more runs were scored in Coors Field than in the Rockies' away games. In all fairness, because of its altitude Coors Field is the most extreme park in modern baseball history, but it illustrates the extent of the effect that parks can have.

Another famous ballpark, Los Angeles's Dodger Stadium, highlights how a park can suppress offense. In 1995 the Dodgers scored 23 percent fewer runs in Dodgers home games (7.7 runs per game) versus Dodgers road games (9.5 runs per game). Many ballparks do not have nearly this effect and no adjustment is necessary, but for some the impact of the park needs to be accounted for when evaluating the ballplayers that play there.

Park effects can be assessed in two different ways. The first method attempts to measure a player's value. As has been shown in the sabermetric literature, one can objectively determine, with reasonable accuracy, how valuable a hitter was to his team's offense. As outlined in appendix 1, this is accomplished by estimating the "run value" of a player's statistics and then putting that value into context (i.e., the number of runs scored per game).

Baker Bowl in Philadelphia, with its short right field wall made of tin, was a notorious hitter's park by the 1920s. The influence of this park shapes the discussion of the value of a player like Chuck Klein, who recorded some monster statistics during the late 1920s and early 1930s for the Phillies. By using context-sensitive statistics that account for the run scoring in the park, we can get a better sense of Klein's value.

Assuming a team plays half its games at home, a player's accomplishments at home are equally as important as those on the road. As long as his achievements are placed in their proper context, a player should be evaluated by the whole of his statistics. In table 1, the second through fourth columns show Klein's runs created per game at home, the average number of runs scored by each team at Baker Bowl, and Klein's offensive winning percentage, which estimates how a team of players who hit like Chuck Klein would perform given the data in the previous two columns. The last three columns provide the same data for Klein in road games.

Table 1   Chuck Klein, 1928–1933

	Home			Away		
	RC/G	R/G	OW%	RC/G	R/G	OW%
1928	11.39	5.87	.790	6.41	4.53	.666
1929	13.35	7.13	.778	8.67	5.12	.742
1930	17.27	7.71	.834	8.55	5.40	.715
1931	15.18	5.36	.889	4.65	4.36	.533
1932	16.55	6.08	.881	5.55	4.39	.615
1933	19.47	5.50	.926	5.20	3.77	.655
Total	15.82	6.28	.864	6.48	4.59	.665

RC/G = runs created per game (game = 25.5 outs)

R/G = runs per game

OW% = Bill James's calculation of offensive winning percentage. The OWpct attempts to estimate the won-lost percentage of a team with nine hitters of similar ability and a league-average pitching staff and fielding ability.

Table 2 Chuck Klein and His Contemporaries

	RC	OW%	OffGms	OW	OL
Chuck Klein					
Home	608	.864	38.4	32.8	5.6
Road	299	.665	46.2	30.1	16.1
Total	907	.743	84.6	62.9	21.7
Mel Ott					
Home	338	.750	42.2	31.0	11.1
Road	394	.788	42.3	33.0	9.3
Total	731	.758	84.5	64.0	20.5
Jimmie Foxx					
Home	483	.857	37.1	31.4	5.7
Road	411	.768	44.6	33.6	11.0
Total	894	.795	81.7	65.0	16.7
Lou Gehrig					
Home	430	.774	44.5	34.0	10.6
Road	579	.864	45.3	38.5	6.8
Total	1009	.806	89.8	72.4	17.4

OffGms is the number of games the player's outs accounted for, and OW and OL allocate those games between wins and losses based on the player's offensive winning percentage.

Thus, while games in the Baker Bowl averaged one to two more runs per game than elsewhere, Klein's performance was extremely valuable, as his runs created per game rose significantly above the effect the park was having on other players. The reasons for his excellence at home are irrelevant when evaluating the level of that excellence.

As an aside, Klein was a pretty good hitter on the road as well. Only once did he have an offensive winning percentage below .600.

To add additional perspective, table 2 compares Klein to several contemporaries on the same basis over the same 1928–1933 time frame.

Though many other great hitters played in the National League at this time for whom we do not have home-road splits, a legitimate case could be made for Klein as the best player in the National League over the 1928–1933 time frame. On the other hand, he falls short of the peaks of players like Gehrig, Ruth, and Hornsby.

The second way of looking at park effects involves assessing how a player's statistics would change if he played in another park. This would be useful for a club in evaluating a player for acquisition. Because of the extreme nature of Coors Field, Rockies general manager Dan O'Dowd has begun to research how particular players might perform in Colorado. We should be cognizant of the difficulty inherent in this endeavor. While a park on average may increase or decrease scoring, translating the nuances to an individual player can be tricky.

Some parks favor left-handed hitters over right handers, others may favor speed over power. Even at this point, determining how another park might affect a player is highly uncertain. Is the player a pull hitter who can take advantage of the new setting or a spray hitter who may not gain a similar benefit? Maybe most important, however, and almost impossible to model, is the fact that players are intelligent and can adapt to their surroundings. For example, Hall of Famer Mel Ott hit an incredible 323 of his career 511 home runs in his home park, the Polo Grounds in New York. As baseball historian Stew Thornley has pointed out, he learned to take advantage of his environment. In his first four years in New York, Ott hit 30 home runs at home and 31 on the road. It makes sense for ball clubs to try and determine which type of player or playing style best fits their home parks, but this is often surprisingly complicated.

Attempting a park-to-park translation, however, makes little sense when trying to assess a player's value to his existing team. For example, assessing Klein's value by attempting to determine what he might hit in a "statistically neutral" park falls into what could be called an alternate universe scenario. Like trying to figure out what would have happened if the South had won the Civil War or Hitler had invaded Britain or Kennedy had not been assassinated, the question of what Klein would have hit in a "statistically neutral" park is a fictional question. Fictional questions can be fun to debate, they can yield insight into a problem, and clearly some responses to the problem are more thought-out and reasonable than others, but as historian David Hackett Fischer has pointed out, they are not empirical problems. A fictional question is not empirically verifiable.

Our perspective on evaluating a player's statistics in a historical context is that they are what they are and we shouldn't try to change them. The statistics do not need to be changed, they need to be put into context, and the two activities are not the same. The fact remains that we really do not know what a player like Klein would have hit if he had played his career somewhere else.

◇ ◇ ◇

Many reasons for the recent offensive explosion have been offered. One is that the new ballparks are smaller or otherwise more favorable to hitters. One way to study this issue is to take a set of parks that haven't changed at all and determine if their park factors have changed over time. Because a ball park is considered a hitter's or pitcher's park in relation to the league's other parks, any change in the relationship between the subject park and the league ought to be due to the composition of the league's other parks.

Our research suggests that the only unchanged ballpark in the AL over the 1990s was Fenway Park in Boston. The installation of the Stadium Club seats in 1989 was the last material change. In the NL several parks may have remained unchanged during the decade. We decided to use Dodger Stadium because neither the dimensions nor the seating capacity changed over the decade 1990–1999.

In the case of Fenway Park, if either the pitchers or the hitters adapted to the new environment change caused by the Stadium Club seating at a different rate, it could skew the results. This seems very unlikely, however. First of all the change to the park factor was so subtle and recognized over such a long period of time that it is unlikely any player tailored his game to the new conditions. Secondly, if in fact any players did alter their approach, there is no reason to believe it would affect the hitters any differently than the pitchers.

Tables 3 and 4 look at the Fenway Park and Dodger Stadium park factors for runs and for home runs over the decade 1990–1999.

While clearly not conclusive, the reduction in the three-year run park factor in Fenway suggests that the new ballparks are indeed having an effect on increased scoring in the American League. That is, Fenway appears to be moving from a park that increases run scoring to one not much above the league average.

The same conclusion cannot be drawn for the National League from the Dodger Stadium data. There does seem some evidence, however, of a run park factor drop in the mid-1990s coinciding with the entrance of the Colorado franchise. The three-year moving average of the run park factor dropped from .95 in 1993, the first year of the Rockies, to a value of .84 or below for the four years from 1995 through 1998. In effect, the entrance of Mile High Stadium, soon replaced by Coors Field, made Dodger Stadium more of an extreme pitcher's park than it had been prior to the Rockies' arrival.

Table 3 Park Factor for Runs, Dodger Stadium and Fenway Park, 1990–1999

	GH	GA	RH	RA	PF	3Yr
			Dodger Stadium			
1990	81	81	674	739	0.91	
1991	81	81	622	608	1.02	
1992	81	81	558	626	0.89	0.94
1993	81	81	648	689	0.94	0.95
1994	55	59	439	602	0.78	0.87
1995	72	72	557	686	0.81	0.84
1996	81	81	597	758	0.79	0.79
1997	73	73	559	664	0.84	0.81
1998	76	73	575	665	0.83	0.82
1999	72	75	677	749	0.94	0.87
			Fenway Park			
1990	81	81	712	651	1.09	
1991	81	81	752	691	1.09	
1992	81	81	669	599	1.12	1.10
1993	81	81	756	628	1.20	1.14
1994	64	51	673	500	1.07	1.13
1995	72	72	747	742	1.01	1.09
1996	81	81	981	868	1.13	1.07
1997	72	75	750	811	0.96	1.03
1998	73	73	731	704	1.04	1.04
1999	72	72	714	669	1.07	1.02

GH =games at home   GA = games away   RH = runs at home—both teams   RA = runs on road—both teams   PF = park factor
3Yr = three-year moving average

Table 4 Park Factor for Home Runs, Dodger Stadium and Fenway Park, 1990–1999

	GH	GA	HRH	HRA	HRPF	3Yr
			Dodger Stadium			
1990	81	81	127	139	0.91	
1991	81	81	103	101	1.02	
1992	81	81	59	95	0.62	0.85
1993	81	81	114	119	0.96	0.87
1994	55	59	96	109	0.94	0.84
1995	72	72	117	144	0.81	0.91
1996	81	81	111	164	0.68	0.81
1997	73	73	136	156	0.87	0.79
1998	76	73	135	140	0.93	0.82
1999	72	75	177	169	1.09	0.96
			Fenway Park			
1990	81	81	105	93	1.13	
1991	81	81	145	128	1.13	
1992	81	81	91	100	0.91	1.06
1993	81	81	107	134	0.80	0.95
1994	64	51	135	105	1.02	0.91
1995	72	72	133	169	0.79	0.87
1996	81	81	214	180	1.19	1.00
1997	72	75	135	164	0.86	0.94
1998	73	73	161	182	0.88	0.98
1999	72	72	132	162	0.81	0.85

GH = games at home   GA = games away   HRH = home runs at home   HRA = home runs on road   HRPF = home run park factor   3yr = three-year moving average

APPENDIX 3

DEFENSIVE EFFICIENCY RECORD

*H*ere we provide the technical calculation of defensive efficiency record (DER). DER is a statistic introduced by Bill James in the 1979 *Baseball Abstract* to measure the ability of a team's fielders to turn balls in play into outs. DER is the ratio of plays made by the defense to total balls in play. Plays made are estimated in two ways and the two are then averaged. The specifics of our DER calculation are outlined below.

Plays Made 1: OppAB - OppH - OppSO - 0.71 x errors + OppSH + OppSF

Plays Made 2: PO - OppSO - DP - 2 x TP - OutfieldAssists - CatcherAssists

PM: (PM1 + PM2)/2

Total Plays: PM + OppH - OppHR + 0.71 x errors

DER: PM/TotBiP

Where:

Opp before an abbreviation refers to opponents.

Note that our calculated values may differ slightly from James's DER figures presented in his *Baseball Abstracts*.

APPENDIX 4

S-CURVE METHODOLOGY

Accuracy Confirmation

The value of the S-curve methodology rests, of course, on whether it can be generalized to most players as opposed to just the couple of examples discussed in chapter 10. The only systematic test of a ballplayer career projection system we are aware of was in Bill James's 1985 *Baseball Abstract*, when he introduced his player projection system, labeled "Brock2." James ran his system on all thirty-three major league players who had at least four hundred or more at-bats in 1964 and were twenty-four, twenty-six, twenty-eight, or thirty-two years of age at the time. This test group gives us a defined set of players on which to run the S-curve analysis and, in addition, a different model with which to compare the S-curve accuracy.

Table 1 below summarizes projection of career runs created totals for the thirty-three players in James's study using the S-curve model. The S-curve projections for each player are generated from the runs created for each player through his age shown in the second column.

The model is more accurate on older players because they have more of their career already "in the bank." For younger players, two different effects are at work that make the projection more difficult: the model most likely has fewer data points to work with and there is more time remaining for unmodeled events such as career-threatening injuries or a sudden developmental jump—as happened, for example, with Willie Stargell.

While acknowledging the many variations in human development and physiology, the S-curve model appears to provide a solid basis for fore-

Table 1 Career RC: Projected and Actual

	Age	S-Curve	Actual
Rico Carty	24	1067	970
Willie Davis	24	1085	1193
Mike Hershberger	24	581	371
Dick McAuliffe	24	1008	826
Ron Santo	24	1823	1376
Willie Stargell	24	776	1502
Zoilo Versalles	24	993	548
Pete Ward	24	1186	415
Carl Yastrzemski	24	1638	2107
Bob Aspromonte	26	661	448
Walter Bond	26	387	158
Orlando Cepeda	26	1805	1364
Johnny Edwards	26	529	504
Curt Flood	26	808	831
Jimmie Hall	26	768	403
Ron Hansen	26	772	490
Rich Rollins	26	889	417
Charlie Smith	26	152	253
Tom Tresh	26	912	584
Billy Williams	26	1658	1667
Joe Christopher	28	292	205
Donn Clendenon	28	449	673
Harmon Killebrew	28	1325	1563
Bobby Richardson	28	515	541
Floyd Robinson	28	450	490
Frank Robinson	28	1923	2061
Tony Taylor	28	799	862
Lee Thomas	28	392	434
Don Blasingame	32	520	571
Eddie Bressoud	32	408	470
Eddie Kasko	32	320	367
Mickey Mantle	32	2173	1939
Eddie Mathews	32	1826	1648

casting a ballplayer's remaining career. One statistically applicable measure of the accuracy of the model is the root mean square of the error (RMSE). The RMSE measures the size of the differences between the projected values and the actual values. The lower the number, the closer the projected values are to the actual and the more accurate the model. As a way of validating the S-curve model, the RMSE for the S-curve was compared to the RMSE for James's Brock2 methodology. The S-curve RMSE was 298 as compared to 350 for Brock2. Additionally, in comparing the two models, the S-curve model projected a career runs created closer to the actual for twenty-one of the thirty-three players.

The point of this assessment is not to argue that the S-curve model is superior to James's projection system but simply to note that it measures up favorably in an objective comparison to the original player projection system. James has refined the Brock2 model over the last fifteen years, although we are not aware of any published tests and his revised method has not been made public. Furthermore the two models have a slightly different utility. Brock2 is designed to use all of a player's batting statistics from the previous several years to project full batting lines for remainder of the player's career. On the one hand, this is a much more difficult task because full batting lines (hits, doubles, home runs, etc.) need to be forecast, not just the overall runs created. On the other hand, Brock2 can use many more inputs in its projection model, including ratios such as strikeouts to walks or doubles to home runs, and how they change over time. The S-curve model uses only a single data point, runs created.

Methodology for the Mathematically Curious

The following formula is used to generate a player's S-curve data points:

$$M/(1 + e^{-(at + af)}) - D$$

Where

t (time): the age of the player

M, a, f, and D: the equation's coefficients

For each player we fit this equation onto the known years of runs created. A computer program finds the coefficients that best fit a particular player by minimizing the sum of squares of the errors; that is, by minimizing the following sum

$$\sum (\text{Mod}_i - \text{Act}_i)^2$$

where

Mod$_i$ is the modeled runs created, and Act$_i$ is the actual runs created, for season i

In order to make the model fit younger players for whom relatively few years of data may be available, the four coefficients are constrained as noted below. The constraints are needed to help shape a player's career. We can be fairly certain, for example, that a player's career will not continue to age fifty no matter how great his first couple of seasons. The model better forecasts remaining runs created by restricting the coefficients to values that result in careers that conform to common sense. Even with the constraints, a wide variety of career shapes can be correctly modeled.

M: Between 400 and 3500

a: Between 0.2 and 0.6 (for very young players the model may let the 0.6 maximum vary slightly)

f: Between -26 and -30 (for young players the model may use an upper constraint other than -30)

D: Between 0 and 1000

Additional technical notes: (1) Years prior to a player's appearance in the majors and years in which the player created less than ten runs are not included in the sum of squares calculation. (2) A nice side effect of the design of this model is that changing the sign of the f coefficient (i.e., -f) produces the model's estimate of the player's peak age.

Example: Frank Robinson at Twenty-nine

After the 1965 season Frank Robinson was twenty-nine years old. As shown in table 2, the model was fit using only his first ten years in the ma-

Table 2 Frank Robinson, 1954–1965

	Age	RC_Car	RC_Mod	Weight	(Car-Mod)^2
1954	18	0	-27	0	0
1955	19	0	49	0	0
1956	20	115	134	1	365
1957	21	234	229	1	23
1958	22	330	334	1	15
1959	23	452	446	1	41
1960	24	564	565	1	2
1961	25	697	689	1	67
1962	26	855	815	1	1549
1963	27	933	942	1	82
1964	28	1054	1065	1	128
1965	29	1171	1185	1	191

jors, 1956 through 1965.

The final column in table 2 shows the square of the errors; in this instance the sum of squares of the errors is 2,462. The computer uses successive iterations to vary the coefficients in an attempt to reduce the sum of squares to the smallest value possible. The coefficients that produce the lowest sum of squares is considered the best fit model. The coefficients for Robinson's best fit model are:

Coefficient	Value
M	2,535
a	0.2
f	-26
D	452

Thus, for example, to calculate the model's forecast for Robinson in 1967 as a thirty-one-year-old we first calculate his forecast career runs created through the end of that season using the formula:

$$2{,}535 / (1 + e^{-(0.2 \times 31 + 0.2 \times -26)}) - 451 = 1{,}401$$

From this value we subtract his forecasted career runs created through 1966 (age thirty):

$$2{,}535 / (1 + e^{-(0.2 \times 30 + 0.2 \times -26)}) - 451 = 1{,}297$$

Therefore, the S-curve model forecasts, on the basis of his seasons through 1965, that Frank Robinson would generate 110 runs created (1,401 - 1,297) in 1967.

APPENDIX 5

WIN PROBABILITY ADDED

*S*everal others have performed analysis using win probabilities, but the re-search has suffered from one of two major limitations: the amount of game data was insufficient or it was generated from simulations, not ac-tual games. In the early 1960s George Lindsay looked at game strategies based on win probability data from 782 1958 AL, NL, and International League games. Such a small number of games does not allow for enough of the nearly 13,000 different situations (i.e., 9 innings x 2 halves to each inning x about 15 score differentials x 23 base/out possibilities). The ta-bles used in this book are generated from the 7,715 major league games played over the four years 1980–1983.

In 1970, E. G. Mills and H. D. Mills authored a book titled *Player Win Averages,* but their win probability tables appear to be based on baseball computer simulations, not actual game data. More recently, in the *Ameri-can Statistician,* Jay Bennett looked at the individual players in the 1919 World Series using a modified version of Lindsay's tables.

In the four seasons of data that we used to generate the win probabili-ty tables, the total number of events (e.g., plate appearances, stolen base attempts) was 613,372. One might think that this would give a large enough sample size for each possible situation to calculate reliable win probabilities. Unfortunately, this is not so. For example, the situation "bot-tom of the seventh, home team ahead by two, no outs, and a runner on third" occurred only nine times (the home team won eight times for an 88.9 percent winning percentage). A situation as common as "bottom of the seventh, two out, runner on first, home team down two" occurred only 221 times.

We addressed this issue by examining the probability of scoring a particular number of runs from each base/out situation over the rest of the inning, adding that number of runs to the current situation and then calculating the probability of winning at the end of the inning based on the new run differential. The earlier example—the home team ahead by two in the bottom of the seventh with a runner on third and no outs—can be used to illustrate the calculation. All cases of a runner on third with no outs occurred 2,356 times; the probability of run scoring over the remainder of that inning is:

Runs:	0	1	2	3	4	5	6	7 or more
	13.6%	44.5%	18.2%	12.5%	6.1%	2.8%	1.3%	1.0%

Thus, adding the above runs to the two already on the scoreboard results in a probability of being ahead at the end of the inning by two of 13.6 percent (i.e., no runs score), by three (i.e., one run scores) 44.5 percent, etc. Each of these is then multiplied by the probability of winning the game when going into the top of the eighth with that run differential. For example, when heading into the top of the eighth up by two (a situation that occurred 778 times in our four years of data), the home club won 90 percent of the time; up by three (occurred 602 times), the home team won 94 percent of the time. After calculating for all possible scenarios, the probability of the home team winning in the example comes out at 94.5 percent. Obviously all identical base/out situations are not created equal, but we believe the sample size is large enough to allow for any imbalances to even out.

◇   ◇   ◇

These win probability tables can offer a new and unique tool to gain insights unavailable from any other type of analysis. For one, they can help in evaluating various strategic choices, like the stolen base, intentional walk, or sacrifice bunt. If, for example, in the bottom of the fourth inning a runner is on first with one out and the home team is behind by a run, should the runner steal? The probability of winning in this situation is 44 percent. If the runner is safe and he moves to second, the probability of winning increases to 46.6 percent; if he's out, the probability of winning the game decreases to 38 percent Thus in this situation the break-even stolen base percentage is 70 percent [(.440 - .380) / (.466 - .380)].

◇ ◇ ◇

One final point needs to be made. This type of player evaluation is entirely situation-dependent and thus measures something slightly different than typical sabermetric statistics, which are situation-independent. In the latter, all hitter events of the same type receive the same weight no matter when or where they occurred. For example, in calculating batting average, a home run, like all hits, receives a weight of one; in calculating slugging percentage a home run receives a value of four; in the sabermetric measure linear weights, a home run is weighted around 1.4. The key, however, is that in each measure a home run is valued the same regardless of when it occurred.

In a situation-dependent measure, events of the same type are not all worth the same; it matters when they occur. In the WPA analysis, for example, a home run in the top of the ninth when ahead or behind by eight runs receives almost no value, while one hit at a clutch moment at the end of the game can receive .50 or more win points.

APPENDIX 6

OFFENSIVE WINNING PERCENTAGE

The statistic used to evaluate prospects in chapter 16 is OW25: projected major league offensive won-lost percentage at age twenty-five. Offensive winning percentage (OWpct) is a statistic developed by Bill James twenty-five years ago to measure the contribution of a player's batting statistics within the context of the game. OWpct estimates the winning percentage of a team with eight other hitters of equal ability and a league-average pitching staff and defense. The statistic is often expressed to the third decimal point because winning percentages are typically shown that way. Given the number of calculations and assumptions involved, OWpct should not really be viewed as accurate to that third decimal place.

The calculation for OWpct is based on Bill James's observation that a team's won-lost percentage can be approximated by the formula:

$$WPct = Runs\ Scored^2 / (Runs\ Scored^2 + Runs\ Against^2)$$

Technical note: James and others have pointed out in further research that an exponent of 1.83 may actually produce a slightly more accurate result than 2. We have elected to use 2 as the exponent because it creates a much cleaner and more intuitive formula and the loss of accuracy is negligible.

In 1999 the New York Yankees finished 98–64, a .605 winning percentage. They scored 900 runs and allowed 731; applying the above formula results in a calculated winning percentage of .603.

For an individual player, "runs against" is the run context of his team's games expressed as runs per game. As used in this book, run context is

Table 1 1999 Toronto Hitting Statistics

	AB	H	2B	3B	HR	BB	SB	CS	AVG
Tony Batista	374	107	25	1	26	22	2	0	.285
Homer Bush	485	155	26	4	5	21	32	8	.320
Jose Cruz	349	84	19	3	14	64	14	4	.241
Carlos Delgado	573	156	39	0	44	86	1	1	.272
Tony Fernandez	485	159	41	0	6	77	6	7	.328
Darrin Fletcher	412	120	26	0	18	26	0	0	.291
Shawn Green	614	190	45	0	42	66	20	7	.309
Willie Greene	226	46	7	0	12	20	0	0	.204
Mike Matheny	163	35	6	0	3	12	0	0	.215
Shannon Stewart	608	185	28	2	11	59	37	14	.304

usually defined as the league average of runs per game adjusted by a park factor. "Runs scored" for the player is defined as the estimate of the number of runs a lineup would score with a similar player hitting in all nine slots.

In order to provide an intuitive feel of OWpct, table 1 shows the 1999 statistics for a selected group of Toronto Blue Jays hitters. Because Toronto's Skydome played as a neutral run park in 1999, the statistics shown give a fair representation of value. Table 2 summarizes the runs created and the offensive winning percentage for these same Blue Jays. As a ref-

Table 2 1999 Toronto OWPcts

			As Blue Jay		If Twin		If Yankee	
	RC	RC/G	RPG	OWP	RPG	OWP	RPG	OWP
Tony Batista	70	6.66	5.27	.616	5.55	.591	4.72	.666
Homer Bush	74	5.58	5.27	.529	5.55	.503	4.72	.583
Jose Cruz	56	5.35	5.27	.508	5.55	.482	4.72	.563
Carlos Delgado	121	7.40	5.27	.664	5.55	.640	4.72	.711
Tony Fernandez	92	7.03	5.27	.640	5.55	.616	4.72	.689
Darrin Fletcher	67	5.86	5.27	.553	5.55	.527	4.72	.607
Shawn Green	137	8.13	5.27	.704	5.55	.682	4.72	.748
Willie Greene	24	3.42	5.27	.297	5.55	.276	4.72	.345
Mike Matheny	14	2.71	5.27	.209	5.55	.192	4.72	.248
Shannon Stewart	94	5.50	5.27	.522	5.55	.496	4.72	.576

OWP = offensive winning percentage

erence, the average number of runs scored per team in AL games in 1999, including the interleague games, was 5.20. Thus, the Toronto context factor of 5.27 indicates a very slight hitter's park. For the sake of perspective, the final four columns indicate the offensive winning percentage had the statistics been produced by a member of the Twins in a more hitter-biased home park or by a member of the Yankees with pitcher-friendly Yankee Stadium as the home venue.

Technical note: Bill James has introduced several runs created formulas over the past twenty-five years. The historical comparisons throughout this book use the most recent formula, introduced in 1998 and summarized in appendix 1. In its most recent incarnation, runs created per game no longer strictly represents the number of runs a team of nine like-hitting players would score and thus cannot technically be used in the OWpct calculation. Therefore, this section uses an older methodology.

APPENDIX 7

MINOR LEAGUE TRANSLATION METHODOLOGY

In chapter 16, we present a method for estimating how a player will perform in the major leagues based on his minor league statistics. The measure OW25 predicts how the hitter will hit in the major leagues at age twenty-five, given his current statistics, his league, his park, and his age.

The specific methodology for the calculation of OW25 involves several steps and is outlined below:

1. Using the raw batting statistics, calculate runs created (RC) using the following formula:

RC = (H + BB - CS) x (TB + 0.05 x BB + 0.55 x SB)/
(AB + BB)

As discussed elsewhere, runs created is a methodology developed by Bill James to estimate the number of runs a player contributed to his team. Over the years he has introduced a number of variants on the formula. The one used in this analysis closely resembles one of his basic formulas but adds a slight batter advancement component for a walk.

2. Calculate the runs created per game (RC/G) using the following formula:

RC/G = RC/(AB - H + CS) x 25.5.

Note that although a baseball game is usually 27 outs per team, a couple of these outs occur on the base paths and are "hidden" from the batting statistics (e.g., a player thrown out attempting to stretch a single into a double). In practice, a team commits about 25.5 "batting" outs (including caught stealing) in a game. Therefore, we convert runs created to a per-game value based on 25.5 outs.

3. *Calculate the team run context (TRC).* For 1998 and 1999 the ream run context is the league average runs scored per game adjusted by a park factor. The park factor derivation essentially follows the method outlined in *Total Baseball* but without a number of the more technical adjustments.

First the basic park effect is calculated using the standard formula:

(Runs scored and allowed per home game)/(Runs scored and allowed per road game)

To this basic park effect we typically add an adjustment to reflect the fact that the road parks do not include the park being rated. After adjustment, the park effect is then converted to a park factor (PF) by adding one and dividing by two to reflect the fact that a team plays half its games at home. Finally, the team run context is calculated by multiplying the league-average runs per game by the park factor.

For 1996 and 1997 the run context was defined as simply the total runs scored in the team's games (i.e., both the player's team and its opponents) per game divided by two—the method outlined in the *Bill James Historical Abstract*.

TRC (1998 & 1999) = League Average Runs/G x PF

TRC (1996 & 1997) = (Team Runs/G + Team Runs Allowed/G)/2

4. *Calculate the OWpct for the batter based on his runs created relative to the team context using the following formula:*

$$OWpct = RCpG^2/(RCpG^2 + TRC^2)$$

5. *Adjust the team context by the major league equivalency of the subject league using the league adjustment factor (LAF).* Specifically, calculate the major league adjusted team context (MLATC) by dividing the team run context in (3) above by the appropriate LAF in table 1.

$$MLATC = TRC/LAF$$

Table 1 League Factors

League Level	Adjustment Factor
AAA	.78
AA	.75
A+ (Calif., Carolina & Florida State)	.65
A (Midwest & Sally)	.60

6. *Calculate the major league equivalent OWpct by substituting the major league adjusted team context from step 5 into the OWpct formula.*

$$\text{Major League Equivalent OWpct} = RCpG^2/(RCpG^2 + MLATC^2)$$

7. *Finally, calculate the player's projected OWpct at age twenty-five (OW25).* The batter's major league equivalent OWpct in step 6 is adjusted by his age adjustment factor (AAF) as shown in the cumulative change column in table 2.

$$\text{OW25} = \text{Major League Equivalent OWpct} \times \text{AAF}$$

The starting point for our research into these adjustment factors is Bill James's formulas for calculating major league equivalencies, James's

Table 2 Age Factors

Age	Year-to-Year Change	Cumulative Change to Age 25
18	1.09	1.56
19	1.08	1.43
20	1.07	1.33
21	1.06	1.24
22	1.06	1.17
23	1.05	1.10
24	1.05	1.05
25	1.04	1.00
26	1.04	.96
27	.97	.93
28	.96	.90

Brock2 formulas, and data presented in *Essential Baseball 1994* by Norm Hitzges and Dave Lawson.

For a player on more than one team in a year, his OWpct for each team is averaged (weighted by at-bats).

BIBLIOGRAPHY

We have listed here the main sources we consulted in researching this book. For ease of use, we have divided the bibliography by chapter after first listing a number of general sources.

ANNUALS

Reach's Official Baseball Guide. A. J. Reach, 1899–1939.
Spalding's Official Baseball Guide. American Sports Publishing, 1899–1941.
The Sporting News Baseball Register. Sporting News Publishing, 1940–2001.
The Sporting News Official Baseball Guide. Sporting News Publishing, 1942–2001.

GENERAL

Bjarkman, Peter C., ed. *Encyclopedia of Major League Baseball: American League.* Carroll & Graf, 1993.
———. *Encyclopedia of Major League Baseball: National League.* Carroll & Graf, 1993.
Cohen, Richard M., et al. *The World Series.* Dial Press, 1979.
Danzig, Alison, and Joe Reichler. *The History of Baseball: Its Great Players, Teams, and Managers.* Prentice Hall, 1959.
Dewey, Donald, and Nicholas Acocella. *The Ball Clubs.* Harper Perennial, 1996.
James, Bill. *The Bill James Historical Baseball Abstract.* Villard, 1986.
———. *The New Bill James Historical Baseball Abstract.* Free Press, 2001.
James, Bill, and Jim Henzler. *Win Shares.* STATS Publishing, 2002.
James, Bill, et al., eds. *Bill James Presents STATS All-Time Major League Handbook.* STATS Publishing, 1998.
———. *Bill James Presents STATS All-Time Baseball Sourcebook.* STATS Publishing, 1998.

Johnson, Lloyd, and Miles Wolff, eds. *The Encyclopedia of Minor League Baseball.* 2d ed. Baseball America, 1997.

Karst, Gene, and Martin J. Jones Jr. *Who's Who in Professional Baseball.* Arlington House, 1973.

Koppett, Leonard. *Koppett's Concise History of Major League Baseball.* Temple, 1998.

Information Concepts. *The Baseball Encyclopedia.* Macmillan, 1969.

Lahman, Sean. "Baseball Player Database." www.baseball1.com

McConnell, Robert, and David Vincent, eds. *SABR Presents the Home Run Encyclopedia.* Macmillan, 1996.

Meany, Tom. *Baseball's Greatest Teams.* Barnes, 1949.

Neft, David S., Richard M. Cohen, and Michael L. Neft. *The Sports Encyclopedia: Baseball 2001.* St. Martin's Griffin, 2001.

Neyer, Rob, and Eddie Epstein. *Baseball Dynasties.* Norton, 2000.

Thorn, John, and Pete Palmer. *The Hidden Game of Baseball: A Revolutionary Approach to Baseball and Its Statistics.* Doubleday, 1984.

Pietrusza, David, Matthew Silverman, and Michael Gershman, eds. *Baseball: The Biographical Encyclopedia.* Total Sports, 2000.

Reichler, Joseph L. *The Baseball Trade Register.* Collier, 1984.

Smith, David, et. al. Retrosheet website. www.retrosheet.org.

Shatzkin, Mike, ed. *The Ballplayers*, 2 vols. Idea Logical Press, 1999.

Thorn, John, Pete Palmer, and Michael Gershman. *Total Baseball.* 7th ed. Total Sports, 2001.

CHAPTER 1

Alexander, Charles C. *John McGraw.* Viking, 1988.

"Brooklyn's Great Team for the Season of 1899."*Brooklyn Eagle,* February 12, 1899.

Creamer, Robert W. "The Old Orioles." In *The Ultimate Baseball Book,* edited by Daniel Okrent and Harris Lewine. Houghton-Mifflin, 1984.

Graham, Frank. *The Brooklyn Dodgers.* Putnam, 1945.

Nemec, David. *The Great Encyclopedia of Nineteenth Century Minor League Baseball.* Donald I. Fine, 1997.

Seymour, Harold. *Baseball: The Early Years.* Oxford University Press, 1960.

Solomon, Burt. *Where They Ain't.* Free Press, 1999.

Voight, David Q. *From Gentleman's Sport to the Commissioner System.* Vol. 1, *American Baseball.* University of Oklahoma Press, 1966.

CHAPTER 2

Alexander, Charles C. *John McGraw.* Penguin Books, 1989.

Alexander, Grover Cleveland. "How I Lost the 1915 World Series." In *The Second Fireside Book of Baseball,* edited by Charles Einstein. Simon & Schuster, 1958.

Seymour, Harold. *Baseball: The Golden Age.* Oxford University Press, 1971.

Sporting News. 1914–1915.

Voight, David Q. *From the Commissioners to Continental Expansion.* Vol. 2, *American Baseball.* University of Oklahoma Press, 1970.

Wright, Marshall D. *The American Association.* McFarland, 1997.

Zingg, Paul J. and Mark D. Medeiros. *Runs, Hits, and an Era: The Pacific Coast League, 1903–58.* University of Illinois Press,1994.

CHAPTER 3

Asinof, Elliot. *Eight Men Out: The Black Sox and the 1919 World Series.* Holt, Rinehart & Winston, 1963.

Barrow, Edward Grant, with James M. Kahn. *My Fifty Years in Baseball.* Coward-McCann, 1951.

Brown, Warren. *The Chicago White Sox.* Putnam, 1952.

Frommer, Harvey. *Shoeless Joe and Ragtime Baseball.* Taylor, 1992.

Gandil, Arnold "Chick," as told to Melvin Durslag. "This Is My Story of the Black Sox Series." *Sports Illustrated,* September 17, 1956.

Ginsberg, Daniel E. *The Fix Is In: A History of Baseball Gambling and Game Fixing Scandals.* McFarland, 1995.

Hern, Gerry. "Eddie Collins Reveals: The Tipoff on the Black Sox." Condensed from the Boston *Post. Baseball Digest,* June 1949.

Kaplan, Jim. *The Fielders.* Redefinition, 1989.

Lindberg, Richard. *Who's on Third? The Chicago White Sox Story.* Icarus Press, 1983.

Sporting News. 1912–1918.

Veeck, Bill, with Ed Linn. *The Hustler's Handbook.* Putnam, 1965.

CHAPTER 4

Marksusen, Bruce, and Ron Visco. "Bucky and the Big Train." *Elysian Fields Quarterly* 17, no. 3 (2000).

Povich, Shirley. *The Washington Senators.* Putnam, 1954.

———. "1924: When Senators Were Kings." *Washington Post,* October, 22, 1994.

Thomas, Henry. *Walter Johnson.* Phenom, 1995.

Thorn, John. *The Relief Pitcher.* Dutton, 1979.

Tygiel, Jules. *Past Time.* Oxford University Press, 2000.

CHAPTER 5

Cairns, Bob. *Pen Men.* St. Martin's Press, 1992.

Deane, Bill. "How They Spelled Relief: A History of Relief Pitching." Photocopy.

Graham, Frank Jr. "The Relief Pitcher Is a Big Shot Now." *Sport.* June 1956.

Greene, Lee. "Suddenly, Wilhelm's a Mystery." *Sport,* September 1959.

Koppett, Leonard. *The Thinking Man's Guide to Baseball.* Dutton, 1967.

James, Bill. *The Bill James Guide to Baseball Managers.* Scribners, 1997.

National Baseball Hall of Fame. File on Hoyt Wilhelm.

Shaap, Dick. "Hoyt Wilhelm, Nothing but Knucklers." *Baseball Stars of 1960.* Pyramid, 1960.

Smith, David W. "From Exile to Specialist: The Evolution of the Relief Pitcher." Paper presented at the annual meeting of the Society for American Baseball Research, June 23, 2000.

Shapiro, Milton. *Heroes of the Bullpen.* Messner, 1967.

Sporting News. *One for the Book.* Sporting News Publishing, 1970.

Thorn, John. *Relief Pitcher.* Dutton, 1979.

Vincent, David, Lyle Spatz, and David W. Smith. *The Midsummer Classic.* Bison Books, 2001.

Young, Dick. "Can a Relief Pitcher Last?" *Sport,* July 1960.

CHAPTER 6

Auker, Elden. *Sleeper Cars and Flannel Uniforms.* Triumph, 2001.

Daniel, W. Harrison. *Jimmie Foxx.* McFarland, 1996.

Hirshberg, Al. *The Red Sox, the Bean, and the Cod.* Waverly House, 1947.

Honig, Donald. *Baseball between the Lines.* Coward, McCann & Geoghegan, 1976.

———. *Baseball When the Grass Was Real.* Coward, McCann & Geoghegan, 1975.

Kaplan, Jim. *Lefty Grove.* Society for American Baseball Research, 2000.

Lieb, Fred. *The Boston Red Sox.* Putnam, 1947.

Thompson, Dick. "The Wes Ferrell Story." In *The National Pastime,* edited by Mark Alvarez. Society for American Baseball Research, 2001.

CHAPTER 7

Creamer, Robert. *Stengel: His Life and Times.* Fireside, 1990.

Dark, Alvin, and John Underwood. *When in Doubt, Fire the Manager: My Life and Times in Baseball.* Dutton, 1980.

Durocher, Leo, with Ed Linn. *Nice Guys Finish Last.* Simon & Schuster, 1975.

Kaese, Harold. *The Boston Braves.* Putnam, 1948.

Kelley, Brent *The Early All-Stars.* McFarland, 1997.

Koppett, Leonard. *The Man in the Dugout.* Crown, 1993.

Lang, Jack. "How Important Is a Manager?" *Sport,* July 1965.

Peary, Danny, ed. *We Played the Game: Sixty-Five Players Remember Baseball's Greatest Era, 1947–1964.* Hyperion, 1994.

Pope, Edwin. *Baseball's Greatest Managers.* Doubleday, 1960.

Rickey, Branch. *Branch Rickey's Little Blue Book.* Edited by John J. Monteleone. Macmillan, 1995.

Voight, David Q. *From Postwar Expansion to the Electronic Age.* Vol. 3, *American Baseball.* Pennsylvania State University Press, 1983.

Westcott, Rich. *Masters of the Diamond: Interviews with Players Who Began Their Careers More Than Fifty Years Ago.* McFarland, 1994.

CHAPTER 8

Golenbock, Peter. *Fenway.* Putnam, 1992.
Halberstam, David. *Summer of '49.* Morrow, 1989.
Hirshberg, Al. *What's the Matter with the Red Sox?* Dodd, Mead, 1973.
———. "Vern Stephens, Junior Red Socker." *Sport,* August 1949.
James, Bill. *The Politics of Glory.* Macmillan, 1994.
Kaese, Harold. "A Little Slug for the Red Sox." *Sport,* June 1950.
Linn, Ed. *Hitter: The Life and Turmoils of Ted Williams.* Harcourt Brace, 1993.
Kaiser, David. *Epic Season.* University of Massachusetts Press, 1998.
Mead, William. *Even the Browns.* Contemporary Books, 1978.
National Baseball Hall of Fame. File on Vern Stephens.
Rummill, Ed. "The Man behind Williams." *Complete Baseball,* Fall 1951.
Seidel, Michael. *Ted Williams: A Baseball Life.* Contemporary Books, 1991.
Stout, Glenn, and Richard Johnson. *Red Sox Century: One Hundred Years of Red Sox Baseball.* Houghton Mifflin, 2000.
Williams, Ted, and John Underwood. *My Turn at Bat.* Simon & Schuster, 1969.

CHAPTER 9

Anderson, Wayne J. *Harmon Killebrew: Baseball's Superstar.* Desert, 1971.
Carew, Rod, with Ira Berkow. *Carew.* Simon & Schuster, 1979.
Devaney, John. "How Mudcat Changed His Spots." *Sport,* September 1965.
Furlong, Bob. "The Feuding Twins: Inside a Team in Turmoil." *Sport,* April 1968.
Greene, Lee. "Baseball Strikes a Talent Bonanza." *Sport,* November 1959.
———. "Jimmie Hall? Who's Jimmie Hall?" *Baseball 1964.* Whitestone, 1964.
Izenberg, Jerry. "Zoilo Versalles: How a Problem Child Becomes an MVP." *Sport,* March 1966.
Kerr, Jon. *Calvin: Baseball's Last Dinosaur.* Wm. C. Brown, 1990.
Miller, Jeff. *Down to the Wire.* Taylor, 1992.
Nichols, Max. "Tony Oliva: Success with an Inside-Out Swing." *Sport,* October 1964.
———. "Sam Mele: A Study in Pressure." *Sport,* April 1966.
———. "The Kaat Organization." *Sport,* December 1966.
Oliva, Tony, with Bob Fowler. *Tony O! The Trials and Triumphs of Tony Oliva.* Hawthorn, 1973.
Roseboro, John, with Bill Libby. *Glory Days with the Dodgers and Other Days with Others.* Atheneum, 1978.
Shecter, Leonard. "A Hitter Has to Have a Killing Desire." *Sport,* September 1964.
Urdahl, Dean. *Touching Base with Our Memories.* North Star, 2001.

Williams, Jim. "Which Is the Real Jim Kaat?" *All Star Sports*, August 1968.
Zanger, Brenda. *Major League Baseball 1972*. Pocket Books, 1972.
Zanger, Brenda, and Dick Kaplan. *Major League Baseball 1971*. Pocket Books, 1971.
Zanger, Jack. " . . . And One Vote for Cesar." *Sport*, June 1968.
———. *Major League Baseball*. Pocket Books, 1965–1970.

CHAPTER 10

Modis, Theodore. *Predictions: Society's Telltale Signature Reveals the Past and Fore-casts the Future*. Simon & Schuster, 1992.

CHAPTER 11

Allen, Dick, and Tim Whitaker. *Crash*. Ticknor & Fields, 1989.
Baseball Guidebook. Maco, 1971.
Baseball Illustrated 1971. Complete Sports Publications, 1971.
Baseball Preview, *Sports Illustrated*, April 12, 1971.
Cataneo, David. *Tony C: The Triumph and Tragedy of Tony Conigliaro*. Rutledge Hill, 1997.
Fimrite, Ron. "For Failure to Give His Best . . . " *Sports Illustrated*, July 5, 1971.
Grand Slam Baseball Annual 1971. Popular Sports, 1971.
Hano, Arnold. "The Lonely War of Alex Johnson." *Sport*, October 1970.
Leggett, William. "A Riot Act Changes the Scene." *Sports Illustrated*, May 3, 1971.
National Baseball Hall of Fame. File on Alex Johnson.
Newhan, Ross *The California Angels*. Hyperion, 2000.
Pluto, Terry. *The Curse of Rocky Colavito*. Fireside, 1995.
Porter, Chris. "Alex." *Los Angeles Times*, June 24, 1990.
Sporting News. 1969–1971.
Sports Quarterly Baseball 1971. Counterpoint, 1971.
Street and Smith's Baseball. Conde Nast, 1971.
True's 1971 Baseball Yearbook. Fawcett, 1971.
Young, Dick. *New York Daily News*, June 18, 1971.

CHAPTER 12

Bergman, Ron. *Mustache Gang*. Dell, 1973.
"A Bolt of Blue Lightning." *Time*, August 23, 1971.
Clark, Tom. *Champagne and Baloney*. Harper & Row, 1975.
Harrelson, Ken, and Al Hirshberg. *Hawk*. Viking, 1968.
James, Bill. *The 1986 Baseball Abstract*. Ballantine, 1985.
Lardner, Rex. "Charlie Finley and Bugs Bunny in K.C." *Sports Illustrated*, June 5, 1961.

Leggett, William. "Dark's Outlook Is Young and Bright." *Sports Illustrated*, March 12, 1967.

Libby, Bill. *Charlie O. and the Angry A's*. Doubleday, 1975.

Libby, Bill, and Vida Blue. *Vida*. Prentice Hall, 1972.

Lowry, Phil. *Green Cathedrals*. Society for American Baseball Research, 1986.

Markuson, Bruce. *Baseball's Last Dynasty*. Masters, 1998.

Michelson, Herbert. *Charlie O*. Bobbs Merrill, 1975.

Shake, Edwin. "A Man and a Mule in Missouri." *Sports Illustrated*, July 27, 1965.

Shecter, Leonard. "Travels with Charley." *Sport*, September 1965.

Smith, Red. *Red Smith on Baseball*. Edited by Ira Berkow. Ivan R. Dee, 2000.

Sport Annual, 1966.

Taubman, Phil. "Charlie Finley: Baseball's Barnum." *Time*, August 18, 1975.

———. "Pyrotechnics by Finley." *Time*, June 3, 1974.

Wise, Bill, ed. *The 1963 Official Baseball Almanac*. Fawcett, 1963.

CHAPTER 13

Felber, Bill. "Relief Pitching Strategy, 1952–92." In *Total Baseball*, 4th ed. Viking Penguin, 1995.

Mills, Eldon G., and Harlan D. Mills. *Player Win Averages: A Computer Guide to Winning Baseball Players*. A. S. Barnes, 1970.

CHAPTER 14

Blair, Jeff. "Mourning Montreal." *Baseball America*, December 23, 2001.

Carter, Gary, with Ken Abraham. *The Gamer*. Word, 1993.

Fimrite, Ron. "His Enthusiasm Is Catching." *Sports Illustrated*, April 4, 1983.

Inside Sports. April 30, 1981.

James, Bill. *The Baseball Abstract*. Self-published, 1979–1981.

———. *The Baseball Abstract*. Ballantine, 1982–1986.

Lee, Bill, with Dick Lally. *The Wrong Stuff*. Viking Press, 1984.

New York Times. August 19, 1985–August 22, 1985; September 3, 1985; September 6, 1985; September 7, 1985; September 10, 1985–September 13, 1985; September 18, 1985; September 20, 1985; September 21, 1985.

Oliver, Al, and Andrew O'Toole. *Baseball's Best-Kept Secret: Al Oliver and His Time in Baseball*. City of Champions, 1997.

Sport. April, 1983

Sports Illustrated. Season preview articles, April 9, 1979; April 7, 1980; April 13, 1981; April 12, 1982; April 3, 1983; April 2, 1984.

Turner, Dan. *The Expos Inside Out*. McClelland & Stewart, 1983.

Waggoner, Glen. "The Best Player in Baseball." *Sport*, June 1983.

Williams, Dick, and Bill Plashke. *No More Mister Nice Guy: A Life of Hardball*. Harcourt Brace Jovanovich, 1990.

Wulf, Steve. "Out but Not Down." *Sports Illustrated*, November 6, 1980.

CHAPTER 15

Baseball Weekly. June 1996–April 1997.
Davenport, Clay. *Baseball Prospectus 1999.* Brassey's Sports, 1999.
Davenport, Clay, et al. *Baseball Prospectus 1996.* Self-published, 1996.
Florida Marlins 2000 Media Guide.
Huckabay, Gary, et al. *Baseball Prospectus 1997.* Ravenlock Media, 1997.
———. *Baseball Prospectus 1998.* Brassey's Sports, 1998.
Kahrl, Chris, et al. *Baseball Prospectus 2000.* Brassey's Sports, 2000.
Keating, Raymond J. "Sports Pork: The Costly Relationship between Major
    League Sports and Government." *Policy Analysis*, April 5, 1999.
Official Site of the Florida Marlins. www.marlins.mlb.com.
Pappas, Doug, ed. *Outside the Lines.* Society for American Baseball Research, Sum-
    mer 1997–Spring 1999.
Rosenbaum, Dave. *If They Don't Win, It's a Shame.* McGregor, 1998.
Sheehan, Joseph S., et al. *Baseball Prospectus 2001.* Brassey's Sports, 2001.
———. *Baseball Prospectus 2002.* Brassey's Sports, 2002.
Street and Smith's Baseball. Conde Nast, 1993–1999.
Zimbalist, Andrew. "A Miami Fish Story." *New York Times*, October 18, 1998.

CHAPTER 16

Baseball America. March 3, 1996; January 5, 1997; March 30, 1997.
Baseball America's Almanac, 1993–1997.
Hitzges, Norm, and Dave Lawson. *Essential Baseball 1994.* Plume, 1994.
Howe Sportsdata. Minor league data files.
James, Bill. *The Baseball Abstract.* Ballantine, 1985.
STATS Inc. and Howe Sportsdata. *Bill James Presents STATS Minor League Hand-
    boiok, 1997–2000.* STATS Publishing 1996–1999.

CHAPTER 17

Atlanta Braves 2001 Media Guide.
Davenport, Clay. *Baseball Prospectus 1999.* Brassey's Sports, 1999.
Davenport, Clay, et al. *Baseball Prospectus 1996.* Self-published, 1996
Glavine, Tom. *None but the Braves.* HarperCollins, 1996.
Huckabay, Gary, et al. *Baseball Prospectus 1997.* Ravenlock, 1997.
———. *Baseball Prospectus 1998.* Brassey's Sports, 1998.
Hope, Bob. *We Could've Finished Last without You.* Longstreet, 1991
Kahrl, Chris, et al. *Baseball Prospectus 2000.* Brassey's Sports, 2000.

Klapisch, Bob, and Pete Van Wieren. *The World Champion Braves.* Turner, 1996.
Sheehan, Joseph S., et al. *Baseball Prospectus 2001.* Brassey's Sports, 2001.
———. *Baseball Prospectus 2002.* Brassey's Sports, 2002.
Zack, Bill. *Tomahawked.* Simon & Schuster, 1993.

APPENDIX 2

Fischer, David Hackett. *Historians' Fallacies: Toward a Logic of Historical Thought.* Harper Torchbooks, 1970.
Thorn, John, and Pete Palmer, eds., with David Reuther. *Total Baseball.* Warner Books, 1989.

APPENDIX 5

Bennett, Jay. "Did Shoeless Joe Jackson Throw the 1919 World Series?" *American Statistician* 47, no. 4 (November 1993).
Lindsey, George R. "The Progress of the Score during a Baseball Game." *American Statistical Association Journal,* September 1961.
Lindsey, George R. "Investigation of Strategies in Baseball." *Operations Research,* July–August 1963.

INDEX

Aaron, Henry, 142, 322
Abbott, Kurt, 299, 307, 309
Abell, Ferdinand, 11, 20
Abernathy, Ted, 92, 108
Adair, Jerry, 191
Adams, Charles, 128, 129
Adams, Jack, 30
Adamson, Joel, 298
Alexander, Dale, 114
Alexander, Doyle, 323
Alexander, Pete, 24, 30, 34–36, 38, 43, 77, 341
Allen, Bernie, 187, 190
Allen, Dick, 221, 228
Allen, Johnny, 114
Allison, Bob, 176, 179, 185, 188, 190, 193, 195–96, 202–3, 355
Almada, Mel, 118, 120–22, 124, 125
Alomar, Roberto, 337
Alomar, Sandy, Sr., 217, 223–24
Alou, Felipe, 253
Alou, Jesus, 212–15, 253
Alou, Matty, 253
Alou, Moises, 304–5, 307, 309
Alston, Walter, 100, 181
Andrews, Ivy, 115
Andrews, Mike, 253
Andujar, Joaquin, 290
Anson, Cap, 78

Anthony, Merle, 229
Antonelli, Johnny, 143
Aparicio, Luis, 103
Archer, Jimmy, 43
Arias, Alex, 298
Arrigo, Jerry, 180
Ashby, Andy, 332, 338
Aspromonte, Bob, 366
Autry, Gene, 131, 218–20, 222, 226
Averill, Earl, 124, 127
Avery, Steve, 323–27, 331, 340
Azcue, Joe, 223

Bagby, Jim, Jr., 126
Bahnsen, Stan, 253
Bair, Doug, 268
Baker, Dusty, 291
Baker, Frank, 36, 57
Baker, Newton, 65
Baker, William, 24, 26, 32, 36–38
Baldshun, Jack, 204
Ball, Phil, 29, 114
Bancroft, Dave, 27, 30, 34–36, 62
Bando, Sal, 224, 243–44, 247–48, 253–54, 256, 258
Banks, Ernie, 168
Banks, George, 180
Barberie, Bret, 298
Barojas, Salome, 273

Barrett, Red, 130, 137, 141–43
Barrow, Ed, 67, 68
Barry, Jack, 36, 84
Barry, Joe, 109
Batista, Tony, 375
Battey, Earl, 176, 179, 187–88, 190, 197–98, 355
Batts, Matt, 160, 163
Bauer, Hank, 103, 153, 163, 236–37
Bavasi, Peter, 219
Beck, Rod, 274
Becker, Beals, 30, 34
Beckett, Josh, 310
Belinsky, Bo, 218
Bell, Beau, 124
Bell, Gary, 191
Bell, Rob, 331, 338
Belle, Albert, 303–4
Belliard, Rafael, 325, 335
Bench, Johnny, 91
Bennett, Jay, 371
Benton, Rube, 65
Benz, Joe, 52, 63
Beradino, Johnny, 165
Berenguer, Juan, 326, 335, 337
Bergesch, Bill, 237
Bergman, Ron, 234
Bernazard, Tony, 283
Berra, Dale, 289
Berra, Yogi, 104, 153, 161, 163, 255
Berry, Ken, 217, 223–24, 226, 231
Bevens, Bill, 153
Bickford, Vern, 140–41, 144
Billingham, Jack, 214
Bishop, Max, 115–16, 119
Black, Joe, 99–101
Blackburne, Lena, 62–63
Blair, Jeff, 281
Blankenship, Cliff, 77
Blasinghame, Don, 366
Blauser, Jeff, 323, 325, 328, 330, 337
Blefary, Curt, 253
Blue, Vida, 247, 249–54, 257–58
Bluege, Ossie, 81–83, 86, 90
Blyleven, Bert, 193

Bodie, Ping, 56
Boles, John, 300, 302
Bond, Walter, 366
Bonds, Barry, 127, 303, 327, 336–37, 342
Bonds, Bobby, 303
Bonilla, Bobby, 304–5, 307
Boone, Bret, 331, 338
Borbon, Pedro, 220, 224
Bosman, Dick, 253
Boswell, Dave, 189–90, 192, 202
Boswell, Thomas, 290
Bottalico, Ricky, 273
Boudreau, Lou, 164, 167–69, 171–74
Boyer, Clete, 236
Boyer, Ken, 104, 191
Bradley, Tom, 223–24, 232
Brahms, Johannes, 205
Breadon, Sam, 131–33
Bream, Sid, 325–26, 335, 339
Brecheen, Harry, 103
Brennan, Ad, 24–25
Bressoud, Eddie, 366
Bristol, Dave, 220, 323
Brodie, Steve, 9
Bronfman, Charles, 276
Brosnan, Jim, 104
Brouthers, Dan, 9–10, 70
Brown, Bobby, 153, 163–64
Brown, Dick, 102
Brown, Kevin, 300, 302, 305, 307, 309
Brown, Larry, 253
Brown, Lloyd, 114–15
Brown, Mordecai, 95
Brown, Ollie, 253
Brown, Roosevelt, 338
Brown, Walter, 47, 51–52, 67
Browning, Pete, 70
Brunet, George, 236
Brush, John T., 6–7, 37, 41
Buford, Don, 182
Buhl, Bob, 143
Burba, Dave, 316
Burkett, Jesse, 8
Burkett, John, 301, 305, 332
Burnett, A. J., 310

Burnitz, Jeromy, 335
Burns, George, 31, 57
Burris, Ray, 280
Bush, Donie, 48, 76, 82–83, 87
Bush, Homer, 375
Bush, Joe, 75
Byrne, Bobby, 25, 30, 35, 154
Byrne, Charles, 6, 11

Cadaret, Greg, 262–64
Cairo, Miguel, 317–18
Caldwell, Mike, 268
Callahan, Jimmy, 53
Callison, Johnny, 197
Cambria, Joe, 178–9
Camelli, Hank, 137
Campanella, Roy, 321
Campaneris, Bert, 239, 243, 253, 258
Campbell, Bill, 272–74
Campbell, Vin, 73
Cangelosi, John, 304, 307
Cantillon, Joe, 77
Cardenas, Leo, 189, 192, 198
Carew, Rod, 190–91, 193, 202, 224
Carnegie, Andrew, 5
Carpenter, Chris, 298
Carr, Charlie, 28
Carr, Chuck, 299–300
Carter, Gary, 276–78, 284–77, 290–93
Carty, Rico, 253, 366
Casey, Doc, 14, 16, 18
Casey, Sean, 315–17, 335
Cash, Dave, 277–78
Cash, Norm, 182, 197
Castilla, Vinny, 332
Castillo, Luis, 302, 304–7
Castillo, Tony, 338
Caudill, Bill, 273
Cepeda, Orlando, 253, 366
Chadwick, Henry, 16
Chance, Dean, 190–91, 218–19
Chandler, Happy, 145
Chandler, Spud, 150, 153
Chapman, Ben, 114, 124–26
Chappell, Larry, 58

Chase, Hal, 57
Chen, Bruce, 332, 338
Chilcott, Steve, 244
Christman, Mark, 166
Christopher, Joe, 366
Cicotte, Eddie, 39, 42, 44, 50, 52, 55, 63–64, 66, 69–72
Cissell, Bill, 115–16, 19
Clark, Jack, 291
Clark, Ron, 198
Clarke, Fred, 17
Clemente, Roberto, 183
Clendenon, Donn, 212–15, 366
Cobb, Ty, 22, 42, 56–58, 63, 70
Cochrane, Witt K, 45
Colavito, Rocky, 185, 191, 242
Colbrunn, Greg, 299, 302, 304–5
Coleman, Jerry, 153, 160, 163
Collins, Eddie, 36, 42, 47, 52–58, 63–66, 68–71, 83, 113–18, 121, 125–27, 149, 151, 152, 341
Collins, Shano, 54, 61–65
Comiskey, Charles, 22, 40–47, 50–53, 58–60, 62–63, 65, 69, 71–72, 78, 341
Comiskey, John, 40
Cone, David, 269
Conigliaro, Billy, 230, 253
Conigliaro, Tony, 191, 217, 223–25, 227–32
Conine, Jeff, 298–300, 302, 304–7, 309
Cook, Dennis, 304, 307, 309
Cooke, Dusty, 120, 122, 124
Cooney, Johnny, 145
Cooper, Mort, 130, 134, 137
Corbett, Doug, 273
Counsell, Craig, 306–7
Covaleski, Stan, 88, 90
Cowan, Billy, 225
Cox, Bobby, 323–25, 337, 339–40
Cramer, Doc, 120–24, 126–27, 152
Crandall, Otis, 95–96
Cravath, Gavvy, 24–25, 30–34, 38, 57, 341
Crawford, Sam, 12, 43
Creamer, Robert, 129

Cromartie, Warren, 277, 279, 282, 284–85, 290–2
Cronin, Joe, 117–23, 125–26, 150, 152, 170, 238, 242, 246
Crosby, Bing, 131
Crosetti, Frank, 114, 150
Cross, Lave, 18–19
Crowder, Enoch, 65
Cruz, Jose, Sr., 291
Cruz, Jose, Jr., 375
Cuellar, Mike, 268
Culler, Dick, 129–30, 139
Cunningham, Bill, 119
Cutshaw, George, 27

Dahlen, Billy, 13–14, 16, 19
Dahlgren, Babe, 118, 120, 122
Daley, Bud, 236
Daley, William R., 238
Dalton, Harry, 232
Daly, Tom, 13–14, 19–20
Danforth, Dave, 59, 64
Danzig, Alison, 39
Dark, Alvin, 137, 139–41, 143–46, 228, 246, 256–57, 265
Daubert, Jake, 30–31, 44
Daulton, Darren, 306–7
Davilillo, Vic, 253
Davis, Ilus, 246
Davis, Mark, 273, 336–37
Davis, Ron, 273
Davis, Tommy, 253
Davis, Willie, 110, 366
Dawson, Andre, 276–77, 279, 281, 284–86, 290–93, 299, 302
Delahanty, Ed, 70
Delgado, Carlos, 375
Delgado, Felix, 243
Demaree, Al, 27, 30, 34, 38
DeMontreville, Gene, 12, 15, 18–19
Dempster, Ryan, 310
DeSautels, Gene, 126
Destrade, Orestes, 298
Dewey, George, 16
DeWitt, Bill, 204, 210–11, 216

Dibble, Rob, 273–74
Dickey, Bill, 114, 122, 125, 150, 154
Dickson, Murry, 131
Dierker, Larry, 268
DiMaggio, Dom, 126, 150–51, 160–61, 163, 170
DiMaggio, Joe, 55, 124–25, 127, 149, 153, 158, 160–61, 163–64, 168, 247
Dipino, Frank, 273
Dobson, Chuck, 243, 245
Dobson, Joe, 150–51
Doby, Larry, 160
Doerr, Bobby, 125–26, 149–50, 160, 163, 168, 170
Dombrowski, Dave, 296–98, 300–304, 306, 309–10, 341, 344
Donaldson, John, 243
Dooin, Red, 25–27
Doolan, Mickey, 25
Doyle, Larry, 31, 57
Doyle, Paul, 93
Dressen, Charlie, 99–100, 102
Dreyfus, Barney, 15, 17, 37
Dropo, Walt, 152
Drysdale, Don, 181
Dugan, Joe, 75
Dugey, Oscar, 27
Duncan, Dave, 243–44, 249–50, 252–53
Dunn, Jack, 11, 14, 20, 81
Duren, Ryne, 236
Durocher, Leo, 101, 103, 133, 139, 143–45
Dye, Jermaine, 329–30, 338

Eastwick, Rawly, 273
Ebbetts, Charles, 11–12, 16, 20, 37, 43
Eckersley, Dennis, 93, 262–65, 269–72
Eckert, William, 246
Edwards, Johnny, 366
Egan, Tom, 219, 223, 232
Eisenreich, Jim, 304, 307
Elliot, Claude, 94
Elliott, Bob, 137–39, 141, 144
Embree, Alan, 338
Engel, Joe, 81–82, 84

Epstein, Eddie, 1, 194
Epstein, Mike, 253
Ermer, Cal, 191–92, 202–3
Esasky, Nick, 324–25
Estrada, Chuck, 103
Etchebarren, Andy, 194
Evans, Billy, 125, 129
Evans, Darrell, 291
Everett, Carl, 298–99
Evers, Johnny, 43

Faber, Urban, 51–52, 55, 63–66, 71–72
Face, Roy, 109
Fanning, Jim, 281–84, 286, 288
Farmer, Ed, 273
Farrell, Duke, 14, 16, 19
Felber, Bill, 266
Feller, Bob, 127
Felsch, Happy, 39, 42, 55–58, 63–65, 68, 70
Fernandez, Alex, 303–5, 307, 309
Fernandez, Nanny, 139
Fernandez, Tony, 375
Ferrell, Rick, 114–17, 121, 125–26
Ferrell, Wes, 116–119, 121–23, 125–26
Ferris, Boo, 151
Fingers, Rollie, 110–11, 243–44, 252–53, 258, 264–66, 269–72
Finley, Carl, 236
Finley, Charles, 145, 218, 233–59, 322
Finley, Charles, Jr., 236
Finley, Shirley, 236
Firpo, Luis, 82
Fischer, David Hackett, 360
Fisher, Eddie, 92, 104–5, 107, 224–25
Fisher, Jack, 103
Fletcher, Darrin, 375
Flood, Curt, 366
Flynn, Doug, 283–85, 292–94
Ford, Whitey, 154
Fornieles, Mike, 92
Forster, Terry, 273
Fosse, Ray, 253
Foster, Eddie, 62
Fournier, Jack, 54, 59–60

Fowler, Art, 202
Fox, Charlie, 277–78
Fox, Howard, 202
Foxx, Jimmie, 117, 120–23, 125–27, 171, 359
Franco, John, 269
Frazee, Harry, 113
Freedman, Andrew, 6–7, 16
Fregosi, Jim, 182, 217, 219, 222–25, 227, 231–32
Frick, Ford, 242
Frick, Henry Clay, 5
Friday, Pat, 236
Frisch, Frankie, 137
Fryman, Woodie, 278, 284
Fuchs, Judge Emil, 128
Furcal, Rafael, 331–32, 334

Gaffney, James, 37
Galarraga, Andres, 330–32, 335
Gandil, Chick, 39, 42, 44, 60, 63, 68, 79
Gant, Ron, 301, 323–28, 339
Garber, Gene, 111
Garcia, Karim, 317–18
Gardner, Larry, 62
Gardner, Mark, 299
Garland, Wayne, 336
Garver, Ned, 171
Gates, Mike, 284
Gehrig, Lou, 1, 120, 122, 125, 242, 359
Gehringer, Charlie, 127
Gentile, Jim, 242
Gibson, Bob, 268
Giles, Brian, 335
Giles, Marcus, 332, 334
Ginsberg, Joe, 104
Glavine, Tom, 323–32, 339
Gleason, Kid, 55, 65–66, 68
Gomez, Lefty, 114, 150
Gonzalez, Tony, 223
Gooden, Dwight, 301
Goodman, Billy, 152, 163
Gordon, Joe, 153, 236, 239
Gordon, Sid, 143–44
Gordon, Tom, 274

Goslin, Goose, 81, 83, 86–87, 89–90, 124
Gossage, Rich, 83, 110–11, 261–64, 266, 268–72, 337
Grabarkewitz, Billy, 253
Graham, Frank, Jr., 100
Grahe, Joe, 274
Grant, Jim, 180–82, 189–90, 192, 203, 253
Graves, Danny, 335
Green, Dick, 242–44, 253
Green, Lenny, 195
Green, Pumpsie, 152
Green, Shawn, 375
Greenberg, Hank, 131
Greene, Willie, 375
Gregg, Eric, 307
Griffin, Doug, 223
Griffin, Mike, 11–14
Griffith, Calvin, 176–81, 188, 191–92, 195, 199, 201, 203, 343
Griffith, Clark, 46, 60, 76–84, 86, 88–89, 117, 121, 177–78, 342
Grimsley, Ross, 278–79
Grissom, Marquis, 328–30, 337–39
Groh, Heinie, 31, 43, 49, 57, 66
Grove, Lefty, 96, 115–23, 126, 127
Guidry, Ron, 268
Guillen, Ozzie, 330
Guinn, Skip, 214
Gullickson, Bill, 276, 279–80, 282, 285, 292
Gutteridge, Don, 166

Haas, Eddie, 323
Haas, Mule, 124
Halberstam, David, 148, 158, 168–69
Hall, Jimmie, 176, 179, 187–88, 190, 194–95, 355, 366
Hall, John, 226
Hallman, Bill, 14
Hamilton, Billy, 70
Hammond, Chris, 302
Hampton, Mike, 336–37
Haney, Fred, 165, 219
Haney, Larry, 253

Hanlon, Ned, 5, 8–20, 91
Hansen, Ron, 366
Harper, Tommy, 253
Harrelson, Ken, 191, 239, 246, 257
Harris, Bucky, 76, 80, 82–84, 86–90, 96, 98, 115, 117–18, 154, 161
Harris, Gene, 273
Harris, Joe, 89
Harris, Mickey, 151
Hart, John, 333
Hartnett, Gabby, 226
Hartsfield, Roy, 144
Harvey, Bryan, 91, 273–74, 297–99
Haynes, Joe, 178
Heath, Jeff, 138, 140–45
Hedges, R.L., 53
Hegan, Mike, 253
Heilmann, Harry, 57
Helms, Wes, 332
Helton, Todd, 317
Henderson, Ken, 323
Hendrick, George, 291
Hendryx, Tim, 56
Henke, Tom, 109, 274
Henrich, Tommy, 53, 161, 163
Henry, Doug, 273
Henry, John (owner), 309–10
Henry, John (catcher), 104
Heridia, Felix, 307
Herman, Billy, 137
Hernandez, Jackie, 190, 198
Hernandez, Keith, 290–91
Hernandez, Livan, 306–7
Hershberger, Mike, 366
Hershisher, Orel, 269
Herzog, Whitey, 240, 289–90
Heydler, John, 131
Hibbard, Greg, 298
Higgins, Pinky, 125–26, 151
Higuera, Teddy, 269
Hill, Jesse, 124
Hiller, John, 110
Hirshberg, Al, 169
Hitchcock, Billy, 152, 167
Hitler, Adolf, 360

Hitzges, Norm, 380
Hoblitzel, Dick, 44
Hodapp, Johnny, 115
Hoffman, Trevor, 264, 298
Hofheinz, Roy, 213–14
Hogue, Bobby, 140–41
Hollandsworth, Todd, 301
Holmes, Darren, 273
Holmes, Tommy, 134, 137, 139, 141, 146
Holt, JIm, 253
Holtzman, Jerome, 92
Holtzman, Ken, 253–54, 257–58
Honeycutt, Rick, 262–64
Hooey, Bob, 132
Hooper, Harry, 57
Hooten, Burt, 268
Hopp, Johnny, 136–37, 139–40
Horlen, Joe, 253
Horner, Bobby, 323
Hornsby, Rogers, 43, 57, 132, 301, 359
Horton, Tony, 228
Hough, Charlie, 273, 298–99
Houk, Ralph, 239
Howard, Elston, 104, 191
Howard, Frank, 182
Howser, Phil, 180
Hoyt, Waite, 1, 75
Hrabosky, Al, 273
Huggins, Miller, 242
Hughes, Jimmy, 13–14, 16–19
Hughson, Tex, 150–51
Huizenga, H. Wayne, 295–97, 302, 304–5, 308–9
Hunter, Brian, 325
Hunter, Jim, 224, 243–45, 247, 250, 253–54, 256–58
Hunter, Torii, 313
Huston, Colonel, 53

Jackson, Danny, 269, 298
Jackson, Joe, 39, 42–44, 47, 56–58, 62–65, 68–71, 73, 127, 341
Jackson, Reggie, 224, 244–45, 247–49, 251, 253–56, 258
Jacobson, Baby Doll, 56, 73–74

James, Bill, 26, 88, 96, 126, 161, 168, 183, 271, 290, 311, 313, 333, 347–54, 358, 364–65, 367, 374, 376, 379
James, Bob, 273
Jarvis, Ray, 223
Jennings, Hughie, 9–10, 12–17, 19
Jethroe, Sam, 144
Jiminez, Manny, 237
Johnson, Alex, 217, 220–22, 224–28, 230–32
Johnson, Arnold, 235–6
Johnson, Ban, 41, 45–46, 50, 67, 72, 78, 89, 113
Johnson, Billy, 153, 164
Johnson, Bob (infielder), 236
Johnson, Bob (outfielder), 121, 124, 127
Johnson, Charles, 297, 299, 302, 305, 307
Johnson, Dave, 194, 304
Johnson, Deron, 253
Johnson, Hank, 115
Johnson, Ken, 236
Johnson, Richard, 168
Johnson, Roy, 120–21
Johnson, Wallace, 283–84
Johnson, Walter, 22, 42, 51, 75, 77, 79–80, 82, 84–85, 87–90
Johnstone, Jay, 223–24, 232, 253
Jolley, Smead, 114–15
Jones, Andruw, 329–32, 334–35, 339
Jones, Chipper, 328–29, 331–32, 334–35, 339
Jones, Doug, 269
Jones, Fielder, 11, 13–14, 19–20, 29
Jones, Jake, 151
Jones, Sam, 75, 87
Joost, Eddie, 136
Jordan, Brian, 331–32, 335, 338
Joyner, Wally, 331, 338
Judge, Joe, 57, 60, 80, 82–83, 85–86, 89–90
Justice, David, 323–27, 329–30, 338

Kaat, Jim, 179, 182, 188–89, 191–93, 201, 224, 243
Kaese, Harold, 129, 168

Kaiser, David, 159–61
Kaline, Al, 182, 185
Kasko, Eddie, 366
Katt, Ray, 102
Kauff, Benny, 36, 57, 73
Keeler, Willie, 9–14, 16, 18–20
Keller, Charlie, 153, 164
Kelley, Joe, 9–10, 12–14, 16, 18–20
Kelly, Roberto, 338
Kelly, Tom, 313
Kennedy, Bob, 247
Kennedy, Brickyard, 11, 14, 17, 20
Kennedy, John F., 360
Kennedy, Monte, 136
Kennedy, Terry, 290
Kern, Jim, 272–73
Kerr, Buddy, 143–44
Kerr, Dickie, 65, 68, 71–72
Kile, Darryl, 336
Killebrew, Harmon, 176, 178–80, 182–
     88, 190, 192–94, 198–99, 203, 224,
     355, 366
Killefer, Bill, 24, 30, 36, 43
Kindall, Jerry, 188, 355
Kinder, Ellis, 99, 152, 167
Kiner, Ralph, 137
Klein, Chuck, 358–360
Klepfer, Ed, 58
Klesko, Ryan, 328–31, 334–35, 338–39
Klimchock, Lou, 236
Kline, Bob, 116
Kline, Ron, 92–93, 108, 190–91
Knabe, Otto, 25
Knepper, Bob, 268
Knight, Ray, 301
Knoop, Bobby, 219
Knowles, Darold, 253, 269–72
Koenig, Fred, 227
Konstanty, Jim, 99, 109
Koosman, Jerry, 268
Koppett, Leonard, 91
Koufax, Sandy, 100–1, 181–82, 189, 251
Kralick, Jack, 180, 200
Kramer, Jack, 152, 167, 171
Krausse, Lew, Jr., 243, 245, 247

Kreevich, Mike, 124
Kroc, Ray, 131
Kryhoski, Dick, 164
Kubiak, Ted, 243
Kuhn, Bowie, 213–14, 248, 251, 255, 258

Labine, Clem, 99–100
LaChance, Candy, 13–14
Lachemann, Rene, 300
Ladd, Pete, 273
LaGrow, Lerrin, 273
Lahman, Sean, 93
Lake, Eddie, 151
Landis, Judge, 39
Lane, Frank, 235–36
Lange, Bill, 55
Lannin, Joe, 52
LaRoche, Dave, 224, 273
LaRussa, Tony, 243–44, 262–64
Lary, Lyn, 117
Lau, Charlie, 250
Lauzerique, George, 243
Lavagetto, Cookie, 179–80, 183
Lawson, Dave, 380
Lazzeri, Tony, 1, 122, 125
Lea, Charlie, 279–80, 282, 285, 292
Leach, Tommy, 17
Lee, Bill, 278, 280, 282–83, 288, 291
LeFlore, Ron, 279–81, 290, 293–94
Leggett, William, 245
Leibold, Nemo, 54, 58, 61, 63–65, 76, 85
Leiter, Al, 300, 302–3, 305, 307
Lemke, Mark, 323, 325, 328, 330
Leyland, Jim, 302, 304, 306–7, 327
Libby, Bill, 249
Lieb, Fred, 19, 67, 75, 120
Liebrandt, Charlie, 325
Lightenberg, Kerry, 274, 334
Lindberg, Richard, 50, 68
Lindblad, Paul, 243
Lindell, Johnny, 153, 164
Lindsay, George, 371
Lindstrom, Fred, 85
Little, Bryan, 284
Lobert, Hans, 25, 27

Locke, William, 23–24
Locker, Bob, 104, 253
Lockhart, Keith, 330–32, 338
Lockwood, Skip, 273
Lofton, Kenny, 330, 338
Loiselle, Rich, 273
Lopat, Eddie, 154, 171
Lopez, Albie, 335
Lopez, Hector, 236
Lopez, Javy, 328–29, 331–32, 334–45, 339
Loria, Jeff, 310
Luderus, Fred, 24, 30, 34, 57
Lupien, Tony, 150
Lyle, Sparky, 110–11, 266
Lyons, Al, 140

Mack, Connie, 36, 50, 52–53, 115–17, 120–21, 177, 242
Maddux, Greg, 127, 269, 307, 327–32, 335–37, 339, 342, 344
Madlock, Bill, 291
Magadan, Dave, 298
Magee, Lee, 36, 43
Magee, Sherry, 24–25, 27, 31, 38
Magoon, George, 13–15
Maisel, Fritz, 62
Maloney, George, 229
Maloney, Jim, 217, 223–24
Maney, Joseph, 129
Mangual, Angel, 253
Manning, Jack, 94
Mantle, Mickey, 184–86, 366
Manush, Heinie, 121–24
Mapes, Cliff, 153, 164
Marberry, Firpo, 82–83, 87–90, 95–98
Marcum, Johnny, 120–22, 126
Marichal, Juan, 268
Marion, Marty, 164, 166, 172–74
Maris, Roger, 236, 248
Marquis, Jason, 334
Marsans, Armando, 56
Marshall, MIke, 110–11
Marshall, Willard, 143–44
Martin, Billy, 192, 197, 201–2, 250

Martin, J.C., 106–7
Martinez, Jesus, 298
Masi, Phil, 134, 137, 139–40
Matheny, Mike, 375
Mathews, Eddie, 142, 191, 366
Mathews, Gary, 323
Mathews, Terry, 299, 301
Mathewson, Christy, 22, 51, 95
Matlack, Jon, 255
Mauch, Gene, 220
Maul, Al, 13, 17
Maxvill, Dal, 253
May, Rudy, 217, 224, 278
Mayer, Erskine, 24, 30, 34, 35
Mazzone, Leo, 337, 339
McAuliffe, Dick, 208–10, 366
McCarthy, Joe, 97, 148, 152, 154, 167, 168, 170–71
McCormick, Frank, 137, 141
McCormick, Mike, 141–42
McCovey, Willie, 207
McDaniel, Lindy, 92, 109, 111
McDowell, Sam, 95
McFarlan, Dan, 13–14
McFarlane, Mike, 325
McGann, Dan, 13, 16
McGinnity, Joe, 13, 16–18, 20, 95
McGlothlin, Jim, 220, 232
McGraw, John, 8, 10, 12, 15, 17–20, 24, 46, 64, 80, 131, 132
McGraw, Tug, 111, 268
McGriff, Fred, 327, 329–30, 337–39, 344
McGuire, Deacon, 16, 19–20
McGwire, Mark, 207
McHale, John, 213. 276, 279, 281, 288–89
McInnis, Stuffy, 73–74
McJames, Doc, 13–14, 17
McKechnie, Bill, 133
McLain, Denny, 253, 268
McMahon, Don, 111, 191
McManus, Marty, 165
McMichael, Greg, 273, 334
McMullen, Ken, 223–24
McMullin, Fred, 40, 42, 44, 63
McNair, Eric, 120–22, 126–27, 152

McNally, Dave, 257
McNamara, John, 248, 250
McNeely, Earl, 84–86, 89
McPhail, Larry, 133
McPhail, Lee, 257
McQuinn, George, 153
Mead, William, 166
Meany, Tom, 1
Meekin, Jouette, 16
Mehl, Ernie, 241
Mele, Sam, 176, 180–82, 190–91, 195, 199, 201–2
Melillo, Oscar, 119, 122–23
Mercker, Kent, 323
Merritt, Jim, 189, 192
Messersmith, Andy, 217, 222–23, 231, 257
Metkovich, Catfish, 151
Milan, Clyde, 56, 77, 79–80, 83, 84
MIller, Bing, 119, 126
Miller, Bob, 192
Miller, Jeff, 191
Miller, Kurt, 298
Miller, Marvin, 227, 246
Miller, Ralph, 14
MIller, Stuffy, 108
Mills, Buster, 126
Mills, E. G., 371
Mills, H. D., 371
Millwood, Kevin, 331–32, 334–45, 340
Milner, John, 289
Mincher, Don, 179, 187, 190, 199, 219, 253, 355
Mitchell, Keith, 327
Mize, Johnny, 153
Modis, Dr. Theodore, 205–6, 208–10
Mogridge, George, 76, 82, 85, 90
Monday, Rick, 243–45, 253, 281
Moran, Pat, 22–23, 26–27, 34–36, 38, 44, 66
Morgan, J. P., 5
Morris, Hal, 311
Moses, Jerry, 223, 226
Moses, Wally, 124, 151
Moss, Damian, 334

Mostil, Johnny, 71
Mozart, Wolfgang A., 209
Mulholland, Terry, 332
Murphy, Dale, 204, 291, 323
Murphy, Eddie, 58
Murphy, Johnny, 97, 114
Murphy, Tom, 223, 273
Murray, Jim, 101, 234
Murtaugh, Danny, 139
Musial, Stan, 167
Myatt, George, 125
Myers, Chief, 43
Myers, Randy, 269–72, 275

Naragon, Hal, 201
Nash, Jim, 243–45
Navin, Frank, 52
Neagle, Denny, 329–31, 337–38, 340
Nelson, Gene, 262–63
Nelson, Tom, 129–30
Nen, Robb, 298–300, 302, 304–5, 307, 309
Ness, Jack, 59–60
Neun, Johnny, 154
Newhouser, Hal, 166
Newsom, Bobo, 125–26, 153
Neyer, Rob, 1, 194
Nichols, Chet, 143
Nichols, Kid, 95
Nichols, Max, 180–81
Niehoff, Bert, 27, 30, 34–35
Niekro, Phil, 95, 105, 107–8, 323
Nixon, Otis, 325–26, 337–38
Nixon, Richard, 251
Nixon, Russ, 102, 193, 323–24
Nops, Jerry, 15
North, Bill, 253
Nossek, Joe, 355

O'Brien, Charlie, 328
O'Brien, Sid, 223
Odom, John, 243–45, 247
O'Dowd, Dan, 359
O'Farrell, Bob, 133
Office, Rowland, 289

Ogden, Curly, 84–85
Oliva, Antonio, 179
Oliva, Tony, 176–77, 179–82, 184–88, 190, 193–94, 198, 202, 224, 355–56
Oliver, Al, 282, 284–87, 290, 292–94
Olson, Greg, 325, 339
O'Malley, Peter, 219
O'Malley, Walter, 218
O'Neil, Steve, 154, 171
O'Rourke, Tim, 9
Ostermueller, Fritz, 121–22
Ott, Mel, 359–60
Owens, Brick, 96

Pacino, Al, 228
Page, Joe, 93, 98–100, 109, 148, 154, 175
Paige, Satchel, 239
Palmeiro, Rafael, 337
Palmer, David, 278, 280, 292
Palmer, Jim, 194, 268
Palmer, Pete, 26, 170, 347–48, 354
Papi, Stan, 278
Pappas, Milt, 103, 204
Parker, Dave, 289
Parnell, Mel, 152, 155
Parrish, Lance, 290
Parrish, Larry, 277, 279–80, 282, 292
Paskert, Dode, 30, 34
Pasqual, Camilo, 177, 179, 182, 189–90
Pasqual, Jorge, 197
Paul, Gabe, 204
Peckinpaugh, Roger, 76, 82–83, 89–90, 123
Pena, Alejandro, 326, 337–38
Pendleton, Terry, 299, 301–2, 305, 311, 325–26, 329, 335, 337–39
Pennock, Herb, 1, 75
Penny, Brad, 310
Perez, Odalis, 332, 338
Perez, Tony, 277, 279, 292
Perini, Lou, 129–31, 136–37, 145–46
Perranoski, Ron, 192
Perry, Gaylord, 268
Perry, Jim, 180, 189, 192–93, 200–201, 203, 224, 253

Pesky, Johnny, 126, 150–52, 160–61, 163–65, 167–68, 170–74
Phillips, Lefty, 220–22, 225–27, 229–30
Phillips, Mike, 284
Pinson, Vada, 230
Pipgras, George, 115–16
Pipp, Wally, 64
Podres, Johnny, 100
Porter, J.W., 105
Potter, Nelson, 141
Povich, Shirley, 78, 88
Powell, Boog, 182, 185
Powell, Jake, 124
Powell, Jay, 307
Puccinelli, George, 124

Quillici, Frank, 355
Quinn, Bob, 113, 128–30, 146
Quinn, John, 130, 136–37, 146
Quisenberry, Dan, 111

Radatz, Dick, 109
Radcliff, Rip, 124
Raines, Tim, 276, 280, 283–85, 289–90, 292
Ramano, John, 197
Ramirez, Manny, 337
Ramos, Pedro, 179
Rapp, Pat, 299, 302, 305
Rariden, Bill, 65
Raschi, Vic, 98–99, 154, 170
Reardon, Jeff, 263, 269–72, 281, 284
Reed, Howie, 236
Reese, Pee Wee, 164, 172–74
Reese, Rich, 192, 199
Regan, Phil, 108
Reichardt, Rick, 219
Reichler, Joe, 39
Reinsdorf, Jerry, 303
Remlinger, Mike, 331, 338
Renko, Steve, 214
Renteria, Edgar, 301, 303, 305, 307
Reuther, Dutch, 88
Reynolds, Allie, 98, 153–54, 169–70
Reynolds, Bob, 220

Reynolds, Carl, 115, 121, 124
Rhodes, Gordon, 115
Rice, Jim, 186, 204, 208–9
Rice, Sam, 57, 73–74, 76, 79, 83–85, 89–90
Richards, Paul, 102–4, 110, 213–14
Richardson, Bobby, 366
Richardson, Spec, 212–14
Rickert, Marv, 142
Rickey, Branch, 113, 132–33, 138–39, 146
Rigney, Bill, 193, 219–20, 222
Risberg, Swede, 39, 42, 44, 62–63, 68
Ritchey, Claude, 17
Rivera, Mariano, 264
Rixey, Eppa, 24–25, 30, 34
Rizzuto, Phil, 149, 153, 158, 160, 163–64, 168–69, 172–74
Robbie, Joe, 297
Robbins, George, 53, 62
Robertson, Billy, 178
Robertson, Jimmy, 178
Robertson, Sherry, 178
Robertson, Thelma, 177
Robinson, Aaron, 153
Robinson, Brooks, 182, 184–85
Robinson, Floyd, 366
Robinson, Frank, 182, 184, 194, 204, 206–8, 210–13, 216, 366–69
Robinson, Jackie, 139, 321
Robinson, Wilbert, 9–10, 12, 18, 20, 27
Robison, Frank, 8, 37
Rockefeller, John D., 5
Rocker, John, 274, 334
Rodriguez, Alex, 337
Rodriguez, Aurelio, 224, 232
Rogers, Steve, 268, 276–78, 280–82, 285–86, 293
Rogers, Will, 85
Rohr, Les, 244
Rojas, Mel, 273
Rolfe, Red, 114, 150
Rollins, Rich, 179, 187–88, 193, 195–96, 355, 366
Rose, Pete, 183, 285
Roseboro, John, 192, 198

Roth, Braggo, 58, 62, 82
Rothrock, Jack, 118
Roush, Edd, 57, 66, 131
Rowell, Bama, 139
Rowland, Pants, 42, 44, 53–55, 58, 60–63, 65, 67
Ruane, Tom, 106, 261
Rudi, Joe, 243–44, 252–53, 258
Ruel, Muddy, 82–83, 85–86, 90, 97
Ruffing, Red, 150, 153
Rugo, Guido, 129
Ruiz, Chico, 220, 226–27, 230
Rummill, Eddie, 161, 171
Runyan, Damon, 95
Ruppert, Colonel Jacob, 1, 53
Russell, Allan, 82–83, 87
Russell, Jim, 140–41, 143, 145
Russell, Reb, 51–52, 55, 63–66
Russell, Rip, 151
Ruth, Babe, 1, 51, 55, 62, 70, 75, 81, 89, 96, 113, 242, 359
Ryan, Connie, 131, 134, 137, 139, 141, 144, 247
Ryan, John, 14
Ryan, Nolan, 232

Sain, Johnny, 133–36, 138, 141–45, 188, 200–1
Salkeld, Bill, 140
Sambito, Joe, 273
Sanborn, Irving, 48, 51, 67
Sanders, Deion, 325
Sanders, Ray, 136, 139
Sanders, Reggie, 331–32, 338
Sanderson, Scott, 276, 278, 280, 282, 292
Sanguillen, Manny, 258
Santiago, Benito, 298
Santo, Ron, 366
Sawyer, Eddie, 99
Schalk, Ray, 42–43, 47–48, 58, 63, 68
Schang, Wally, 75
Schatzeder, Dan, 278–79, 292
Schmidt, Jason, 329, 337–38
Schmidt, Mike, 290–91
Schoendienst, Red, 220

Schooler, Mike, 273–74
Schuerholz, John, 289, 324–27, 329–31, 336–37, 339–40, 344
Scott, Everett, 44, 75
Scott, Gary, 298
Scott, Jim, 52, 63
Scott, Mike, 269
Scott, Rodney, 278, 281, 283–4
Seaton, Tom, 24, 25
Seaver, Tom, 268
Seitz, Peter, 257
Seitzer, Kevin, 324
Selig, Bud, 39
Selkirk, George, 124–25
Sewell, Luke, 165, 167
Sexon, Richie, 335
Shapiro, Ron, 288
Shawkey, Bob, 36, 74
Shea, Specs, 153
Sheckard, Jimmy, 11, 13–14, 17–19
Sheffield, Gary, 298–302, 304–5, 307, 332, 338
Shindle, Billy, 9, 14
Shore, Ernie, 96
Shoun, Clyde, 141
Siebern, Norm, 239
Siebert, Sonny, 253
Sievers, Roy, 179
Simmons, Al, 124
Simmons, Ted, 326–27
Simpson, Dick, 204
Singer, Bill, 268
Sisler, George, 29, 57
Sisti, Sibbi, 141, 144
Slaught, Don, 325
Smiley, Don, 296, 305, 308–9
Smith, Charlie, 366
Smith, David W, 93
Smith, Dwight, 328
Smith, Lee, 263
Smith, Lonnie, 290, 325
Smith, Red, 237
Smoltz, John, 323–32, 339
Snider, Duke, 100, 282, 321
Snyder, Paul, 323, 339

Snyder, Russ, 236
Soden, Arthur, 6
Solomon, Burt, 16
Solters, Moose, 124
Somers, Charles, 52, 58
Sosa, Elias, 278
Southworth, Billy, 131–33, 135–38, 140, 142, 144–47
Southworth, Billy, Jr, 133
Spahn, Warren, 129, 134–36, 138, 141–42, 144, 145
Speaker, Tris, 36, 42, 55–58, 63, 70, 73–74
Speier, Chris, 277–79, 281, 284–85, 292–93
Spencer, Jim, 217, 223–24
Spillner, Dan, 273
Spink, Alfred, 40–41
Spink, J. G. Taylor, 120
Stange, Lee, 180
Stanhouse, Don, 273
Stanky, Eddie, 138, 140–46
Stanton, Mike, 273, 323, 334
Stargell, Willie, 365–56
Staub, Rusty, 212–15
Stengel, Casey, 98, 100, 129, 148, 154, 161, 164, 169
Stephens, Vern, 149, 152, 160, 163–74
Stephenson, John, 231
Stewart, Shannon, 375
Stirnweiss, Snuffy, 153, 164
Stobbs, Chuck, 152
Stock, Milt, 27, 30, 35
Stoddard, Tim, 273
Stone, John, 124
Stoneham, Horace, 237–38
Stout, Glenn, 168
Strawberry, Darryl, 301, 336–37
Strong, Curtis, 289
Strunk, Amos, 56
Sullivan, Ted, 40–41
Sullivan, William, Jr., 130
Surhoff, B. J., 332
Sutter, Bruce, 111
Swan, Craig, 268
Swank, Bill, 33

Sweeney, Mike, 311–15
Symington, Stuart, 233, 246–47

Tabeau, Patsy, 8
Tabor, Jim, 150
Taft, Charles, 37
Tanner, Chuck, 258, 261–62, 323
Tatum, Jarvis, 223
Tatum, Ken, 93, 222–24, 232, 268
Tavares, Frank, 284
Taylor, Tony, 366
Tebbetts, Birdie, 151, 163
Tekulve, Kent, 111, 261–62
Tenace, Gene, 244, 254, 258
Terry, Bill, 133
Terry, Ralph, 236
Terry, Zeb, 62–63
Thigpen, Bobby, 273–74
Thomas, Lee, 366
Thomas, Roy, 280
Thorn, John, 26
Thornley, Stew, 360
Tiant, Luis, 78
Tinker, Joe, 29
Torborg, Jeff, 223, 226
Torgeson, Earl, 136–39, 141, 144, 145
Torre, Joe, 214–15, 323
Tovar, Cesar, 180, 193, 198–200, 203, 253
Trammell, Alan, 80
Treadway, George, 9
Treadway, Jeff, 325
Tresh, Tom, 366
Triandos, Gus, 104
Trillo, Manny, 254–45
Trout, Dizzy, 166
Tucker, Michael, 330–31, 338
Turner, Dan, 281, 283, 293
Turner, Ted, 322

Ueberroth, Peter, 288
Uhlaender, Ted, 193, 198
Urdahl, Dean, 187

Valdespino, Sandy, 179, 355
Valentine, Ellis, 277, 279–82, 289–92

Van Haltren, George, 9
Veach, Bobby, 57, 64, 73, 74
Veeck, Bill, 42–43, 322
Veras, Quilvio, 299, 302, 305, 331, 338
Veres, Randy, 299
Versalles, Zoilo, 176–77, 179, 187–88, 190, 192–93, 196–97, 355, 366
Vincent, Fay, 297
Viola, Frank, 269
Virdon, Bill, 284–86
Voight, David Q, 16, 146
Voiselle, Bill, 137, 141–43
Von Der Ahe, Chris, 7, 40–41
Von Der Horst, Harry, 6, 8, 10–11, 15, 20
Vosmik, Joe, 124

Waddell, Rube, 17
Waggoner, Glenn, 290
Wagner, Charlie, 150
Wagner, Hal, 151
Wagner, Hans, 15, 17, 22, 43, 48, 70, 172
Wagner, Heinie, 48
Wagner, Leon, 219
Walberg, Rube, 116
Walker, Gee, 124
Walker, Jerry, 103
Walker, Larry, 337
Walker, Tilly, 56
Walker, Todd, 315–17
Wallach, Tim, 276, 282, 284–86, 290, 292
Wallenda, Karl, 322
Walsh, Dick, 218–227, 230–32
Walsh, Ed, 47, 51–52, 55, 95
Ward, Duane, 109, 273–74
Ward, Pete, 366
Warstler, Rabbit, 113, 116
Weart, William, 26
Weatherly, Roy, 124
Weathers, David, 301
Weaver, Buck, 39, 42–43, 48–49, 54–55, 58, 62–64, 68–70
Webb, Red, 143
Weeghman, Charles, 29
Weiland, Bob, 115
Weiss, Walt, 330, 335

Welch, Raquel, 228
Werber, Billy, 114–15, 117, 121–23, 126
West, Sammy, 124
Westrum, Wes, 104
Wheat, Zack, 31, 57, 73–74, 131
Whisenant, Matt, 298
Whitaker, Lou, 80
White, Devon, 300, 305, 307, 309
Whitted, George, 27, 30, 34
Wickersham, Dave, 236
Wilhelm, Hoyt, 100–109, 111, 269–72
Williams, Billy, 253, 366
Williams, Dib, 119
Williams, Dick, 250–51, 253, 255–56, 265, 277–78, 280–81, 283, 286–87, 289, 291–93
Williams, Lefty, 39, 42, 55–58, 63–65, 69–70, 72
Williams, Ted, 105, 125–26, 149–51, 161, 163–64, 167–68
Wilson, Hack, 204
Wilson, Jack, 126
Winfield, Dave, 337
Wohlers, Mark, 273, 334
Wolfgang, Red, 55
Wood, Wilbur, 104–5
Woodling, Gene, 153, 163

Workman, Chuck, 134
Worthington, Al, 189–90
Wright, Clyde, 217, 222–23, 226
Wulf, Steve, 276
Wynn, Early, 178
Wynne, Billy, 223

Yastrzemski, Carl, 161, 182, 200, 239, 366
Yawkey, Tom, 112–17, 120–21, 123, 125–28, 149, 151
Yawkey, William, 52, 113
Yeager, Joe, 11, 14
York, Rudy, 151
Yost, Eddie, 179
Young, Cy, 8
Young, Nick, 6
Youngs, Ross, 57
Yount, Robin, 290

Zachary, Tom, 82, 85, 90
Zarilla, Al, 163
Zimbalist, Andrew, 308–9
Zimmer, Don, 187
Zimmerman, Heinie, 31, 49, 65
Zimmerman, Jerry, 192
Zuk, Bob, 244

ABOUT THE AUTHORS

MARK L. ARMOUR has been studying baseball since 1968, when he turned eight years old and his hero, Carl Yastrzemski, hit .301 and won the American League batting title. Mark has been blessed to be a devotee of the Boston Red Sox, who have provided him his most important education. He has contributed baseball articles to several websites and to the publications of the Society for American Baseball Research. Between ball games, Mark has worked in the software business for the past twenty years in Rhode Island, Massachusetts, and Oregon. In his free nonbaseball time, he rides his bicycle and reads history. He lives with his family in Corvallis, Oregon.

DANIEL R. LEVITT, a lifelong Twins fan, has enjoyed researching baseball questions for many years. Published articles include the discovery that Ferdie Schupp should be credited with the record for the lowest single-season ERA and evidence that today's pitchers throw just as many pitches per season as their deadball-era counterparts despite fewer innings. When not trying to solve baseball questions, Dan manages the capital markets for a national commercial real estate firm that principally offers design-build and development services. To get outside in the summer without golf clubs, Dan plays on a nineteenth-century-vintage baseball team that travels around the upper Midwest. He lives in Minneapolis with his wife and children.